Sita's Daughters

Sita's Daughters: Coming Out of Purdah

THE RAJPUT WOMEN OF KHALAPUR REVISITED

Leigh Minturn

WITH THE ASSISTANCE OF
Swaran Kapoor

New York   Oxford
OXFORD UNIVERSITY PRESS
1993

Oxford University Press

Oxford   New York   Toronto
Delhi   Bombay   Calcutta   Madras   Karachi
Kuala Lumpur   Singapore   Hong Kong   Tokyo
Nairobi   Dar es Salaam   Cape Town
Melbourne   Auckland   Madrid

and associated companies in
Berlin   Ibadan

Library of Congress Cataloging-in-Publication Data

Minturn, Leigh.
Sita's daughters : coming out of Purdah : the Rajput
women of Khalapur revisited / Leigh Minturn ; with the assistance of Swaran
Kapoor.
p.   cm.   Includes bibliographical references and index.
ISBN 0-19-507823-3. — ISBN 0-19-508035-1 (pbk.)
1. Women, Rajput—India—Khalapur—Social conditions.
2. Women, Rajput—India—Khalapur—Economic conditions.
3. Women, Rajput—India—Khalapur—Family relationships.
4. Purdah—India—Khalapur. 5. Caste—India—Khalapur. 6. Dowry—India—Khalapur.
7. Khalapur (India)—Religions life and customs.
8. Khalapur (India)—Social life and customs. I. Kapoor, Swaran. II. Title.
DS432.R3M56 1993
305.42′697054—dc20   92-22147

1 3 5 7 9 8 6 4 2

Printed in the United States of America
on acid-free paper

I dedicate this book to the women it describes, my friends, who twice welcomed an inquisitive stranger into their homes, adopted me as a daughter of the village, and shared with me their hospitality, their stories, and their friendship. I hope that my rendition of their lives does them justice.

I also dedicate the book to the memory of my assistant, Swaran Kapour.

ACKNOWLEDGMENTS

Ethnographic research involves the joint cooperation of persons in the researcher's own country and community as well as those where the research is carried out. I owe debts of gratitude to many people who have helped me with my field research, data analysis, interpretation, and writing.

My field trip and expenses for this research were financed by fellowships from the Ford Foundation, the Fullbright Foundation, and a grant from the University of Colorado Council on Research and Creative Activity to pay the salaries of interpreters. The administrators and staffs of both the Ford and Fullbright foundations in Delhi were helpful in facilitating my stay in India. The Ford Foundation personnel arranged for me to reside at their hostel in Delhi and helped me obtain supplies. Mr. Ramakrishna of the Fullbright office contacted Swaran Kapoor, whom I hired as my interpreter. She assisted me in dealings with Indian officials, in clearing some equipment through customs, and in helping with my exit permits. The Fullbright Foundation arranged to affiliate me with Lady Irwin College in Delhi. The president of Lady Irwin College, Dr. Durga Delkar, was hospitable and helpful when I came to Delhi on visits.

In Khalapur, Kirpall Singh Tanwar, principal of the Khalapur Intercollege, graciously turned over two rooms in the Purana Project House for myself and Swaran Kapoor to use as our residence and kitchen. All of the faculty and their wives residing at the house helped us settle in and made us feel at home. Mahender Singh of the intercollege faculty was particularly helpful concerning the maintenance of our equipment and facilities.

Swaran Kapoor assisted me in communicating with village women, in the preparation and translation of interviews, and in the organization and labeling of photographs. She remained in Khalapur for 3 months after I returned to the United States in order to complete some interviews with our preselected sample of respondents. Regrettably, Swaran Kapoor died in the spring of 1992.

Dr. Michael Mahar, of the Oriental studies department at the University of Arizona in Tucson, is the custodian of the Khalapur files from the Cornell research project conducted during 1950–60. Dr. Mahar gave me copies of photographic material from the files and the translated copies of letters from Luxmi to her mother, Draupadi. Mala Sinha provided me with newspaper accounts and articles on the sati of 1987.

Drs. Shelly Calisher and Desmond Cartwright of the psychology department at the University of Colorado at Boulder, read early drafts of my manuscript and made helpful editorial suggestions. Dr. Dennis McGilvray, of the anthropology department at the University of Colorado at Boulder, read and commented on my chapter on religion. Dr. Kathleen L'Armand did a splendidly thorough review of the entire manuscript.

Two secretaries, Bee Peterson, Barbara Krause, have worked on this text, patiently editing and reediting and copying and recopying its many drafts. A third secretary, Mary Ann Tucker, reviewed the final editing and compiled the index. Jonathan O. Roberts provided us with invaluable advice on software and formatting.

I am particularly grateful to Amar Nath and his family. He served as a primary informant for John Hitchcock and Michael Mahar, in the belief that aiding American field-workers is part of his karma, or duty, in this lifetime. Swaran Kapoor and I ate our lunches in his men's quarters when the congestion created by curious children in his women's quarters became overbearing. Amar Nath's daughter-in-law, Dhooli, cooked our lunches under the supervision of his wife, Draupadi. Dhooli and Draupadi brought our lunches from the women's to the men's quarters, and kept us company while we ate them. Both women served as valuable informants.

Finally, my greatest debt of gratitude is owed to Sita's daughters, the Rajput women of Khalapur, who welcomed me back with warmth and enthusiasm and offered their patience, understanding, and friendship to the inquisitive stranger who twice came, uninvited, to write about their lives. I hope that my account has done them justice.

Boulder, Colo.   L.M.
May 1992

CONTENTS

Sita's Daughters

Introduction

HISTORY

Khalapur is a village in the Indian state of Uttar Pradesh. It is located about 100 miles north of Delhi. Khalapur is in the Gangetic plain, an area of fertile land that has sustained agriculture for millennia. The largest caste group are Rajputs, descendants of conquerors from Rajastan, who invaded and settled in this area about 400 years ago. Over 20 other caste groups and a community of Muslims constitute the rest of the Khalapur population. Before 1952 the Rajput families in the region were Zamindars, rulers and owners of large tracts of land, who administered their landholdings, agricultural workers, and other servant caste groups in a system similar to that of feudal lords in Europe. In 1952 the Indian government passed the Zamindar Abolition Act, a land redistribution law that gave land to tenant farmers who had worked it for more than 10 years. During the time of my first field trip, many Rajput families were engaged in court battles over landholdings and were moving their tenant farmers from one field to another to prevent them from exercising claims of ownership.

In the fifties Khalapur was one field station for an extensive research project funded by the Ford Foundation and administered by anthropology professors at Cornell University. This project had field sites in Peru and Thailand as well as India. The senior investigator for the Indian research was Professor Morris Opler. Khalapur was selected because it had been chosen as a target village for an Indian government agricultural and village development program. At that time a government agricultural extension worker and midwife resided in the village. One research goal, the responsibility of John Hitchcock, was to evaluate the effect of this government effort on farming and health.

John Hitchcock served as project field director for Khalapur. During his first year in Khalapur he supervised the construction of a project house and walled compound about 500 yards from the village and across the road from the local intercollege. The project house, situated in the center of the walled enclosure, contained a kitchen, dining room, bath and shower, and eight bedrooms. A smaller unit in one corner of the compound housed resident cooks. When our population of researchers outgrew the available number of rooms, a few tents on concrete blocks

3

were put up within the compound walls. I lived in one of the tents during my first field study. An artesian well provided water; a small garden and a few banana trees supplied some of our fruits and vegetables. When the Cornell Research Project closed, this facility, named the Cornell Purana Project House, was given to the intercollege to house faculty and resident students.

Morris Opler accepted my request to work at his Indian field station, with the proviso that I contribute my field notes to his central file on Khalapur. My first field trip to Khalapur occurred in 1954–55 when the Cornell project was in full swing and John Hitchcock was the resident Khalapur director. A number of American and Indian field researchers were working in Khalapur at this time, and our combined publications have given Khalapur in general, and the dominant Rajput caste in particular, a unique place in the literature on Indian village studies.

During my first field trip I was one of six field researchers doing coordinated socialization studies in six different countries. This research project, also sponsored by the Ford Foundation, was planned by John and Beatrice Whiting of Harvard University, Irvin Child of Yale University, and William Lambert of Cornell University. Beatrice Whiting was the project director. Research sites in Kenya, Okinawa, the Philippines, Mexico, and New England were included in this study.

The aim of this research was to collect comparable information on socialization practices and children's behavior for cross-cultural comparisons. All researchers participated in designing the interviews and observation schedules. The resulting instructions and instruments were issued in a field manual from which all field teams worked. After the field research had been completed, the manual, with commentary from field teams, was published as the first book in the paperback reissue of the ethnographic reports (Whiting, Child, & Lambert, 1966).

Our instructions were to select a homogeneous neighborhood within each field setting; I selected a neighborhood of Rajput families living at the edge of the village nearest to the Cornell Project House. My first report, "The Rajputs of Khalapur" (Leigh Minturn & John T. Hitchcock), was published as one chapter in *Six Cultures: Studies of Child Rearing* (B. Whiting, 1963) and reissued in 1966 as one of six paperback books.

The comparative study of socialization in these six communities, based on interviews with mothers and entitled *Mothers of Six Cultures: Antecedents of Child Rearing*, by Leigh Minturn and William W. Lambert, was published in 1964. For several years *Mothers of Six Cultures* was the only cross-cultural description of women's roles. The final volume of this study, by Beatrice and John Whiting, *Children of Six Cultures: A Psycho-Cultural Analysis*, based on our observations of child behavior, was published in 1975.

Although Khalapur was studied extensively in the fifties, little had been published on changes in subsequent decades. In the sixties the development of hybrid grains with much higher yields than older varieties produced the so-called green revolution. These new grains and modern farming methods enabled Khalapur farmers to move from subsistence to commercial agriculture and provided a basis for increased prosperity, which in turn led to modernization in other aspects of village life. Education, particularly for daughters, became more common. Bus service directly to Khalapur enabled people to travel more. New local businesses sold commercial goods not previously available in local stores.

I returned to Khalapur in 1974–75, funded by Ford and Fulbright fellowships, to study changes in the status of Rajput women from 1955 to 1975. Khalapur is a conservative village, and Rajput families living there cloister their wives and observe the customs of the purdah tradition. These customs involve the veiling of women's faces and bodies, women's subservient postures when speaking to men, isolation of wives from family men older than their husbands, husband–wife separation, and ritual deference of young wives to their mothers-in-law and other senior women. Marriages are arranged by parents and are considered to be final at the marriage ceremony, although most brides do not live with their husbands for several years after this ceremony. Khalapur Rajputs do not allow widows to remarry, and in 1975 some families still had virgin widows.

The timing of my second field study was fortuitous, because the most dramatic decline in the observance of the complex system of respect–avoidance customs of the purdah tradition occurred during the 20-year period between my two visits. The decline in the observance of purdah had been fostered by prosperity and modernization. Increases in women's level of education, access to health facilities, control of finances, autonomy in their husbands' households, mobility outside of their husbands' households, and even changes in their religious observances have come about as a result of a decrease in purdah.

In 1975 I worked with the same families I had described in 1955. I was able to document important changes in village life in general, and in Rajput women's roles in particular, that would have been impossible to document if I had not observed, interviewed, and photographed these families 20 years earlier.

METHODS

My methods included ethnographic description, case histories, systematic sampling, and structured interviewing. I used general informant interviews to develop structured interviews on several important topics and used these interviews on a sample of pairs of mothers-in-law and daughters-in-law. The interview topics included changes in the amount of dowry over two generations, changes in wives' control of dowry distribution, and family planning. The most detailed interviews concerned reports of the current degree of purdah observance as opposed to the degree observed by mothers and mothers-in-law. Retrospective interviews with older women allowed me to obtain descriptions of purdah over three generations. Sample women were also asked about their reactions to changes in purdah observance. My field notes and photographs from 1955 document both accuracy and error in the retrospective reports of the older women.

When reading ethnographies, I have often been frustrated by the tendency for the individual identities of the people described to disappear in the descriptions of their customs and roles. I think this problem may be particularly acute in descrip-

tions of the lives of women oppressed by the societal standards of their ethnographers. Some descriptions of Indian women leave them silent, cloistered, and
oppressed in the confines of their segregated quarters without conveying the lively
activities taking place in women's courtyards or the lively nature of the women
themselves. When I reread my first ethnography before returning to Khalapur in
1975, I found that the personalities and individual lives of my friends had been
"embalmed" in my text.

The Rajput women I knew were variously proud, honorable, hospitable, funny,
bawdy, brave, timid, greedy, generous, and conniving. Their stories include accounts of heroism, loyalty, courage, jealousy, deception, and strife. In my second
study I was determined to preserve the individuality of these extraordinary women,
and I employ several techniques to personalize this text. Each chapter begins with
relevant quotes from interviews. In order to allow these women to "speak for
themselves" as much as possible, the texts of most chapters include extensive
quotes from interview material. In a final chapter I review material from previous
chapters to present a profile of the women's major values and behavior traits.

I include extensive case history material to illustrate general points. In an early
chapter I describe the members of one wealthy and one poor family. I present case
history material about members of these two families in several chapters to illustrate
the effect of wealth on their lives. An account of the worth and composition dowries
of brides from both families illustrates the range of dowry wealth among families of
this group of Rajputs. Details of the difficulties of a poor wife in the wealthy family
and a child bride in the poor family are described.

To illustrate the importance placed on women's honor, I contrast an account of
the death of an unmarried girl, as the consequence of an illicit affair, with the story
of the flight of a poor wife, wrongly accused of infidelity by her wealthy husband,
to her father's house and her husband's difficulties in negotiating for her return. In a
similar exercise I illustrate the difficulties of the widow's roles with a detailed
account of the tragic plight of three widows in a family without men. One widow, a
sister of the deceased headman of the family, left her own husband 30 years ago to
wage extended and unsuccessful court battles for control of her brother's family
land.

THEORY

An important theoretical concept in cultural research is the distinction between etic
and emic. The term *etic* comes from phonetics, the study of universal language
sounds, while *emic* comes from phonemics, the study of language sounds with
meanings unique to particular languages. In etic research, investigation and data
interpretation are guided by a preselected theory, while emic investigation attempts
to discover the ideas of people in the society being studied and interpret data in
indigenous terms.

Most ethnographers utilize both approaches, because the choice of topics to be studied is partly predetermined and partly the result of phenomena unique to the population under investigation. Similarly, interpretation is determined by both pre-existing paradigms and unique aspects of field data.

I call my approach *emic feminism*. The topic of my study, women's roles and status, was selected in part because of scholarly interest generated by the new women's movements. Some new interests and research of feminist scholars guided my inquiry and interpretation, and my theoretical paradigms come primarily from women scholars. I report changes in women's lives in their own terms and interpret them with a combination of emic ideas and the guidelines of feminist scholarship. The resulting report is woman–based. (Unless otherwise noted, epigraphs are taken from interviews with the women.)

One scholarly paradigm I use extensively is the distinction between the public realm of male activity and power, and the private, or domestic, realm of female activity and power. Cloistered Rajput women live their married lives within the confines of their courtyards. Their private realm is made more private by the exclusion of married men from women's quarters. Mothers-in-law are the chief executives of these living and work places. They direct the work of their daughters-in-law and make most of the decisions about the organization and performance of women's activities. Women's influence on the public realm is indirect, through influence on family men. Mothers have traditionally exerted considerable influence over their sons, an access to male power being threatened by increased husband–wife intimacy.

A second important paradigm in my analysis is the distinction between power status and deferential status. Power status refers to the ability to exert influence over others. Power, in some form, is the basis of most status distinctions. Most material benefits and privileges—access to money and goods—for example, accrue to persons in powerful roles. Deference refers to ritualized customs acknowledging status differences; for example, eating first; being served special food; and observing certain forms of address, postures, and seating arrangements. Deferential status customs are usually directed to powerful people in recognition of their power. The respect–avoidance purdah customs that young wives observe with members of their husbands' families are deferential status customs.

However, one group of deferential status customs that applies almost exclusively to women—cloistering, chaperoning, and limiting access to public places—is ostensibly based on an assumption of powerlessness. The rationale for these practices is that women cannot protect themselves, are unable to handle their own financial affairs, and must be protected by family men from seduction and exploitation. Cloistering, chaperoning, and limited mobility are customs observed by upper-class women. Working-class women in all societies are less sheltered and more mobile because their work roles necessitate such freedom. It is my contention that the latent purpose of these customs is to prevent wealthy women from high-status, influential families from employing their wealth and influence independently of family men.

Many groups of Indian women, including women in my sample, represent a cultural extreme in the practice of cloistering. Cloistering of women is the most obvious aspect of purdah. Married Rajput women are confined by custom to the courtyards of their husbands' families until their children are grown and married. When they visit in the village they go in groups, and when they travel to their parental villages they are escorted by men of their husbands' or fathers' families. For the same reasons they cannot testify in court, even in their own behalf. I found that cloistering and purdah customs profoundly affected attitudes towards marriage, education for girls, and women's nature by reinforcing a female subservience that made most women incapable of opposing men or resisting male advances. The system engendered unrealistic fears of all strange men and made women fearful of traveling even short distances by themselves. Sex segregation and arranged marriages provided the background for unrealistically romantic fantasies about prospective spouses. The only political activity of these women was voting, and they voted according to their husbands' directions. They could not by custom serve on village councils or legislatures because they would be in the company of men. Legislation protecting women's rights and property foundered on the barriers of purdah customs.

I am aware of the sensitivity of urban, educated Indians to Western analysis of their customs. Fortunately, I have an official body of information with which my findings can be compared. My fieldwork began in 1974, the same year that the Indian government published *Towards Equality,* a national report on the status of Indian women. In the last chapter of the present study I compare my results with the findings of that report, relying on the Uttar Pradesh norms wherever possible. Since my research is contemporary with the report, my findings are that the situation of women I knew was similar to conditions reported by the government investigators.

Some feminist scholars will be dissatisfied with my defense of traditional customs, the emphasis on the complaints of mothers-in-law about the "new shamelessness," and my lack of feminist analysis and critique. The extensive utilization of feminist polemic would impose inappropriate etic ideas on these accounts, ideas with which the women I describe are not familiar and which they would not, in general, accept.

This book is written for both Indian and Western audiences. To this end I have attempted to make traditional Indian customs comprehensible to an American audience without sacrificing accuracy. In assessing my obligation to various groups of people who will read my account, I recognize that their viewpoints will be divergent, and what pleases some will displease others. As a scholar my primary obligation is to the truth, as I can best report it. As a guest and friend of those about whom I write, my allegiance belongs to the women whose patience, time, and friendship made this effort possible. I have used fictitious names for people I describe, altered irrelevant details of incidents reported, and delayed publication to protect my informants from unnecessary invasion of their privacy.

Finally, I have chosen the title *Sita's Daughters* because I think it is the one which the women I knew would most prefer. Sita is the wife of Rama, an earthly manifestation of the great god Vishnu and the hero of the Hindu epic, the Ramayana. In Hinduism Sita is the ideal Hindu wife: patient, obedient, and chaste.

She is a mythological role model for Indian women in general and Rajput women in particular. Rajputs claim Rama as their mythical ancestor, and Khalapur Rajput women usually referred to a personified god as "Ram" and "Sita-Ram"; indeed, the latter was their most frequent mantra. Sita is the most important culture heroine for the women I knew; her values and her life are the model for their ideals. Rajput women have a proud and honorable heritage which they bear with pride and honor. Sita is their mythical clan mother, and they, in turn, are her ideational daughters.

I

CONSTANCY AND CHANGE

This part describes the physical surroundings of Khalapur, the relationships of Khalapur Rajputs with other caste groups and other Rajput clans and general changes in village life from 1955 to 1975. In the 20 years separating my field trips, the "green revolution," brought about by the introduction of hybrid grains, had shifted Khalapur's economy from subsistence to commercial agriculture and brought new prosperity to the Rajput families. Unlike their fathers, who disdained farming, young Rajput men worked in their fields.

This new prosperity formed the basis for a number of changes. New houses had been built, clothing styles had changed, and a variety of commercial goods were sold in Khalapur. The people, including the young women, were much more modern than they had been in 1955. Girls as well as boys went to school. Literacy for both men and women had become a necessary asset for a good marriage. In most households the mothers-in-law were illiterate, while their daughters-in-law were literate.

The houses of our families consisted of men's quarters (*choopars*), women's quarters (*bughars*), and animal compounds (*ghers*). These structures, including their function in ensuring the privacy of cloistered wives, are described, as are recent architectural adaptations to overcrowding, including two-story *choopars* and private apartments on the roofs of *bughars*.

The new prosperity had increased individual initiative, which sometimes threatened the solidarity of the traditional joint family. This, in turn, sometimes led to division of houses and land. At the end of chapter 1 we introduce two families whose members appear throughout the book. That of Gopal, Puran, and Mussaddi is a very wealthy family whose wives occupied one of the oldest, largest, and grandest women's quarters in Khalapur. Friction among the male cousins had led to the construction of new *choopars*, but no one wanted to relinquish claim to their share of their stately *bughar*. The second family, that of the brothers Daya, Kela, and Kanak, is poor. When the wives of this family quarreled, their modest *bughar* was divided, and one family built a new house in the family *gher*.

11

The two parts of this double courtyard are separated by the entrance to the street, leading to a round cattle feeder. Two buffaloes can be seen lying in front of the feeder. Two dogs stand in the far courtyard. A man, wearing a Ghandi cap, sits waiting for his food. One of his sisters walks away to bring him his meal, while another stands watching. A *chuula* can be seen in the lower left corner. A brass serving tray leans against the *chuula* wall. A sacred basil bush, draped with laundered clothes, grows in the corner. One cot is piled with bedding and two are standing on their sides, forming a purdah screen. In the far courtyard one glimpses the entrance to a bedroom and wall storage niches. Two rooms on the roofs of adjacent *bughars* appear at the upper right (1955).

1

The Khalapur Rajputs, 1955 to 1975

If the Ganges flows by your door, you are foolish not to take a bath.

It was on a hot September afternoon, 20 years to the week after my first field trip to Khalapur, that I found myself, with my new assistant, Swaran Kapoor, traveling once again from the railroad station in Bhudana to Khalapur. We still traveled in a horse-drawn cart, but the road was now paved, so the ride was considerably less bumpy. I was returning to a village that was larger and more prosperous than it had been during my 1955 visit. The Khalapur of 1975 also had a faster pace and more sophistication than the one I had left. The population had doubled since 1955, from 5,000 to 10,000. Rajputs continued to be the largest and dominant caste. The population of children between the ages of 3 and 10 had tripled in the families I studied. The increase in children was evident throughout the village. On my first visit I had the impression that the journey from Delhi to Khalapur was a journey back in time; on my second visit I was impressed with the degree to which Khalapur had moved forward in time. The river of modernity was flowing by the village, and the villagers, not being fools, were bathing in it.

I had come to study changes in the lives and status of the cloistered Rajput women. The description of these changes is the subject of this book. Changes in the roles of one sex cannot occur without changes in the roles of the other. In a society as male dominated as that of the Khalapur Rajputs, changes in the roles of women could not have occurred without tacit male approval. The changes in sex roles occurred in the context of general changes in the country and the village.

THE SETTING

I begin with descriptions of the geographical and cultural setting, and the changes in the setting from 1955 to 1975. Khalapur is in the Saharanpur district of the state of

13

Uttar Pradesh. (Figure 1.1 shows the location of the Saharanpur district.) Our 1955 description of the setting follows:

> South of the Himalayas, the great mountain chain which forms a natural boundary between India and countries to the north, lies a vast alluvial plain. It is watered by the broad, slow-moving Ganges and its tributaries. The region is very fertile and its western half—most of it now a part of the state of Uttar Pradesh was the cradle of Indian classical civilization. Khalapur, one of the many thousands of villages in Uttar Pradesh, lies between the Ganges and its large tributary river Jumna. The village is about 90 miles north of Delhi and is so close to the Himalayas that the foothills and snow-covered peaks are visible on clear days. . . .
>
> The climate is monsoonal, and a hot, wet summer is followed by a comfortably warm winter and a very hot, dry spring. In April or early May, after the winter crops have been harvested, a scorching wind from the western desert begins to blow. It is ladened with dust picked up from the barren fields. The atmosphere becomes yellow and opaque and dust is everywhere. Small twisters sometimes whirl across the plain, and occasional dust storms blacken the sky and lower the visibility to a few hundred yards. In the heat of the day, temperatures rise to 110 °F or higher.
>
> Violent thunder and hail storms often precede the summer monsoon by a month or more. These harbingers of the longer and steadier rains are called the "little monsoon" and sometimes cause severe damage to any grain which is still standing in the fields. The heavy rain-bearing clouds of the true monsoon arrive toward the end of June, and from then until the end of September almost all of the 40-inch average yearly rainfall occurs. The usual pattern is rain for a day or two, followed by a few days of sunshine, with each succeeding day becoming increasingly humid and hot, so that the renewal of rain is a welcome relief. Throughout the monsoon insects are abundant, and toward the last of the period the incidence of malaria shows a marked rise.
>
> With the retreat of the monsoon in September, temperatures gradually fall. By November and December nights are cool, and occasionally there may be a light frost. There is some rainfall during the winter, and during these wet periods the weather can be uncomfortably damp and chilly. On the whole, however, the winter months are moderate, clear, and very pleasant. . . .
>
> Like most villages in the area, Khalapur shows many evidences of [its] prolonged Muslim and west Asian contact. The custom of purdah, or seclusion of women, which the high status village families observed probably was taken over from the Muslims. A Hindu temple was recently built in Khalapur, but prior to this the most prominent religious structure was a large domed memorial to a Muslim saint. Hindustani, the language of the villagers, is a blend derived from Sanskrit, Arabic, and Persian. Prior to the adoption of a different script after independence, the schoolchildren learned a Persian form of writing, and most official records also were maintained in this script. Nearly 400, or approximately 8%, of Khalapur's population are followers of Islam, and their number includes some of the landowning families.
>
> The center of Muslim and west Asian influence in the neighborhood of Khalapur is Bhudana, a town of some 25,000. Once an important seat of Muslim provincial rule, it lies about 4 miles northeast of the village and today houses a world-famous center of Islamic learning.

(Minturn & Hitchcock, 1966, pp. 1–4)

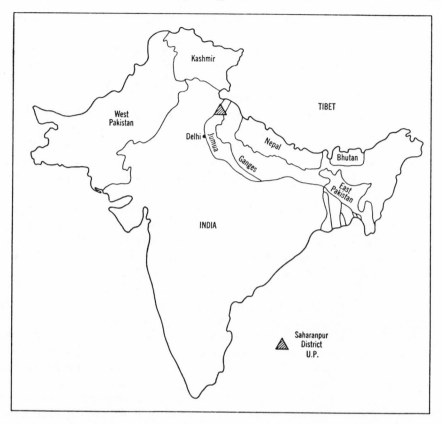

Figure 1.1 *Map of India indicating location of Saharanpur district. (From Minturn & Hitchcock, 1966, p. 2.)*

KHALAPUR

The first landmark I recognized on my second visit was the mango grove at the outskirts of the village. The monkeys still chattered in the trees, and the ancestor shrine still stood in their shade, but the peacocks were gone. Power lines along the road now brought electricity to the village, and tube wells with their pumps could be seen in the fields. New cultivation methods had changed the landscape. Most of the large irrigation dikes, which had occupied about one fifth of the fields, were gone, and those that remained were small. Traffic on the road was heavier and more varied than before. Bullocks still trotted briskly, pulling carts filled with grain from the fields to the village. Men still walked to the fields, and children still brought grain back on their heads. The increase in sugarcane production had increased the number of slow, strong buffaloes pulling their heavy carts on the 4-mile trip to the Bhudana sugar mill. New vehicles were also evident. Bicycles, rare in 1955, were seen more frequently, and some wealthy farmers drove their bright red tractors to their fields. The manager of the new bank drove to work in his car. A bus from Delhi ran directly to Khalapur once a day, and buses to the railway town of Bhudana ran several times a day.

Changes on the village road could be heard as well as seen. The horns of cars and buses occasionally pierced the air. Irrigation pumps pounded a steady beat in many fields. From the fields the lilting tinkling of the cattle bells was occasionally drowned out by the blare of transistor radios.

Nearing the village I noticed more women on the road than formerly. The girls attending the intercollege (the local school teaching Grades 8 through 12), dressed in their uniforms of blue tunics, white pants, and scarves, walked with married women whose faces were covered by their saris. A woman in a bright yellow *burka* (the outer garment covering the entire body) reminded me that Khalapur has a community of Muslims in its midst.

In 1955 the Cornell-Purnea Project House, the cooperative seed store, and the intercollege were the only buildings on the road near Khalapur. In 1975 a number of new buildings could be seen. The intercollege that was being expanded in 1955 had been expanded further, and a new building was under construction. A new elementary school, bank, and medical dispensary had been built. A machine for grinding sugarcane was in use, adding its mechanical thumping to the beat of the irrigation pumps. Several small roadside stands served take-out food to the field-workers, who used to depend on their families to bring lunch to the fields. One of several new village stores sold a variety of household items, ranging from plastic shoes to cooking oil and washing powder. In addition to these commercial buildings, there were several new cattle compounds along the road, and the threshing field where boys used to play hockey was covered with these new buildings.

When we reached the edge of the village, the effects of a light monsoon were evident in the low water level in the *khala* (pond) under the bridge at this entrance to the village. When I arrived in 1954, the bridge was flooded and we had to wade across, but this September the water level was about 12 feet below the bridge.

Our 1975 study was conducted in the same neighborhood in which we had worked in 1955, situated nearest to the bridge which connected the road to Bhudhana. Rajput families from three lineages live in this area. All of the families we had studied in 1955 still lived in the same neighborhood. The streets were still a maze of irregular dirt paths. More water buffalo carts and some tractors added to the congestion of bullock carts and people, and increased traffic made the streets more dangerous than they had been. Most of the children's empty play spaces had been taken up by new buildings. During our second visit, a child was run over and killed by a buffalo cart.

However, the traffic jam of cattle on the footbridge, where the Bhudana road enters Khalapur, is a problem of the past. In 1955 several hundred cattle were driven over this footbridge every morning, to graze on the stubble of fallow fields and the brush growing on the irrigation dikes. They were driven back again each evening, creating a bovine bottleneck twice a day. In 1975 the larger fields necessitated by tractor cultivation had eliminated most dikes; intensive cultivation and double cropping used all the land throughout the year, so fields were seldom fallow, and cattle were kept in village compounds and fed on fodder.

Women still visited from house to house by going along the flat roofs that connect many rows of women's quarters. This "high road" allows women to leave their houses without coming into contact with men.

CASTE AND THE *JAJMANI* SYSTEM

Traditionally the residents of Indian villages constitute an economically independent unit. Traditional occupations are alotted to particular caste groups, which are linked to each other in an economic system known as the *jajmani* system. The demands of the market economy were changing this system in 1955, and in this year we described the Rajput's place in the *jajmani* system as follows:

> The Rajputs and the other caste groups of Khalapur form a complex web of economic interdependence. Each Rajput family is dependent for services on families belonging to nine other caste groups, and these families in turn are dependent on the Rajput families they serve for most of their food. Water carriers and sweepers come to a Rajput house every day, the former to bring the daily water supply—a task of special importance, for wives cannot leave the courtyard—and the latter to clean the latrines or carry off refuse, a job which only an Untouchable can do. Every family, in addition, is served by a carpenter, blacksmith, barber, potter, washerman, and leather worker. Carpenters and blacksmiths make and repair agricultural implements; barbers shave, cut hair and fingernails, and play a key role on ceremonial occasions; potters make a large variety of clay pots and other utensils, including the jugs in which water is carried and stores; the washerman washes clothing and bedding; sweepers make cow dung cakes and carry away refuse, and the women also act as midwives. The leather worker removes dead cattle and supplies his clientele with a few simple leather articles, such as a whiplash and parts of the bullocks' harnesses.
>
> Each family also has a Brahmin priest who assists on ceremonial occasions. Some priests . . . have given up their traditional role and obtain a living from their land. Only a few priests in the village devote all of their time to ritual matters. These are the Brahmins who know how to read and write and how to conduct the marriage ceremonies. The remainder of the priests divide their time between their farms and the ritual needs of their clientele, the majority of whom are Rajputs. Today priests are called less often than they were in the past. A major reason for this was the Arya Samaj movement. It had an anti-priest bias and taught that each family head was himself capable of carrying out any religious rites which were necessary. The coming of the schools also weakened the position of the Brahmins, who in the past were prime repositories of whatever learning was found in Khalapur. These developments have made an increasing number of Rajput families reluctant to give the full traditional payment to their Brahmin priest. The priests, in response to these changes, have shown an increasing tendency to give up their traditional calling. And were it not for the fact that the women are much more conservative religiously than the men, it would seem that the decline in the functional importance of the Brahmin would be even more marked. An index of women's greater conservatism in ritual matters is the fact that, unlike most men, they will bathe and wash their hair if they inadvertently come into contact with an Untouchable.
>
> Part of the payment for services performed by members of these nine caste groups consists of a number of customary benefits provided by each of the families

served. These include such things as food on many ceremonial occasions throughout the year and the right to cut fodder and fuel from the fields. The major payment
consists of grain. These payments are made twice a year, after each of the two food-
grain harvests.

This system of economic interdependence, known in its widest ramifications as
the *jajmani* system, is based on mutual need and lack of economic alternatives. The
system was based on a subsistence rather than a money economy, and many of the
strains to which it now is subject arise both from the growing number of different
jobs which are open to villagers and from the increasing use of money.

(Minturn & Hitchcock, 1966, pp. 17–18)

The green revolution, which transformed India between my two visits, had
largely completed the process of moving villagers from a barter to a cash economy
and weakened the *jajmani* system. Commercial goods, purchased in neighboring
towns, had replaced some goods made by village craftsmen. The craftsmanship of
the village goldsmith was thought to be inferior to the skill of Bhudana goldsmiths.
The weavers, tailors, potters, and blacksmiths had become increasingly tangential.
Weavers still made material for sheets and quilts, but most clothing was made of
commercial material, woven in factories. In 1955 only a few houses had pumps; in
1975 most Rajput houses had pumps within the courtyards, so the water carriers no
longer made their daily rounds. The demand for water pots had decreased the
potters' work, but village potters still made cooking pots and the oil lamps for the
festival of Divali.

Rajput use of low-caste servants had diminished. Many women, and some
young bachelors, did their own laundry, eliminating the service of the washermen.
Sweepers still came to clean latrines, but a shortage of cow dung, brought on by
increased family size and number of *chuula*s (cooking hearths), had led a number of
women to make the cow dung fuel cakes themselves, because they thought their
sweeper women wasted dung. Brahmin women were still called to cook for festivals, but in some families women of the household made their sacred Hooii
paintings instead of hiring Brahmins for this task.

THE KHALAPUR RAJPUTS

Rajput relations with Rajputs from other villages are regulated by membership in
endogenous kin groups called *jati*. Many customs stem from the fact that the
Khalapur Rajputs belong to a highly ranked jati. While relations with servant
families from other castes had changed, the Rajput's *jati* system, the basis of their
marriage arrangements, had remained essentially unchanged from the description
given in our first book:

> People who are not well acquainted with Indian society think of the caste system as
> a fivefold division consisting of Brahmins, or priests; Ksatriya, or warrior-rulers;
> Vaisya, or merchants; sudra, or artisans, servants, and laborers; and Untouchables,
> or persons who are regarded, somewhat paradoxically, as being entirely outside the
> system. If such divisions ever really existed and served as a means of organizing
> society, it was many centuries ago in ancient India. Today the basic unit of the caste
> system is a social grouping called the *jati*. A *jati* is a group one joins by being born

into it and it is the group from which one takes a husband or wife. There are many thousands of *jati*. They vary greatly in the size of their membership, as well as in the size of the area where these members are concentrated.

The *jati* do have some connection with the fivefold divisions thought to have existed in ancient India. These divisions were ranked, and the first three—the priests, warrior-rulers, and traders—had the highest status. Only the members of these three orders were permitted to hear the sacred Sanskritic texts. Since they went through a period of training believed to give greater spiritual insight, they were known as the "twice-born," and as a mark of their status they wore the "sacred thread," a circlet of string draped over one shoulder. Today most *jati* in India associate themselves with one or another of the five ancient divisions, and many claim descent from an illustrious personage believed to have been a member of the "twice-born" orders. The twin concepts of *dharma* and *karma* are of basic importance in the ideology of the caste system. The concept of *dharma* has a wealth of connotation but a core meaning is "a way of life appropriate to one's status." Quite simply it means that a potter should be a good potter and should follow the rules governing relations between himself and other members of his *jati*, and of other *jati*. By doing this he wins for himself, by the workings of *karma*, a better station in his next reincarnation. He is a potter in this life because of deeds he performed or failed to perform in his last. Besides accounting for one's status, the concept of *karma* accounts for the good or ill fortune one may suffer during the course of one's life. Although the full meaning of these terms is untranslatable *dharma* connotes duty and *karma* connotes fate. Both ideas have religious sanction.

· · ·

Almost all North Indian villages are composed of persons belonging to a number of *jati*. In Khalapur some 30 are represented. They vary among themselves in the extent and definition of their social organization. The Rajputs in Khalapur, for example, are clearly and explicitly a portion of one of the clans in their *jati*. They always have lived in the village, and only a few outsiders have ever been able to obtain any of the land.

(Minturn & Hitchcock, 1966, pp. 6–10, 16–17)

The history of the Khalapur Rajputs is a fascinating one, one which we now retell:

Landowners, who were the subject of this study, belong to a *jati* claiming descent from the ancient warrior-rulers, or Ksatriya. Throughout Indian history there have been groups of kinsmen who at various times and places have achieved political power. Generally these kinsmen were organized as patrilineal clans, that is, they were groups of men, all of whom believed that they could trace their descent, if they went back far enough in the male line, to a single man who was the progenitor of them all. The children of these men, both boys and girls, were also members of the clan. The wives, however, were not, for it was the rule that they had to come from a different clan. A powerful clan generally validated its claim to the status of Ksatriya by securing a genealogy. In the genealogy the descent of all members of the clan was traced back to one or another of the semidivine Ksatriya heroes whose lives and deeds were recorded in the ancient Sanskritic epic literature. And when members sought wives, they picked them from among clans that had established similar claim.

As a matter of historical fact, it is probable that many of the clans which achieved this status are descended from invading tribes that entered India from Central Asia prior to the arrival of the Muslims. Later, during the period of Muslim invasions, many of these clans, now calling themselves Rajputs, or "sons of princes," fled to Rajputana, a dry and forbidding mountainous area to the south-west of Khalapur. The kingdoms they established there were in existence through-out the Muslim period and continued as seats of Rajput courtly splendor until India became independent. These kingdoms were a center for resistance to Muslim rule, and the heroism and derring-do of Rajput groups and individuals today are an important part of folk tradition throughout India. . . .

It is impossible to say with any certainty from which area the Rajput clan to which the landowners of Khalapur belong came. According to their own traditions, they moved into North India from Central India sometime during the early centuries of Muslim rule. Their numbers swelled, and as opportunity arose they took up land in northwest India, in the region where the Ganges and Jumna debouch onto the plains. Calculations based on their genealogy suggest that Khalapur, as part of a general southward movement, was taken by a clansman and his sons sometime during the fifteenth century. The descendants of this man, with their wives and children, now number over 2,000. No other caste group in Khalapur is as large by half, and the few other caste groups claiming equal length of residence in the village say they came as retainers of the founding family. Today the Rajputs hold over 90% of the land and regard the village as theirs by right of conquest and 400 years of possession.

Following the usual pattern, the Khalapur Rajputs and the other members of the clan to which they belong—many of whom have a similar position in a large number of surrounding villages—validate their claim to Ksatriya status by means of a written genealogy. This is kept by a professional genealogist whose family has served in such a capacity for generations. His home is in Rajputana, so that he forms a link with the heartland of Rajput tradition. He journeys once a year to visit various clan villages and keeps a careful record of births and deaths in the male line. His charts trace the male line back through a succession of historical and mythical figures to Rama, the divine hero of the epic poem Ramayana.

Throughout the nineteenth century the Rajputs of Khalapur and their kinsmen in nearby villages were a problem to the British because of their cattle thieving, their marauding for grain (especially when crops were poor), and their unremitting resistance to revenue collectors. The police and some government officials still speak of Khalapur as a criminal village, and some of the village Rajputs still do augment their incomes through cattle theft.

Things the Rajputs say about themselves show how they tend to create their self-image in terms of their putative and, to a degree, their actual past. For in-stance, during a conversation in the village it was remarked that a highly placed official was a good administrator. "And why not?" replied a Rajput man. "He is a Rajput. He belongs to a ruling race, and they have been doing this work since time immemorial."

(Minturn & Hitchcock, 1966, pp. 10–12)

Cattle thieving, which had given Khalapur the reputation of a criminal village, was largely a thing of the past. With the green revolution, the use of high-yield grains, chemical fertilizers, and increased irrigation greatly increased food produc-tion. Sugarcane, the principal cash crop, had become a stable source of income for most farmers, and many sold a variety of grains to the government. Competition for land had increased, so owners still guarded their crops, as they had in previous times, to prevent theft or burning.

The most important change for the women had been the effect of modern agriculture on their men's self-image as the martial Rajputs, since the seclusion of women was an integral part of this martial tradition. The prosperity of the new grains had enabled families to educate most of their sons. These sons wanted literate wives who, in turn, resisted traditional purdah restrictions. In 1955 some Rajput men had thought of purdah as a protection for uneducated women, so the shift to educated brides diminished, in their minds, the necessity for strict purdah.

Khalapur Rajputs had acted as feudal landlords, known as Zamindars. The Zamindar Abolition Act and the Land Reforms Act had been passed in 1952, just two years before our first field trip. Wealthy Rajput men of that time saw themselves as warriors and landowners and sat in turbaned splendor on their men's platforms, disdaining farmwork as beneath them. Many former Zamindars were involved in lawsuits over land and were moving their former low-caste sharecroppers from one area to another, because the new laws gave tenants ownership of land they had farmed for 10 years. For some wealthy families, who had relied entirely on low-caste servants to farm their holdings, this legal provision caused the loss of most of their land. Only the wealthy landowners could afford to hire servants and use part of their land for the production of excess grain to sell or for the principal cash crop of sugarcane. Therefore, many were forced to farm their own land, labor that they considered demeaning. In 1955 we knew one man who had learned to plow when he was over 40, and another who said that Muslim conquerers had given Rajputs small plots of land so that regular contact with plows and bullocks would make them patient and calm and, like the earth they plowed, broken and scattered. "Rajputs," he added, "should be given their own work, and that work is not beating the hind end of a bullock."

Hitchcock describes the ideal of the martial Rajput as follows:

> The idea of the martial Rajput as an ideal of conduct was never accepted by every Rajput, and during the past century and a half its power in this respect has been very much weakened by the establishment of more peaceful, orderly, and prosperous conditions in this section of North India. Like the eighteenth-century fortress in the center of the village, a structure now crumbling in ruins, the qualities and forms of behavior embodied in the idea are now much less useful as guides to conduct than they were during former periods of intermittent warfare and social disruption. The martial Rajput as an ideal of behavior has also been weakened by the Arya Samaj movement of socio-religious reform and more recently by the example of such national leaders as Gandhi. There are many of the educated younger men in the village who regard the martial Rajput as something of an anachronism. They see his long mustaches, high turban, and heavy wire-bound staff—what Steed so aptly calls "an insistent, self-styled physical appearance and dress symbolically denoting strength"—as symbols of a passing day. These young men express their allegiance to different values by closely cropping their mustaches, and by wearing *khaddar* and Gandhi caps—the latter symbol causing the more martial of the older Rajputs, privately at least, to speak of them somewhat derisively as *topi-walas*. It must be remembered, in short, that I am illustrating a concept which is only more or less, and now and then, descriptive of any one of the 2,000 or so members of the Rajput population of the village of Khalapur.

(Hitchcock, 1958, pp. 216–217)

In 1975 few young men subscribed to this nostalgic image. The legal land battles, so common in 1955, had often been successful, and Rajputs had regained some of their lost land. The move to modern agriculture made the land a source of profit, as well as subsistence, and brought the sons of Rajput families into the fields to work along with field hands. The nostalgic self-image of the warrior had been replaced with that of the modern commercial farmer. Whereas a martial Rajput in 1955 protested that farming was not Rajput work but had been forced on them to make them docile and broken like plowed land, a Rajput woman in 1975 protested the allocation of land to low castes on the grounds that farming was Rajput work. The "tinge of the princely and the medieval" had been replaced with an air of the modern and prosperous.

Most farmers still plowed with bullocks, but a number of wealthy families had tractors. The cultivation of the new hybrid grains produced much higher yields so that, in 1975, most landowners were able to use some fields for raising sugarcane, and many had surplus food crops to sell. The hybrid grains and a profitable sugar market had increased the income of most Rajput families and many of their servant families. The intensive cultivation required by these new grains had also increased the work. The midwinter lull between the harvest of the fall crops and the sowing of the spring crops had disappeared. Farmers now planted three and sometimes four crops a year. Even the large men's platforms, which in 1955 usually had groups of elderly men seated on their spacious platforms, were usually empty in 1975.

In the fifties, Khalapur Rajput men largely ignored the introduction of the government's agricultural improvement program. Some had not been to their fields in years. In 1975 they worked the fields themselves or supervised the work of hired hands. Sons of men who had grown only the traditional crops, relying on their own seed for the next year's planting, now planted the new hybrid grains, which must be changed every few years, and regularly used the government services that their fathers ignored. Their knowledge of the latest seed strains and cultivation methods was up-to-date and accurate. They had also learned to use machines. Sons who had been raised with bullock carts ran tractors, tube wells, and pumping stations. The labor of sons had become the most important asset in a family's fortunes.

In the past, wealthy families freed one son from farmwork to oversee local politics and arrange marriages. In 1975 wealthy families aspired to educate one or more sons through college so that they could be employed off the land. A number of families already had college-educated sons. Because of the depressed economy, some of these men had returned to Khalapur to work the family land with their brothers. They brought their wives with them, and these women, accustomed to city living, sometimes had difficulty adjusting to the authority of the *sasu* (mother-in-law) in a joint-family setting.

Sons and fathers still shared a fierce devotion to their landholdings. The shift to commercial farming had made the land more valuable and intensified the land disputes. During the winter of 1975 three violent confrontations occurred over land disputes. These are described in chapter 5.

We interviewed women about the family landholdings, and many reported that the family no longer had enough land to support the families of their sons when the sons marry and have children. Most of them planned to buy more land. Since little land is up for sale and its price increases with demand, one may anticipate that land disputes will become worse as population pressures increase.

KINSHIP TERMS

The Hindu kinship system is unilateral, rather than bilateral, like English kinship terms, and thus Hindi kinship terms cannot be accurately translated into English. The translation problem may be illustrated by the English terms *brother-in-law* and *sister-in-law*, which are particularly vague. *Brother-in-law* may refer to: (a) the brother of one's husband, (b) the brother of one's wife, (c) the husband of one's sister, or (d) the husband of one's wife's sister. *Sister-in-law* may refer to: (a) the sister of one's husband, (b) the sister of one's wife, (c) the wife of one's brother, or (d) the wife of one's husband's brother. These encompassing terms assume equal status and role relationships among all the kin included in this term. In Hindu families with a patrilineal kinship system and an extended family household, each of these kin has different status and role relationships with respect to each other, as well as different kin names. Kin relationships are essential to family social structure, and people usually refer to relatives by kinship terms, rather than names, because speaking the names of older relatives is disrespectful. Wives, referring to their high-status *affinal* relatives, are particularly careful to use kin terms rather than names.

Unilateral kinship terms differentiate between paternal and maternal relatives (e.g., there are different words for maternal and paternal grandparents, aunts, and uncles). Hindi kinship terms do not differentiate among relatives of similar status, living in the same household (e.g., *bahen* means sister or female paternal cousin, and *bahai* means brother or male paternal cousin), but they do differentiate among household relatives with different statuses.

The birth order of the family men determines the role relationships among family members. Within a generation, Hindi kinship terms differentiate among relatives of different status, living in the same household, including brothers-in-law and sisters-in-law. *Jaith* is the term for older brothers or paternal cousins, and *dewar* is the term for younger brothers or paternal cousins. Wives of *jaith*s are called *jethani*, and wives of *dewar*s are called *derani*. Similarly, uncles older than one's father are called *chacha*, and their wives *chachi*, while uncles younger than one's father are called *taaya* and their wives *taayi*.

Wives do not use the term *husband*, referring to them, if at all, by circuitous descriptions. *Bahu*s (daughters-in-law) are expected to keep purdah restrictions from their *soosar*s (fathers-in-law) and all of his brothers (*taaya*s and *chacha*s), since they are all of a generation older than the husband. *Bahu*s also keep purdah from *jaith*s but not from *dewar*s. *Bahu*s may have informal joking relations with *dewar*s, but formalized joking relations between *bahu*s and *dewar*s, while present in other castes, are not recognized by Khalapur Rajputs.

Deference is accorded by *bahu*s to all wives of kinsmen from whom they keep purdah. Although deference among *bahu*s of the same generation is minimal, they use the terms *jethani* and *derani* to refer to sisters-in-law of senior or junior status. Wives are likely to come from the same villages. It is considered convenient and desirable to arrange marriages with women in the same family, so many *bahu*s have grown up together. If quarrels over household matters do not develop, relationships among *bahu*s are informal and friendly.

Sons are married in order of their birth, unless lack of education or some other factor prevents some sons from finding brides; therefore, wives of older men are usually older than the wives of younger men. However, all women marry in their late teens or early 20s, so second wives of widowers may be younger than their *derani*s. Nevertheless, their formal status is determined by the birth order of their husbands, although their actual authority is usually diminished by their youth.

All husbands' sisters have higher status in their natal households than all brothers' wives, and thus, whether they are older or younger sisters of the husband. Husbands' sisters are *nanad*s and brothers' wives are *bhabhi*s. *Bhabhi*s and *nanad*s never come from the same villages and live most of their adult lives in separate villages. *Bhabhi*s are expected to bring gifts to *nanad*s on designated occasions throughout their lifetimes, while *nanad*s are never expected to bring gifts to *bhabhi*s. Relationships among these sisters-in-law are formal and may be strained.

Because of the noncomparability of English and Hindi kin names, and because the description of purdah customs necessitates the accurate designation of the kin relationship of individuals, we use the Hindi kinship terms throughout the book. The terms used frequently appear, along with their translations, in Table 1.1; for the

Table 1.1 Kinship Terms

Hindi	English
baap	father
maa	mother
beta	son, or nephew
beti	daughter, or niece
bahai	brother, male paternal cousin
bahen	sister, female paternal cousin
bahu	daughter-in-law
soosar	father-in-law
sasu	mother-n-law
taaya	father's elder brother, or paternal cousin
taayi	wife of father's elder brother, or paternal cousin
chacha	father's younger brother, or paternal cousin
chachi	wife of father's younger brother, or paternal cousin
nanad	husband's sister
bhabhi	brother's wife
jaith	husband's elder brother, or paternal cousin
jethani	wife of husband's elder brother, or paternal cousin
dewar	husband's younger brother, or paternal cousin
derani	wife of husband's younger brother, or paternal cousin

sake of simplicity we have included only those necessary to understand the complexity of purdah restrictions.

CLOTHING

Clothing styles had changed for men, women, and children when we returned 1975. The fighting staffs, bristling, handlebar moustaches, and red turbans that had been the mark of the martial Rajput were worn only by men 50 years or older. Young men were clean shaven or had small moustaches and did not carry staffs. The 6- or 7-inch tuft of hair, worn by men and boys on the back of the head, was only 1 or 2 inches in length and usually unnoticeable. Young Rajput men had replaced the colorful, dashing turbans worn by their fathers with wool mufflers wrapped around the head for warmth or padding, when carrying loads. What they lost in style they gained in time, since wrapping a turban is a complex process. Most men and boys still wore dhotis (cloth wrapped around the waist and between the legs), but many young men had adopted the city dress of trousers and sports shirts, particularly when traveling away from home.

Most married women wore commercial saris made from brightly printed cotton. The Gandhi ashram was still in operation, and women still spun cotton and sold their thread to the ashram, but only a few of the older women still wore the plain, white, homespun saris, with their narrow colored borders, that had been the standard dress during my first visit. While colorful, the new saris were of much thinner material than the homespun saris that Gandhi had encouraged in his efforts to make villagers self-sufficient.

Older women still wore loose cotton shirts, with the shirttails hanging over the waists of their saris, but most young wives had adopted the bare-midriff sari blouse of the city. Although women still wore their saris over their heads as they went about their work, when I took pictures of young women, as I often did, they posed, city style, with their saris over their shoulders and their heads bare. I was reminded that, during my first stay, the only wife who dared to have her picture taken bareheaded was beaten by her irate husband.

Tunics and pants were still the usual dress of unmarried women, but the cut of these garments had changed. In 1955 pants had waistlines with a circumference of 3 yards. This excess material was pulled to the front of the body with a drawstring, giving an effect I called "instant pregnancy." The pants worn by young women in 1975 were cut to fit the waist and hips, emphasizing rather than hiding their slim figures.

Silver belts and toe rings had gone out of fashion and were stored in locked trunks, to be sold as silver when women needed money. A few wealthy wives wore gold chains at their waists. Women still wore silver anklets and gold earrings. Most married women still wore silver wedding rings on their second toes, although some mature women removed these when their daughters were married. Glass bangles were still the mark of married women but were worn more frequently by small girls.

Gold nose and front-tooth plugs had been out of fashion for some time and were seen on only a few of the oldest women.

Tattooing of the hands and wrists had gone out of fashion. The tattooed wrist-watches had been replaced by real ones, but on festival days women still made henna designs on their palms and around their feet. The *bindi,* a beauty spot worn on the forehead, had become common with young married women.

The elaborate hairdo of small braids, shining with mustard oil, that were woven together at the back of the head at the base of a long plait had been replaced by a single braid. The old elaborate hairdos were time-consuming to braid and had to be done by another woman. Because of the difficulty of their preparation, they re-mained untouched for a week or more between washings, and the oiled hair drew lice. In 1975 women washed their hair more often and braided it themselves. The familiar sight of women picking lice out of each other's hair had disappeared with the oiled hairstyle. Some of the girls attending the intercollege had adopted the city hairstyle of two braids. They were sometimes called "the ones with two braids" by conservative women, suspicious of their education and city styles.

Children's clothing, particularly that of girls, had undergone dramatic change. Many young wives made their own blouses and their children's clothes on their dowry sewing machines. Instead of the simple white cotton shirts, formerly worn by young girls and boys, the children of these young mothers were outfitted with bright dresses for girls and shirts and pants for boys. The young women also knitted more than wives of the previous generation, and children's sweaters had largely replaced the quilted jackets of former times. Infant adornment had also changed. Boys no longer wore elaborate charm necklaces to protect them from the evil eye, and mothers were less concerned about this danger than they had been in 1955. Few babies wore kohl under their eyes, and the frequent eye infections once spread by the kohl pot had disappeared.

Although toys were still rare, some children had small commercial toys such as trucks, in addition to the baby rattles and homemade cloth dolls of former times. Baskets of toys had become a standard part of dowry goods; these were given to children of the bridegroom's family.

CHOOPARS, BUGHARS, AND GHERS

Houses were still organized into *choopar*s (men's quarters), *bughar*s (women's quarters), and *gher*s (cattle compounds). Figure 1.2 shows the floor plan of a typical *choopar* and *gher,* and Figure 1.3 a floor plan of a *bughar* with a double courtyard. *Choopar*s have open platforms in front and rooms in the back. The *choopar* plat-forms of wealthy families are large, built of brick, and 4 or 5 feet above the street, with stairways leading to them. Large *choopar*s usually have a sizable central room in front of the individual bedrooms, where men can entertain guests during rainy weather. The platforms of poor families may be small adobe structures built at street level. Men sleep and spend most of their leisure time in their *choopar*s. *Choopar*s give men a vantage point from which to see whatever is going on in their street and hail anyone passing by.

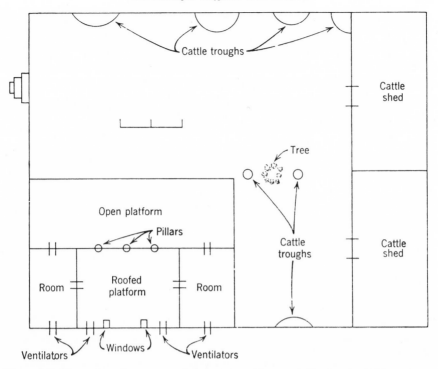

Figure 1.2 *Floor plan of* choopar *and* gher. *(From Minturn & Hitchcock, 1966, p. 21.)*

Unlike *choopars*, *bughars* are built to shield women from the gaze of any passerby. Women's rooms are built around an enclosed courtyard. The room adjacent to the street is often used for a milk cow, and the door of this room to the street is usually not aligned with the room's door to the courtyard, so that a passerby cannot look directly into the courtyard. The bedrooms are windowless or have small peepholes. They are used for storage and for sleeping during rainy weather. The women's activities take place in the open courtyards when it is sunny. Most courtyards have roofed portals along one side that give shelter during rainy seasons. A family's *bughar* may be built adjacent to, or across the street from, the family *choopar*. Quarrels among wives sometimes lead to the division of a *bughar* courtyard or the construction of two or more *bughars*, while the family men still share the same *choopar*.

Family *ghers* may be at the entrances of *bughars* or beside the *choopars*. In 1955 men with a particularly good pair of bullocks usually tethered them in a conspicuous site beside their *choopar;* in 1975 tractors were similarly displayed by wealthy families.

Inside the village new brick or cement-block houses and *ghers* had replaced most of the adobe homes in Rajput neighborhoods. In 1955 a number of families had adobe *bughars* even when their *choopars* were brick; in 1975 most *bughars* were also brick, without the mud courtyard floors that had made women's work in

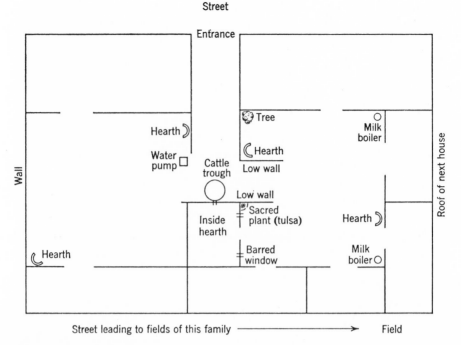

Figure 1.3 *Floor plan of* bughar *with double courtyard. (From Minturn & Hitchcock, 1966, p. 23.)*

rainy seasons unpleasant and unhealthy. In 1975 many Rajput homes had electric light in both *choopars* and *bughars*, although it was more common in *choopars*. Although bulbs were small and widely spaced, they provided welcome light to the dark covered courtyard porticoes and windowless bedrooms.

By the time of our second visit, a number of families had constructed two-story *choopars*. Only the young men, from whom most wives need not be secluded, used the second stories; nevertheless, some women still objected to this invasion of their cloistered privacy, and small brick walls had been built on the roofs of a few *bughars* adjacent to these new two-story *choopars* to shield women working on the roof from the intruding gaze of men. In contrast to these new shields for old customs, a number of courtyard roofs had single rooms built on them, away from the cloistering restrictions of the courtyards, for housing young married couples.

The principal article of furniture was still the hemp cot laced onto a bamboo frame. Cots were still used for sleeping and for drying grain as well as dishes. With the loosening of cloistering restrictions, they were less likely to be placed on their sides to shield a young wife from the family men, which we observed in the fifties. In 1975 some dowries included wooden chairs and beds, but these were usually in the bedrooms. Woven sitting mats were still used by many women. *Choopars* were also furnished with cots and, for wealthy families, chairs.

Cooking was still done on the small *chuulas*—U-shaped mud hearths about 12 inches square and 8 inches high. *Chuula*s are built against a courtyard wall, or in a roofed enclosure, protecting them from rain. The round-bottom cooking pots are put directly on the *chuula*. Milk was still boiled in pots placed in *chuula*s, and cow dung was still used as fuel.

Bughar courtyards were still the sites for the threshing and winnowing of grain. Small metal threshing cups were set into most courtyard floors. Threshing poles, with metal sheathing on one end, were stored in the *bughar*s, and women singly or in groups pounded grain placed in the threshing cups to husk it. Winnowing baskets as well as cooking utensils were a standard part of *bughar* equipment. Spinning wheels were still used regularly. A number of *bughar*s also had hand-operated sewing machines, brought as dowry by young brides.

The Rajput ideal is a patrilocal joint family whose members farm land collectively and shared living quarters and a common *chuula*. In fact, quarrels among wives are likely to result in the establishment of separate *chuula*s and the division of a *bughar*. The family men may share their *choopar* and farm their land collectively, even when they have established separate households for their wives. The conflicts engendered by differences in the membership of families sharing *bughar*s, *choopar*s, and land were briefly described in our first report:

> There are fewer men's dwellings, for related men from neighboring courtyards may share the same platform. Four brothers, for example, with wives living in three different courtyards, shared the same sleeping quarters and spent many leisure hours together there.
>
> After the courtyard and men's house groups, a third important social unit is the joint farm family—the group of males who own and work land in common, plus their wives and children. Although the ideal pattern is for brothers to continue to own and operate the father's farm after his death, in practice brothers usually divide the land. The joint farm family, therefore, tends to be a smaller social unit than either of the two groups who share a sleeping area.
>
> Lack of congruence among the membership of these three social units is often the result of quarrels between the wives confined in the same courtyard, a situation leading them to exaggerate small annoyances. The easiest and least disruptive solution of such tension is for the conjugal family to build a separate hearth within the courtyard. Sometimes, however, the courtyard is divided into separate compartments by building a wall down the center, or a completely new women's dwelling unit may be constructed. The men may continue to share the same men's dwelling and may continue to own land in common.
>
> At the beginning of a cycle, a courtyard may consist of a mother and father, a married son, and his wife and children. They eat together at a common hearth and share a single women's house. The men and adolescent boys share a single men's dwelling, own land in common, and work together in the fields. Ideally the young sons will marry and continue to live with their parents and raise their children in the common courtyard. The ideal, however, is seldom realized for long.
>
> The first break in the pattern usually comes when a man and his wife decide to have a separate hearth. This step may be taken with overt good nature and willingness on both sides and may be rationalized on the basis of convenience. More frequently, however, as mentioned above, it results from tension and quarrels among the women. It is a weakness of the ideal extended family that fractionating is inevitable but not accepted emotionally.

Although not always regarded as desirable, separate hearths are no real threat to the extended family, for basic patterns of authority and of property allocation and economic cooperation are not broken. The older women still have charge of giving out the daily ration of food. The father runs the farm. Further division, however, is a threat to basic patterns. The division of the courtyard into two sections by building a wall, or the setting up of a new household, entails the division of property: The milk cattle, furniture, and food. Now the *sasu* [mother-in-law] no longer has to be approached for the daily ration, and the young wife has a source of pocket money, for she can sell small amounts of grain at the store and spend the money for bangles without permission of her sasu. At this stage, however, land remains intact.

Further divisions may be more drastic. The land may be divided up among brothers, or brothers and cousins, at the death of the older generation, thus setting up separate joint farm families. The men may still share a dwelling and their wives a courtyard, but the economy of each family is now distinct.

(Minturn & Hitchcock, 1966, pp. 25–26)

Prosperity had enabled a number of men to construct new buildings for themselves, their families, and their cattle. The construction of *bughar*s was a more frequent addition. Therefore, the lack of congruence between the people sharing a *choopar,* a *bughar,* and a joint-family farm, as described in 1955, had increased, escalating the conflicts inherent in these situations.

Construction of new buildings had not kept pace with the increased population, and thus although there were more dwellings than formerly, they were usually more crowded in 1975 than they had been in 1955. Table 1.2 shows the numbers and percentages of extended, stem, and nuclear families in the two periods. Nuclear families consist of a husband, a wife, and their children; stem families have one or two additional relatives, usually an elderly parent or parents; extended families are ones in which two or more couples and their children live in the same household. The total number of houses occupied by the families of the study had increased from 38 in 1955 to 52 in 1975. However, the number of extended family households had increased from 22 to 38 (16%), while the number of nuclear family households had decreased from 12 to 10 (12.5%). The number of stem families remained essentially the same.

Table 1.3 shows the average number of males and females connected to *bughar*s in 1955 and 1975. The numbers for both sexes are listed separately for those over the age of 6, when children enter school, and for preschool children, aged 5 or younger. The figures show that, for those over 6 years, the average number of males

Table 1.2 Family Composition

	1955		1975		1955–1975	
	N	%	*N*	%	*N*	%
Extended	22	58	38	73	+16	+15
Stem	4	10.5	4	8	0	−2.5
Nuclear	12	31.5	10	19	−2	−12.5
Total	38	100.0	52	100		

Table 1.3 Average Number of People per Courtyard

	1955			1975		
	N	%	M	N	%	M
Age 6+ years						
Males	184	51	4.8	296	43	5.7
Females	118	33	3.1	256	37	4.9
Total	302	84	7.9	552	80	10.6
Age 0–5 years						
Males	30	8	0.8	63	9	1.2
Females	29	8	0.8	77	11	1.9
Total	59	16	1.6	140	20	3.1
Grand total	361	100	9.5	692	100	13.3
Courtyards		38			52	

per *bughar* had risen from 4.8 to 5.7 and the average number of females had risen from 3.1 to 4.9. The average increase in the number of older children and adults was 2.7. The average number of preschool children had increased from 0.8 to 1.2 for boys and from 0.8 to 1.9 for girls, or an average increase of 1.2 young children. The average number of family members of both sexes and all ages had risen from 9.5 to 13.3, or an increase of 3.8.

While these numbers are not large, one or two additional children in an enclosed *bughar,* or one or two additional people to cook for on a *chuula,* represented an increase in *bughar* congestion and *bahu* work load that was great enough to heighten interpersonal antagonisms in some families. This increase in *bughar* population was often more marked in wealthy families who occupied large, expensive, brick households that sheltered large extended families, because each man wanted to ensure his claim, than in poor families where small adobe structures had been left to one group after a family quarrel.

Extremes of this dimension may be seen in the families of the wealthy Gopal, Puran, and Mussaddi and the poor brothers Suchet, Kela, Daya, and Kanak. These two families represent extremes of wealth. Some of the sons of Gopal and his brothers had built large men's quarters for themselves and their sons, but the women of the family, despite some bitter quarrels, shared the most crowded courtyard of any of our families, because the *bughar* was one of the oldest and finest in Khalapur. Built of fired brick, with Mogul-style fluted arches and elaborate woodwork, it was a mansion to which none of the heirs would relinquish their claim.

The four poor brothers—Suchet, Kela, Daya, and Kanak—had a small adobe building in their women's quarters, and their *choopar*s were little more than a low adobe platform at the door of their *bughar*. Kela's quarrelsome wife had displaced the families of Daya and Kanak before 1954 and had separated from Suchet by 1974. The original *bughar* was divided into three small courtyards, which were occupied by the families of Suchet, Kela, and Kanak, while Daya built a small house in the family cattle compound.

We knew both families well, and will be referring to them throughout the book. We introduce them now. Their family composition in 1975 is shown in Figures 1.4 and 1.5.

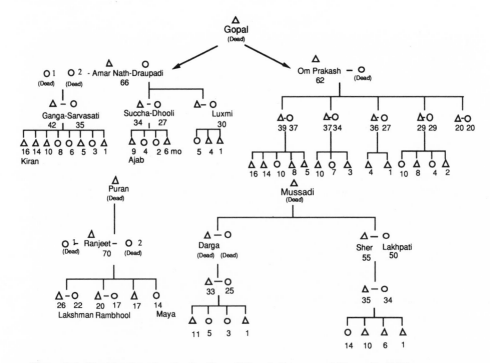

Figure 1.4 *Kinship chart for the families of Gopal, Puran, and Mussadi, 1975.*

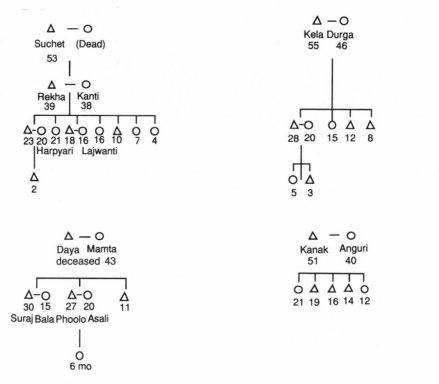

Figure 1.5 *Kinship chart for the families of Suchet, Kela, Daya, and Kanak, 1975.*

32

TWO FAMILIES
The Families of Gopal, Puran, and Mussadi

Gopal had been one of the wealthiest and most powerful of Khalapur's Zamindars. He had died before our first visit but was still a formidable memory. His family was one of the wealthiest and most conservative in our sample. In 1955 the women of his household were the only ones who would not allow me to take any photographs of them. His two sons, Amar Nath and Om Prakash, were alive during both of our visits. Both men were principal informants for John Hitchcock. Amar Nath had decided that it was his karma for this lifetime to help the Americans studying his village. He served as host to Michael Mahar, who stayed in Amar Nat's *choopar* during his visits. Swaran Kapoor and I ate in this *choopar* during the winter of 1974–75.

Both brothers drank heavily, and Amar Nath also took opium. Amar Nath was the eldest son but lacked the leadership qualities of Om Prakash, who was a village official in 1955. Amar Nath and Om Prakash had built separate *choopars* by 1955, but their wives shared one half of a double courtyard in one of the oldest and largest of Khalapur's *bughars*. Each side of this courtyard is about 30 feet square.

In 1955 Om Prakash had five sons, only one of whom was married. Amar Nath had been widowed twice and was married to his third wife, Draupadi. He had a married son, Ganga, by his first wife. In 1955 Ganga had recently been married to his wife, Sarvasati, but had no children. Amar Nath and Draupadi had one son, Succha, and a daughter, Luxmi, both unmarried.

When we returned in 1975, Ganga had eight children, five sons and three daughters. During our absence, Succha had married a woman who died giving birth to her first child, leaving her husband widowed and childless. When we returned in 1974 Succha was married to his second wife, Dhooli, who had given him one son and two daughters. A second son was born during the winter of 1974–75. Luxmi had married and had two sons and one daughter.

Ganga was prosperous and had built a house across the street from the family home. His wife, Sarvasati, still lived in the joint *bughar*. Sarvasati said that she would be lonely in a house by herself, but others said that Ganga did not want to move his family until after his father's death, so that he could retain full claim to his portion of the family home. Ganga farmed his land and kept his finances separate from those of his father and younger half brother, because Draupadi had alienated Ganga from his father by adopting his eldest son, Kiran, when Kiran's mother, Sarvasati, could not nurse him.

Succha had not been so fortunate. During the sixties, after the sudden death of his first wife, he was mentally ill for several years. The farming of his father's land was neglected until he recovered. Amar Nath did not farm his land, and their finances were severely reduced during the period of Succha's illness. Because of their reduced wealth and Succha's illness, Amar Nath was unable to obtain a wealthy second wife for his son. Succha's second wife, Dhooli, came from a poor family and suffered by comparison with her wealthy sisters-in-law. Succha finally recovered and went back to work. In 1975 he told us: "In the last 2 years Lakshmi [the goddess of wealth] has smiled on me, and now I have plenty of money."

Draupadi came from a wealthy family and told us that her grandmother bragged that she was wealthy enough to buy brides for the pillars of her house. Of all the women, Draupadi was the shrewdest at gaining the loyalty of family men. She had alienated Ganga from his father, taken over his firstborn sons as her own, and retained the loyalty of Succha and his firstborn son, Ajab. Draupadi was often at odds with Succha's second wife, Dhooli, because he blamed Dhooli for Succha's mental illness. Also, the contrast between her poor *bahu* and the wealthy *bahus* of Amar Nath's brother, Om Prakash, and cousins Ranjeet, Darga, and Sher was an embarrassment to the wealthy Draupadi and no doubt contributed to her dislike of Dhooli. (The details of Draupadi's co-opting of Kiran and Ajab are reported in chapter 12.)

Draupadi had been very successful in maximizing her advantages in a difficult position. She married Amar Nath, the eldest son of the eldest son Gopal, and would have been clearly senior in status in relation to the wife of Amar Nath's brother, Om Prakash, and to the wives of his cousins Darga, Ranjeet, and Sher, except that she was Amar Nath's third wife and considerably younger than any of the other senior wives. This age discrepancy made her status with these other *sasus* somewhat ambiguous. Until the death of Om Prakash's wife, Draupadi had to be particularly careful of her relationships with her elder *derani*. Om Prakash has five married sons, all of whom, in addition to Ganga, are Succha's rivals for control of the family land, and house when their fathers die.

In 1975 Om Prakash's wife was dead, so Draupadi was the undisputed senior woman of her courtyard. Om Prakash had become a confirmed alcoholic, and on more than one occasion Amar Nath had used his walking stick to beat his younger brother for his disreputable behavior. Om Prakash spent much of his time visiting the families of his *bahus* and imposing on their traditional hospitality for food and drink. Draupadi sometimes took over the mother-in-law role for Om Prakash's daughters-in-law, and her assertiveness was appreciated by them when the drunken Om Prakash wandered into the *bughar*. During one of our visits Om Prakash came in and, standing over one of his son's wives, who was cooking at her *chuula* and constrained by custom not to stand up, uncover her face, or speak in the presence of her father-in-law, complained that he was cold at night without his wife and suggested that she divorce his son and marry him. Such a remark would be improper for a father-in-law in any society; in Rajput society, where women's virtue is essential and gossip is rampant, it was not only salacious but potentially dangerous. When she heard Om Prakash's proposal, Draupadi stood up, walked over to Om Prakash, and, looking straight at him, ordered him out of the *bughar*. He went without a word of protest, and the relieved daughter-in-law breathed a grateful thanks.

Amar Nath failed his responsibilities as the eldest son, neglected his fields, and spent his time on his *choopar*, drinking and taking opium. With her husband in a habitual stupor, Draupadi had to take on responsibilities that should have been handled by her husband. Succha ran away several times during his illness, and it was Draupadi, not Amar Nath, who traveled widely searching for him. She assumed unusual financial responsibilities and was largely responsible for providing her daughter, Luxmi, with the expensive presents expected of a wealthy *bahu*.

Draupadi was unusually aggressive and outspoken. She was the only wife who openly criticized her husband or expressed concern for his health. Despite his faults, she seemed to be genuinely fond of Amar Nath. Intelligent and humorous, she was, despite her shrewd and often manipulative behavior, one of the most likable women we knew.

The other half of the double courtyard of this *bughar* was occupied by the families of three cousins of Amar Nath and Om Prakash, descendants of Gopal's two brothers, Puran and Mussadi. Nothing divided the two halves of this courtyard except the low walls around two *chuulas*, projecting a few feet on either side of the courtyard. However, the women's behavior represented one of the best examples of the "invisible walls" between *bughar* sections. Except on ceremonial occasions, the wives of Amar Nath and Om Prakash never crossed into the courtyard of their husbands' cousins, and the wives of Sher, Darga, and Ranjeet in turn stayed on their side of the courtyard. Even within their courtyard sections, each woman generally confined her activities to the few feet of space surrounding her *chuula*. These conventions of respect for the space of other wives allow women to maintain a degree of privacy and reduce friction in the crowded quarters to which they are confined.

In 1955 Puran was already dead. His son, Ranjeet, had two wives, having married a second time because his first wife was barren. His senior wife had given her consent to this second marriage because of the taunts of her fellow *bahus* that their sons would inherit Ranjeet's land. Fair skin is the primary criterion of beauty among Indians, so important that it overrides good features and bearing; the dark complexion of Ranjeet's junior wife was no doubt an important reason for her inability to make a more favorable marriage. The two wives got along amicably and rejoiced in Lakshman.

In 1955 Sher and Darga, sons of the widower Mussadi, were the senior men of the other two families sharing this half of the courtyard. Although Sher and Darga had only one son each, neither had slept with their wives for years. Both sons were unmarried in 1955. Ranjeet's son was said to be the offspring of Mussadi, who had raped Ranjeet's wife.

In 1955 Mussadi was still alive at age 65 and was one of the most colorful examples of a martial Rajput at that time. In his youth he had fallen in love with a Muslim prostitute in Bhudana. Hitchcock recounts the results of this infatuation:

> The girl eventually married a rich merchant. When the merchant failed to fulfill a number of promises he made, she decided to leave him and informed her Rajput friend by messenger that she needed help. One night the young man with a large group of companions, all of them on horseback, rode into the town where she was living and abducted her.
>
> (Hitchcock, 1958, pp. 220–221)

The mistress lived in Mussadi's *bughar* with the wives of his sons and nephews for many years, until she made the mistake of asking for a share of the family land. Mussadi's sons and nephews objected to this unprecedented request, and she was promptly sent back to her own people. After she left the *bughar,* she still came to visit at festivals and had come to mourn Mussadi when he died. She died in 1972.

Sher had a reputation for cattle theft and other crimes, although he had never been on trial. Before 1954 the wives of Sher and Ranjeet had fought so bitterly that Ranjeet's wife had put burning coals on one of Mrs. Sher's trunks and burned some of her dowry clothes. Sher replaced the clothes but would not let his wife separate her household, although he could have afforded to build a new *bughar*.

In 1955 Mussadi was the only *soosar* (father-in-law) of the family and Luxmi was the only daughter of the house. The five senior men and the married sons of Amar Nath and Om Prakash totaled seven married men. The unmarried sons of Amar Nath, Ranjeet, Sher, and Darga and Om Prakash's four unmarried sons totaled eight unmarried men in the family. The wives of Amar Nath and Om Prakash were *sasu*s (mothers-in-law). Ranjeet's first wife is counted as a mother-in-law in Figure 1.4 because she directed the work of her junior co-wife, and his second wife is counted as a daughter-in-law.

By 1975 Mussadi, Darga and his wife, and both of Ranjeet's wives had died, leaving Sher's wife, Lakhpati, as the senior woman of her courtyard. All of the sons had married. Darga's son had two sons and two daughters, and Sher's son had three sons and one daughter.

The second Mrs. Ranjeet had died before her older co-wife but had given birth to two more sons and a daughter, Maya, before her death. The senior wife had raised her stepchildren with care and affection until her death. The two elder sons were married but had no children. All four children had inherited their mother's dark complexion. Ranjeet, a 70-year-old widower, had arranged the marriage of Maya when she was only 13 years old because he wanted to see his dark-skinned daughter settled before he died. Maya was preparing for her permanent move to her husband's house during our second visit.

Table 1.4 shows the increase in this joint family from 1955 to 1975. The total number of people being fed from the double courtyard had risen from 25 to 64. The number of women residents in the *bughar* had increased from 9 to 24. The number of children aged 10 or younger had jumped tenfold, from 3 to 29. The women still occupied the same *bughar* and fed all of the family members from the courtyard

Table 1.4 Household Members of the Families of Gopal, Puran, and Mussadi, 1955 and 1975

	1955		1975	
	N	%	N	%
Males				
Fathers-in-law	1	4	4	6
Sons, married	7	28	11	17
Sons, unmarried	8	32	25	39
Total males	16	64	40	62
Females				
Mothers-in-law	3	12	2	3
Daughters-in-law	5	20	9	14
Daughters, unmarried	1	4	13	20
Total females	9	36	24	37
Total people	25	100	64	99

*chuula*s. A room built for Om Prakash's eldest son and his wife was the only addition to the *bughar* space.

The addition of so many women and small children greatly increased the confusion and noise in the courtyard. To make matters worse, two of the children were abnormal: one, an almost comatose boy of 3, was nursed for long periods by his mother while he moaned monotonously, and the other, a hyperactive girl of 5, rushed constantly about, stopping in front of adults to make faces and agitated gestures before rushing off again.

Despite the hectic congestion, the traditional desire for children prevailed. Draupadi told us there had been a long period when none of the family wives gave birth; then the Hitchcocks gave them a doll, and after that several women conceived. One particularly hectic morning, after I had taken two rolls of pictures of children demanding more and more photos, I jokingly suggested to Draupadi that she get rid of the doll. She laughed heartily and said that I should bring them another doll so the family could have even more children.

The courtyard occupied by the families of Sher, Darga, and Ranjeet had been electrified but still had an adobe floor, which became particularly muddy during the rainy season because of the unusual congestion in this *bughar*. The *bughar* shared by Amar Nath and Om Prakash was paved, but Amar Nath had refused to have it electrified. Although Amar Nath refused to have his *bughar* electrified, he had electrified his *choopar*. Sher, who would not build his wife her own house, had moved out of his cousin's *choopar* and built himself one of the largest *choopar*s in the village. The family women were not happy about this situation but were unable to persuade their husbands to remedy it. When I asked Lakhpati and her *bahu* if their muddy courtyard floor was not uncomfortable, they both agreed and said that they had often asked to have it repaired. In a rare criticism, Lakhpati's *bahu* commented, "If men refuse to make repairs, wives can die in poor *bughar*s." Dhooli had run an electric wire from the electrified courtyard to her room, but the wire had been broken and not replaced. She complained to me about this and asked me to have her room electrified. My request and payment for the service finally persuaded Amar Nath to electrify his *bughar*.

The joint ownership of this *bughar* was one reason for the reluctance of anyone to improve it. All of the families had a stake in the *bughar*, so they continued to occupy it, but because the house was jointly owned, no one wanted to invest in it. When Amar Nath accepted my offer to pay for the *bughar*'s electrification, Draupadi and Succha complained to me that this expense would benefit Ganga's family, who shared the *bughar*. They dismissed the request of the poor Dhooli as unimportant and preferred to have their quarters dark rather than share the benefit of electricity with their rival.

The Families of Suchet, Daya, Kela, and Kanak

The brothers Suchet, Daya, Kela, and Kanak were so poor that they had to "buy" their brides—that is, pay the brides' families to subsidize their dowry, because they had not received any marriage offers from families of brides with dowries. Daya's wife, Mamta, and Kela's wife, Durga, were sisters, married to two brothers, an arrangement that simplified marriage negotiations. Mamta was a kind and gentle woman, but Durga was ill-tempered and quarrelsome. Before we met them in 1955, Durga had driven Mamta and her family out of the courtyard by refusing to let Mamta's children eat in it, saying that they made it dirty. The evicted couple, with their daughter and three sons, were living in the cattle compound in the poorest conditions of any family in our study. Durga had also quarreled with Kanak's wife, Anguri, saying that the family had paid so much for Anguri when she married Kanak that they were unable to repair their house. As a result of the quarrel, Kanak had built a wall separating the *bughar*. The division left Anguri and her infant daughter with a courtyard only 5 feet wide and 12 feet deep, the smallest we visited, but she preferred her cramped quarters to sharing the *bughar* with the ill-tempered Durga.

In 1955 Durga had one son and one daughter. She shared her courtyard with the wife of Suchet's son, who had three small children, two daughters and one son. During the winter the two women quarreled and strung a clothesline across the courtyard, well supplied with sheets and quilts, as a makeshift division.

In 1955 Mamta kept less seclusion from her husband than any other woman. She had two sons, one daughter, and a baby girl born during the winter of 1955. (This baby died in 1956 and is not shown in Figure 1.5.) She was worried about the family's ability to earn enough money to get the daughters married, although the oldest girl was only 14. Her two boys, Suraj and Phoolo, had no education because they were needed in their father's fields. They carried heavy loads of fodder daily from the fields to their cattle compound. Despite their poverty they were one of the friendliest families and seemed to be one of the happiest. Mamta was a ritual sister of Sher's wife, Lakhpati, and so fond of Lakhpati that she said, "When I die, I hope to go to my ritual sister. We are very good friends."

Table 1.5 shows the composition of the original undivided household and the four households in 1975. Figure 1.5 shows the kinship relations of the family

Table 1.5 Household Members of the Families of Suchet, Daya, Kela, and Kanak, 1955 and 1975

			1975							
	1955		Suchet		Kela		Daya		Kanak	
Kanak	N	%	N	%	N	%	N	%	N	%
Males										
Fathers-in-law	0	0	2	15	1	11	0	0	1	14
Sons, married	4	22	2	15	1	11	2	29	0	0
Sons, unmarried	4	22	2	15	3	33	1	14	3	43
Total males	8	44	6	45	5	55	3	43	4	57
Females										
Mothers-in-law	0	0	1	8	1	11	1	14	1	14
Daughters-in-law	4	22	2	15	1	11	2	29	0	0
Daughters, unmarried	6	34	4	31	2	22	1	14	2	29
Total females	10	56	7	54	4	44	4	57	3	43
Total people	18	100	13	99	9	99	7	100	7	100

members in 1974–75. Before the separation of the *bughar* prior to 1954, the married members of the family consisted of the four brothers, their wives, Suchet's eldest son, and his wife. All four wives are counted as daughters-in-law because none of them had married children. There were four unmarried sons and seven unmarried daughters living in the household.

By 1975 Durga and Suchet's *bahu*s had divided their courtyard into two separate residences. Suchet's eldest son, Rekha, had three sons and four daughters. His two eldest sons were married, and the senior son had an infant boy; his two eldest daughters married in the spring of 1975. Durga's eldest son was married with two small children. An unmarried daughter and two unmarried sons also lived in their parents' household.

Mrs. Kanak had given birth to three sons and two daughters, all of whom were unmarried. Weakened by long confinement to her tiny courtyard, she died of tuberculosis in the winter of 1975. Mamta took over the child care of the two youngest children, saying "How can I let these poor orphaned children be without a mother?"

By 1975 Mamta's husband, Daya, had died. His family was still poor, but they had built a house in the neighborhood. Suraj, Phoolo, and the daughter had married. Phoolo and his wife had a baby boy. One 11-year-old son also lived in the household. The warmth of Mamta and her sons was unchanged. I recognized Suraj by his smile the first time I saw him, and one of my last memories when I left was of Phoolo, with his young son on his shoulder, waving good-bye.

CONCLUSIONS

The prosperity brought about by the green revolution accounts for the majority of the changes in Khalapur's material culture; the new brick homes, additional schools and shops, the bank, and the overall increase in acceptance of modern goods and customs stem from the increased prosperity brought about by the new agriculture. In wealthy families like Gopal's household, this prosperity has intensified family disputes over property, as the family maintains its extended household. In poorer families like Suchet's, separation into smaller family units has resulted from quarrels. The poor in most societies are more mobile than the rich. A simple house is easy to replace and may not be worth fighting over, but an ancestral mansion may become the focus of prolonged disputes among the heirs. The dispute over possession of the *bughar* of Gopal, Puran, and Mussadi, when their surviving sons Amar Nat, Om Prakash, and Ranjeet die, promises to be a bitter one.

These physical changes reflect changes in the people. The increased prosperity of the green revolution enabled Rajput families to educate all their sons and virtually all their daughters. Bus service enabled people to travel more frequently and easily. Young men and women, whose parents were afraid of city traffic, travel with ease to nearby towns and cities. With increased ease of transportation, marriages are often arranged with brides living in villages farther away from Khalapur than those of the brides of previous generations. Many of these new brides came from the district of Meerut and had been raised in more modern and urban families than those of

Khalapur. Wives brought in from cities and villages near urban areas brought new modern customs to their *bughars*.

The result was a marked increase in the ability of people to cope with change and new products. The changes had affected women as well as men. Many families had at least one college-educated son who was employed away from Khalapur as a teacher, government worker, or soldier. Educated sons usually married educated women. Their education, and their city residence with only their husbands and children, made these daughters-in-law particularly potent sources of change when they joined their husbands' extended families. In the fifties an educated daughter-in-law was rare and she was forced to comply with the traditional customs of the illiterate women. In the seventies, educated daughters-in-law outnumbered the un-educated ones. They not only passed their knowledge on to the uneducated women of their *bughars* but set the norms of their *bughars*, raised the aspirations of their illiterate sisters-in-law, and often changed the customs of their mothers-in-law. The resulting difference in sophistication of the women was striking. They had greatly increased knowledge about topics as diverse as geography, politics, and physiology. The following examples illustrate the degree of change.

In 1955 several women had asked me whether or not it was true that when it is day in India it is night in America. I answered the question several times before I realized the implications of the question: These women did not know that the world is round! No one asked this question in 1975. In 1955 I had to abandon plans to interview women about the structure of their government because they knew so little about it. One elderly woman thought India was still run by the British East India Company. In 1975 we found that all the Rajput women voted and knew that Indira Gandi was prime minister. In 1955 women knew no method of birth control other than abstinence. Several said they had heard that American women knew a way to keep from having children and wanted to know what it was. In 1975 several *bahus* criticized the resident nurse for promoting tubal ligations, since the operation did not help with the spacing of children, and complained that birth control pills were not available in the Khalapur dispensary.

In virtually every aspect of their lives, the Rajputs of Khalapur are partaking of the river of modernity that has flowed into their region. These changes in attitudes, behavior, and customs, particularly changes in the women, are the subject of this book. They have been brought about by increases in affluence, education, and access to urban goods and services. As we will see, they are fundamental, exten-sive, and probably irreversible.

II

TWO VILLAGES: PARENTS'
HAVEN, HUSBAND'S PRISON

Chapter 2 focuses on the status of women as daughters in their parental homes and as daughters-in-law in their husbands' homes, and their transition at marriage from their parental to their marital residences. The trauma of this transition is described and illustrated through excerpts from letters of a new bride to her mother and accounts of ghost possession and depression in the brides.

Khalapur Rajputs select their brides from, and marry their daughters into, a limited number of villages. Therefore, more married women had relatives from their own villages living in Khalapur. The presence of these "hometown" women helped to ease the transition of most wives to their new, strange marital residences.

When we asked women how many other women from their home village had married Khalapur men, answers usually ranged from "dozens" to "hundreds." Women do not necessarily know all of their hometown relatives, and thus it is difficult to assess from such general answers how much support *bahus* might receive from their hometown sisters. In order to obtain a more accurate estimate of the number of close relatives women had in the vicinity, we interviewed a sample of 71 women in detail about the number and type of female consanguineous relatives living in Khalapur.

Women may also adopt ritual sisters, who serve as friends and confidantes in their husbands' villages. We surveyed 140 daughters-in-law and found that 37, or 26% of the sample, had ritual sisters. Most women had only one ritual sister, but seven women had two and one woman had three. Ritual sisters are always of the same generation but are seldom relatives. Of the 12 pairs of sisters in the sample, only 2 were cousins. Cousins, like sisters, are often raised in the same *bughar;* therefore, they have a sisterhood relationship that does not need ritual recognition. The functions of both real and ritual female relatives are described in chapter 2.

When scandal or poverty makes it difficult for the groom's family to arrange marriages for their sons, brides are taken from strange villages rather than the ones usually selected for marriage arrangements. These wives can be identified by the absence of female blood relatives living in Khalapur. Circumstances surrounding three deviant marriages are described in detail at the end of chapter 2.

Rajput wives are subjected to the restrictions of cloistering and a complex set of respect–avoidance customs with their senior affinal relatives, as well as distancing customs that restrict their relationships with their own husbands. These customs are collectively called *purdah*, a word that literally translates as *curtain* or *veil*. Purdah customs are common among high-caste Hindus and Muslims throughout North India. A description of these customs in other communities may be found in several publications (Jacobson, 1982; Mandlebaum, 1988; Sharma, 1978). However, none of these accounts reports changes in purdah restrictions over a generation, and none records women's reactions to these customs and the changes in them. The decrease in the observance of purdah customs is the crux of the changes in the status of cloistered women.

Detailed information concerning women's reports of their lives and changes affecting them is relatively rare, particularly where women are rural and illiterate. Our account is based largely on such information. To document these changes and women's reactions to them, we interviewed 15 pairs of mothers-in-law and daughters-in-law. The age of each woman interviewed was recorded from census figures. Eleven of the senior women are in their 40s, and three are in the 50- to 80-year range. Ten of the daughters-in-law are in their 20s, and five are in their 30s. Each woman was asked to compare the amount of purdah she kept with the amount kept by her mother and mother-in-law. Therefore, the interviews with mothers-in-law report on purdah customs over three generations.

The most extensive interviews were conducted with the mothers-in-law. I was often able to check their descriptions of practices of 20 years ago with 1955 field notes and pictures. Comparisons indicated that some mothers-in-law were exaggerating both the purdah restrictions of their generation and the degree to which purdah had lessened for their daughters-in-law (see appendix A). Therefore, while some questions in the daughter-in-law interview were chosen to match those of the mother-in-law interview, others were designed to document actual behavior of the younger women. Some answers of daughters-in-law (e.g., that the observance of purdah customs had lessened considerably within the *bughars*) confirmed the reports of the mothers-in-law. Other reports from mothers-in-law (e.g., that daughters-in-law worked in the fields or demanded separation of cooking facilities shortly after marriage) were contradicted by responses of the younger women (see appendix B).

Chapter 3 describes the customs of traditional purdah and the changes that have occurred in them. General questions about the degree of purdah each woman kept were followed by specific questions concerning the change in avoidance by themselves versus their mothers to different types of family members—that is, fathers-in-law and other senior family men, women, particularly mothers-in-law, husbands, brothers, and patrilineal male cousins older and younger than the husbands, as well as persons outside the family (e.g., servants and salesmen). Changes in freedom of movement were covered by questions concerning mobility in Khalapur, work outside the *bughar*, and the frequency of visits to parental villages.

Chapter 4 describes women's explanations of the causes of the decrease in purdah and their evaluations of the changes. When asked to identify the causes of the changes in purdah observance, Bhagwan, or the will of god, was usually the first answer. When we probed for more secular causes, education, prosperity, and increased transportation were cited most frequently.

Evaluation questions began by assessing the women's evaluations of general changes in purdah customs and went on to elicit their opinions concerning changes in specific practices—that is, deference to older men and women, husbands, servants, and outsiders. Relations between *sasus* and *bahus* were documented through questions about obedience of *bahus*, their authority over the children, and how well the women got along. Finally, women were asked whether they thought the changes were good or bad, and whether their new freedom made daughters-in-law happier than women of previous generations had been.

Chapters 3 and 4 describe the changes in customs and attitudes that are basic to the changes in beliefs, behavior, and roles as they are described in subsequent chapters of this book.

Two young women dance at the birth ceremony of a family son. A daughter dances with her sari on the back of her head and a daughter-in-law with her sari pulled over her face, forming a *gungat*. These two dancers illustrate the difference in veiling between daughters and daughters-in-law (1975).

2

Marriage: From Daughter to Wife

A daughter is a guest in her parents' home.
Going to the husband's house is like going to jail.

Whyte's cross-cultural study of the relative status of men and women in preindustrial societies finds several clusters of variables measuring components of status
in different cultural realms—for example, economic, kinship, sexual behavior
(Whyte, 1978). However, Whyte does not address status variation of women in their
parental versus their marital homes. Women in exogamous societies marry out of
their natal communities into the communities of their husbands. Among many
Hindus, women's status as wives is lower than their status as daughters. One would
expect this difference to appear in most exogamous societies and to be particularly
marked in elite groups where the patrilineage is of paramount importance. This dual
aspect of women's status is crucial for understanding the lives of the women in our
study.

Marriage among Khalapur Rajputs is not only exogamous but hypergamous.
Wives are taken from *jati*s of lower rank, and daughters are married into *jati*s of
higher rank, than the Khalapur *jati*. Because Rajputs from the same *jati* tend to live
in the same villages, these marriage rules prohibit daughters from marrying men
from their own village or marrying into the same villages from which wives are
taken. Women continue to belong to their parental *jati* after marriage; therefore, the
jati of a daughter is higher in rank than the *jati* of her mother and her brothers'
wives.

Because marriage within one's parental village is impossible, Rajput women
live their lives in two villages—their parental village, where they grow up, and their
husband's village, into which they marry. Until she has grown sons and her own
parents are dead, a woman's primary emotional affiliation is to her natal relatives.
The strongest emotional bonds between men and women are those between brother
and sister and mother and son, rather than between husband and wife. The customs
of purdah, described in chapter 3, restrict the interaction of wives with their husbands and other members of their husband's household. These restrictions are
designed to ensure that the alliance between husband and wife is subordinated to the
alliance of men with their consanguineous kinsmen. Women do not keep purdah

restrictions in their natal village and therefore prefer to visit their parents whenever possible.

Changes in status as a function of age, also ignored in Whyte's study, are the second most important determinants of women's status. Each new wife enters her husband's house at the lowest status and advances as she has children, particularly sons, and as younger wives come into the courtyard. As *sasu* a woman is traditionally in charge of the household finances and directs the work of her *bahu*s. This control is lessening as daughters-in-law opt for more autonomy over their own affairs.

The increase in women's status with increasing age occurs in most societies (Guttman, 1985). Rajput women show several of the general characteristics listed by Guttman: (a) After menopause, women are not a sexual threat and have increased mobility, (b) mothers may gain increased power through their grown sons, and (c) mothers-in-law gain servants in their daughters-in-law.

CHOOSING A GROOM
Formal Negotiations by Men

Usually it is the bride's family who seek a husband for their daughter. Formal marriage arrangements are made by senior male relatives. A description of these formal arrangements appears in our first study:

> A family must arrange marriages for all of its daughters. A failure to do so is unheard of in the village and would be met with severe censure. There is not the same social pressure to see that all of the sons are married, but a family will make every effort to get wives for them, especially the eldest. Girls are generally married at 16 or 17. The marriage of a boy may be delayed until he is 18 or 20, especially if he is a student.
>
> When a girl is old enough to be married, her family must begin the search for a suitable groom. Marriage negotiations are sometimes conducted by the girl's father, particularly if he is the head of the house. But it is more usual for the father to obtain the help of elderly relatives. Information about eligible boys is often obtained when a member of the family, or a relative, goes to another village to attend a marriage.
>
> The range of choice is limited by a number of factors. Since some Rajput clans are more highly regarded than others, the negotiators will try to make an alliance with a family belonging to a clan of high standing. Another limiting factor is the location of the groom's village in relation to Khalapur. Traditionally wives have come from the south, and daughters have been given in marriage to the north and northwest. Distance is also a consideration, and few marriages are made in villages which lie beyond a radius of about 100 miles. Most Rajput villages very close to Khalapur are eliminated because the Rajputs in them are clan brothers.
>
> Within these limitations, the selection of a suitable groom requires a delicate balancing of many factors. The reputation of the groom, his age, health, looks, and schooling are important. The relative social and economic standing of the two families must be weighed. It is desirable, if possible, for the girl's family to make an alliance with a family having a somewhat higher status than hers, since this

enhances their prestige in their own village and ensures that the bride will not be discontent with her husband's social standing. But aspirations of this kind must be trimmed according to the amount of dowry which her family can afford and, finally and most important, by a decision as to whether the girl would be well taken care of, both as a wife and a widow.

(Minturn & Hitchcock, 1966, p. 35)

Informal Negotiations by Women

These marriage customs result in families of each village seeking husbands for their daughters from a limited number of other villages. As a result of this localization, most wives know other women from their parental villages who also married into Khalapur. Because the selection of a groom involves balancing many factors, the bride's family seeks as much information as possible about prospective grooms and their families. Women already married into families under consideration are the major source of such information. Therefore, the first, informal contacts are frequently made by a female relative who is already married into the village of the prospective groom.

The presence of relatives or friends in the husbands' village helps alleviate the strain of living with strangers. Some female relatives may be *sasus*, and exempted from purdah restrictions, and are free to visit young *bahus* to whom they are related. They are confidantes for problems with the in-law's families. They may bring and take messages to their natal homes when they return for visits, share local customs with each other, and join to celebrate some festivals not recognized in Khalapur.

Table 2.1 shows that 43 (60%) of the women interviewed had one or more sisters in Khalapur. This figure includes seven pairs of sisters who married brothers. Table 2.1 also shows that 15 (21%) of the women had a cousin, 11 (15%) an aunt, and 5 (7%) a niece living in Khalapur. Only 24 (34%) of the women we interviewed had no female relatives in the village. Table 2.2 shows that the number of relatives in Khalapur ranged from one to four; 28 women (39%) had one relative, 10 (14%) had two, 5 (7%) had three, and 4 (6%) had four relatives in Khalapur.

In order to determine how near these relatives lived to our informants, we asked whether their relatives were married into the same *bughar* as the informant, married

Table 2.1 Identification of Female Consanguineous Relatives Living in Khalapur (N = 71)

	N	%
Sisters	43*	60
Cousins	15	21
Aunts	11	15
Nieces	5	7
No relatives	24	34
Total	98	

*This figure includes 7 pairs of sisters married to brothers. Since women may have more than one type of relative living in Khalapur, the N is greater than 71.

Table 2.2 Number of Female Consanguineous
Relatives in Khalapur

	N	%
Zero	24	34
One	28	39
Two	10	14
Three	5	7
Four	4	6
Total	71	100

Table 2.3 Location of Female Consanguineous
Relatives in Khalapur

	N	%
Same household	16	27
Same neighborhood	18	30
Different neighborhood	26	43
Total	60	100

Table 2.4 Marriage Arrangements by Female
Relatives

	Marriage Arranged for		Marriage Arranged by	
	N	%	N	%
Sister	4	31	2	15
Cousin	6	46	1	8
Aunt	3	23	10	77
Total	13	100	13	100

to a man of the same lineage as the informant's husband (which would mean they were living in the same neighborhood), or married into another Khalapur *putti* (living in another part of the village). Table 2.3 shows that 16 (27%) of the women had a relative in the same *bughar,* 18 (30%) had a relative in the same neighborhood, and 26 (43%) had a relative in another *putti.* It is important to note that although female relatives often lived in the same *bughar* and might be *taayi*s or *chachi*s, *bahu*s (daughters-in-law) were never blood relatives of their own *sasu*s (mothers-in-law). The intimacy of a shared natal village would interfere with the authority of *sasu*s over their sons' wives.

Sometimes women taken an active role in arranging marriages for their relatives. We found that one third of the women we interviewed either arranged marriages for, or had their marriages arranged by, a woman relative already married into Khalapur. Table 2.4 shows the designated relationship of the relatives involved in marriage arrangements. It is interesting to note that 77% of the women had their marriages arranged by an aunt, but 77% of the women reporting arranging marriages for other relatives are sisters or cousins. The data are based on too few cases to make definitive conclusions but seem to indicate some shift in marriage contact from aunts to sisters or cousins.

MARRIAGE CEREMONIES

Marriages are celebrated in two stages: the *shadi,* or marriage ceremony, and the *gauna,* when brides move permanently into their husband's villages. *Shadi*s are usually held during the spring and summer, when food is plentiful and the weather is warm. For 3 days the groom camps outside the village with his *bharat* or grooms party. The *bharat* is as large a number of young male relatives as his family can afford to send. Old Rajput women tell of one groom's father, in the days when they were Zamindars, who rode his horse around the village of his son's bride, dropping gold coins as he went, until he had ringed the entire village with his largess. The days of such displays of regal wealth are over, but *bharat*s of wealthy families may still number several hundred. Since many *bharat* members are unmarried men, fathers with daughters of marriageable age inspect the men of the *bharat* for prospective bridegrooms. On the third day the marriage ceremony is performed and the bride leaves with her groom amid much weeping and many farewells—although the bride stays in her husband's village for only a few weeks and the marriage is usually not consummated at this time. After this brief visit, the bride returns to her parental village and usually remains for about 1 year; if she is young or her family is still assembling her dowry, this period may be as long as 7 years. If a husband dies between the time of the *shadi* and the *gauna,* his bride becomes a virgin widow and is not remarried.

For Khalapur Rajputs, the sacred thread ceremony for men is performed as part of the *shadi* ceremony. The sacred thread ceremony is traditional for all high-caste Hindu men, namely, Brahmins, Kashatriya, and Vaish. In this ceremony a young man is ritually adorned with a white cord worn over the right shoulder and across the chest and back, which is tied at the left side of the waist. The ceremony symbolizes a man's religious coming of age and his "twice-born" high-caste status. Devout Hindu men wear their sacred threads throughout their adult lives. There is no comparable ceremony for high-caste Hindu women.

There is no ceremony for the *gauna,* when the bride goes to take up permanent residence in her husband's village. After the *gauna* a woman usually remains in her husband's village until after the birth of her first child. She then visits her parents to show them the new grandchild. Visits are repeated after the birth of each child, when a relative dies, and for some ceremonial occasions. Young wives may spend one third to one half of the first 5 years of their marriage visiting their parental homes and will continue to make visits throughout their lives. They usually bring their children with them for these visits, particularly their sons, whom they are reluctant to leave behind. As a consequence, the children develop emotional ties with their mothers' relatives; these ties are particularly important for men, who use their mothers' villages as places of refuge if they get into trouble in Khalapur.

A description of wedding arrangements and the display of a new bride appears in our earlier book. The weeping of the brides had become less dramatic by 1975 and the display more informal, but the structure of the negotiations remained unchanged.

> When a decision has been reached and a boy's family has agreed to the match, a ceremony is held at the men's quarters of the boy's family. The negotiators who represent the family of the girl present a sum of money to the groom-to-be, plus small token payments to the members of his family and some of his family servants. Since the status of a wife's family is always subordinate to the status of the groom's, this aspect of the new relationship is shown by the very respectful and deferential way in which the elderly representative of the bride-to-be's family presents the gift of money to the groom-to-be. It is also clearly symbolized by the eating pattern. Since members of a girl's family are not supposed to take food in the village of her husband, when food is served at the end of the ceremony by the family of the groom-to-be, the representatives of the bride-to-be's family refrain from eating. This is an indication that the preliminary marriage agreement has been sealed.
>
> An auspicious date for the marriage is determined by astrological calculations made by a Brahmin in the village of the bride, and the groom's family is informed of the date by letter carried by the bride's barber.
>
> As the date approaches, both the family of the groom and the family of the bride have much to do. The head of the groom's family must see that arrangements are made for the ceremony and feasting which will take place before the groom sets out for the bride's village. Those who are to attend the groom as members of his marriage party must be informed and arrangements made for their transportation. . . .
>
> A number of preliminary ceremonies center about the bride and the groom separately, but the most important ceremonies take place when the groom and his party have come to the village of the bride, where they remain for three days of ritual and feasting. On the third day the groom and his party leave the village, taking the bride with them. The new bride seldom stays at her husband's village for more than a month or two. The date of her return to her parents' home is decided during the marriage ceremonies, and at the appointed time her brother or some other male member of her family comes to get her. She may remain in her parents' village for as long as three years, but she usually stays no longer than a year. When she again returns to her husband's home, she takes a large number of gifts for the members of her in-laws' family. She does not return to her own village until the birth of her first child.
>
> Although children do not participate directly in the marriage preparations and ceremonies, they have ample chance to view the proceedings from first to last. For months before the marriage, the conversation of the women centers around the event. In the bride's family the women are busy making baskets, bowls, and mats. The children see the preparations and mounting excitement. At the various ceremonies leading up to the wedding and at the wedding itself, the children, in restless, giggling groups, hover in the background, watching with eager interest.
>
> The marriage proceedings are particularly significant for children in that they provide a clear and dramatic picture of the drastic changes in a girl's life following her marriage. During the ceremony which marks the sending of a letter to the groom's house to set the date of the wedding, the girl, hidden in some dark corner of the house, weeps, by herself. This weeping is not a ritual mourning but a genuine expression of grief.

(Minturn & Hitchcock, 1966, pp. 58–59)

Ceremonies for the groom begin when he leaves his home village for his wedding. The first, the Baan ceremony, is attended by the groom and the men and women of his family. A special type of decoration called *manda bandhan,* made of long dried grass and tied in several places with red thread, is hung along the top of the door to the marriage chamber. When the groom returns in marriage with his bride, he unties this grass.

During the Baan ceremony, the groom sits on a mat facing east to the rising sun. A Brahmin man puts a *tikka* mark on the groom's forehead and ties a *kangana* around his wrist. The *kangana* is a sacred colored cord with which a piece of tumeric, a betel nut, an iron ring, and a few mustard seeds have been tied into a handkerchief. Gurshari is held the day after Baan, on the day that the groom leaves for his wedding. The groom is mounted on a horse and wears a headdress with a tinsel veil, because he goes in purdah when he leaves for his marriage. The groom's procession, the *bharat,* visits the Bhumia, the Piir, and the Siva temple. Offerings are made and the family Brahmin performs a *puja* at all three shrines. The groom's sisters and his brothers' wives put kohl, a black paste, under his eyes to ward off the evil eye. The groom gives his sisters a small amount of money in payment for this service. After the groom has visited the shrines he cannot reenter his house until he returns with his bride. *Bharat* parties used to travel by horseback, but in recent years they usually have gone by chartered bus.

Several hundred people come to feast and attend the ceremony, which usually takes place shortly after midnight. The ceremony is performed by a Brahmin, with many prayers and blessings. The bride and groom circle a fire several times to symbolize their union. They look into a mirror to see each other's faces for the first time.

A *tikka* ceremony is held on the morning of the marriage day. All the relatives of the bride's family put marks of yellow pigment on the groom's forehead and offer him money. Before the bride departs for her husband's home, her forehead is marked with pigment, and she is given some money to start her new life.

When the couple return to the groom's house, ceremonies are held to bless them and protect the bride. As the couple approach the house, the groom's *jethani,* or family barber woman, puts kohl under the bride's eyes to ward off the evil eye. When they reach the gate of the house, the groom's mother takes the jug of water and encircles the heads of the bride and groom several times to purify and bless them. The bride and groom touch the feet of all the family elders in traditional gestures of respectful greeting.

After the groom unties the *manda bandhan* tied to the doorway of the newlywed's room and throws it away, the couple are seated comfortably in the courtyard. The Brahmin removes the *kangana* cords tied to their wrists, and they are asked to "open the *kangana*" for each other. In a ceremony that symbolizes the strength of the marriage bond, each of them holds a gold ring tightly in one hand while the other one opens the hand. Then the couple are taken to a well where a *puja* is performed. They are given two small sticks, and each is asked to beat the other one seven times with their sticks. This symbolizes the recognition that newlyweds fight with each other and then make love, and the belief that there can be no deep love between them unless they fight. The *kangana* ceremony concludes with the bride and groom putting a few grains of rice into each other's hands. Both are fed sweets and dates. Some coins are passed among their heads and given to the barber women. The couple, having feasted heavily at the bride's house, are usually given a light supper as their first meal in the groom's house.

All of the ceremonies surrounding weddings recognize the importance of the occasion, emphasizing the relative status of the bride and groom, and the potential danger that each one faces in the villages of their in-laws.

The contrast between the emotions surrounding marriages of sons and daughters is expressed in songs sung on these occasions. Songs sung at daughters' weddings refer to the weeping bride who must leave the shelter of her home to live with strangers. The lyrics of three such songs are recorded here. References to motors and wristwatches in two of the songs indicate that they are modern. Two songs refer to the bride as a foundling, expressing the anxiety of being without parents in her husband's house.

> O foundling your looks are like a picture
>   Grandfather is searching for a husband but the foundling is weeping.
> O foundling your looks are like a picture
>   Elder uncle is searching for a husband, but the foundling is weeping.
> O foundling your looks are like a picture
>   Younger uncle is searching for a husband, but the foundling is weeping.
> O foundling your looks are like a picture
>   Brother is searching for a husband for you, but the foundling is weeping.
> O foundling your looks are like a picture
>   Brother-in-law is searching for a husband, but the foundling is weeping.

A second example also uses the image of a foundling:

> The foundling makes a noise like a motor.
>   "Grandfather come running, the groom is taking me away!"
> The foundling cries that a foreigner is taking her away.
>   "Jaith come running, the groom is taking me away!"
> The foundling cries
>   "Brother you come running, the groom is taking me away!"

While mournful songs are sung when a daughter leaves her parental home, songs at the marriage of a son are joyful.

> The in-laws' house of the groom is in Janakpuri
> Friends sing happy songs.
> The grandfather of the groom is in gay dress, elder uncle
>   is well dressed in the marriage party.
> The groom is dressed like Lord Rama.
> Friends keep him and *bharat* in front of all.
> The in-laws' house of the groom is in Janakpuri.
> Friends sing happy songs.
>
> The elder uncle of the groom and younger uncle of the groom
>   are gracing the marriage party,
> but the groom looks like Lord Rama.

Friends keep Rama in front of all.
The in-laws' house of the groom is in Janakpuri.
Friends sing happy songs.

The younger uncle of the groom and brother of the groom
    are the beauty of the marriage party,
but the groom looks like Lord Rama,
Friends keep Rama in front of all.
The in-laws' house of the groom is in Janakpuri.
Friends sing happy songs.

The brother of the groom and the brother-in-law of the groom
    are decorating the marriage party,
but the groom looks like Lord Rama.
Friends keep Rama in front of all.
The in-laws' house of the groom is in Janakpuri.
Friends sing happy songs.
The brother-in-law of the groom and his maternal uncle
    are gracing the marriage party,
but the groom looks like Lord Rama.
Friends keep Rama in front of all.

THE TRANSITION

A girl's status rises markedly as soon as her *shadi* has taken place. She is now a married woman, visiting her family. As a married woman, she is allowed to roam about the village and surround, free of supervision. Groups of young women who have had their initial fixings or *shadi*s frequently drop in on neighborhood *bughars*. Because they will soon leave, they are always treated as welcome guests. They may also wander out of the village into the fields, where men are working.

The interval between the *shadi* and the *gauna* is probably the most relaxed and joyful time of a Rajput woman's life. It may also be the most perilous. Although married and free of the restrictions of unmarried girls, these brides are still naive virgins. In 1975 some of these young women had become somewhat arrogant and stopped showing respect for their elders. Ranjeet's daughter, Maya, a bride of only 14 years, became particularly "swell headed" from her new status. Rajput customs reflect ritualistic status more closely than realistic considerations, and the unchaperoned freedom of young brides ignores the reality that affairs between young women and their cousins do occur. While rare, these seductions are recognized in some local songs: "O, cousin, I am coming to bring you food. / O, cousins, do not seduce me in the fields."

In 1955 we described the initial arrival of brides to their husbands' houses as follows:

When a new bride enters her husband's house, she is put "on display" every afternoon for several days. All the women of the family's lineage are invited to see her and her dowry. The bride, her sari pulled over her head and face, sits huddled on the courtyard floor. One by one the visiting women lift her veil and peer at her face, while the bride, with lowered eyelids, struggles to turn away. Having seen the bride and perhaps commented on her looks, the visitor turns to an inspection of the dowry. The mother-in-law displays the various items and tells her visitors how many utensils and pieces of clothing the bride has brought to the house. Each woman is comparing the dowry to those of other families, and the older women may verbalize these comparisons and make slighting remarks about the quantity and quality of the goods, or they may praise the dowry to the detriment of some other family who has recently acquired a bride. By the middle of the afternoon, the courtyard is full of women busily talking to each other and catching up on the latest news. No one speaks to the bride, and it would be shameless for her to join the conversation. She must not even be caught looking at any of the visitors. Although she may peek through her sari while it is over her face, she does not lift it, and she must keep her eyes lowered when anyone lifts her veil to look at her. The children, both those of the family and those who have come with their mothers, watch the proceedings, and occasionally a little girl, with a troubled expression on her young face, stands thoughtfully viewing the silent figure huddled in the midst of the chattering women.

(Minturn & Hitchcock, 1966, p. 60)

The decrease in the severity of purdah and the custom of displaying the dowry goods of *bahus* in enclosed rooms had diminished this ordeal in 1975. The decrease in purdah was dramatically demonstrated by the change in the visibility of brides. In 1955 I was not permitted to take pictures of any new brides, even though all were completely covered by their saris. My only photographic record of the bride display was a picture of a small girl who had wrapped one of her mother's saris around her and was sitting on the courtyard floor imitating a new bride on display in her home. In 1975 I photographed a new bride, sitting on a cot, with her wedding sari pulled back from her forehead and her face fully exposed. Standing next to her is her young *nanad*, whose *shadi* was about to be performed, utilizing the bride's dowry goods. The *nanad*, still wearing the tunic and pants of unmarried girls, has her scarf covering no more of her head than the sari of the new bride. This bride had arrived for her *gauna*, so she was past the stage of being put on display. Nevertheless, the change was dramatic.

TRANSITION TRAUMA

In 1955 I sometimes found prospective brides weeping silently in bedroom corners while senior women discussed plans for their marriages. In the decades between 1955 and 1975, the attitude of brides-to-be had been transformed from terror and silent weeping to giggling anticipation. Older women said that educated brides were no longer afraid of going to their husbands' homes. However, brides were still homesick during the first months of their marriages, and symptoms of emotional distress were most common in young women on the verge of, or during the early years of, marriage.

A personal expression of this anxiety is recorded in the letters written in 1968 by Amar Nath's 18-year-old daughter, Luxmi, to her mother during the first 6 weeks after her *gauna* (see pp. 69–71). Luxmi had married a handsome young man of a wealthy family and received a substantial dowry. We do not have the letters written by her mother, Draupadi, but we know that she was not alarmed by her daughter's letters and evidently considered them to be a normal expression of separation anxiety. In 1975 Draupadi told us that Luxmi had made a good marriage and was very happy.

Throughout her letters Luxmi includes lists of people, household members, friends, and servants whom she misses and asks that her greetings, *namistees*, be conveyed to them. She often refers to missing her younger brother, Kiran. She wants to return home before some *bahu*s return to their parental homes for visits. She asks to be called home for the wedding of some neighbors' daughters. She repeatedly asks Draupadi whether there will be a wedding in her parental village and says that she wants to attend this wedding, although such visits are not usual. Although she has just been married, she argues that one seldom gets the opportunity to attend weddings.

Luxmi repeatedly complains that her mother has not written in a long time and asks whether her father and aunts have forgotten her, although she has been gone for less than 6 weeks. Although brides do not usually return from their *gauna*s until after the birth of their first child, she begs to be called home immediately, says that her clothes are packed, and that she has been waiting at the railroad station. She repeatedly demands that her older brother, Succha, should be sent with several adult male cousins to bring her home. After three brothers and cousins do come for a visit, she writes that she has been depressed since the men left and blames Succha for not insisting that she be brought home and for telling her that she must listen to her in-laws.

She says that she does not eat and spends all of her time weeping. She threatens that she will die, "be in the house of Rama," if she is not brought home. She also threatens to curse her devoted brother, Succha, if her demands are not met. Luxmi describes herself as being like "a fish fluttering in a little water," "a snake with a frog in its mouth," and "a parrot in a cage."

She complains about her in-laws, saying that they are cross with her for not eating, and implies that her parents did not arrange a good marriage by saying that the in-laws are not the good people they had been thought to be. She fears that her letters have not been delivered, or have been tampered with, and writes curses against anyone other than her parents opening her letters. She also asks her mother, several times, whether she believes the lies presumably being written by her husband and other members of her in-laws' household. Luxmi's messages are sometimes inconsistent; for example, in one letter she says that she has been "locked in a cage" since coming to her husband's house, and in the next sentence says that she has been to the market many times since her arrival. When not complaining, Luxmi expresses excessive concern over several trivial matters: her mother's infected hand, a lost key, her father's drinking, who will take over her chore of cleaning the courtyard. She asks that her sandals and the license for her radio be sent to her.

Luxmi's letters sound desperate and demanding; however, they were not a matter of concern for her unusually doting mother. Despite her pathetic letters, Luxmi did not suffer any emotional breakdown. During our 1975 visit we came upon a house where women were weeping because they had just received a letter from a recently married daughter saying that she was weeping and felt so sad that she wanted to grow wings and fly home. Apparently, letters from brides that express extreme homesickness are not unusual.

Some brides exhibit abnormal behavior, and many develop ailments of some kind during the stress of early marital years. The most frequent ailments are possession and temporary coma, but sometimes brides become severely depressed and may commit suicide.

Possession

During our 1975 visit, Maya, Rajeet's daughter, became possessed on several occasions by the ghost of her brother. Although Maya had a large dowry and need not have feared her reception by her in-laws, she possessed two traits that may have made her unusually anxious about her marriage—youth and a dark complexion. Khalapur Rajputs usually marry daughters when they are 18 to 22 years old. At 14, Maya was the youngest married daughter of our families. Her father had decided on her early marriage because, as a man of 70 years and twice a widower, he wanted to assure his daughter's future before his death.

Maya was the daughter of Ranjeet's second wife and, like her older brothers, had inherited their mother's dark complexion. Among Indians, light skin is the most essential attribute of beauty. Because Maya's bridegroom had a light complexion, some of the family women teased her cruelly, saying that her husband was beautiful and he had married a donkey. Some said the bridegroom had refused to have anything to do with Maya after seeing her during her *shadi* visit.

The possessions took place 22 days before Maya's *gauna,* when she was due to leave for permanent residence in her husband's house. The family had received word that Maya's husband's grandfather had just died. Maya wanted to go for the funeral services, but her father would not send her because brides are customarily not sent for funerals in their husbands' homes until after their *gauna.*

Maya's symptoms were hysterical convulsions that began during the night, awakening the entire household, and went on for 4½ hours. Her jaws were locked, and she was laughing. It took several family men, summoned from their *choopar*, to hold her down. Draupadi and Lakhpadi began worshiping Maya, on the assumption that she was possessed by a goddess. When this failed to calm her, they slapped her and demanded to know who was possessing her. When no one answered, they decided that she was not possessed by either a goddess or a ghost.

On the following day Maya was taken to a doctor in Bhudana. She returned complaining of a pain in her abdomen and difficulty speaking. That afternoon she again became hysterical and challenged the wife of one of her brothers to a fight. Again the family men were called to calm her.

During this possession the family women were successful in persuading the ghost to identify itself by burning an ill-smelling spice in a tali. The ghost identified himself as Maya's half brother, the deceased son of Ranjeet's first wife, who said he was unhappy because his family had not built him a *pitar* (ancestor shrine) where he might live, be offered milk, and preside over the feeding of Brahmins in his honor.

Draupadi thought Maya was only pretending to be possessed, because brothers never possess their sisters. A family ghost wants to remain with its family, and sisters must leave the household and village. Therefore, possession of a sister, particularly one who was about to move to her husband's house, would not accomplish his aim. Draupadi described Maya as immature and foolish, saying, "Since she has nothing to do she goes around and hears these stories of how women become possessed and are treated very well. She did this so that she would be sent to her in-laws. She does not want to meet her husband, but to mourn the death of his grandfather." Acting on her suspicion, Draupadi challenged the spirit, asking, "Why have you appeared in Maya, why do you not appear in her older brother or his wife?" She reasoned that if the ghost did not appear in Maya's brother or his wife, it proved that Maya was lying.

Apparently, Maya became aware of Draupadi's suspicions, because 2 days later she was possessed by two women who claimed that they had come because someone in the household thought Maya was lying about being possessed by her brother. After this declaration Maya lost consciousness. On this occasion Draupadi first challenged the ghosts, declaring, "We are not afraid of ghosts," and then denied that she thought Maya was lying. A Muslim teacher who was visiting in the family *choopar* blessed some water and sent it into the *bughar*.

Maya regained consciousness when this blessed water was sprinkled in her face. She said she felt a heavy weight on her head and wanted to cry. When we asked whether she was anxious about going to live with strangers, she denied being afraid and said that she was glad her *gauna* was coming. She suffered no further possessions before leaving her natal home.

A *pitar*'s function is to provide a home for wayward spirits, so that they will not haunt the *bughars* and possess family members. The women in Maya's family finally agreed to accept the ghost's identification. They followed the customary procedure of promising to build the spirit a house during the period of the dark of the moon and extracted a promise from the ghost not to return if his house was built. The family was unable to afford the expense of a shrine until Maya's *gauna* had been paid for, but as a gesture of good faith they placed two bricks in a family field at the future site of the shrine they planned to build in about 2 months.

Coma

A temporary coma, usually lasting 24 to 36 hours, is one response to stress. During this time a woman goes to bed and loses consciousness. Usually no doctor is summoned for such comas; the woman is allowed to simply "sleep it off" and is not disturbed, unless the coma lasts longer than 36 hours. In 1955 one wife was particularly likely to take to her bed after a fight with the *bahu* with whom she shared her *bughar*. In 1975 we found no reported cases of coma. Probably the educated *bahu*s of the new generation were able to deal with conflict more directly.

Depression

Khajani, one of the girls in the sample of our 1955 study, suffered a severe depression 1 year after her marriage. She was married to a telephone operator for the Indian air force and lived with her husband on several military bases. Some relatives thought that the attack was brought on by seeing a massacre at one of the bases. One doctor had diagnosed her as suffering from the evil eye. Khajani was childless after 6 years of marriage. Because of the importance of children for Indian women, her latest doctor was treating her for infertility, apparently on the assumption that pregnancy would end her depression. An operation for infertility had been performed the previous summer, and she was still under treatment for infertility when we saw her.

Khajani's symptoms began with antisocial behavior and disobedience to her *sasu*. She would not offer her seat to visitors, cut up her clothes, and refused to do anything her *sasu* told her to do. In 1974 she could not cook or do her work well. Khajani talked to herself but usually would not talk to other people except her husband. Her husband kept her with him rather than leaving her with his family and had reportedly spent thousands of rupees in trying to cure her.

Khajani visited her parents' home while we were there, and we were able to visit with her one afternoon. She had just returned from a visit to a Bhudana doctor. She was unusually well dressed and well groomed. She wore a red chiffon sari, coat and shawl, nail polish, and *bindi*. She spoke quietly but was quite rational. She said that she remembered me and was glad that I had returned. She followed directions very slowly and sometimes answered questions several minutes after they were asked.

Suicide

Hindus believe in reincarnation, and thus suicide is seen as the shedding of one life for another. While certainly not desirable, suicide is not the serious sin for Hindus that it is for Christians, who believe that God has given them only one life. Suicide rates among Indian women are higher than in many other countries. The usual method of suicide is drowning in a village well. In 1955 a prominent Rajput man was known jokingly as "son of jump-in-the-well" because his mother, when a young bride, had jumped into the well near their house several times, hanging onto a protruding brick to keep from drowning. Women sometimes poured kerosene on themselves, and burned themselves alive, a practice that gives credence to the bride burnings of recent years. The presence of modern insecticides in villages has increased the incidence of suicide by poison.

These female ailments may be seen as culturally accepted reactions to the stress of young wives living in the confinement of *bughar*s, away from their relatives, and under the supervision of sometimes hostile *sasu*s. When this stress becomes too great, women engage in extreme behavior, such as possession, which temporarily suspends their status and makes them the center of attention, or they lapse into a coma that removes them from their duties and from contact with the other household women. Kajani's illness, a serious depression, was more debilitating and had lasted for a far longer period of time than the more usual possession or coma; nevertheless, it followed the pattern of stress-reducing behavior typical of women's ailments.

It is obvious that the behavior of both Maya and Khajani attracted attention and sympathy. Maya received the full attention of the family members she was about to leave, as they exorcised her ghost, and she obtained a shrine for the spirit of her half brother. Khajani's illness allowed her to avoid both her *sasu* and her household duties. Instead of living away from her husband, under the supervision of her *sasu*, she lived with and was cared for by an unusually doting spouse.

These examples represent extreme traumatization of brides. The vast majority of women do, of course, adjust to their new surroundings and thrive in them. Indeed the strength and fortitude of women in the face of confinement and low status are among their most impressive traits, to which we will refer in later chapters. It is the daughter who must "leave the nest" while sons remain at home. Therefore, daughters must be prepared to function on their own by the time they marry, while sons cannot do this while their parents are alive. In most cases both have the support of relatives: the men that of the patrilineage for sons, and related wives for daughters.

*NANAD*S AND *BHABHI*S

Because of hypergamous marriage and the primary importance of patrilineage, a woman's status as *nanad* (husband's sister) is always higher than her status as *bhabhi* (brother's wife). Wives represent links between patrilineages, but daughters are members of the patrilineage; therefore daughters always have higher status than wives. This difference in status is reflected in the two terms for sister-in-law. When a *bhabhi* gives birth to a son, she is expected to invite her married *nanad*s to visit their new nephew and give each *nanad* a present of gold jewelry, a custom that may seriously reduce the *bhabhi*'s bridal jewelry. Sometimes these mandatory presents cause long-term resentment.

Daughters are considered guests in their parental homes. In 1955 mothers seldom taught their daughters to cook or do housework, saying that they would have to work so hard in their husbands' homes that they should not be expected to work before they married. In 1975 some mothers were teaching their daughters basic homemaking skills before marriage, but married daughters did nothing except take care of their own children when visiting their parental homes. Their presence brought extra mouths to feed for the hardworking *bahu*s who must cook for them and their children.

The brother–sister relationship is considered sacred and is celebrated each year with a festival. The 1955 description of the warmth of the brother–sister relationship and this festival is still accurate:

> The relationship between a brother and his sister or female cousins also seems warmer and less restrained than the marital one and is considered sacred. A sister, even after marriage, may sit with her face uncovered and converse freely with her male relatives. There are ceremonial days when the strength of this bond is publicly recognized. On Brother's Day sisters fast for the health of their brothers and receive a present of a few rupees from their brothers in return for these good wishes. This festival occurs shortly after the festival honoring a locally worshipped goddess. When the clay figure of the goddess, which has been plastered on the courtyard wall, is removed, a smaller figure of her brother is put up in her place.
>
> (Minturn & Hitchcock, 1966, p. 36)

Bennet's comments on the significance of brother's day, as celebrated in the Nepalese village she studied, also apply to Khalapur.

> As a consanguineal woman, the sister has absolute purity which even the faithful wife . . . cannot match. No matter how "pure" an affinal woman may be—in terms of her virginity at the time of marriage, or her subsequent faithfulness to her husband—she still cannot have the ideal categorical purity which a sister has to her consanguineal kin. This purity is the basis of her sacred filiafocal status and of her power to bless her brother with long life.
>
> (Bennett, 1983, pp. 250–251)

Women also fast for husbands and sons, but these fasts are not accompanied by celebrations. The brother's day ceremony celebrates the sacred bond between brothers and sisters, and emphasizes the primacy of patrilineal kin over other kinship connections.

SISTERHOOD: RELATIONAL AND RITUAL

*Bahu*s without relatives in Khalapur do not have the female contacts with their natal villages that most women share. However, they may approximate these advantages by adopting a ritual sister. In 1975 we interviewed extensively about the details of this custom and took a census of women in 38 Rajput families to determine which ones had ritual sisters and what factors influenced their decision to enter into this relationship.

We found that women mutually choose each other for this relationship because they have become good friends. The sisterhood is formalized when the women exchange gifts on brother's day. This ceremony signifies their mutual adoption of each other as sisters. After this initial exchange, sisters are expected to exchange gifts every brother's day. The gifts usually include grain and clothing. Women also listed sweets, cosmetics, soap, ribbons, combs, and bindis as gifts they had exchanged. Some sisters also offer a jar of water to the sun as part of the ceremony. In addition to exchanging gifts with each other, ritual sisters usually give presents at the births and marriages of their friend's children, as would real sisters. Older ritual sisters may help each other's daughters with gifts of money for their dowry expenses.

Ritual sisters are allowed to visit each other as if they were real sisters, and could do so even in the days of strict purdah. They may also call on each other for work when a husband's family has some ceremony that requires entertaining guests. Two women nursed ritual sisters through extended illnesses. In one case, the attending woman was a trained nurse; in the other, the patient had a real sister living in the same courtyard but evidently was closer to her ritual sister than to her real sister.

Most ritual sisterhoods persist throughout the lifetimes of the women involved. However, three sisters broke off the custom of gift exchange when there was a poor harvest and they could not afford to give away grain or buy presents. Once broken,

Table 2.5 Social Distance of Ritual Sister Pairs in Husband's Lineage

	N	%
Ritual sisters with husbands from same lineage	16	47
Ritual sisters with husbands from different lineages	14	41
Ritual sisters from different caste or religion	4	12
Total	34	100

Table 2.6 Determinants of Ritual Sister Choice

	N	%
Ritual sisters became friends after marriage	22	65
Ritual sisters became friends before marriage	12	35
Total	34	100

the gift exchange was not resumed. The friendship may continue without the ritual, or the sisters may stop seeing each other.

Two women expressed beliefs that the karma of ritual sisters is transferable. One said that she did not have a ritual sister because the Vedas said that one could acquire the effect of the good or bad deeds of a ritual sister. Another, a virgin widow, said that she did not have one because she "is a trouble to people."

Table 2.5 shows that 47% of the ritual sister pairs have husbands from the same lineage, while 41% have husbands from different lineages. Two women had ritual sisters from their parental village belonging to other castes, and two had ritual sisters who were Khalapur Muslims. In both of these cases, the women's husbands were friends. Only three women had ritual sisters who were not living in Khalapur.

Table 2.6 shows that 22 women became friends after marriage (60%), 12 (32.5%) without any reported intermediary and 10 (27%) because their husbands were friends. Twelve women (35%) had become friends with their ritual sisters shortly before marriage. They usually chose a woman who was also expected to marry into Khalapur. The three women with ritual sisters married into other villages had made friends before their marriage with girls whom they expected would also marry into their future husband's village; subsequently, either their own or the sister's marital location had been altered.

In 1975 some women said that more ritual sisters break up now than in past years because they are more likely to complain about the quality of goods exchanged, while others said there were more ritual sister pairs now because purdah restrictions have lessened and people have more money. In order to check these reports, we totaled the number of women with ritual sisters, as a function of age. Table 2.7 shows no change in the incidence of this custom over time; 26% of women over 40 and 24% of those under 40 have ritual sisters.

On the assumption that a ritual sister may serve as a substitute for a real sister, we compared the incidence of this custom for women with and without consanguineous female relatives living in Khalapur. Table 2.8 shows a significant relationship between presence of a ritual sister and absence of a blood relative in

Table 2.7 Presence of Ritual Sister and Presence of Female
Consanguineous Relatives in Khalapur

	Ritual Sister					
	Yes		No		Total	
Age	N	%	N	%	N	%
Over 40 years	14	26	40	74	54	38
Under 40 years	21	24	68	76	89	62
Total	35		108		143	100

Table 2.8 Presence of Ritual Sister and Female Consanguineous
Relatives Living in Village

	Ritual Sister					
	Yes		No		Total	
Relatives in Village	N	%	N	%	N	%
Yes	13	18	29	41	42	59
No	18	25	11	16	29	41
Total	31	43	40	57	71	100

$\chi^2 = 6.75, p < .01.$

Table 2.9 Presence of Ritual Sister and Birth Order of Husband

	Yes		No		Total	
Husband's Birth Order	N	%	N	%	N	%
Only or firstborn child	16	35	10	22	26	57
Middle or last-born child	18	39	2	4	20	43
Total	34	74	12	26	46	100

$\chi^2 = 4.75, p < .05.$

Khalapur ($\chi^2 = 6.75, p \le .01$). It seems, therefore, that a ritual sister serves as a substitute sister for *bahu*s without blood relatives in Khalapur. This finding led us to look closely at women who had two or more ritual sisters and at women who had neither resident female relatives nor ritual sisters.

Of the women with more than one ritual sister, five had relatives in Khalapur and three did not. Therefore, having two ritual sisters is not related to the presence or absence of relatives in the vicinity. In all of these cases, one woman of the diad had only one ritual sister. Evidently, some women are chosen by more than one other woman for this relationship and accept more than one ritual sister.

Twelve women had neither relatives nor ritual sisters in Khalapur. Table 2.9 shows that these women were more likely to be married to only sons or firstborn sons than were women with ritual sisters or relatives in Khalapur ($\chi^2 = 4.75, p \le .05$). Sons are always married in order of their birth; therefore, the wife of the eldest son is the first daughter-in-law to enter her mother-in-law's courtyard. The wife of an only son is, of course, the only *bahu* assisting her *sasu*. These women may be prevented from taking ritual sisters because of heavy household responsibilities.

The absence of a ritual sister, like the absence of resident female relatives, may indicate that the woman or her husband's family are socially undesirable and therefore avoided by their neighbors. We have noted the isolated virgin widow who said that she had not sought a ritual sister because she is unlucky. Our sisterhood census also revealed that the wives in the *bughar* where there was a suicide in 1955 did not have ritual sisters or female relatives residing in Khalapur.

Our data indicate that, unlike female relatives, who may live in the same *bughar,* ritual sisters *never* live in the same *bughar.* They may have the same affinal relatives, if their husbands come from the same lineage, but they always have different *sasus. Bahus* with ritual sisters have friends outside of their households with whom they may visit when their lives as *bahus* become burdensome. The sisterhood allows problems with husbands, *sasus, nanads,* and *jethanis* to be shared with a confidante living in another *bughar.* The value of a ritual sister as a confidante was the one most often mentioned and was clearly considered to be more important than the help with work or money that a ritual sister may provide.

DEVIANT MARRIAGES

When families seek husbands for their daughters they try to avoid matches with undesirable men. When wives come from villages and *jatis* other than the ones that usually marry their daughters to Khalapur men, it indicates that the husband's family had to seek a bride for their son because they had received no inquiries from families of prospective brides. Some problem with the man or his family made him an undesirable marriage choice for families with access to village gossip. Wives of these deviant marriages come from families who settled their daughter in a strange village because they could not arrange a better marriage for her. Lack of education, poverty, and scandal are the primary reasons why a family may have to seek brides for their sons.

A family scandal makes marriage difficult for all of the unmarried men of the extended family, and often men from a family where there has been a scandal must take brides from villages where they are not known. If it is serious, the entire family may be "outcasted" by their *khandan.* Other Rajput families will not eat with or marry into an outcasted family; the latter are treated like members of the untouchable groups, who are outside of the traditional caste system. In 1955 a family that had been outcasted for some years married a son, already in his 30s, after several years of searching for a bride.

Educated men are more desirable husbands, particularly for educated women. In the past, poor families were unable to afford to send all of their sons to school, and many illiterate men remained bachelors. Paradoxically, poor families who cannot attract wives with dowries for their sons may be forced to "buy" their wives from families too poor to provide dowries for their daughters. The term "buying a wife" is used to describe indirect dowry, the custom whereby the groom's family gives money to the bride's family, who use some of it to provide a dowry and keep some of it (Goody, 1973). Such marriages are disgraceful for both husband and wife, so purchased wives are often chosen from strange villages in order to minimize the resulting gossip.

A poor widower is an undesirable bridegroom; when his deceased wife has no eligible sister or cousin to serve as a replacement wife, he may have great difficulty finding a bride. These men are particularly likely to take poor girls as second wives and to finance these marriages with indirect dowry payments.

We were able to obtain detailed information about several deviant marriages. Three case histories illustrate typical problems of such unions.

Nakali, the Suicide

In 1955 a *bahu* named Nakali committed suicide under circumstances that reflected unfavorably on her *sasu*. In 1975 we had the opportunity to document the marriage arrangements of a family stigmatized by this scandal.

In 1955 Nakali had not been on good terms with her husband or her *sasu* for some time. Her husband, whom some described as "a bit mad," had once burned her badly with coals because he suspected her of having an affair with his *jaith*. She had recently gone home to her parents without telling anyone and then returned with her brother without being called. Her *sasu*, who was typically cross with her *bahus*, had been particularly cruel to Nakali since her return.

Nakali had only one son, aged 10 at the time of her death. She envied *bahus* with more children and thought that her *sasu* favored other grandsons over hers. Nakali was ill at the time of her suicide, and her son was suffering from smallpox. She became angry when neither her husband nor her *sasu* would bring them medicine, and refused to cook.

In the evening, when her husband returned from the fields, he beat Nakali with his staff until his mother warned him to stop, not because he would hurt his wife but because he would anger the smallpox goddess. At that point Nakali became so angry that she shouted at her husband, "If you do not kill me today, you are not a Rajput but a Chamer." Her irate husband was caught between his mother's warning and his wife's taunt. He stalked out of the *bughar* saying, "I will not kill you. Go jump into the well."

After her husband's departure, Nakali told her *sasu* that she was leaving the *bughar* to jump into the well, as her husband had directed; when the angry *sasu* retorted that she would not have the nerve to kill herself, Nakali walked out of the *bughar* into the twilight. Her *sasu* sat waiting with the other household women for Nakali's return. When she did not return promptly the *sasu* began to worry, but the other *bahus* reminded her that Nakali had threatened suicide many times before. While they waited, Nakali carried out her threat.

Nakali went to a nearby well, tied her sari over her face, and jumped in. A man seated on a nearby *choopar* saw her but thought he had seen a ghost. By the time the women had given the alarm, it was too late. When Nakali was pulled from the well, she was dead. By the time the police arrived from Bhudana, the body was lying beside the well, covered with a sheet, and a large crowed had gathered. Women from nearby houses, including Nakali's, watched from the rooftops or peered through half-closed doors. Relatives were so reluctant to admit to the facts that the men would not tell the police which house Nakali lived in, although her husband and several other family men were present. When the police—angry at the lack of cooperation—finally completed their report and left, several men bailed all of the water out of the well before it was used again. The ritual pollution of a body was a matter of more concern than the germs harbored in the open well.

Nakali's suicide struck at the core of *sasu–bahu* relationship. *Sasus* were reluctant to either criticize or defend their fellow *sasu,* and *bahus* sat frightened and silent while the news spread. The negligent *sasu* was criticized chiefly because she allowed Nakali to violate purdah restrictions. Although Nakali's face was covered by her knotted sari, her petticoat was pulled up when the men pulled her from the well. Women were horrified that the body of a Rajput woman had been exposed where "everyone could see her." One said that Nakali should have taken poison in the privacy of her room, another protested that it is not the work of a Rajput *bahu* to go out of the house. The women agreed that men in the family would not be able to find wives because no one would marry their daughter to a member of a household where a *bahu* had been driven to suicide. When I returned in 1975, I found that their predictions had proved correct.

Although in his early 30s and the father of only one son, Nakali's husband never remarried. Years passed before brides were found for any of the family men. Finally a marriage was arranged by a prestigious village man who assured the family of the bride that she would be safe and cared for. Once this man was married, other weddings followed. However, none of the *bahus* in this *bughar* had women relatives in Khalapur; not only were they from strange villages, but no two *bahus* within the *bughar* came from the same village. This was the only household in our sample where all of the *bahus* were strangers to each other at marriage. Furthermore, during our 1975 visit, the guilty *sasu,* who under normal circumstances would have been directing the work of her *bahus* and their children, regularly sat alone in the street outside the door of her *bughar,* apparently exiled by her *bahus* because of her cruel treatment of Nakali.

Dhooli, the Poor Bride

Men from wealthy families can usually find brides and second wives but may have to arrange marriages with uneducated women from poor families when potential husbands have serious liabilities. Poor *bahus* in wealthy families are particularly disadvantaged because of the contrast between them and other household women. Such was the case of Dhooli, the second wife of Succha, Amar Nath's son, who had been psychotic for several years. While Dhooli had not been purchased through indirect dowry, her family was much poorer than the families of other wives in her *bughar.*

Succha was out of town when his first wife died in childbirth. He saw the fire of the funeral pyre as he entered Khalapur and asked a passing man, "Who has died?" He was told that the pyre was for his wife. Succha became sick for 6 months, but recovered. His marriage to Dhooli was arranged 1 year after the death of his first wife. Sometime later he became psychotic and aggressive on the night of the wedding of his sister, Luxmi. At first his aggression was directed at his wife. He would enter the *bughar,* complain about the food, and break the cooking pots— behavior that was interpreted as unusually angry but not mad. The family became more concerned when Succha attacked his father with a knife, but still thought he was only angry. However, when Succha entered the Siva temple and broke the sacred idols, he was soon surrounded by a mob of angry villagers who dragged him home and demanded that he be confined to the house. For several years he had to be chained, although he escaped periodically, wandering by train throughout India. His behavior was so aberrant that not even Luxmi's relatives would take him in.

Succha's mother, Draupadi, went on several trips looking for him, and the family spent thousands of rupees on his treatment. Amar Nath had not farmed his fields in years deprived of Succha's labor, he became poor during his son's illness. The family's poverty made keeping up dowry payments to Luxmi's wealthy relatives difficult. Succha was finally sent to a doctor who cured him, and he was a rational, dutiful, hardworking son at the time of our visit.

Dhooli married into a wealthy and prestigious family and lived in the most elegant but most crowded *bughar* in our sample. Several *sasus* and all of the other *bahus* in her husband's family were educated, and all were wealthy. She was not on good terms with her *sasu, nanad,* husband, or eldest son. Her parents were dead, and her brothers were poor, so she had not been home in 8 years.

Dhooli was also the only *bahu* without earrings. *Sasus* customarily give their own earrings to poor *bahus*, to protect their sons from gossip about marriage to a poor bride. However, Draupadi still wore her own gold earrings. Because Dhooli complained about her lack of earrings several times, I bought her a pair of gold earrings. When I gave them to her, she immediately hid them in her sari. Draupadi took the first opportunity to ask why I had bought earrings for Dhooli. I replied that I had given them to Dhooli because she often cooked for us, and because she was unhappy about not having earrings to wear.

The two women told us different stories to explain the absence of Dhooli's earrings. Dhooli said that her wedding earrings had been given to Luxmi, and that she had another pair of earrings but Succha had knocked one off while hitting her and she could not find it. Draupadi claimed that Dhooli had come as a bride without earrings, although earrings are considered to be the minimal amount of jewelry for a Rajput bride. According to Draupadi, Dhooli had become insulted soon after her marriage, when Draupadi said, "No one marries their daughter without earrings, but you have come without them." At the time of Succha's wedding Draupadi's family sent the pair of earrings, which Draupadi wore. Draupadi said that she had offered these earrings to Dhooli and later offered her another pair, but Dhooli refused them, saying, "Since my parents did not give me earrings, I will not take them from you." Apparently the absence of earrings had become an issue of pride with Dhooli, as she tried, despite her poverty, to maintain her dignity and family pride in the household of wealthy women.

Draupadi contended that Dhooli refused to wear jewelry in order to protest against gifts given to Luxmi, and that she beat her head against the wall when anything was given to Luxmi. Her final comment was that Dhooli would wear the earrings now that I had given her a pair. In fact Dhooli did wear them, but not regularly, as is customary.

It was Dhooli who cooked our lunch, and Swaran Kapoor and I bought her a shawl, in appreciation of her effort. When Draupadi saw it she said, "I like my daughter better than my *bahu.*" Interpreting this to mean that she meant to give Dhooli's shawl to Luxmi, Swaran Kapoor and I each bought another shawl for

Luxmi and instructed Draupadi to let Dhooli keep her present. When we explained this to Dhooli, she burst into tears, saying,

> "Everything good is given to Luxmi. Even my wedding earrings were given to her. My parents are dead and my brothers cannot afford to give me more jewelry. I cannot ask what has happened to my parents' jewelry. My husband will not defend me."

Luxmi's, Draupadi's daughter, was insensitive to Dhooli's distress and abused her privilege of receiving gifts. At the birth of Dhooli's first son, Luxmi took Dhooli's only valuable piece of jewelry, a *tikka* (a gold ornament worn on the forehead), lent to her by Draupadi, and threw it on the ground, saying that it was not enough. When Dhooli gave birth to a son during our visit, she refused to call Luxmi for the customary visit, despite strong objections from Draupadi. Draupadi finally insisted on bringing her daughter for a visit and called her without Dhooli's consent.

Dhooli was crying on the day Luxmi arrived, because Sher's wife had said that Luxmi brought many gifts to Dhooli. Dhooli retorted that Luxmi knit sweaters for her own sons but gave her nothing. Dhooli and Luxmi got along amicably during the visit, but Dhooli complained bitterly about the presents Luxmi was given to take back to her husband's house. Luxmi's greed embarrassed even her devoted mother, to whom she wrote, shortly after we had given her our two shawls, to ask for yet another shawl, on the pretext that her *sasu* had asked why she had not been sent a shawl for the winter.

Dhooli's situation was particularly unfortunate because of the wealth of her fellow *bahus* and the unusually poor relations between her and her husband, *nanad*, and *sasu*. However, her plight was not atypical of poor *bahus*.

Bala, the Child Bride

The most dramatic example of the problems of arranging marriages without knowledge of the husband's family was the marriage of Suraj, the eldest of three sons of Daya's widow, Mamta. As described in chapter 1, Mamta and her sister Durga had married the brothers Daya and Kela. Both had been purchased for 600 rupees each. When the third brother, Kanak, married, the bride's family wanted 3,000 rupees, and both married brothers contributed to the sum, leaving them even poorer. Durga was soon fighting with her sisters-in-law and refused to let Mamta's children eat in the *bughar*.

Daya and his family moved into their *gher,* taking nothing with them from the joint *bughar,* and built another small house. The breakup of the *bughar* caused a quarrel between Daya and his elder brother, Kela. Daya died before the marriage of their only daughter, leaving his widow with a daughter and three young sons.

When a man dies leaving young children, the responsibility for arranging their marriages falls to the deceased's brothers, particularly his older brothers. However, if a man's nephews remain unmarried and childless, their land goes to their paternal uncles or cousins upon their death. Therefore, some uncles of orphaned boys attempt to prevent their marriage, hoping eventually to take possession of their land.

Kela, already estranged from Daya's family, refused to help with his nephews' marriage arrangements.

The marriage of their older sister in the years before they reached adulthood impoverished the family further. Faced with the prospect of permanent bachelorhood for himself and his brother, Suraj, at age 23, bought his wife, Bala, from her two brothers. A primary schoolteacher had arranged to have a neighbor marry this girl, but when her brothers came to visit, the neighbor refused to pay their price of 3,000 rupees. The two men stayed in Khalapur for 4 days, without anyone giving them food, until one of them met Suraj. Seeing an opportunity to arrange for his own marriage, Suraj said that he would pay the brothers 3,000 rupees and marry their sister himself. The two visitors stayed in Suraj's family *choopar* for 4 days and, pleased with his hospitality, agreed to give him their sister in marriage.

Their family came from a distant village, and Suraj had no way to check on the accuracy of the information given by his bride's brothers. They left Khalapur with Suraj's written word that he would marry their sister, and his payment of 3,000 rupees. As is customary, the marriage took place in the bride's village, without any previous meeting between the prospective newlyweds, and Suraj returned to Khalapur with his tiny veiled bride. It was not until Mamta saw her new *bahu* without her *chaddar* (headcloth) and *gungat* (veil) that she discovered that the bride whose brothers said was 18 years old was actually still a child of about 7 years! (Bala did not know her own age, and was married for 5 years before her first menstruation.) Since the family could not retrieve their money, they kept the young bride. The situation would have been disastrous for Bala but for the unusual kindness of Mamta and the patience of Suraj.

Mamta fed Bala milk, dates, and almonds, despite their cost, so that she would grow up quickly. The *sasu* kept Bala in her bed until she matured and moved her to Suraj's bed when Bala began to menstruate. During the time that Bala was maturing, Suraj, now a married man, was able to arrange a marriage for his younger brother, Phoolo. Phoolo's bride, Asali, having married when she was mature, was older than Bala and gave birth to a daughter soon after her marriage. Under the direction of their kindly *sasu,* these two *bahus* shared their work with unusual harmony.

Asali did not know how to cook when she was first married. Mamta spent much of her time in the family's orchard guarding their guava crop and was not in the *bughar* to instruct her new *bahu.* Mamta had already taught Bala to cook, and she told Asali she need only spin, and could leave the cooking to her young *jethani.* However, when Asali learned to cook from watching Bala she took over this laborious work, saying that since she was the *derani* of the family, she ought to be the one to do the cooking. Under this new arrangement, Bala did the housework and tended Asali's baby daughter. It was the only household where a *bahu* was the primary caretaker of the child of another *bahu.* During my visit Bala became pregnant, and when I left the family was happily awaiting the birth of her child.

CONCLUSIONS

Rajput marriage is a social and economic alliance between two families. Families seek to marry children into families with wealth and prestige, and without scandals.

It is assumed that if the family is a good one any bride or groom selected from it will be a person of good character. Therefore, any misbehavior of a family member reflects on the reputation of his or her family, lineage, and indeed entire village. Concern for correct and moral behavior of family members, particularly young ones, represents a concern for the good name of the family.

The bride's family provides money and goods to the groom's family throughout her lifetime. A *bahu* is expected to bring presents to her husband's relatives whenever she returns from visits to her parents. This economic obligation provides a check on the coveted visits to parental homes.

The custom of not allowing husbands and wives to meet before marriage is an initial step in a series of practices minimizing husband–wife contact. Women seldom saw their husbands, particularly in the early days of marriage, but spent their early married lives confined in *bughar*s with other women of the husband's family. Their adjustment to the women of their *bughar*s, particularly their *sasu*s, was more important than husband–wife attachment.

A wife is marginal to her husband's family until she has borne sons to perpetuate his lineage. Primary loyalties and affection between men and women are expected to be between mother and son and brother and sister rather than between husband and wife. The superiority of *nanad*s' status over that of *bahu*s emphasizes the solidarity of natal kin.

The practices serving to separate husbands and wives collectively constitute purdah. As these restrictions lessen, husband–wife intimacy increases, presenting a threat to a man's ties with his mother and sisters. When the *sasu* dies, conflicts among *bahu*s are likely to become more intense. These conflicts are the most frequent reasons for separating households, a procedure that may lead to a division of brothers' jointly held land. Therefore, the influence of discontented wives upon their husbands poses a threat to the stability of the extended family.

Although the transition from the status of a guest in one's parental home to that of a servant in one's husband's home is a difficult one, it is eased by frequent and extended visits to the parental village, and by female relatives and ritual sisters in the husband's village who provide sympathetic allies and safety valves for women subjected to the restrictions of purdah. Nevertheless, the transition is temporarily traumatic for most women, and causes serious breakdowns for some.

EXCERPTS FROM LUXMI'S LETTERS TO HER MOTHER

Respectful Mother,
Respectful salutations,

Most humbly it is submitted that I am well here. Well here is what I want to say. I have posted a letter addressed to Father. You try to send Succha. Don't forget. Mother dear, I do not like here at all. I have not eaten yet. Here everybody is annoyed with me because I don't eat. But I am homesick. . . . I am fluttering like a fish in a little water.

You are saying that you won't call me home for four years. In four years' time I will be dead and gone to the houe of Rama. Why did you write that!? When I read this letter, my heart was saddened on hearing the words "four years." Mother dear, not a day has passed when I have not wept, while missing you.

He [husband] is not here. He has gone to another town. Mother dear, I am writing to you this letter after three days. Mother dear, I have not liked it here.

Mother dear, don't listen to anyone. Send someone here. Mother dear, I don't understand the work here. Call me soon. My *sasu* does not have a happy temperament. She seems to be jealous. Only when you have called me will I eat my fill. Mother dear, I miss Kiran a lot. . . .

Mother dear, you had said that you will call me after nineteen days. Why did you take so many days? I have already packed my clothes for coming. . . .

Mother dear, tell me this, do you believe my letters or do you believe the false things written by anyone in the world? Mother dear, if I lance my heart and show it to you, will you believe me then or not?

Mother dear, my sandals got to me today. Mother dear, send me another pair of sandals. I was using the sandals that were given to me at the time of my wedding, and one is torn now. . . .

Mother dear, all the women here are going to go away. I will be left alone. Mother dear, try to call me soon. Mother dear, I have not liked it here at all. I weep day and night. You have completely forgotten me. Mother dear, I miss my home a lot. You be sure to send Succha and M. at the earliest possible time. Mother dear, be sure to send them. Don't forget. . . .

All the people here say, "When someone will come to take you, we will send you." Mother dear, why have you forgotten me so soon? I remember you and cry day and night. . . .

Mother dear, [names 4 men of the family] had come. I was very happy. But when they went away, leaving me behind, I cried a lot for two days and did not eat food. Now I have had fever for the last four days. There is a constant pain in my eyes, and because of constant crying my eyes have swollen.

Mother dear, I do not like it here at all. I have been locked in a cage like a parrot. Mother dear, after having come here, I have been to the market many times. Mother dear, send a letter here on behalf of Father, asking these people be sure to bring me back home soon. Mother dear, call me back home before the girls [names some neighbor's girls] get married. Don't forget. . . . Call me before the weddings of the girls. Mother dear, one very seldom gets the opportunity to see a wedding.

Mother dear, all of you must have gone to the fair. I could not go. I was left wandering. Mother dear, I missed the food of the fair a lot. Mother dear, the wives of all my brothers [names brothers and male paternal cousins] must have gone to the mela and they must have missed me. The day when the fair was held, I thought of you a lot.

Mother dear, when is U. [a neighbor's girl] getting married? Has T. [a neighbor's man] been engaged yet or not? Let me know. Mother dear, convey my "Namistee" to Auntie dear and O. [male cousin] and A. [mother's sister] and to all the brothers. What (a boy or a girl) has been borne to O's wife? Mother dear, convey "Namistee" to the aunt from Kheri putti, and "Namistee" to her husband, love to their children. I miss J. [a friend] very much. Has K [a friend] gone or she is still there? Mother dear, convey my "Namistee" to [names 4 friends] "Namistee" to K. B. Banya [their Banya servant]. I miss his peanuts a lot. Greetings to the wife of K. B. "Namistee" to [names four friends]. Greetings to all the wives at the house of U, the wife of J. S. Love to their children. "Namistee" to S's mother [mother of a neighbor's girl] and both the *bahus*. Excuse me if I have written anything wrong; forget it.

Please convey my greeting with the folded hands to [names 11 *bahus*] I miss all the *bahus*. I wonder if they also miss me. I wrote before also to all the *bahus*, but none wrote back to me. Are all the *bahus* annoyed with me? Well, I was also testing a little just to see who misses me. Greetings to the aunts. I miss all the aunts a lot. "Namistee" to [names 10 male cousins]. All the brothers [names brothers and cousins] have forgotten me. Love to [names 6 children of the family]. Love to Kiran. Love to [names 3 male cousins]. Love to little C. [a child of the family]. Love to [names 7 more family members]. Greetings to all the uncles. Forgive my faults. Don't forget.

I have also given up drinking milk, Mother dear. There was a reason for it. When I come, I will tell you. . . . Will you go to maternal uncle's house? Mother dear, I will also go to maternal uncle's house to the wedding. . . .

The radio that you had given to me, where is its license? If it is there, please do send it. If it is not there, then try to get one issued and send it here.

Mother dear, I was very sad to know about your hand being septic. Mother dear, there was nothing in my control, when Succha began to say (during his visit) that "You must listen to your in-laws." He must have been told "no" once [Luxmi could not return home so soon] and then he did not pursue it. Mother dear, I cried a lot for two days. What to do? I am restless like a fish in a little water. I do not like it here at all. My condition is that like a snake who has a frog in his mouth. . . .

Tell me about the Father's condition. He must be drinking a lot. Father dear, I miss a lot the cleaning at home. I miss Kiran a lot. And mother dear, what has happened to your hand? Mother dear, did you find your money? And did you find the key or not? . . .

Mother dear, you don't lose anything, nor do the people here. I am the one in between who is suffering. Mother dear, we have not found the kind of people we wanted. We have met troublesome kind [of] people. There they looked like very good people. After I came here, I found them to be quite different. . . .

Ever since I have come here I have not eaten well. Mother dear, I have become quite weak. I am always burning within my heart (I am always sad). I cannot tell my troubles to anyone because it would be insulting myself. . . .

Except for Mother dear, no one else should open this letter. They will have [a] curse of God on them.

Your daughter,

Luxmi

Don't forget. Greetings to Mother.

Do not try to open without Mother and Father. (written outside of the cover of the letter)

A veiled mother, wearing a homespun sari, winnows grain while her young son watches. Behind her a cot lies on its side. A milk *chuula* is in the corner. A lofa vine grows on the left wall and a Sanjii figure decorates the right wall (1955).

3

Purdah: Respect–Avoidance, Dominance–Submission

> My father-in-law never heard my voice.
> My husband never saw my face.
> I never saw the gate to my husband's house.

This quotation, recorded in 1954, is typical of the descriptions of restrictions imposed by the complex customs of purdah on Rajput women of that time. Purdah is a severe form of cloistering women, observed by high-caste Hindus. This chapter describes these customs and their significance for the regulation of social interaction, the maintenance of traditional authority, and the solidarity of the extended family. I refer to purdah customs as a keystone custom complex because they are, in my opinion, such important regulators of traditional role relationships that their demise may cause that tradition to collapse. The anger and anxiety expressed by older women over such seemingly trivial matters as a 4- to 5-inch difference in the degree to which the sari covers the faces of their *bahu*s, conversation between their sons and *bahu*s, or the practice of some *bahu*s of sitting on cots, at the same level as older women, instead of on floor mats can only be understood in terms of the symbolic significance of these practices.

Caste is the key custom complex that regulates social interactions among persons of different lineages, occupations, and social positions; purdah is the key custom complex that regulates social interaction between men and women and among female relatives. Purdah and caste rules are complex, interactive, and inclusive. Deferential customs for both caste and purdah distinctions revolve around food, clothing, seating arrangements, and work roles. Both sets of customs maintain authority and status, and ensure obedience of subordinates to superiors by instituting ritual separation between persons of different status ranks and elaborate expressions of deference by subordinates to superiors.

Caste restrictions guard against the disruptive intrusions of outsiders into the caste group by curtailing social interaction with and marriage to persons outside of one's own caste. Purdah restrictions guard against disruptive intrusions of brides into the extended family by limiting social interaction of wives with their husbands and with senior men and women of the family. These communication restrictions between husband and wife serve as marriage dilution customs. They subordinate the bonds between husbands and wives to the bonds of sons to their blood relatives.

VEILED, SILENT, AND BOWED

In 1955 we described purdah customs as follows:

> Men have the power to veto any suggestions made by women. Women are discouraged from getting more than a rudimentary education. Most men wish to keep their wives in purdah, although it is a luxury, since to do this the men must do without their help in the fields and hire servants to help them run the house. The men control even the physical movements of their wives. A man, if angry or inconsiderate, may beat his wife, refuse to try and provide medical care, and may even prevent or cut short her visits to her own home, or refuse to call her back from a visit to her own family.
>
> The subordinate status of women is further emphasized by the custom that women must crouch on the floor and pull their saris over their faces when in the presence of their husband or any man older than their husband. This custom is so pervasive that young women usually cover their faces even in front of older low-caste serving men. This is a sign of respect for the man's status. Covering the face in the presence of one's husband is also a sign of respect for his mother, another of the customs designed to protect the mother–son relationship from being threatened by the son's attachment to his wife. When a man has entered the house for his meal, he will quickly retire into a room or behind the wall of his hearth. The women are then free to move about their business quietly. His meal will usually be served to him by his mother, if she is living, or by an adult sister. Only if some woman of his own family is not present or does not wish to assert her prerogative will his wife be allowed to serve his meal.
>
> Because of this custom, the men always announce their presence with a warning cough before entering the household and when possible, send a boy or the youngest male present on errands to the courtyard, since the younger the man, the fewer are the women who must keep purdah from him. When the eldest male enters, the entire *bughar* is immobilized until he has been safely attended. In nuclear families, the wife usually does not cover her face before her husband, but only because the man usually requests her not to continue this custom.
>
> The symbols of women's status inferiority are easy to perceive. The ameliorating factor in the status inequality of such a social organization, however, is the strength of the bonds which exist between mothers and sons and between sisters and brothers. Adult males are taught that they should be respectful and considerate to their mothers and because of their early, prolonged intimate contact with her are influenced by her wishes. The mother feeds her son even after he is married and even has strong influence on his marital life. She runs the family as long as she wishes to assume the responsibility.
>
> Ideally a man and his wife are not allowed to talk to each other in front of the older members of the family. Since the *sasu* is virtually always present in the courtyard and the young wife cannot leave the courtyard, this means in effect that the young couple may converse only surreptitiously at night.

A husband is not supposed to show any open concern for his wife's welfare; this is the responsibility of his parents. If the wife is sick, the *sasu* and *soosar* see that she goes to a doctor; if they do not, neither she nor her husband should complain. The villagers report one or two cases where a woman has remained childless for years and despite the great importance of having children, has not seen a doctor because the husband was too shy to ask his negligent parents to take her.

The restrictions, imposed on husband and wife in the presence of others, particularly the mother-in-law, are to avoid jealousy and conflict and to ensure that the extended family takes precedence in importance to the nuclear.

(Minturn & Hitchcock, 1966, p. 35)

The first response of Rajput women describing changes in purdah usually referred to the degree to which women keep their faces covered by the portion of their saris worn over their heads. This sari "veil" is called the *gungat*. When they left the *bughar* women used to wear an additional white cotton head cloth called the *chaddar,* so that their heads were doubly veiled. When talking to husbands or family men older than their husbands, women squatted, so that conversation took place with the woman in a crouching position. The *gungat*, the crouching position, and restrictions on talking are customs that are interrelated and practiced together.

Only a movie could convey the dramatic change that occurred in *bughar*s when elder men entered. I still retain a memory of my first experience with this custom. I was sitting on a charpoy talking with a group of women in a large *bughar*. The conversation was animated and loud. Suddenly and apparently without warning, the women slid from the couch and crouched on the floor, drawing their saris over their faces as they descended. In an instant, our animated companions were transformed into silent, huddled, shrouded figures. I looked around in complete bewilderment and saw an elder man at the doorway. Later I asked the women how they could tell when a man was coming. They replied that men announce their presence by a low cough as they enter. Since *bughar*s are always noisy, it seemed impossible that such a quiet sound would be noticed, but within a month I could hear it too.

The stillness of these tiny women when men are in the *bughar* caused an American friend of an anthropologist to ask, when first escorted into the *bughar* of the family with whom he was staying, "Why are these piles of laundry lying around the *bughar* floor?" The question is not absurd to anyone who has witnessed the crouch-freeze position of women when men are present.

Rationale for Purdah

All the purdah restrictions are ostensibly observed to honor wives or other family members. The respect–avoidance customs within the family are ways in which the wives honor their husbands, other family men, and the older women of the household, particularly their *sasus*.

The elaborate respect–avoidance customs between husbands and wives and between *bahus* and *sasus* clearly indicate that prevention of adultery is not the exclusive or even the primary function of purdah. However, these customs are most frequently justified as a means of keeping women safe from rape or seduction.

Despite the absence of Muslim dominance in the area for more than a century, the presence of Muslim men who raped women is cited by men as the reason for adopting these customs, which are viewed by Rajputs as being of Muslim origin.

In 1955 men generally assumed that if purdah were abandoned their wives would leave them. Although marriages are arranged between couples who have not seen each other, men also argued that if there were no purdah, ugly men would be unable to get married. The anxiety of the men about their wives leaving them was a pathetic aspect of purdah. From interviewing the women I felt sure that these fears were, in general, unfounded. Some women did not get along with their husbands and most had occasional quarrels with them; in fact, most of the women were genuinely fond of their husbands and were good and faithful wives, but purdah restrictions prevented husbands from seeing this. Restrictions were universally disliked by young wives, who usually wanted to return to the freedom of their parental homes. The pull on young wives was away from their husbands, whereas husbands' motivation was to keep wives with them. Wives were usually able to gauge husbands' affection by the strength of the men's protests against women's leaving and by how they were treated while in their husbands' homes, but the wives were so subordinate and their behavior so totally determined by deferential customs that the husbands seemed unable to judge their wives' attachment to them.

The extreme isolation of young wives from the *jaith*s and *soosar*s recognizes the potential of these senior men to become seducers. This possibility was recognized, in 1955, by a standard joke among Rajput men that the *bughar*s were so dark at night that men sometimes got into the wrong bed by mistake. More than one woman repeated this tale to me as a matter for serious concern. Although the courtyards were indeed dark at night before the introduction of electricity, each woman had her own room or sleeping place in the courtyard, and it seemed unlikely that a man would accidentally mistake his wife's bed or its occupant. The prevalence of the story, however, indicates that such events have occurred, perhaps not by mistake. We heard a few reports of *soosar*s seducing their *bahu*s. Sher's only son was said to be the illegitimate son of his grandfather, Mussadi, a claim supported by the fact that Sher had not entered his *bughar* or seen his wife since that pregnancy.

Despite the accepted rationale that purdah is necessary to prevent adultery, there was a general feeling that purdah was not effective in accomplishing this aim, and suspicion about the slightest sign of scandal was widespread. More than one woman said that if a woman wished to have an affair she would find some way of avoiding the purdah.

Husband–Wife Separation

In a cross-cultural study, Broude measured the dimension of marital intimacy and aloofness, using a composite scale of the degree to which "husband and wife eat and sleep together, talk and joke freely, share household duties, including baby tending, and generally lead a life of close companionship" (Broude, 1987, p. 51). She reports that the Khalapur Rajputs have the most aloof husband–wife relationships among her sample of 140 societies. Broude finds that aloof marriages occur where individuals have a close kin network independent of marriage and where people have permanent residences that give them a home base. Both of these conditions prevail for Khalapur Rajputs. Aloof marriages, and cloistering of wives, are also characteristic of a number of warrior groups.

Purdah customs are designed to separate husbands and wives, so that wives cannot disrupt the authority of their *sasus*. In addition to the public customs restricting husband–wife interaction, traditional purdah imposed on married couples extensive periods of abstinence from sexual intercourse. Customs and cramped living quarters also restricted intercourse when wives were in residence in their husbands' homes. Families made an effort to reserve a room for newlywed couples for several months, but in many small houses *bahus* and *sasus* shared the same bedroom. *Sasus* regulated the sex lives of their sons and *bahus* by deciding on the timing of marital visits. Husbands came from their *choopars* to visit their wives and then returned to them.

Although Rajputs certainly recognize the pleasurable nature of sexual activity, they regard reproduction as the primary function of intercourse. Certain days were considered to be auspicious or inauspicious for conception. One elderly woman attributed her reproductive success in having three sons and no daughters to the strict observance of sexual abstinence on inauspicious days when couples were not supposed to have intercourse.

Traditionally, Rajputs observed a postpartum taboo of 2 years, although in 1955 the women said the taboo was not always observed. In 1955 I compared the birth rates of mothers over and under the age of 35 and found a significant increase in the number of children born less than 2 years, versus more than 3 years apart, indicating that the taboo was being neglected by younger couples. In 1975 vasectomies and intrauterine loops had replaced abstinence as birth control methods for younger couples.

Khalapur Rajputs marry in their late teens or early 20s, so a couple may be in their late 30s or early 40s when their children get married. The high mortality rate in childbirth makes second marriages for men fairly common, and since women never remarry, a man of any age takes a young bride. In a few families where widowers with grown sons had remarried, *sasus* were only a few years older than their *bahus*. Nevertheless, a husband and wife are supposed to cease all intercourse after their children are married, and a *sasu* who becomes pregnant after she has grandchildren creates embarrassment for herself and her family.

Custom also prohibits remarriage for widows, who are expected to remain in their husbands' homes but are unwelcome burdens. They are under the authority of the family *soosars* and *jaiths* and dependent on them for support; therefore, they are powerless to resist sexual advances by these men. The chapter on widows describes in detail the tragic effects of the prohibition on widow remarriage in combination with the cultural assumption that widows are immoral.

These combined restrictions result in long periods of sexual abstinence for married couples, and it is not surprising that the village abounds with tales of scandal both general and specific. It was very difficult to assess the validity of such rumors, since the women themselves admitted that people were always suspicious and willing to believe the worst.

The Paradox of a Double Standard

Although adultery for wives is prohibited, Rajput men may relieve long periods of sexual abstinence by visiting prostitutes in nearby towns or using the village Chamar (sweeper) women as prostitutes. The dichotomy between virtuous and immoral women is reflected in the behavior of Indian men towards any woman not observing traditional customs. Because women are expected to be cloistered and veiled, and to travel only in the company of a male relative, men have no norms of restraint for women who do not observe these customs. Men are also immature, by Western norms, in their behavior towards women. Young men in their 20s behave like junior high school boys in showing off and teasing passing girls. This harrassment makes independent movement difficult for women, and is sufficient grounds for many families to keep their daughters from traveling without men, even to shop or attend a movie, or, more seriously, to keep them out of high school or coeducational colleges.

The seclusion of women makes them somewhat mysterious to men. Women generally know as much about men's activities as they care to, and can peer out of windows in the *bughar* walls at anything of interest in the street, but men cannot observe the women's activities. On more than one occasion we saw a young man of a family sneak a curious look into the *bughar* when women were singing and dancing for some festival. One man expressed this danger fostered by the seclusion of women by observing: "Purdah makes women more attractive. Men have illicit relations through curiosity." Therefore, purdah restrictions produce the paradox of all double standards for sexual activity: Women are, on the one hand, harassed and vilified for not conforming to restrictive norms and, on the other hand, rendered more attractive and more vulnerable to seduction by the seclusion that purports to protect them.

CHANGES IN PURDAH

The British colonial administration passed a number of laws to protect women but did little to disrupt the indigenous social structure. Its aim was to rule, not to reform, so the institutions of caste and purdah were not seriously challenged until after independence in 1947. Among the first actions of the Indian government were land reform, caste reform, and efforts to educate and liberate women from the restrictions of early marriage and purdah. These programs continue to be central to efforts of the Indian government to modernize the country. The *bahus* we interviewed in 1975 were the first postindependence generation, raised with the reforms of the independent government.

While purdah restrictions were decreasing when the present generation of *sasus* were children, the major changes occurred between 1955 and 1975. My second visit to Khalapur, therefore, was well timed to document these changes. The impact of the decrease in purdah restrictions on the roles and status of *sasus* must be assessed against their expectations of the rewards to *sasus* of the traditional system. In the past, each *sasu* directed the work of her *bahus*, telling them what to do and when to do it. If a *sasu* disagreed with the way a *bahu* was raising her grandchildren, she might send the young woman back to her parents and keep the grandchildren with her. Education of young women and more modern times had decreased purdah restrictions, mandating obedience of *bahus* to their *sasus* and avoidance of their husbands.

In the past, *bahus* were silent and veiled before their *sasus*. When *sasus* returned from visits outside the *bughars*, *bahus* sometimes massaged their feet and lower legs. In 1955 young wives massaged me, although we were the same age; in 1975 this did not occur, although I was in the *sasu* generation.

In the past, *bahus* cooked the food and *sasus* took it, served their husbands and sons, ate their own meal, and only then gave the remaining food to her *bahus*. Young *bahus* preferred to cook only for their husbands and children. Although most *bughars* still had joint *chuulas*, *chuula* separation had become a major complaint of *sasus* in 1975. Any woman can build a *chuula* in about 1 hour; therefore, the resistance to *chuula* separation is based not on the expense or effort of its construction but on the threat to the unity of the joint family.

In 1955 I described the status change that came for *bahus* with the death of their *sasu:*

> After the death of the *sasu*, a woman can talk to her husband in the presence of her sisters-in-law. When her sons marry, she assumes a new and prestigious role. She is now in charge of the young women and is released by virtue of his relative age from many of the restrictions of purdah. Age in the *bughar* brings respect, and every bride can look forward to the day when she assumes this role.
>
> (Minturn & Hitchcock, 1966, p. 35)

In their youth, these older women did look forward to this day, but their expectations were not fulfilled. Their educated sons and *bahus*, reared under a host of modern influences, had abandoned many of the customs that legitimate the *sasu*'s authority and ensure that the mother–son alliance will be stronger than the husband–wife bond. In losing their authority over their sons, they were also losing control of family finances. They were caught up in changes for which they were unprepared, and they had indeed been denied the deference and authority which, in their youth, they accorded to their *sasus*.

Overall Changes in Purdah Observance

In 1975, in order to assess overall changes in purdah restrictions over three generations, we asked each *sasu* whether or not she kept less purdah than her mother did when she was a child, and whether her *bahus* kept less purdah than she herself did as a young *bahu*. The answers to these two questions are summarized in Table 3.1. The "other" coding contains cases in which mothers were dead when the informant was a child. The comparison from preceding to succeeding generation shows that half of

Table 3.1 Reports by Mothers-in-Law About Changes in Purdah over Three Generations

	More		Same		Less		Other	
	N	%	N	%	N	%	N	%
Mother-in-law to self at self's age	1	5	4	21	10	53	4	21
Self to daughter-in-law at daughter-in-law's age	0	0	0	0	19	100	0	0

Table 3.2 Reports of Daughter-in-Law About Changes in Purdah from Mothers to Self

	More		Same		Less		Other	
	N	%	N	%	N	%	N	%
General	1	7	3	20	11	73	0	0
For fathers-in-law	1	7	8	53	5	33	1	7
For mothers-in-law	2	13	4	27	8	53	1	7
For husbands	2	13	4	27	9	60	0	0

the *sasu*s reported keeping less purdah than their mothers, but all reported that their *bahu*s kept less purdah than they did as young wives, indicating that the major changes have come in the *bahu*'s generation.

The answers indicate that the degree of change in the amount of purdah kept in front of *soosar*s is less than the degree of change for *sasu*s and husbands. Fifty-three percent of the women reported that they kept the same amount of purdah from their *soosar*s as their mothers did, while 33% reported keeping less. These percentages are reversed for husbands and *sasu*s; 27% reported keeping the same amount of purdah from both husbands and *sasu*s, while 53% reported keeping less purdah from their *sasu*s and 60% reported keeping less from their husbands than did their mothers (Table 3.2). The distributions for the husband and *sasu* rows are identical, except for one case coded "other," representing a woman whose grandmother was dead when she was a child, so that she could not make the comparison. Since seclusion from husbands honors the *sasu*, one would expect the changes for these two types of relatives to be linked.

*Bahu*s were also asked to compare the amount of purdah kept by themselves with that kept by their mothers, and their answers agree with the assessment of the *sasu*s. Table 3.2 shows that 73% reported keeping less purdah than their mothers, 20% reported keeping the same amount, and only one *bahu*, raised in a city, reported keeping more purdah in Khalapur than in her parental home.

Some general comments of the *sasu*s are summarized in the following statement:

> The days are gone when there was purdah. The world is changing. Previously no one could enter the *bughar* of others. Now anybody can come in anytime. When there was purdah, ladies did not move out of the house nor did they move in the presence of their *soosar, sasu,* elder brother-in-law, or husband. In our *sasu*'s time we could not appear in the presence of any men.

her. Now she may threaten to slap him. That is good. She may
ap him in front of other people. That is also good.

younger generation that is expected to keep stricter purdah,
stoms makes observance of purdah to husbands by the older
reversal of the age status. One *sasu* changed her own purdah
f this paradox:

covered from my husband even up to now but when I observed that
does not do that and talks to her husband in my presence while I kept
red, I stopped covering my face from my husband. So, I do not like
s of these days.

answer of a *bahu* confirm the decrease in purdah kept from husbands:

to my husband even in the presence of others, but my mother could not
r husband when we were young children. In the presence of my husband I
ing on a cot, not a low chair. Although, so far, I have never eaten in the
e of my husband, I can talk to my husband anytime I want, although
y else may be present. My mother could not talk to my father. She kept her
overed from her husband, while I do not. Women in my mother's time were
t blind. Because of the thick *chaddar* they could not see properly. My mother
serve meals to her *soosar* and brothers-in-law but she could not serve meals
r own husband. Either the husband would serve himself or be served by any
an of the house, except his own wife. Now I can serve my husband myself.
re are many men nowadays who eat only what their own wives serve them.

e decline in purdah kept from husbands is particularly marked for couples
ave lived in cities while the husband was employed and have now returned to
arental home for visits or because of unemployment. *Sasu*s are particularly
y to complain about such young women. However, the reports of the *bahu*s
w that they adapt their behavior to life in the extended family. One such wife
e the following answer:

My husband is employed and I went away from home to live with him. Then I did
not keep any purdah from him. I used to talk to him and worked in his presence.
But when I am here in the joint family house I cannot talk to him in the presence of
others.

Deference

Deference to *Sasus*

The *sasu*s had lost much of the deference previously accorded to them and had also
lost or abdicated some of their power vis-à-vis control over their sons' wives, their
grandchildren, and family finances. For many *sasu*s the loss of status was partly
voluntary. Because almost all sons married, there were more *bahu*s and grandchildren to look after, and some *sasu*s preferred to delegate authority in exchange
for free time for themselves. *Bahu*s were now educated, and *sasu*s sometimes

Previously we dressed much more modestly. Before we were covered from head
to toe. Now our *bahu*s wear the city sari blouse, their backs and tummies are naked,
their braids show, and their breasts are moving. Our nose plug was never visible to
the old women. Previously the clothes were thick and we used to cover our faces
completely even before *sasu*s and elder sisters-in-law. Now men may say, "Look at
that woman with the beautiful naked tummy."

General statements by *bahu*s, such as the one following, confirm the descriptions of the older women:

The difference in the purdah that I keep and that which my mother used to keep is
like the difference between earth and sky. Older ladies of the village, at my age,
used to keep so much purdah that they covered their faces even before low-caste
women. Previously women did not go to the fields at all. Now those who are older
can go. Women whose families are separated from the joint family may go to help
their husbands, because there are no men to help. Women who are in joint families
only go to the fields to pick vegetables and cotton. Previously women did not do
that.
    If a child had passed feces which the mother was going to clean and suddenly
the *soosar* entered, then she used to sit immediately, even on the feces, and keep
sitting until the *soosar* moved away.
    Now I can go into the cattle compound but my mother could not go there unless
it was essential. I make the cow dung cakes in the cattle compound, but my mother
could not do this. If it was necessary for my mother to go outside the house she
used to wrap herself in a thick *chaddar*.

Several types of exaggeration appear repeatedly in these statements. The frequent reference to sitting in filth and excrement reflects the Hindu's abhorrence for
ritual pollution. Even under conditions of strict purdah, women could step to a clean
spot before crouching. In 1955 I never saw a woman crouch in filth, nor was that
possibility a matter of concern. In my 1975 visit I never saw a husband and wife sit
together in the courtyard.
    One woman gave an extreme answer describing possible conflict resulting from
lack of purdah:

If the *sasu* is angry and has scolded you, the good thing is not to reply and keep
quiet. But if the *bahu* is shameless and cannot tolerate the scolding and replies back
to the *sasu*, then the purdah will automatically be lessened. If the *sasu* has come
from the outside and is tired, and has asked her *bahu* to bring something and the
bahu says "I am not your servant. Get yourself what you want," then the *sasu* feels
very bad and tells her own husband that the *bahu* has insulted her. Then again the
bahu replies, "Don't think that I will do anything for you in the future. Do not give
me orders." Then there is no purdah, because the *bahu* has not only talked in the
presence of her *sasu* but in the presence of her *soosar*. Like this the purdah can
decrease.

This hypothetical situation is most unlikely, but the answer pinpoints a major
function of purdah: enforcing obedience to authority. If *bahu*s cannot talk, they
cannot talk back, but if they can speak, they may speak their minds.

Husband–Wife Intimacy

In 1975 young husbands preferred more intimacy with their wives, and some wives prepared and served food for their own husbands and children. *Bahu*s asked for their own *chuula*s, and with them a separate food supply, sooner than they had in previous generations.

In the past couples often had to share sleeping quarters with each other or with the mother-in-law. The increased prosperity had enabled most Rajput families to expand their houses, so that each married couple had a private room and some had private apartments in the *bughar* roofs. These separate quarters enabled wives to talk privately with their husbands and, frequently, to gain their support in disagreements with *sasu*s. The increased intimacy between husbands and wives was particularly irksome to *sasu*s, whose early days of marriage were dominated by *sasu*s who controlled virtually all interaction with husbands, including their sexual encounters.

*Sasu*s described restrictions from their husbands as follows:

> Previously we could not talk to our husbands when their parents were alive. Sometimes for 2 years or so we could not talk to our husbands nor even look at them because in the presence of our brothers-in-law we had to keep our faces covered. We were very much troubled with the long thick *chaddar* which we had to keep on most of the time. But now some *bahu*s keep only half of their faces covered when their husbands are present and others do not even cover their faces at all, only their heads. Now they keep sitting on the cots even in the presence of others. Some *bahu*s now go to their husband saying, "husband, husband" in the presence of everyone. Those who are educated sit with the husbands even in the presence of elders. Those who are too brave have much fun. They sit on chairs with their husbands and do not keep purdah for *sasu*s or *jethani*s. Previously you only used to meet your husband during the night, not during the day.

> I never showed my face to my husband during the day and at night when he came it was dark. We could not see each other's face in darkness; even though we reproduced we had not seen the face of each other. Now most have electricity in their rooms and if they don't, they have a lantern or a candle.

> For 12 years after I lost my *sasu* I only gave things to my husband through my children, and not directly. It was only after my children were old enough to go to the fields that I started giving things to my husband myself.

> Previously we never gave food to our husbands. Only the *sasu* or *nanad* could give food to the husband. I used to keep so much purdah that if my husband came home to get anything I never used to give it to him. His daughter or his sister, brother, or nephew could give it.

> Now in some families the husbands and wives eat together. In former days the women never ate until the men had finished eating. In former days men used to die at an old age but they would say that they had never seen the faces of their wives. Now *bahu*s keep their faces uncovered and even eat with their husbands. I know husbands and wives who have no purdah when they sleep together, but in the presence of purdah is to show respect to other people [e.g., senior relatives].

> I never let my husband look into my eyes. I let him do whatever he liked but I always kept my face covered. Even when he beat me to get me to uncover my face I

did not do it. When at the ti... said, "Poor lady, I am... covered my face a little... though I did not even have... and my husband as well. T... his wife and his sisters all d...

At the time that this woman... *Sasu*s' comments about the i... particularly barbed:

> I used to sleep inside my room even i... while I was sleeping. Now the *bahu*s s... in-law. We used to consider the time fo... this matter. We did not meet our husban... days old or when there was no moon or fu... to be good for conceiving and you could get... hands. Now they do not bother to avoid mee... days. Indeed they do not even wait for night... rules and bore two sons and no daughters, be... correct times.
>
> Moreover, *bahu*s have grown so shameless th... sleeping in the same room where the *bahu* and husb... talking and do not have consideration that their *sas*... talk. They go on talking shamelessly. Now I do not li... as my *bahu*.

> Previously the new *bahu* was given a separate room fo... marriage, then she slept with other women; now she keeps... husband can come during the day or night and stay all nig... separate room and they are shameless.

One *sasu* viewed the change in husband–wife intimacy with...

> Previously, if a husband came to his wife and someone caught h... back to the chopar. Now they come galloping like horses. Previously... to see their wives with their shoes in their hand. Now they make a big... clap, clap—with their shoes.

Some older women joked about the new shameless *bahu*s:

> Now they are so forward that, if their husbands are having a fight, they wil... with a stick to help. They will go to the roof and throw bricks at their husb... enemies. Many women have broken the heads of men by throwing bricks w... their husbands were fighting.

One *sasu* reported that women could now defend themselves:

> Now one advantage is that previously a woman could not defend herself if some

man tried to seduce... even threaten to s...

Since it is the... laxness in their cu... generation seem a... customs because...

I kept my face... even my *bah*... my face cov... these chang...

Again the...

I can talk... talk to h... keep sit... presenc... anybo... face c... almos... could... to h... wo... Th...

Th... who... the... like... sho... ga...

agreed that *bahu*s were more skilled at handling money than their uneducated elders. The increase in the number of wives and children in the courtyards made it difficult, if not impossible, for one woman to cook for the entire family, legitimating the need for separate hearths and separate food storage facilities.

In addition to decreasing the respect traditionally accorded *sasu*s, *bahu*s have appropriated control of their own food supply and money from their parents, resources traditionally controlled by the *sasu*. In 1955 *sasu*s took all money and gifts brought by *bahu*s returning from their parental homes. By 1975, however, wives kept money they brought from home instead of giving it to their *sasu*s. This meant that in some families it was the *sasu* who was without funds while her *bahu*s had money to spend on personal luxuries, clothes, and toys for their children. Most *sasu*s seemed to regard this situation as inevitable. They preferred to give their *bahu*s autonomy in minor matters, thus avoiding petty conflict and reserving their authority for more serious disputes, where their wishes usually still prevailed.

Answers of the older women describe the strict purdah they kept in the presence of their *sasu*s:

> Previously the *bahu*s could eat only when they were given food by *sasu*s or sisters-in-law. Now they take food without even asking their *sasu*s if they may eat. Those who come from good families will respect their *sasu*s but some of those who are educated do not respect them. Previously they cooked the food but could not eat it themselves. Before, the *sasu* always used to eat first, but nowadays they eat before we eat. The other day when I was crying it was because I did not have my meals for the last 3 days because my *bahu* had not offered me the food. If I want to take anything my *bahu* cannot come in my way. I am all-powerful but I was crying and did not eat because my *bahu* did not ask me to eat. In my day if a *sasu* asked me to stand on a particular spot, I would not move an inch from that spot in any circumstance without further approval of my *sasu*.

> When my *sasu* was sick, I used to sit with her the whole day and keep on crying. I was worried because I could not do without her, we had so much affection for each other. The moment I finished my kitchen work I used to come to her service. Now there is no affection between *sasu*s and *bahu*s. Previously I used to bathe my *sasu* and massage her also. Now they do not do this for us.

Some houses were still strict and followed the old customs, as described by two women:

> My elder son was married some 17 years ago and they have six children, but so far my *bahu* has neither talked before me nor walked before me.

> If the *sasu* or *jethani* came in the *bahu* would cover her face, at least up to the nose, and sit, whereas, nowadays in some houses the *sasu* may sit on a low chair while the *bahu* sleeps on the charpoy. Our nose plug was never visible to these older women.

Some typical answers of the eight young women who said they kept less purdah from their *sasu*s than their mothers did are as follows:

> She could not sit on a cot, while I do not mind sitting on a cot even when my *sasu* is

sitting on a low chair. When I am angry I can talk back and even fight, while my mother never talked loudly to anyone.

Not even one third of what my mother kept from her *sasu*. My mother kept that amount of purdah from her *sasu* which we nowadays keep from our *soosar*s. I have no purdah from my *sasu*.

I do not keep purdah from my *sasu*. In the very beginning I had a *gungat* in the presence of my *sasu* but she did not let me keep my face covered. She did not like this purdah. Therefore, I do not cover my face from her while my mother still keeps purdah from her *sasu*.

My grandmother died before I was born. Mother used to observe purdah from her *jethani*s. She used to keep a *gungat* from older women, but we cannot keep our faces covered. We only cover our faces when men enter the house. In the beginning when I came after my *shadi* and *guana*, I covered my face from my *sasu* for 3 or 4 years. But how long can I continue doing this? Now I have stopped doing that.

The two *bahu*s who kept more purdah than their mothers gave these explanations:

In my mother's place women keep their faces covered, but can move and go on working in the presence of elders, but here, in this village, women not only cover their faces, but at once sit, whenever they are in the presence of elders. If they must, then they walk while squatting, but they do not walk. When my *sasu* comes, I also sit and do not walk, while my mother did not even cover her face from her *sasu*. This is due to different customs in different places. In Meerut district women do not have much purdah.

My mother keeps some purdah from her *sasu*, but I observe far more purdah than my mother did. The reason was that my father was the only son and my grandmother was very fond of him. She did not like my mother to sit idle and keep strict purdah. My mother could talk to her *sasu* and could talk to my father in the *sasu*'s presence.

A change in the method of showing respect was reflected in another answer: "I do not think that one should look into the face of an older person, but one need not cover the face in front of the *sasu*." For this young woman the *gungat* had been replaced by downcast eyes, a traditional sign of demure demeanor in the Western world.

It is clear from these answers that the *sasu*s still had the final say in the degree of purdah kept to them. The influence of household customs was expressed by one *bahu*: "I keep the same purdah from my *sasu* that I saw other women keeping from their *sasu*s."

Deference to Older Men

For several reasons purdah customs have changed least where deference to senior family men is concerned: The older men are the most prestigious members of the family and therefore would be most offended by breaches in traditional customs of courtesy; since their presence inhibits the actions of their *bahu*s they seldom enter the *bughar,* and thus there is little reason to change behavior that defers to them; finally, seclusion of young *bahu*s from these older men also protects women from incestuous sexual advances from men whose position of authority makes them difficult to disobey.

Nevertheless, there was a decrease in traditional deference accorded even to the senior men. In 1955 *bahu*s covered their faces and did not stand or speak in the presence of *sasu*s or husbands. When older men entered the courtyard, *bahu*s remained immobile until these men left. In 1975 *bahu*s moved freely, with un-covered faces, in the presence of older women and their husbands, and continued their work, with saris pulled over their faces, in the presence of older men.

The senior men continued to stay out of the *bughar*s as much as possible. Usually these men visited with their friends on their spacious *choopar*s, discussing politics, business, and marriage arrangements. However, one *soosar,* too poor to have a large *choopar* or the prestige of many friends, sat alone day after day, staring sightless into space. He had gone blind in his declining years. His sons were busy in the fields, and he was barred from the friendly chatter of his wife and *bahu*s. Even though he could not see them, custom demanded that he stay out of their *bughar* since the women could not talk among themselves without dishonoring him. We always greeted him as we passed; he started to hear a woman's voice in greeting, and replied with a short, dignified *"namastee"* (the traditional greeting). The lonely isolation of this blind patriarch was a poignant reminder that men who shut women in shut themselves out.

The minimal change in deference to older family men reflected their status and their absence from the *bughar.* However, women's descriptions of changes in these customs, and our observations, indicate that this deference had diminished. One *sasu* described the changes as follows:

> We could not move before the elders. If we had to move we moved while squatting. If a *soosar* or brother-in-law entered the house the *bahu* used to sit immediately even if it was raining or burning sunshine. As long as the man remained at home, she could not move even her hands or feet.
>
> Previously *bahu*s were covered from head to toe and if the *soosar* and brothers-in-law came they stopped their work and kept sitting. They sat until the men finished their food and moved only when the men were gone. Sometimes they had to sit in excrement or filth when the men came into the house.
>
> Now *bahu*s cover only their faces in the presence of elders. Previously *bahu*s kept their faces covered at all times. Now if the men have to stay at home for a long time *bahu*s go on with their work saying, "How long can I waste my time like this?" If we were sitting on a low chair and our *soosar* came in the *bughar* then we would get down on the floor. But now *bahu*s keep sitting on their cot while their husbands, poor fellows, sit on the floor. Previously we could not sit higher than any of the men.

A *bahu*'s description confirms these practices:

> When men came into the house, *bahu*s used to stop spinning, cooking, or whatever work they were doing, and sit covering their heads, hands, feet, everything. A dog might come and eat the milk but she could not move. The *soosar*s and *jaith*s never

heard the voices of the *bahu*s. If men were eating in the kitchen and there was blazing sun or rain we could not move. If we had to walk at all, we walked while crouching to take shelter.

The description of a wife sitting on a cot while her husband sits on the floor is an extreme exaggeration, but the dramatic crouch-freeze position assumed by women when men entered the *bughar* in 1955 was gone completely during our second visit. Women stopped talking and pulled their saris over their faces when men entered, but they quietly continued their work.

Deference to Sons

The greater deference accorded to sons is reflected in one mother's report of a difference in the amount of *gungat* she used in the presence of her son and daughters: "I keep my face covered from my husband in the presence of my sons but not in the presence of my daughters. I never keep my face completely uncovered from my husband, even when we are alone."

Deference to Outsiders

Each Rajput family has servants from other castes, who may visit fairly regularly. The only servants who outrank Rajputs, by caste, are the Brahmins, who are always accorded the respect due their priestly caste. Caste rules prohibit taking food from persons of lower caste, so Brahmin women come to cook for ceremonies that require feeding many people. Brahmin women also come each year to renew the sacred wall paintings in the women's bedrooms. For some occasions the Brahmin family priest may be called to chant Sanskrit prayers in the *bughar*.

At the low end of the hierarchy are the outcaste Chamars, untouchable women who come to clean out the family latrines. The only sweeper woman who enters the *bughar* proper is the *dai* (midwife). The *dai* usually does not deliver infants, a task that the older women are willing to do themselves, but she is always called to cut the cord, dispose of the afterbirth, and change bandages until the mother stops hemorrhaging. In 1955 each Rajput family had a Jhinvar (water carrier) who made daily rounds, bringing water from the communal wells to the secluded Rajput women. In 1975 tube wells and pumps had been installed in most *bughar*s, and daughters brought water for the *bughar*s without tube wells.

The only nonfamily men who entered *bughar*s were the village priest, traveling holy men, and doctors. Salesmen hawked their wares outside the *bughar* door, with the exception of the bangle salesmen, who must fit the fragile glass bracelets to the wrists of his customers. Bangles must fit tightly around the wrists, to prevent breaking, so the salesman must squeeze the women's hands to force the bangles onto the wrists.

I can attest to the dramatic change in the cloistering kept from women from outside the household by the difference in the degree of *gungat* kept when talking to me and my interpreter. In 1955 I interviewed many young women who held their saris closed in front of their faces, leaving only a slit for them to see through. When

I returned in 1975, even though I was now a member of the older generation, these "one-eyed women," as I used to call them, had disappeared; all women talked to us with their faces uncovered. One woman commented on deference to these *bughar* visitors:

> We also could not show our faces to women of the outside. Previously we used to keep purdah even before the low-caste servants. Now the *bahu*s do not do this. In our time if we wanted to buy bangles we had to squat behind the charpoy and put our hands through its lacing so that the bangle salesman could not see us. Nowadays the young women who want to buy bangles simply go directly to the bangles salesman without hiding from him.
>
> I was beaten by my *sasu* when I was a child because I did not salute a low-caste woman or a Muslim who used to sell oil for our family. I thought my *sasu* might not like my being intimate with an outside woman but my *sasu* took the wooden hookah lying nearby and struck me with it very sharply. I did not know the reason, which was explained by an aunt of mine who happened to be sitting there along with the others. My aunt told me that even when the sweeper comes in the house you should wish her "*namistee*" and never commit that mistake again because in that case my *sasu* may break my bones.

One daughter-in-law confirmed the change in the method of buying bangles: "At my age my *sasu* used to get her bangles by putting her hands through the laces of the charpoy."

Mobility

In Khalapur

Purdah customs restrict the movements of women outside the *bughar,* particularly that of *bahu*s. Some *sasu*s described changes in these restrictions as follows:

> *Bahu*s could not go to the roof or go out of the house to observe something in those days. We did not come up and sit on the roofs or even open the door and see a wedding party or something else going by the house. Previously if there was a procession or someone with a performing monkey the *bahu* would peep through the cracks in the door to see it. Now they go into the street to see it.

> Women nowadays visit around the village much more than we used to. In our times women had to go and see a new bridegroom in a marriage from some distance; they could not go even when a single man was in the street unless he went away. Now no one cares for these things. Day and night women wander around the village. Before, if women were going to a wedding or something, and their *taaya* happened to meet them in the way, they would sit at once not even considering that there was mud or water or anything and they would continue sitting even in the rain until the *taaya* went away.

> Even though I had no *sasu* I never saw the gate to my husband's home. Now women go to see movies and they also go to the market. Previously if there was some marriage, five or six women would get together and go in a group; now *bahu*s can go alone. When we went to marriages before, we went only during the night. Now even the newlyweds go out during the day. Nowadays *sasu*s sit at home and

the *bahu*s move about the village. They may also go to visit other houses even when there is no particular function; we would never have done that. Before we used to go out only with our *sasu*s; now *bahu*s go together without their *sasu* going along. Now women roam about the village and don't put on a *chaddar* over their sari. If a *bahu* had to go somewhere out of the village, she was sent in a bullock cart that was draped and covered on all sides, but now she may go jointly with men in a *thonga* anywhere.

One big change in purdah is that previously the *bahu*s did not leave the house even for elimination [latrines used to be in the house]. If *bahu*s did go out to eliminate they only went at night and in groups. Now they may go out during the day. In former days if a woman felt she had to eliminate in the morning, she fasted all day so that she could be prevented from doing this and only went out of the house at night. Now they may go to the fields to eliminate. So if a man and a woman see each other squatting in the fields, where is the purdah?

When the *bahu*s were asked about mobility it became obvious that the *sasu*s were exaggerating the amount of time that young women left the house. Four young women said that they never visited any other house. One said that she went to the adjoining house of her husband's brother, which would have been permissible in earlier years. The remaining *bahu*s described going to marriages and birth ceremonies, which were appropriate occasions for visiting even under strict purdah.

We also asked, "When did you last go out of the house?" and "Where did you go?" The answers to these questions indicated that young women were visiting outside their *bughar* on other than ceremonial occasions. Some said that they went to visit relatives or friends in the village, particularly ritual sisters; the time that each woman last left the *bughar* varied from the previous day to 6 months earlier.

Outside of Khalapur

All *sasu*s said that *bahu*s visited their parental homes more than they did when they were young. However, only six *bahu*s said that they visited their parents more than their mothers did, while three said they visited with the same frequency and four said they visited less. These differences may reflect exaggeration by the *sasu*s or a difference between purdah customs as practiced in Khalapur and the less conservative home villages of some *bahu*s.

Our interview with 43 wives shows that visits to locations other than natal and marital villages are still relatively rare (see Table 3.3). The most frequent town visited was Bhudana, the market town 4 miles from Khalapur, which 37% of the women had seen. Meerut had been visited by 23% of the wives, many of whom came from towns near that city. Other places had been visited by 26% of the wives; these were mostly holy cities where large fairs are held. Finally, 14% of the women had visited no towns other than their residential villages.

Only 25 of the women interviewed told us how many towns they had visited. The maximum number of towns visited by women was four. Only 12% of the wives interviewed had visited either three or four towns, 20% had visited two locations, and 32% had visited only one, other than their natal and marital villages. Clearly, travel was still a rare event for Khalapur wives. However, literacy had enabled

Table 3.3 Mobility of Women to Towns Other
Than Residential Towns

	N	%
Towns visited		
Bhudana	16	37
Meerut	10	23
' Other	11	26
None	6	14
Total	43	100
Number of towns visited		
0	6	24
1	8	32
2	5	20
3	3	12
4	3	12
Total	25	100

women to buy tickets and read signs for ticket windows and railroad stops, so they were capable of traveling alone.

MEDIA AND POLITICS

In the report on my visit of 1955 I commented, "Although women may vote they cannot attend political meetings and inform themselves" (Minturn & Hitchcock, 1966, p. 34). In the years between my visits to Khalapur, the invention of the transistor radio had brought the outside world into most *bughar*s. Transistor radios were more common than radios that need to be plugged into an electric socket, even in houses with electricity. Women were interviewed in groups concerning their access to radio programs; Table 3.4 shows the frequency with which women listened to radio programs and their program preferences. Only 36% of the households interviewed had radios in the *bughar,* but 63% had radios in the *choopar*s. A few men had their radios hooked up to loudspeaker systems. The radio from Sher's *choopar* blared continuously into the family *bughar.* In other households women borrowed their men's radios and listened fairly regularly. In Amar Nath's *bughar* a newborn girl often had a radio placed next to her, presumably to keep her quiet. Virtually all of the women (86%) listened to radio programs, sometimes visiting neighbors to listen when their families did not own radios. The two women who said they did not listen came from families that did not own radios.

Music was by far the most popular type of program, preferred by 57% of the women. Women also had access to news, women's programs, often about family planning, and religious programs. This new medium brought information about popular music, current events, and government policies into the cloistered *bughar*s, to literate and illiterate alike. Exposure to news programs, however, had not changed women's obedience to their husbands where voting was concerned. Without exception women said that they always "put their stamp where their husbands said to put it" and voted for the Congress party, as their husbands directed. None of

Table 3.4 Exposure to Radio Programs

	N	%
Radio ownership		
Radio in family	7	36
Radio in men's quarters	12	63
Total	19	100
NA	34	
Radio listening		
Does not listen	2	14
Listens	12	86
Total	14	100
NA	34	
Preference for radio programs		
News	4	19
Women's programs	3	14
Music	12	57
Religious	2	10
Total	21	100
NA	46	

the women interviewed knew why the family men liked the Congress party, and some commented that Prime Minister Gandhi's policy requiring them to sell some of their crop to the government at a fixed price was hard on farmers. All women were registered to vote; indeed, they sometimes substituted for wives who were away visiting their parental families and cast two votes. Since women were veiled, this practice was fairly common among village families who strongly support a local candidate.

In the years between my visits, laws enabling women to serve on village *panchayats* (town councils) had been passed, although no women had served on the Khalapur *panchayat*. Most women did not know about this law, and all disapproved of women "sitting in the presence of men." One *sasu* said that a woman who would do this was "naked and shameless." Another commented: "We cannot succeed in the household *panchayat*. What would we do in the village *panchayat?* When we fight among ourselves, we cannot reach an end, so what can we do sitting with men?"

The women's objections to women who sit with men did not extend to the wife of the intercollege principal, who was serving on the district board. The principal and his wife were well respected, and most women said it was a good thing to have this woman representing the district in this manner. However, they were not interested in assuming such responsibilities for themselves. They did not think themselves qualified to sit with men on the town council even if such activity were proper.

CONCLUSIONS

Purdah customs are a complex set of rules that assure that a wife maintains a respectful social distance from and subservience to her husband and his senior relatives. Although the customs are justified by reference to the necessity of protecting women from seduction or rape, they are designed primarily to protect the consanguineous extended family from disruption by affinal wives. The interviews indicate that all aspects of purdah observance have decreased—the least for practices associated with older family men and most for practices separating husbands and wives. *Bahus* visited their parents more frequently than in former years, although visits to other towns were rare and limited. Radios have brought new ideas into the *bughars* but have not yet affected women's political behavior.

The husband–wife separation customs reported in 1955 were so severe for Khalapur Rajputs that they scored as having the most aloof marriages in Broude's sample of 140 societies (Broude, 1987). Broude finds that marriages are aloof where people have nonmarital kin networks and permanent home towns. As we will see in chapter 5, profit agriculture has strained joint-family ties. In 1975 some young, educated Khalapur men had jobs in cities and lived there with their wives for much of their time. Therefore, the shift to greater intimacy between husbands and wives can be predicted from Broude's data.

The increased husband–wife intimacy observed in 1975 was not great enough to change the group's position on Broude's scale. Nevertheless, many *sasus* saw the change as a threat to their influence over their sons and hence their authority. The respect–avoidance customs observed by *bahus* with their *sasus* had also decreased during this period, further diminishing *sasus*' traditional status. The change occurred primarily in the observance of deferential customs; in fact, most *sasus* still reigned supreme in their *bughars*.

The observance of respect–avoidance customs had changed least for the senior men. Isolation of young wives from the powerful male family heads was still considered prudent. In 1975 wives continued to work quietly when senior men were present, a change that most women regarded as a practical improvement, but wives still did not stand or speak in the presence of senior men.

The protection of wives from men outside the family, which restricts their mobility, was widely believed to be particularly necessary for uneducated and naive women; therefore, the increased education of *bahus* has been one justification for the decrease in the severity of purdah restrictions in recent years. In the next chapter we report on the attitudes of women regarding the decrease in traditional purdah restrictions.

In 1955 plowing was done with bullocks pulling simple plows made in Khalapur. In 1975 the prosperity resulting from new hybrid grains enabled many wealthy families to buy tractors. Increased agricultural production is vital to the village economy and an adequate supply of food is essential to India's huge urban population.

4

Changing Times

The days are gone when there was purdah.

The world is changing.

The preceding statements, taken from our 1975 interviews, exemplify the attitudes of most older women about changes in the last generation. The *bahu*s left the courtyard and visited other houses more frequently than they did in former times. New commercial products, unfamiliar to *sasu*s, were purchased and used by young women, many of whom disregarded the customary confinement to the *bughar* and walked to village stores. Traditionally young Rajput women could leave the *bughar* to visit or shop only if they were daughters of village families, and except for ceremonial occasions wives of Khalapur Rajputs were confined to their *bughar*s until their sons married and they became *sasu*s. In 1955 some *bahu*s had not left their *bughar*s in years. One young wife of a conservative husband had been confined to her small *bughar* for 8 years, even though she had no *sasu* or *bahu*s to share her isolation. Such isolated women were completely dependent on visits from neighbor women for company.

All of these changes allowed the younger generation of *bahu*s more autonomy and freedom of movement than their predecessors. They were no longer immobilized in the presence of older men, could move and speak freely in the presence of older women, and wore clothing that permitted greater visibility, even when saris must be pulled over their faces. The seemingly trivial objections of *sasu*s to the demise of purdah restrictions must be evaluated in the context of their threat to traditional norms of deference and respect.

When we asked the women what they thought was causing the changes in purdah customs, they typically said *bhagwan*, the formless, supreme godhead. They meant that the changes were God's will. All the women recognized that changes were not the result of individual decisions but of massive social changes, *bhagwan*. Detailed interviews concerning the reasons for changes elicited more worldly explanations.

REASONS FOR CHANGES

Specific probe questions about three frequently cited causes for change—increased education, affluence, and transportation—were included in the standardized interviews and asked of all the women. In addition to these frequently cited influences, women mentioned Indian independence, the creation of Pakistan after partition, Indira Gandhi's position as prime minister, the coming of American anthropologists to the village, and the increase in *bahu*s from the urban Meerut district as influences that lessened purdah restrictions.

Education

It was generally believed by both generations that the lessening of purdah for young wives had come about because the young educated men did not want their wives to keep as much purdah as their fathers desired. One *sasu* feared the influence of city customs on the village:

> Now the *sasu* will keep her face covered and the daughter-in-law will not cover her face. Both are obeying their husband's wishes. Men today do not want their wives to keep any purdah while men previously wanted their wives to keep more purdah. Previously education for women was not a good thing. Now it is a good thing because educated men want educated wives. Now men want their wives to sit at parties and eat in the presence of outsiders. They make their wives move in the cars in the presence of other men. They want their wives to eat with them from the same dish as the Americans do.

Another complained that her conservative son was disliked by his wife:

> Nowadays those boys who allow their wives not to keep purdah in the presence of their elders are liked and appreciated by their wives. But those who do not allow their wives to uncover their faces in the presence of elders are disliked by their wives. My son is very simple and conservative; he does not talk to his wife in our presence. He does not like his wife uncovering her face, so my *bahu* does not like my son. If he were like the boys of today who do not like purdah, then this *bahu* would have been happy. I prefer to talk to my own family and not to anybody else. My *bahu* has no regard for my son because he does not like this shameless purdahlessness. But generally nowadays boys do not want their wives to keep purdah and this is the cause for these changes. Young men want their wives to roam about as their sisters do. Previously city people got their daughters educated and now village boys want educated wives. And they want to move with them hand in hand.

Increased education of the wives was seen by some older women as a factor in reducing purdah:

> Educated women do not want to keep purdah. Previously there were separate

schools for boys and girls, but now they go to school together. With coeducation there must be less purdah.

The wife of my younger son is educated, and just after the marriage I found her sitting on a cot talking to the brother of my elder son's wife with her face uncovered. I did not like this and went away since I didn't wish to scold my *bahu* in front of an outside visitor. The next morning she was ready to go home to her parents and I told her if you will not keep purdah as I do I will not take you back as my *bahu*. Then she touched her ears to my feet and took a pledge that she would not give me cause for complaint again. Since then she has kept strict purdah and I have no further complaints about her. Now the educated sons who are in service and work away from the village take their wives with them instead of leaving them with their parents as they did in former days. So there is no question of purdah because the husband and wife may be living alone.

Education is the main cause for these changes. Now you are educated, so you are sitting without covering your head. Had you been uneducated you might also be keeping your head and face covered. My daughter says that there is no life when she is in purdah. The daughters come after marriage and if their husbands keep hand in hand the wives are happy but if the husbands feel shy, our daughters say that their lives have been spoiled.

One woman reported on her reaction to the eating customs of a city family traveling with her by train:

Once my sister and I were traveling on a train where there was an educated couple and two children also traveling in the same compartment. After some time .they started taking their meals. The man was eating one piece of bread while at the same time the woman was eating two. She was not even ashamed of eating double the amount that her husband was eating. We were laughing and surprised at how the world has grown shameless due to education. In some families the *bahu*s learn from them and imitate them [i.e., educated women].

Although the women regarded increased education of both sons and daughters as a major factor in the decrease in purdah, they usually reported that both educated and uneducated sons and *bahu*s obeyed their elders to about the same degree. While they considered education to be an important factor in the decrease in purdah, they apparently did not regard it as important in increasing household strife. Some women pointed out that educated women may know better how to please their in-laws than women who "know nothing."

A few women cited the fact that young people were simply less shy than they were in former times as the cause of the decrease in purdah. It is difficult to see quite what has brought about this change, but our observations confirm it. The young men and women who were about to be married or newly married certainly seemed less shy and anxious than young people were 20 years earlier. One suspects that this is a result of education that has exposed boys and girls to children of the opposite sex who are not close relatives.

*Bahu*s agreed that the disapproval of husbands and the education of wives were primary factors in the decrease of purdah. Ten women said that their husbands disliked purdah, and several mentioned particularly the aversion to "useless purdah," referring to deferential customs which the husbands thought had no practical value. Nine *bahu*s said that educated women preferred less purdah, while three said there was no difference between educated and uneducated women, in this regard.

Affluence

Another reason cited for the lessening of purdah was money. *Sasu*s often saw the new affluence as a threat to family solidarity:

> It is the sons who want to separate their *chuula*s now because they want a separate income. It is because of the sons and not of the *bahu*s. The parents tell their boys not to go to the pictures and circuses, and they will not give their sons money for this. The money the sons earn they keep and they don't give it to their parents. Now they may take money from their parents but they do not give it to their parents.

> We have more expenses now and what they earn is not sufficient for them. Nowadays the expenses are more complicated. Previously parents made one set of clothing for each person in the family for the whole year. Now people want more clothing, more fashionable clothing, soap, cosmetics, money for movies, etcetera. Now people may wear fashionable dresses, but you will not find a single penny in their pockets. Parents are unable to keep track of all of this for all of their children and find it easier to divide their income.

> People now pose at being rich and showy but they do not have even enough to eat, while previously people used to eat pure butter and pure rich food but never made a show of anything. People had money in earlier days also. They used to eat the food they grew and wear the clothes which they had made of cotton, that they produced in their own fields.

> I used to wear homespun clothes. The people have grown fashionable now and they buy their clothes. Previously, women did not use cream, powder, scented oil; we had only soda for washing. We wore padded cloth vests in the winter. Now the people have sweaters, mufflers, and blankets. Also, the boys now wear pants instead of dhotis. All of these things cost money. Now if one brother has money he is happily eating and the other who does not have enough to eat is watching.

> Previously, one brother would help the other, but now nobody helps anybody. Nowadays, the *bahu* behaves as if she is the *sasu* and the *sasu* as if she is the *bahu*.

Transportation

The bus and *thonga* (horse-drawn cart) service now available to Khalapur had led to greater mobility. It was possible for women to visit their parental homes or go shopping in Bhudana, the market town 4 miles away, without being driven by a man of the family in a bullock cart. Women generally agreed that this increased ease of transportation had enabled them to travel more frequently:

> Yes, previously, there were bullock carts only. Now there are buses, horse carts, in

fact, everything. Many women do not even wait for their husbands to go along with them; they may travel alone. Because there is bus and *thonga* service from the village, now *bahu*s can go out. I have never been to Bhudana, but my *bahu* has just gone there to purchase some cloth. Previously we had no money for purchases, but now there is money so they keep going to Bhudana to buy things. Ladies move in buses and go into the cities and they meet with other women in the cities who are not in purdah so they follow them and imitate their ways. Because of buses people move and they see things in other places and want to imitate them. People used to go on foot. They started early in the morning and came late in the evening. Now even the beggars come and go on the bus. [The last statement is correct. Several beggars traveled regularly from Bhudana to Khalapur on the bus.] Women also go to see the movies and the fairs. Nowadays people do not have enough to eat but at the same time they have forgotten to walk. Previously people used to walk miles and miles day and night. Now there are buses for Bhudana and even further. From home women go up to the bus stand covering their heads and faces, but when they sit in the bus, they uncover their faces. Now they sit in the buses or *thonga*s so near the other men and travel alone. Previously they used to sit in the bullock cart all alone with the bullock cart wrapped and then only would they travel. The bus and *thonga* service has caused changes in traveling.

Women who were in purdah and were traveling could not say anything even if a thief took their luggage and even if they saw them. This made men want to have their women keep less purdah. Sometimes a woman who was following her husband with her head in heavy veil would get lost and follow the wrong man. That way she lost both her husband and her honor so that men did not want their waives to keep purdah while they were traveling.

Although undocumented, the story of a wife following a strange man in a crowded station and losing her way and her virtue was frequently cited by men as a reason for abandoning the *chaddar* that limited a woman's vision. One woman, when asked about the likelihood of such an incident occurring, said: "How is that possible? Now I am looking at the ground, but I could see my husband's feet, if my eyes were not broken." It does seem most unlikely that women who can recognize the cough of a man at their doorstep over the din of women, children, and animals would not quickly learn to recognize their husbands' feet, shoes, and walk when their safety depends on it. However, this story, like the threat of rape by Muslins, is a convenient justification for changing tradition. Since purdah customs are ostensibly designed to protect feminine virtue, these customs may safely be abandoned if they threaten that virtue.

Nine *bahu*s agreed that increased transportation had lessened purdah, while four said it made no difference. Only two of the older *bahu*s had traveled by bus alone. Regarding travel one young woman said:

Previously no woman used to travel, but nowadays they do all sorts of shopping for the marriage of daughters. So it has become convenient for them to travel by bus or cart. I do not like to go alone anywhere. Once I went to get my eyes examined with my sons, when my husband could not go. When I go to my mother's place my husband goes with me.

EVALUATION OF CHANGES
Obedience

The *sasu*s generally agreed that their *bahu*s did not obey them as well as they had obeyed their own *sasu*s. This insubordination had caused some resentment:

> Nowadays no *bahu* obeys her *sasu*. Some rare *bahu*s might be obeying her. *Bahu*s behave as if they are *sasu*s these days. During our day every *bahu* obeyed her *sasu*. Previously among 1,000 *bahu*s, there would be 1 who would not obey her *sasu*. Now in 1,000 there is 1 who does obey. I saw a house where the *sasu* was doing the household chores and was crying also. That is because the *bahu* was not obeying. Now if the *sasu* asks her *bahu* to do some work, she will complain to her husband saying, "Your mother scolds me and asks me to do a lot of work." Then the husband will question his mother instead of insulting his young wife for lying in the bed when her *sasu* is working. This is because their husbands don't object to their wives moving about the village and the *bahu*s do not feel any necessity to ask their *sasu*s whether they can go to any home or not. There is no shame nowadays.

> We used to work late at night and got up at 4:30 a.m. We got only 1 or 2 hours of sleep. Now the *bahu* gets up at 5:00 a.m. and goes to bed at 8:00 p.m. Now they call their *sasu*s a co-wife and they sometimes pull their braids. Nowadays one cannot say anything to one's *bahu*s otherwise their husbands will tear off our ears.

> Previously *bahu*s obeyed better than they do now. Now they may even cut off the hair of the *sasu*s. Before there was more affection between *bahu*s and *sasu*s. *Bahu*s used to obey us and we could work according to our own choice. *Bahu*s now may obey their *sasu* but not in every piece of work.

Happiness

Answers to the question "Do you think that the young *bahu*s are happier now than you were when you kept stricter purdah?" were varied. Two *sasu*s replied that they were happier in former times. One cited the fact that the new *bahu*s have many more decisions to make than they did and that they must sometimes work in the fields: "Now young women have to bother about so many things, they have to go to the fields and they get more tired than we were." The second woman who made this claim seemed to be basing the statement on her own preferences rather than the preferences of the *bahu*s: "I was happy in purdah and the *bahu*s are not happy with less purdah. *Bahu*s are only good when they are in purdah."

Five *sasu*s said that they and their *bahu*s were equally happy because people are happy with the behavior to which they are accustomed. The comments of three are included here:

> I was happy with more purdah and the *bahu*s are happy with less purdah. In my time all the *bahu*s were in purdah and none of the *bahu*s now are in purdah. We were happy in it and they are happy out of it.

> I was happy in my purdah and the *bahu*s are happy in less purdah. Now they spread their legs [has sex with her husband] before the *sasu* and the *sasu* turns her face away from them. I used to sleep inside the room even in summer. Now the *bahu*s

sleep in the courtyard. I used to be afraid that someone would see me while I was sleeping. Now the *bahu*s spread their legs before their *sasu*s and have no shame. But they are very happy.

We were happy in our strict purdah because we had seen our elders observing purdah. But nowadays, *bahu*s are happy in less purdah. I did not live to even move while crawling. Due to shyness and shame, we did not like to be without purdah and stand in the presence of men.

Because of our strict purdah sometimes we had to leave many things in the kitchen such as milk. If the milk was boiling on the hearth we could not stand up in the presence of men in the house and take that milk tumbler off the hearth. For such losses we never bothered.

Seven *sasu*s who said that the younger generation was happy in less purdah cited some of the suffering they went through under the strict purdah customs that prevailed when they were young. Three of them commented as follows:

The *bahu*s are happier. We had to keep such strict purdah and we were not happy because we could not stand and had to walk while squatting. We had to cover our face all the time and we spent hours staring at the ground. We were not happy.

Now *bahu*s are happier than we were in purdah. Previously *bahu*s did not know this was my husband, and the husband did not know this was my wife. Previously we were not at all happy. Women who were simple would cook all day and serve the whole family. If the husband came like a thief once a month, then the *bahu* enjoyed him. Now they have the best possible clothes and food and enjoy themselves and are much happier. Previously, *sasu*s were jealous. Now I feel happy when my *bahu* is happy.

*Bahu*s are happy in less purdah nowadays. We used to cover our faces for hours in summer and had drops and drops of sweat but could not uncover our faces. But nowadays, *bahu*s, whenever they feel like it, uncover even their heads. So they are happy.

Better or Worse?

When asked to judge whether the changes in purdah were good or bad, 13 of the 15 *sasu*s (88%) thought they were not good but realized that they could not reverse *bhagwan*:

Although we do not like these things we are not going to change the world. Everybody does as he or she likes. I do not like these changes. My liking or disliking is of no importance. If we express our dislike the women of today comment that *sasu*s are jealous of their *bahu*s; if the *bahu*s are not covering their faces and they eat with their husbands and are happy, then the *sasu*s are unhappy. I feel very angry in these days of the shameless ways of women. An educated woman said that *sasu*s should be happy if their sons and *bahu*s live happily and love each other. Then I told her that every woman has love for her husband. I also had affection for my husband but we had some shyness and shame which people do not have nowadays.

> The changes are not good. The old ways were better. If the *sasu* is not considerate enough to look after her *bahu* then only the *bahu* wants to separate. Otherwise why should they want to separate?

> Yes, how can I say that they are bad? I don't like it but everybody else likes it. Then my disliking is useless. So why should I say these changes are bad?

Two older women who said the changes were good gave no explanation for their answers; the third commented as follows: "It is good that the *bahu*s are in good clothes, eat well, and enjoy themselves. Previously men after their marriage never went to visit their in-laws. They used to feel shy, but now they go to visit their in-laws frequently."

Of the *bahu*s interviewed, seven said the changes were good, three that they were bad, and two gave mixed answers. Ten *bahu*s said they were happier than their mothers (66%), four that they were equally happy (27%), and one that the older generation was happier (7%). Therefore, while the younger women were generally in favor of the changes, they were by no means unanimous in their support.

*Bahu*s were also varied in their preferences for the amount of purdah they wanted their daughters to keep, although none wanted them to keep more purdah than they themselves kept. Most recognized that the husband's family would make this decision. One woman gave a conditional answer: "If my daughter gets married in a village, then she will have as much purdah as I do. If she goes to the city with a husband who is in the service then she will have less." Another seemed concerned about her daughter's reputation: "I would like my daughter to keep as much purdah as I do and serve her in-laws well." The most extreme reaction was the following: "I want that there should be no purdah for anybody. My brother was saying that we should look for husbands for our daughters in the city, so that our daughters would not have to keep any purdah."

Sasu–Bahu Relations

We asked each *sasu* whether she got along as well with her *bahu* as she had with her own former *sasu*. A number of women could not answer this question because their *sasu*s had died before their marriage. Of those who did answer it, nine said *sasu*s and *bahu*s were getting along as well now as they did formerly, one said that she got along better with her *sasu*, one said that she got along better with her *bahu*, and one gave an indefinite answer. Some of the answers of the women who said that intergenerational relations were as good as formerly are as follows:

> I do not live very well with my *bahu*, but my *sasu* was very bad. She used to beat me with anything she caught if she observed that my face was not completely covered even in the presence of ladies. If my sari was a bit away from my body my *sasu* used to beat me with a stick. But now my *bahu* goes on talking in the presence of others. I do not like her. When a *sasu* comes in from outside, the *bahu* should massage her legs. She should give a welcome smile and ask her what is to be cooked for the family. If the *bahu* does not do all this then what can a *sasu* do for her *bahu*? I have some affection for my *bahu* but that is only like two annas out of a

rupee because my *bahu* has no affection and respect for me. How can I love her? She will have as much as she gives.

Another woman who got along better said of her relationships:

I get along with my *bahu*s as well as I did with my *sasu*. I was alone with my *sasu* but I have five *bahu*s. My *bahu*s and I have some fights then my son comes and she talks to him first. My son cannot tolerate it if my *bahu* shouts at me in my own house. [This woman did have the support of her son, who took her side in any dispute with his wife.]

A third woman solved the problem by not interfering:

I have always been alone and busy with my own work. I do not forbid the *bahu*s to do anything. I get along well with my *sasu* and also with my *bahu*s because I do not say anything. Educated daughters can slap you if you have any fears. I do not have any fears so I do not get slapped. When I was a young bride, other *sasu*s and *bahu*s used to get along very nicely.

Some of the answers of the women who say that people got along better in their younger days were based simply on the greater authority of the *sasu*s in that time. One woman said:

Now the world is changing swiftly. The early days are gone. During those days *bahu*s and *sasu*s got along well. Previously if the *sasu* saw the face of the *bahu* uncovered or not completely covered she would start beating the *bahu*. But nowadays there is no consideration for such things.

One woman said that in early days there was more affection between *sasu*s and *bahu*s so that the *bahu*s obeyed better. Another woman said:

Formerly whatever the *sasu*s used to say the *bahu*s used to grasp it and follow the same guidelines forever. But nowadays, *bahu*s do whatever they like. They do not listen to their *sasu*s. Everyone is not alike. There are some who still obey their *sasu*s.

It would seem that these women were citing the greater disobedience of *bahu*s as a reason for believing relations were better in earlier days. One wonders if they really felt that way when they were young or whether they gave this answer for the benefit of their *bahu*s, who, unfortunately, were usually present during the interviews.

The one woman who said that things had improved got along unusually well with her *bahu*s and apparently had had a particularly cruel *sasu*. This is what she had to say:

My *sasu* was a hard-natured lady, and I was afraid of her. She uses to beat me on my back until I bled. I never even touched my brothers-in-law. My *sasu* used to beat me if I uncovered my face at all. She used to beat me if she even saw me with her son. She would cover her face and keep purdah from all men as if they were her elder brothers-in-law. Sometimes she would not even speak to her own sons for 2 years. My *bahu*s are the best in the whole village and even if some outside person teaches them to go against me, they will not listen.

We also asked the *bahu*s whether they felt they got along with their *sasu*s as well as their mothers had gotten along with their grandmothers. Seven said that they got along better, two that it was worse, and two that it was the same. The four remaining women could not answer because their grandmothers had died before they were born or when they were very young.

CONCLUSIONS

Extended families have a tendency to divide, as married sons with families establish their own households, and the customs of husband–wife separation are designed to prevent this splintering. The anxiety of *sasu*s over this new intimacy is not merely a reaction to their decreased authority, but reflects a genuine concern for their own economic welfare and the preservation of the extended family's financial and social position.

One might expect, from the extensiveness of the complaints expressed in these interviews, that the changes reported have seriously strained relations between *sasu*s and *bahu*s. However, women's evaluations of these changes, reported in chapter 5, indicate that this is not the case. *Sasu*s recognize that these are widespread changes in customary behavior, brought on by a variety of outside cultural influences. Because of this understanding they do not view *bahu*s as insubordinate rebels and do not blame them for conforming to new norms. Their overall explanation for the social forces producing the changes may be summarized in the term *Bhagwan*, God's will.

These answers, particularly those of the older women, seem surprising in view of the extensive complaints about the demise of purdah. *Sasu*s were virtually unanimous in their realization that the changes were the result of a variety of influences and that their *bahu*s are not personally to blame. It may be that the recognition that the wishes of their sons were a primary cause of the new freedom for *bahu*s soothed the *sasu*s' resentment. It is possible that the rare experience of the interview had allowed them to "blow off steam" and mitigated the ire of these final answers. However, I do not think that either of these factors is significant. I think the answers are best understood as realistic descriptions of difficult adjustments to changes in basic values. Changes in purdah lead to changes in many other aspects of family life. Family roles are fundamental to the social structure of all societies. When they change, the structure of the family creaks and crumbles until a new equilibrium is reached.

But while all this is taking place, meals must be cooked, men must be fed, children must be tended, and marriages must be arranged. Even if the brides are educated, modern women from Meerut, *sasu*s must get along with them. If the *bahu*s have gone from shy to shameless, if they imitate new customs of the city or of foreigners, the fault is not with them but with Bhagwan. It is foolish to get angry with Bhagwan. Bhagwan is inexorable, unavoidable, and impersonal. One reacts to it as one would to a strong wind: One holds down that which is most precious, lets small things blow away like chaff, and holds the course of one's life steady against it.

In the following chapters we will examine the changes that Bhagwan has brought, women's reactions to these changes, and their adaptations to the modernization of village life.

III

ECONOMY

The two chapters of Part III present the basic information concerning the economics that affect the women of our study. Chapter 5 describes the basic economy whereby men inherit land and women are given large dowries. Laws passed in this century give daughters the right to claim portions of the family land and protect women's rights to their dowry goods. These laws have given women increased economic power, but run contrary to traditional norms. In 1975, most women were aware of their legal rights to land inheritance and dowry control but were only beginning to exercise them. Women's attitudes about land inheritance and dowry are documented in this chapter.

Rajputs are reluctant to disclose their wealth and landholdings, even to family members. Several women said that their husbands had not told them how much land they owned. Therefore, we included these questions in the family planning interview, asking whether the family had enough land to support their sons and their sons' present and future families. In answering these questions some women gave information about the amount of their landholdings, but more importantly, they revealed their estimation of problems of land shortage facing their families (see appendix E).

A detailed description of dowry goods and their distribution was obtained from 10 mothers-in-law and 12 daughters-in-law (see appendixes A and B). The amounts of dowry given at the initial fixing of a marriage, the *shadi*, or marriage ceremony, and the *gauna*, when the bride goes to live permanently with her husband, are described. Wives were also expected to bring money and goods whenever they returned from visits to their parents' houses. The functions of this custom and changes in wives' control of these funds are recorded. The increase in dowry expenses for this generation is documented through comparisons of dowries of mothers-in-law and daughters-in-law. Wives' mandatory gifts of jewelry to husbands' sisters, at the birth of sons, and for the sisters' weddings and the weddings of their daughters are described.

Questions about attitudes concerning daughters' inheritance of land and information about dowry were included in an economic control interview, given to 42 women. Women's opinions concerning dowry increase, control of dowry goods by wives, and land claims by daughters were obtained from this interview (see appendix D). Chapter 5 ends with detailed descriptions of some dowries in the wealthy family of Gopal, Puran, and Mussadi and the poor family of Daya, Kela, and Kanak.

Chapter 6 describes the domestic economy, including work assignments, the division of cooking hearths, and the distribution of dowry goods at marriage and in gifts throughout women's lives. In the economic control interview 42 women were asked how much of their dowry goods and jewelry they had given away, who received the gifts, and for what occasions. This interview also included questions about preferences for control of dowry goods by these women and their daughters.

Chapter 6 concludes with a description of the distribution of household funds, other than money brought from wives, also obtained from the economic control interview. These funds come from the sale of small quantities of grain, from loans, and from spinning. We interviewed these 42 women about their spinning, the amount they earned, and how they spent the money. We also asked whether the money for clothing, school supplies, and other incidentals came from their parents' or their husbands' families.

Family members inspect the dowry display of a daughter in the courtyard of a large, brick *bughar*. Papier-mâché bowls appear in the foreground and metal utensils are to the right. Neatly tied sets of clothes and quilts are a spread on cots that fill most of the courtyard area (1955).

5

Land and Dowry: Modern Laws, Traditional Beliefs

A daughter grows old, but the custom of giving to her never grows old.

If my daughters ask for their shares of the land, most of the land will go from us. Land is only for the men.

There is no affection between brothers and sisters, if sisters take their shares of the land.

Traditionally sons inherited land, while daughters' inheritance was given in dowry goods and jewelry. Landholdings passed from father to son, and gold jewelry passed from mother to daughter. Traditionally, dowry goods and food supplies were controlled by *sasus*. Dowry goods came from *bahus* and were distributed to daughters and other household members by *sasus*. Although traditional law gave sons the right to claim their share of the family land when they reached adulthood, this right was seldom exercised. Land, crops, and money from their sale was owned by *soosars*. Therefore, elder men controlled the land, and elder women controlled the distribution of household goods. Elders of either sex might control some or all of the household money.

While a man's most valuable asset is his land, a woman's most valuable possession is her gold and silver jewelry, which she guards most carefully and gives away with the greatest reluctance. Gold has been hoarded by Indian women and passed down from generation to generation along the female line for millennia. Even before dowry protection legislation, custom discouraged husbands from selling their wives' jewelry. Traditionally, Indian gold jewelry was made from 22-carat gold, making much of it too soft to be worn. In recent years the government banned the manufacture of 22-carat gold, making 18-carat gold the highest percentage that can be legally produced. Old 22-carat jewelry is retained, guarded, and melted down for smaller pieces when gifts are mandated.

Women's control over land is indirect, this despite successive legislation to ensure their property rights. By custom, widows retain control of the family land during their lifetimes and pass their inheritance to their sons. The Hindu Women's

Property Act of 1937 legalized the right of widows to administer property while their sons were still minors. However, widows could not sell the land, only administer it. The Hindu Succession Act of 1956 enabled daughters, widows, and mothers to inherit land on an equal footing with sons. However, few women, particularly daughters, exercise this right.

Widows jealously guard their land ownership as a means of keeping the loyalty of sons, whose wives may urge them to set up separate households after the death of their fathers. When a daughter claims land, it means that her husband, a member of a different *jati,* must join the village community or, at the very least, see to the management of some of its land. Regardless of its legality, such a situation is a very serious breach of village custom, which has always held that no wife, daughter, or daughter's husband could inherit land.

Dowry protection laws have been as difficult to enforce as women's rights to land inheritance. In 1961 the government passed a dowry prohibition act, but enforcing it has proved to be impossible. In fact, dowries have increased in recent years, although they remain about 1 year's family income. The new laws have changed people's perception of the dowry. In 1955 dowry was seen as a series of gifts to the daughter, to which she had no legal claim. In 1975 dowry was more likely to be regarded as a rightful substitute for inheritance, and several women said that larger dowries were being given to discourage daughters from claiming family land. The difficulty with dowry as inheritance is that it is usually given while the parents are still living, and daughters have no legal claim to it.

Dowry includes gifts to members of the husband's family, which must be given at marriage and whenever wives return from visits to their parental homes. The population increase means that husbands' families usually have more people who must receive gifts. The increase in daughters, resulting from the cessation of female infanticide in the twenties and more equal health care for sons and daughters of the more recent generations, means that families have more daughters to marry than they did in previous generations. Therefore, daughters, who were always viewed as expensive, have become an increasing drain on their families' finances. There are more of them, they need larger dowries, and they may now claim portions of the family land. The source of daughters' dowry goods provided by incoming *bahu*s is threatened by the dowry protection act and the assertiveness of young *bahu*s in guarding their possessions.

These changes in the economic power structure give more power over money and possessions to women, particularly young women. Like the decrease in purdah customs, these changes have upset the traditional distribution of power by changing the regulations governing the distribution of wealth. The new laws and changing customs are threatening the economic stability of the joint family. This chapter describes the reactions of women to changes in dowry size, control of distribution of dowry goods, and land inheritance by daughters.

Few Khalapur daughters have actually claimed their land inheritance, recognizing that this would cause alienation from their parents and brothers; therefore, the new land inheritance laws have not seriously altered the traditional male inheritance of land. Dowries, however, have increased in Khalapur, as well as in other areas of India, and the resultant drain on family finances was a matter of increased concern.

The scandal of killing brides whose families' fail to make dowry payments, which has attracted international attention and brought about marches and reform efforts from Indian women, is an urban phenomenon, concentrated largely in Delhi. The large urban population and the use of professional marriage brokers make it possible for families to find second wives for sons, even when the first wife has been murdered. The family-based system of marriage arrangement described in chapter 2 makes it more difficult for such a family to find new wives for any family men. However, the problem of killing brides for their dowries has appeared in Khalapur. One woman told us that three Khalapur families had murdered brides for their dowries, and that rich families could get large dowries on second marriages, even when the first bride had been murdered.

Among these landholders, wives are most likely to be killed for their husbands' portion of the land, since land is more valuable than dowry goods. I recorded one case of the murder of a bride from Khalapur, in a detailed account from the mother of the murder victim. The bride entered a family where her *sasu* was already dead and the household under the control of her *taayi*. When she became pregnant, this *taayi* set her on fire and killed her, in order to retain her nephew's potential land inheritance for her own sons. The dead woman's mother reported that the shame and distress of the *soosar* were so great that he tried to immolate himself on the murdered woman's funeral pyre, that her daughter's widower had said he would not remarry, and that his three unmarried brothers had said they would not marry. The reluctance of the brothers to marry was presumably based on a reluctance to put brides under the jurisdiction of their murderous *taayi*. However, since such actions would ensure that the sons of the evil *taayi* would inherit all of the family land, it was more likely that the dead bride's *soosar* would separate his land and house from his brother, to ensure the safety of future brides.

The motive for this murder was land inheritance and the intended victim the unborn child. The *taayi* was certainly not attempting to further her nephew's fortunes by killing his wife so that he could marry again and obtain an additional dowry. However, the *taayi* took all the dowry goods from the house and hid them, so that the *bahu*'s family could not reclaim them. We did not obtain a clear answer as to why they could not be recovered, even from the distraught *soosar*. The dead girl's mother said that they would have burned their daughter's dowry if it had been recovered.

We inquired about situations involving other *bahu*s, where one might have expected dowries to be returned, such as the case of the suicide Nakali whose *sasu* was responsible for allowing her to leave the *bughar*. We found no instance in which any portion of dowry goods had been returned to the bride's family, irrespective of the degree of bride abuse.

LAND INHERITANCE

Although traditional law permits land division, sons seldom divide landholdings until after the death of both parents, and then only if they are quarreling. Fathers usually retire from fieldwork when their sons are old enough to take over the work but retain ownership of the land. Joint ownership allows families to share farm equipment and cooperate in cultivation. Even when farm equipment and labor are not shared, the land may be held in joint ownership. In many families, senior men and their sons farm portions of their ancestral land and use or market their crops separately, without changing the land records to legally separate their holdings. Table 5.1 shows that 84% of the families studied had not divided their land.

By traditional law, if a man had no sons, his estate passed to his brothers and their children—that is, to his paternal nephews. These inheritance rules ensured that land ownership remained with men of the same lineage, thus excluding persons who were not members of the village *khandan* from landownership. These inheritance rules account for the fact that Khalapur Rajputs have been able to maintain control of their land through the vicissitudes of the past 400 years, including, most recently, the Zamindar Abolition Act. The patrilineal inheritance rule is still adhered to with deep emotion, despite the changes in inheritance laws. Land disputes may persist over long periods of time, resulting in violence and lawsuits. Several instances of such confrontations occurred during my two field trips. In chapter 10 I describe in detail the long-term efforts of a sister to reclaim the land of her deceased brother from a wealthy and powerful family.

A dramatic example of a brother's opposition to his sister's receiving land occurred during our second study, when Rambhool, the second son of Ranjeet, a cousin of Amar Nath, attempted suicide, a rare course of action for Rajput men, when Ranjeet proposed giving his only sister, Maya, a share of land in addition to her dowry. Maya had had her *shadi,* and her brother's labor had contributed heavily to her dowry. It is unclear whether the suicide was a genuine attempt that failed or a false attempt; in any case it was effective in changing the father's plans.

A land dispute that had been troublesome in 1955 caused a fight in 1974. In 1954 Abhaye was considering a lawsuit against his two brothers and five nephews over the division of their land. The dispute was further complicated because a sister of these five nephews had broken the taboo on land claims by daughters, claimed her portion of the family land, and returned to Khalapur with her husband, who farmed it for her. This brother-in-law was bitterly resented by the nephews and their families.

At that time Abhaye's wife claimed that the nephews had tried to kill her husband while he was working in his fields and that only the intervention of village men had saved his life. Abhaye took the matter to a Bhudana judge but did not get a hearing. Villagers are suspicious of officials, and the delay encouraged the men to mediate among themselves. The next day the family men agreed on a settlement. Abhaye received 11 *bigha*s of disputed land, while 5 *bigha*s that Abhaye had already cultivated and an additional 15 *bigha*s he had claimed went to his nephews.

By 1974 the family land had been farmed separately for 20 years, and the three brothers were finally about to record their divided holdings at the land records office, when Abhaye claimed that his brothers had moved the boundary ditch between their fields a little each year, encroaching on his land, so that their land area

Table 5.1 Division of Family Land

	N	%
Divided	5	16
Undivided	26	84
Total	31	100

would be recorded as larger than their rightful share. Sometime previously Abhaye had called his two brothers into the fields along with the two top village officials, and had tried to fix the boundary with the two officials acting as witnesses. However, his brothers refused and the officials would not take action, leading Abhaye to conclude that they took bribes from his brothers.

In December 1974 two of Abhaye's sons went into their uncles' fields when only younger sons of their uncles were working and moved the border back to its original position. When they returned the next day to work their fields, they were ambushed by two of their uncles and five of the uncles' sons, all armed with fighting staffs. The unarmed and outnumbered brothers could only defend themselves with stalks of sugarcane. All three had to go to the hospital for treatment. When we left in 1975, this dispute still had not been settled.

A second incident occurred during the winter of 1974–75 when the men of one lineage set fire to about 20 carts of fodder that families from another lineage had stored on their land. That dispute also went back many years. Two years before the fire, Seema, one of the men whose fodder was burned, had received a permanent head injury that left him unable to talk, and a woman of his family had been beaten by the men who had burned the fodder. Neighbors also said that Seema's elder brother had been killed 50 to 60 years earlier by these same men. The speechless Seema and two of his grown nephews were attacked again the day after the fire, and Seema was sent to the hospital in Bhudana with a cracked bone in his hand.

With the advent of modern technology, access to new farm equipment may also lead to disputes. Such a confrontation occurred between Succha and his cousins in the spring of 1975. Neither Ganga nor Succha, the sons of Amar Nath, had their own tube wells or tractors, but Sher, perhaps the wealthiest man in Khalapur, owned both. Sher's three sons refused to let their cousins, Ganga and Succha, use their father's tube well for irrigation of their adjoining fields. Since the hybrid grains required regular irrigation, this breakdown in joint-family cooperation forced Succha to install a tube well on his father's property.

Succha had sunk his tube well pipe, at a cost of 3,000 rupees, and connected it to a pump borrowed from a neighbor but had not yet purchased a pumping motor. His fields needed watering, and Sher's sons reluctantly agreed to let Succha use their tractor motor to start his pump. One of Sher's sons insisted on driving the tractor himself, and, instead of stopping the tractor at the pipe, he kept going, attempting to bury the pipe and destroy the pump. He stopped when one of his brothers reproved him, saying, "Succha is not taking anything from us," and Succha successfully ordered his cousin to get down from the tractor.

Succha behaved more generously with his estranged brother. He let Ganga use his chaff cutter and planned to let Ganga use his new tube well. Expressing the ideal of joint-family cooperation, Succha explained, "After all, we are sons of the same father, and even if he has behaved badly, from my side, I will treat him well."

ATTITUDES ABOUT DAUGHTERS INHERITING LAND

When interviewing about family planning, we began by asking women if their husbands' landholdings were large enough to support the families of their sons when the latter married. We found that 19% of the women did not know the extent of their husband's landholdings. One woman said, "Landholdings are known to men only." Another commented, "I do not know the actual landholding. If we women ask our husbands anything about land, they do not tell us, but simply ignore us." Apparently a number of husbands kept this information from their wives to deter them from claiming land as widows.

Some families have lost land through lawsuits or bad management by the family men, as described in the following answers to our interview questions:

> At present the land is sufficient for my family but the whole of the earning is being drained in fighting court cases and in paying interest to the moneylender, with whom my ornaments were mortgaged many years ago. One case is against S., who is getting a new house built for his son on our land which he claimed illegally. They are getting the house built even when their claim to the land has not been declared in the court yet. All these things are taxing my strength.

> The land is nominal with us. Both of these brothers [her husband and his brother] used to sell their land and eat and drink. They never worked their land. We have only 30 to 40 *bigha*s left now. That is why my son had to take everything under his control. My husband did not even bother to feed grass to the bullocks and they died of hunger. If my elder son gets employment, then only can we think of purchasing some land. At present it is difficult to feed everybody properly at home.

> We have only 20 *bigha*s with us. We had joint land of some 600 *bigha*s, but our *soosar* gave the land in alms to Brahmins and others, because he himself was unable to look after it properly. Now, with division the shares are very small.

> Her husband is very irresponsible [indicating another bahu]. He runs away for 10 to 20 days without informing anybody at home, so that he does not have to toil the joint fields. On top of that, he takes money on loan which his father has to repay. He does not even care for his family and wife, who has become a skeleton because of these worries.

Despite these difficulties, most wives do not approve of daughters' claiming land. Table 5.2 shows that 61% of the Khalapur wives whom we interviewed knew that daughters could claim a share of their father's land, but 71% thought such claims were bad. One justification for this conclusion was the belief that the daughters' shares of the estate, represented in dowry payments, were usually larger than (67%) or equal to (10%) the sons' shares, even though the daughters did not contribute any farm labor. Only 10% of the women interviewed thought that daughters' shares were less than those of the sons (see appendix D, questions 16, 16a, and 17).

> I have not heard of this law. It is not good. Land is only for brothers. If sisters want to get that also it is very bad on their parts, because if there are seven sisters and one brother, then the brother will be left with practically nothing.

> Yes, daughters may take more than her brother's share of land because he has to earn money and sister has to take all her life and even after her death her children continue to visit the grandparents and get occasional gifts.

Yes, those who belong to rich parents may get more than the share of their brothers in the parental land.

It is not only the daughter who gets gifts in *shadi, gauna, chuchak,* etcetera, from her parents but daughter's daughters also get money and many things when they go to the grandparents' house after her marriage. Therefore, daughter always gets more than the brother's share in the land. Brother simply works on the land and earns money and sister simply takes away the gifts from the parents every time and at all occasions.

Yes, she may take more than her brother's share of land. It is not less than giving her a share of land. When once a daughter is married, then you have to pay the tax throughout your life. First you spend a lot on the marriage, then on *gauna, chuchak,* at the birth of nephews and then when they are married, as well as on the marriages of her own children. Every time she gets presents when she comes to her parents' house.

A woman who thought that daughters inherit less than sons reasoned as follows: "Sisters do not get more than brother's share of land. Because the brother and his family are enjoying the produce. The sister gets some occasionally, but the land is still with the brother."

The more important justification for believing that daughters should not claim land is the recognition that such a claim would damage the sacred sister–brother relationship and threaten the traditional welcome of the *nanad* in her parental home.

Table 5.2 Daughters' Land Claims

1. Do you know that a daughter can claim a share of the land along with her brothers?

	N	%
Yes	19	61
No	9	29
NA	3	10
Total	31	100

2. Do you think this is good or bad?

	N	%
Good	9	30
Bad	22	71
Total	31	100

3. Is the share that daughters receive in gifts at *shadi, gauna, chuchak,* and so on, usually more or less than her brothers' portion of the land?

	N	%
More	21	67
Less	3	10
Equal	4	10
Depends on the family	3	10
NA	1	3
Total	32	100

The comments of women opposing land inheritance by daughters on this basis included the following:

> This I do not like. When parents give presents to their daughters throughout their lives and invite them also quite often, at all important occasions, then why should they claim the share of land? If they claim the share, then who would invite them and give them gifts and other presents from time to time? There would be no affection but only hatred for each other.

> Yes, I have heard of this law. But it is not good. If she claims her share of land from parents' property then who is going to invite her from her in-laws' place? Then she loses the right to come to her brothers and parents. Brothers would also say that if our sister has claimed her share of land then what for does she come here?

Women who favored land inheritance by daughters reasoned that it ensures a sister's welcome in her brother's house:

> Yes, I have heard of this law. People give so much in dowry so that daughters do not claim their share of land.

> It is good to get a share of land with the brother, because if she does not get proper respect in her husband's house at least she gets that respect in her parents' place in getting the land there. She may be getting more than the brother's share of land. But if she gets a share of land equal to her brother, then how can she get dowry?
>
> Q. What is good, then—to take a share of land or dowry?
>
> A. It is good to take dowry so that the sister can come every now and then, and some presents as well, and can know about the welfare of her parents' family. And if she can claim her share in land also, then her brother has to invite her home for fear that his sister may claim the land, and the sister can also say that she is getting the dowry against her share of land. Otherwise the brother is not giving any alms to the sister after the death of the parents.

> Who gives share of land to the daughters? Nobody gives! If it is a law then it is good because there are many brothers who never invite their sisters, so that they may not have to give them anything. But if the daughter is invited by the parents and given something they like, then daughter should not get any share from her brother's land.

Another woman denied the possibility that a sister will not be invited home unless she is difficult:

> Q. Some brothers do not invite their sisters. In that case what should happen?
>
> A. The daughters who are well behaved and work in their parents' houses for the brothers and the *nanad*s are always remembered and invited, but those who do not help their brothers' family in any way with their service and are not well behaved and criticize their *nanad*s or nephews are not welcome and are not invited. Therefore all want work and service.

All of the women in one house agreed that widow and daughter inheritance are incompatible.

> A girl should not claim the property of her parents because she gets a share of land

in the name of her husband in her in-laws' place and they why should she claim her parental land? It is bad.

DOWRY

The status of a Rajput woman in her husband's household, and the frequency of her cherished visits to her parental village, depend on her dowry. Gifts and alms usually flow from high-prestige to low-prestige persons. Rajput families give food to all of their low-caste servants on feast days. Wealthy and prominent people are expected to give generously to poorer persons. An exception to this practice is the flow of money and dowry goods from the families of brides into the higher-status families of their husbands. However, the rule applies when families of *bahus* are compared. Daughters from wealthy homes are given good dowries and are married into wealthy families, while the daughters of poor homes are married into poor families, with minimal dowries, or become the second wives of wealthy widowers.

Dowry includes money, goods given by parents and relatives, and items made by brides. For months before their *shadis* and *gaunas*, brides are busy knitting sweaters and making papier-mâché bowls and cloth hanging decorations for their dowries. A bride whose father has many brothers and cousins, particularly if they are *soosars* with married sons who must contribute to her dowry, will receive more gifts than a bride whose father has few brothers and cousins, or young ones who are not yet *soosars*. A bride with married brothers draws from the dowries of her *bhabhis* (brothers' wives) while a bride with no brothers or unmarried brothers does not have these resources.

The amount of jewelry worn by brides at their weddings and during the early months of marriage reflects on the prestige of the husband's family; therefore, new brides often have their jewelry augmented by gifts from their *sasus*. However, this jewelry is usually taken back after the display of the new bride is over.

Dowry gifts such as jewelry may be given to any of the husband's female relatives, but the primary direction of dowry gifts is from *bhabhis* to *nanads*. The amount of dowry goods that a woman receives throughout her lifetime depends on the proportionate number of her brothers and sisters, and on the number of brothers who marry before or after her. A woman with several brothers, particularly older, married brothers, and few or no sisters will receive more from her *bhabhis* than a woman with fewer brothers, younger brothers, or several sisters. The amount of dowry goods that a woman is able to retain, therefore, depends on the number of her *nanads* and whether they were married before or after her marriage. The *bahu* with few *nanads*, or with *nanads* who married before she entered the household, will retain more of her dowry goods than one who marries a man with several unmarried sisters.

Initial Fixing

The flow of money and goods from the family of the bride to the family of her husband begins with the "initial fixing" of the marriage arrangements and continues throughout her lifetime. The value of presents that a *bahu* brings from her parents decreases as she gets older, but she is always expected to bring gifts to her husband's relatives whenever she returns from her parents' house. For this reason, the frequency of visits of married daughters to their parental homes depends on their families' wealth. Parents of poor families seldom call their daughters home for visits, and poor *bahus* may stay for years at a time in their husbands' homes before going home for visits, while daughters from wealthy families visit their parents more often. Wealthy *bahus*, therefore, not only bring large dowries when they marry but also bring money and goods to their husbands' families throughout their lifetimes and bring them more frequently than do poor *bahus*.

Shadi and *Gauna*

Often the "initial fixing" marriage agreement involves a payment of money and goods. When negotiations are completed, the marriage takes place in two stages: the *shadi*, when the bride comes to the husband's home for a few weeks, and the *gauna*, or *chala*, when she usually comes to live permanently. After the *gauna*, a Khalapur Rajput bride usually does not return to her husband's home until after the birth of her first child. Money and property are brought by the bride on both occasions. The majority of the money and gifts of clothing for members of the husband's family are delivered at the time of the *shadi*, while the bride's trousseau, household utensils, furniture, and personal possessions are brought with her at the *gauna*.

It is understood that dowry goods such as clothing and utensils will be distributed by the *sasu*, usually to provide for the dowries of her own daughters. Families try to marry sons before daughters, and bring *bhabhis* home for a daughter's wedding, so that the dowry goods of the *bhabhi* can be utilized for her *nanad*. Married daughters are not invited home, since gifts from them when they returned to their husbands' houses would add to the family expenses. Therefore, married daughters do not attend the weddings of their younger sisters and cousins.

Dowry protection laws passed in the intervening 20 years between my two visits to Khalapur probably accounted for changes in the method of dowry display. In 1955 families displayed dowry goods of both brides and daughters in the open courtyards of the *bughars*. In 1975 the incoming dowry goods of brides were piled up in the dark, enclosed bedrooms, while the outgoing dowry goods of daughters were still displayed in the open courtyards. This made it more difficult for visitors to examine the dowries of brides and to identify goods later displayed in daughters' dowries. I assume that families in 1975 were more reluctant to publicly admit that they utilized *bahus*' dowry goods for their own daughters, although the practice continued. The new method of display saves *bahus* from the more blatant comparisons of their dowry goods with those of other *bahus*.

DOWRY INCREASE

Table 5.3 shows the tabulation of marriage payments at *shadi* and *gauna* for a sample of 10 *sasus* and 12 *bahus*. Virtually all women could tell us exactly how much they brought in their dowries, and most could tell us how much had been

Table 5.3 Classification of Dowry Items of *Sasus* and *Bahus* at Initial Fixing, *Shadi*, and *Gauna*

	Shadi				Gauna			
	Sasus $n = 10$		*Bahus* $n = 12$		*Sasus* $n = 10$		*Bahus* $n = 12$	
	M	R	M	R	M	R	M	R
Rupees								
a. Initial fixing	120_5	1–351	447_{11}	0–1,650	—	—	—	—
b. *Shadi*	233	0–625	929	300–3,100	25_1	—	75_1	—
Total	292	0–851	1,555	301–4,775				
Number of jewelry items	11	0–23	9_{12}	0–15	2_4	1–3	2_5	1–3
Clothing & bedding	38	1–120	64	11–101	45_9	5–100	51_{10}	0–150
Utensils	30	15–16	55	0–125	9_5	5–11	25_4	9–41
Furniture & appliances	0	0	4_6	1–9	0	0	2_3	2–4
Bicycle	0	0	1_8	0	0	0	0	0
Other	1_1	0	2.5_5	1–4	2_5	1–3	2_5	2–3

M = mean; R = range; subscripts indicate reduced *n* because of nonresponse.

Table 5.4 Proportions of Gold and Silver Jewelry Items
for *Sasu*s and *Bahu*s

	Sasu			Bahu		
	M	%	R	M	%	R
Gold	5.3	20	0–10	6.2	57	0–19
Silver	21.6	80	0–35	4.7	43	0–17

given away. It was usually poor women who were vague in their reports, and we sometimes suspected that they did not want to reveal how little they had contributed (see appendix C for dowry classification codes).

Comparison of the dowries of *sasu*s and *bahu*s clearly shows an increase in dowry goods for the younger generation. Only 5 of the 10 *sasu*s reported an initial fixing payment, whereas 11 of the 12 *bahu*s reported initial payments. Not only had initial fixing payments doubled in frequency, they had almost quadrupled in amount. The average payment at initial fixing had risen from 120 rupees for *sasu*s to 447 rupees for *bahu*s. Similar increases had occurred for *shadi* payments, which had risen from an average of 233 rupees for *sasu*s to 929 rupees for *bahu*s. The average amount paid in fixing plus *shadi* had increased 500%, from 292 rupees for *sasu*s to 1,555 rupees for *bahu*s.

The number of dowry goods had also increased. *Bahu*s were brining about twice as many sets of clothing and utensils as their *sasu*s. Furthermore, one half of the *bahu*s brought furniture and three fourths gave their husbands bicycles, items that were absent from *sasu* dowries. On the other hand, one wealthy *sasu* had brought a cow and calf, and another a horse and camel in their dowries, whereas no *bahu* dowries included animals.

The only category of dowry items that had decreased slightly over the previous generation was jewelry; *sasu*s brought an average of 11 jewelry items, while *bahu*s brought an average of 9 (Table 5.3). However, the heavy silver belts and anklets worn in the fifties had gone out of style, and the bulk jewelry had shifted from silver to gold. Table 5.4 shows that only 20% of *sasu* jewelry, as opposed to 57% of *bahu* jewelry, was gold. Silver jewelry items are usually heavier than gold items, and we do not have information on the weight of items or the relative price of gold and silver when women married. Therefore, it is not possible to accurately assess the relative value of *sasu* and *bahu* jewelry. However, the increase in gold items in *bahu* dowries must surely counterbalance the slight decrease in the number of their jewelry pieces; thus, the value of the jewelry in *bahu*s' dowries was at least equal to, and probably greater than, the value of the jewelry in the dowries of *sasu*s.

ATTITUDES ABOUT DOWRY

Table 5.5 shows that Rajput women have mixed feelings about increased dowries. When interviewed, 48% said that big dowries were bad, while 39% said they were good; however, 87% approved of the government's efforts to eliminate dowries (see appendix D, questions 14, 15, and 15a). The ambivalence in the answers about

Table 5.5 Attitudes About Dowry

1. People say that dowries are getting bigger. Do you think that is good or bad?

	N	%
Good	12	39
Bad	15	48
Both good and bad	3	10
NA	1	3
Total	31	100

2. The Indian government is trying to stop dowries. Do you think this is good or bad?

	N	%
Good	27	87
Bad	4	13
Total	31	100

3. Would you like your daughter to have more control over her dowry than you had?

	N	%
Yes	6	19
No	24	78
Other	1	3
Total	31	100

dowry size is based on the recognition that, on the one hand, dowries are hard to ban and large dowries are basic to a *bahu*'s status and contribute to her father's prestige and that, on the other hand, *bahus* with small dowries are often treated badly by their in-laws. One woman, who recognizes that dowry payments cannot be stopped, stated the problem as follows: "Dowry cannot be stopped. Those who want to will give stealthily. Those who have more to give will definitely give to their daughters in marriage. Those who are poor will also give their daughters as much as they can."

The primary reason given by those opposed to large dowries was that they put poor families and brides at a disadvantage:

A big dowry is good and bad. It is good because everyone praises a father who gives much to his daughter in her marriage. But if one does not have much to give, then one is helpless.

Q. What is good, then? Big dowry is good or not?

A. This depends upon the individual. Marriage can be performed even with five utensils and five sets of clothes.

Q. But then people do not praise the family, and many women have said that a bride does not get good behavior or respect from the in-laws if she does not bring a big dowry?

A. No, all this depends on the bride herself and her treatment with her in-laws. There are many who get so much from the parents, even then do not get good treatment from in-laws, and there are many others who bring nothing from parents and nobody even utters anything to her about these things.

A big dowry is bad because there are many families who say that our *bahu* has not brought as big dowry as some other *bahu* has brought. So they murder the daughter-in-law and get the sons married again to get a big dowry. Therefore, big dowry is not good.

Those who are poor, the bigger dowry is bad for them. Where from could they bring money for the dowries of their daughters? You live in Delhi and tell Indira Gandhi to reduce the dowry. Those who are rich should give less dowry, so that all daughters of rich as well as of poor parents get the same amount of dowry. Because the daughters who bring less dowry are not welcomed by their in-laws and they behave badly towards them and leave them to their parents and those who are daughters of rich people, they take a lot of big dowry and they get proper respect from their in-laws and everybody likes them and praises them for the big dowry they bring.

It is good that government is trying to stop the dowry system, because all daughters will get proper respect in their in-laws' house. There would be no comparison with dowries from other places. Today we went to see two brides in Gulal *patti*. One is from a rich family of a contractor. The bride brought a gun, a scooter for the groom, and many other costly items. The house is full of articles. In the other house, the bride is beautiful but her dowry is poor. Therefore, the *sasu* was commenting, "What is there to be shown? There is nothing which I can show." The *nanad*s were saying that the material of their saris that the new *bahu* had given them was as poor as the cloth meant for percolating tea.

Now what is the condition of the new bride, who was listening to everything? On the first day of her marriage in her house of in-laws this was happening to her. If there were no dowry then these things would not happen. There would be proper welcome to all *bahu*s.

This will be the best thing to stop the dowry completely. By this all daughters will get good treatment in their in-laws' house. There would be no distinction of rich and poor.

Some women had heard of recent cases of bride murder and cited them as a reason for opposing large dowries:

Those who cannot afford to give big dowry to their daughters do not get proper treatment and those who can get proper welcome at in-laws' place. If the dowry is not big, even those girls who are beautiful, educated, and talented are sometimes sent back by their in-laws and are never taken back, or they murder her and tell people that either she committed a suicide or died accidentally of fever or during childbirth or caught fire in the kitchen, etcetera. Therefore, if government is trying to stop dowry, it is good.

One woman, referring to the fact that *bhabhi*s' dowry goods are often shifted to the dowries of *nanad*s and may pass through many families without being used, cited waste as a reason for opposing dowries:

It is good if government is trying to stop dowry. In Punjab dowries are stopped but here people do not care and ignore the law and give big dowries. I like this law because the big hoardings of clothes given in the marriage are a sheer waste. They are simply kept in the boxes and after some years are of no use because the clothes do not fit and they are eaten by the moths or other insects, and colors also fade.

Comments of women favoring dowries cited the necessity of brides having clothes, jewelry, and household equipment:

It is not good to come to the in-law's house without any dowry in marriage.

People have started giving more to their daughters. That is good. If somebody has more, he may give more to his daughters but it is good to give more, so that he [the father] may get appreciation for giving more to his daughter, and daughter also gets proper welcome and respect in her in-laws' because of bringing more from her father.

DOWRIES IN THE HOUSE OF GOPAL

The dowries of wealthy Indian women are illustrated by a detailed account of the dowries of some of the women of Gopal's household, including the contributions of household women to two daughters of the family. (Charts of the household members descended from Gopal and his brothers are included in chapter 1.) In this account we describe the dowry goods of the two surviving *sasus*—Lakhpati, the wife of Sher, and Draupadi, the wife of Amar Nath; of the two wives of Draupadi's son, Succha; of Draupadi's daughter, Luxmi; and of Ranjeet's daughter, Maya.

Lakhpati's Dowry

Sher's wife, Lakhpati, brought the largest dowry of the six senior women in the *bughar*. For her *shadi* she brought 200 rupees, a horse, and a camel. (The camel frightened the cattle and had to be sold.) She gave her *sasu* a gold ring, earrings, and one pair of thick bangles, and brought 100 dress pieces for family members and 85 utensils. At the time of Lakhpati's marriage, four saris for a bride at *shadi* was maximum; she brought two.

For her *gauna*, 3 years later, Lakhpati brought 25 saris, blouses, *chaddar*s, and petticoats for herself, one "dress" (i.e., sari, blouse, and petticoat material for women and shirt and dhoti material for men) for each member of the family (i.e., her husband, his two brothers, and their families), for a total of 125. She brought 25 utensils, one large bed, two trunks, and one suitcase, fans, toys, and household decorations. Her jewelry included silver bracelets, anklets, necklaces, and a belt, gold thumb rings and earrings—two pairs for the upper ears and two pairs for the earlobes.

Draupadi's Dowry

Draupadi came from a wealth family and received an unusually large dowry for a third wife. Draupadi's initial fixing price was only 1 rupee, but she married before large fixing amounts became customary. For her *shadi* she brought 350 silver rupees for her bridegroom, a cow and calf, 60 sets of clothes, and 31 utensils. Her gold jewelry included a gold *tikka,* a nose ring, a nose plug, a heavy necklace, and a pair of earrings. In silver jewelry she brought a pair of earrings, three pairs of buttons, three pairs of bangles and one pair of bracelets for the upper arms, a pair of hand ornaments, two necklaces, one belt, one set of cuff links, a pair of foot ornaments, and three pairs of toe rings. For her *gauna* Draupadi brought an additional 6 pieces of gold and 30 pieces of silver jewelry, as well as 60 sets of clothes, 11 utensils, and a variety of small items such as soap, oil, fans, and toys.

Draupadi had made *chuchak* payments for only two sons. At the birth of the eldest son of her stepson, Ganga, she gave Ganga a gold ring, a pair of gold earrings, and some clothes. When Succha was born Draupadi gave a pair of silver bangles and 10 or 15 sets of clothes to Amar Nath's sister. When a nephew was born, she gave one pair of silver bangles.

Draupadi is an excellent example of the wealthy *bahu* who can "guard herself by giving cash and buying presents." A shrewd woman, she guarded her jewelry well, giving modest amounts for *chuchak* payments. Even allowing for other gifts, one may assume that at the time of Luxmi's wedding Draupadi was still in possession of much of her jewelry and probably contributed some of her own collection to Luxmi's dowry.

Champa's Dowry

Champa's dowry was modest for the bride of a wealthy and prestigious household. Her initial fixing price was 300 rupees, plus 1 rupee for each household member, for a total of 50 rupees. At her *shadi* Champa arrived with 300 rupees, 80 sets of clothes, 45 utensils, a gold necklace and earrings, a silver necklace, a pair of silver bangle bracelets, and a pair of silver anklets. Champa added 51 sets of clothes, a wooden trunk, and a tin trunk when she came for her *gauna*. Champa's clothing and utensils had been used by the time she died, but her jewelry passed to Succha and was probably available to Draupadi to pass on to Luxmi.

Dhooli's Dowry

Dhooli had the smallest dowry of any woman we interviewed, including other second wives, who usually bring small dowries. The initial fixing price for her marriage was only 1 rupee, a token amount. For her *shadi* she brought 300 rupees, 11 sets of clothing, and 11 utensils. She was the only bride who brought nothing with her at her *gauna,* and she was unable to make the expected contributions to Luxmi's marriage expenses.

Luxmi's Dowry

Draupadi and Amar Nath did not have large dowries from Dhooli or from Succha's deceased first wife, Champa, to draw on for their daughter's dowry. Draupadi described Luxmi's dowry as moderate—"Rich people would give more, poor people less," she said. In fact, Luxmi's dowry, and that of her cousin Maya are at the top range of our sample of eight daughters' dowries, presented in Table 5.6. From preliminary talks through the *gauna*, Luxmi's family spent 50,000 to 60,000 rupees on her marriage. Luxmi's initial fixing price was 1,200 rupees. For her *shadi* her bridegroom arrived with a party of 500 men, the largest groom's party we recorded. The bridegroom was given a horse with richly decorated trappings, a bicycle, a gold ring, and five silver utensils. Each member of his party was given 2 rupees, a towel, and a brass cup. Luxmi's *shadi* goods included a sofa set, a table and two chairs, a large bed, a sewing machine, a radio, a suitcase, a bedroll, and 101 utensils.

Sher's wife, Lakhpati, gave Luxmi one gold ring, a cow and calf, with a richly decorated covering cloth for the cow, cloth for a suit for the bridegroom, and 25 rupees. Sher and Lakhpati also paid for one meal for the groom and his party, at a cost of about 600 rupees.

Luxmi also brought 25 sets of clothing for herself and 100 sets of clothing for her husband's relatives to her *shadi*. Her gold jewelry consisted of a *tikka*, a thick necklace, a pair of thick bangle bracelets, two pairs of earrings, and four rings. Her silver jewelry was four pairs of anklets, a belt, a hand ornament, and a handful of toe rings. She was also given a wristwatch.

Just 7 days after Luxmi's *shadi* the oldest son of her uncle Om Prakash was married. Om Prakash invited Luxmi and her groom back to this wedding and gave them another bicycle, a cotton suit for the groom, a shawl, an ordinary sari, and two utensils. No doubt these gifts substituted for Om Prakash's contribution to Luxmi's *shadi*.

For her *gauna* Luxmi was given an armoire, an 8-foot wooden trunk, a tin trunk, an electric stove, a camera, a transistor radio, 21 utensils, 31 dresses for herself and 80 for her husband's family, 10 kilos of laundry soap and 10 kilos of toilet soap, many toys and combs, small baskets, and five or six hand mirrors. At this time Lakhpati contributed six sets of clothes and about 25 rupees.

The rift between Amar Nath and Ganga, caused by Draupadi's adoption of Ganga's eldest son, was so bitter than Ganga's wife, Sarvasati, did not contribute to

Table 5.6 Classification of Dowry Money and Goods at Initial Fixing and *Shadi* to Daughters and *Bahus*

RS	Daughters N = 8		Bahus N = 12	
	M	R	M	R
a. Initial fixing	592_6	5–120.7	447_{11}	0–1,650
b. *Shadi*	1,685	305–4,500	929	300–3,100
Total	2,277	310–6,200	1,555	301–4,775
Number of jewelry items	12	5–26	9	0–15
Clothing and bedding	72_7	35–139	64	11–101
Utensils	58	25–121	55	0–125
Furniture and appliances	2.25	0–8	4_6	1–9
Bicycle and animals	1	0–4	1_8	0

M = mean; R = range; subscripts indicate reduced N.

Luxmi's marriage. The failure of Ganga's wife to contribute to the dowry of her husband's half sister contrasts sharply with our reports of contributions to more distant relatives (e.g., granddaughter of husband's brother, father-in-law's sisters) by women living in more harmonious families, and illustrates the cost of alienation from relatives.

Maya's Dowry

Maya, the 14-year-old daughter of Sher's brother, Ranjeet, also received a large dowry. For Maya's *shadi* she had brought to her bridegroom's house 4,400 rupees, a horse, a radio, a gold ring, a wristwatch, 121 utensils, a sofa set, an armoire, a pressure cooker, an electric stove, a table fan, a sewing machine, and a machine to roll *chapatis*. Her gold jewelry included a *tikka*, earrings, two rings, a collar, and two pairs of heavy gold anklets. Her silver jewelry included a chain belt and a hand ornament (a bracelet connected by chains to a disk worn on the back of the hand, which is connected by chains to two silver rings), and two pairs of anklets. She also brought two silver bells. She took 11 dresses for herself and 121 for members of her bridegroom's family. Her groom's grandfather was given a silver glass, a wool shawl, and 100 rupees. Her groom brought 60 men in his *bharat,* and each one was given two rupees and 1 brass glass.

In 1974–75 Maya was preparing for her *gauna*. In the spring Maya's older brother's wife was called back for her *gauna* so that her dowry goods could be utilized for Maya's *gauna*. Over 100 sets of clothes from the *bahu*'s dowry were to be contributed to Maya's dowry. For her *gauna* Maya was being given 50 utensils, 121 sets of clothes for her groom's family and about 35 sets for herself, and another pair of earrings and anklets. Minor gifts—including straw fans, combs, toys, thread wrappers and straw loops for sewing machines, a large doll, and house decorations—were being collected for Maya.

Because Om Prakash has no daughters, the five wives of his sons were in the fortunate position of *bahus* without *nanads*. They were expected to make contributions to Maya's dowry, but these obligations were not as definite or as expensive as the obligations to contribute to *nanads*' weddings.

Although Draupadi claimed that Luxmi's dowry was moderate, the dowries of both Luxmi and Maya were at the top of the range of daughters' dowry goods that we recorded (see Table 5.6).

Dhooli's Resentment

The comparison of Dhooli's dowry with those of Luxmi and Maya documents the unfavorable economic position of a poor bride married into a household of wealthy women. (Dhooli's resentment of her wealthy *nanad*, Luxmi, has been described in chapter 2.) Luxmi's wedding took place several years after Dhooli's and drew on the labor and finances of her husband, Succha, as well as the financial resources of other family members. Against the background of their respective dowries, one can understand why Dhooli resented so fiercely being forced to give Luxmi her only *tikka,* and her lack of earrings, when even Luxmi's infant daughter had been given gold earrings and silver anklets. Dhooli was given 4 saris a year, while at least 25 saris were given to Luxmi each time she returned to her husband. She had no clothes to give her daughters, while gifts were lavished on Luxmi's children. Luxmi had an electric stove and fan, but Dhooli did not have even an electric light in her room.

The difference in gifts received by Dhooli and Luxmi continued after Luxmi's marriage. During the time that Succha was ill and his parents poor, Luxmi returned for a number of visits and was always given 20 to 30 sets of clothing when she returned to her husband's house. Dhooli's brothers seldom called her home, so she could not augment her clothing or contribute goods and money to her husband's family.

Chuchak payments received by the two women reflect the differential wealth of their families. Even when her first son was born, Dhooli received no jewelry from her brothers' wives. She said that they were also poor, but the absence of any *chuchak* gifts was most unusual, as was the length of time between her visits to her brothers' homes. It seems likely that this discontented woman was at odds with her own *bhabhi*s, and possibly with her brothers.

Because of Succha's illness, Luxmi's parents were too poor to give expensive *chuchak* payments for her first two children. Even so, they gave their first grand-daughter a pair of gold earrings and a pair of silver anklets. The family finances had recovered by the time Luxmi's second son was born and, on this occasion, she received 115 sets of clothing, several quilts, a tin trunk, a table, an electric fan, 11 utensils, and 500 rupees.

Dhooli's refusal, during our visit, to call on Luxmi for the birth of her second son stemmed from the resentment she still harbored over Luxmi's *chuchak* demand of her *tikka* when Dhooli's first son was born. The responses of other women concerning *chuchak* payments indicated that Luxmi was unusually greedy. The son born to Dhooli in 1975 was her fourth child, and her second son. One can easily understand why Dhooli, after over 10 years of marriage and the contribution of two grandsons, to a *sasu* who had only one son to provide her with grandsons, thought she had a right to expect better treatment from her *sasu* and her husband.

The practice of giving gifts to a daughter, and not to a daughter-in-law, is in accordance with custom; however, when one compares Dhooli's dowry with those of Luxmi and other women in her *bughar,* one can sympathize with Dhooli's distress. Although Rajput wives are expected to be supported by their parental families and do not usually receive goods or money from their in-laws, the neglect of Dhooli and her daughters was extreme. Customs are modified to fit unusual circumstances. While *bahu*s and their children are ordinarily not supplied with clothes, exceptions are made for poor *bahu*s, particularly after they have borne children. Grandmothers do buy clothes for young granddaughters. Dhooli was the only *bahu* in a prosperous family without gold earrings. Some *sasu*s from poorer families went without earrings, having given them in *chuchak* payments, daughters' dowries, or to poor *bahu*s, but Draupadi was the only *sasu* who wore earrings while her *bahu* had none, and that display of vanity was contrary to custom.

On the other hand, the other women of the household generally sided with Draupadi and convention, and Dhooli had no support from them in her complaints. Dhooli had made a very good marriage for a bride from a poor family. She lived in one of Khalapur's finest houses, had plenty to eat, and did not need to help with the fieldwork. Her children would make good marriages, financed by her husband's wealthy relatives. She did not contribute, as expected, to Luxmi's marriage. The *tikka* Luxmi claimed was loaned to Dhooli by Draupadi, not given to her by her parents. Many of the presents given to Luxmi were meant to be distributed among her husband's relatives, so Dhooli's contention that "everything good is given to Luxmi" was somewhat unfair.

Draupadi's loyalty to her own children was in accordance with convention. She had won the battle for her son's affections. She defended her son and blamed Dhooli for his illness. She helped to arrange Luxmi's marriage into a wealthy and prestigious family. She used her resources and drew on the resources of Amar Nath's wealthy relatives to finance her daughter's dowry. Despite the financial setback resulting from Succha's mental breakdown, she protected her daughter's status in her in-laws' household by sending Luxmi back to her husband with the gifts they would expect.

Dhooli was unwise to express her resentment of gifts to her *nanad*. In so doing she had threatened the unity of the blood kin, identified herself as an unusually dangerous wife, and incurred the anger of her husband and her *sasu*. Luxmi was also unwise in alienating her *bhabhi* so completely. Despite her isolation, Dhooli held firm to her refusal to invite Luxmi after the birth of her second son and enlisted some support for her refusal from Succha, who had just put in his tube well and was reluctant to pay for Luxmi's visit. It was only after I agreed to contribute to the expenses that Draupadi sent for her daughter. Luxmi was sent home with gifts from Draupadi but did not take any *chuchak* present from Dhooli for this second nephew. It seemed likely that after Draupadi's death, Luxmi's visits to her brother's home would be few and far between.

DOWRIES IN THE HOUSE OF SUCHET

Two of Suchet's granddaughters, Harpyari, aged 21, and Lajwanti, aged 16, were married in a double ceremony in the spring of 1975. The bridegrooms were unrelated but came from the same town. The double *shadi* reduced expenses, and the selection of grooms from the same community simplified marriage negotiations and ensured the sisters a common marital residence, as it had for their aunts Mamta and Durga. Children are usually married in birth order, regardless of sex, but Harpyari's wedding had been delayed until after the wife of her younger brother had returned from her *gauna*, bringing goods and money that could be used for the dowries of the two daughters. Consistent with the poverty of this family, the sisters' identical dowries were the lowest we recorded for Khalapur daughters. Each bridegroom received a wristwatch, a gold ring, and 253 rupees. Each daughter received a wristwatch, a pair of gold rings, two pairs of silver anklets and foot rings, 51 sets of clothes, 25 utensils, and 105 rupees. There was no gossip about the grooms buying these wives, so presumably the modest dowries had been financed by their father, Rekha, and mother, Kanti.

Misfortune, as well as poverty, plagued this wedding. A cart of one of the bridegrooms turned over, and several injured members of the groom's party had to be taken to the dispensary for treatment. To make matters worse, the brides' grandfather, Suchet, died in his sleep the day before the wedding. Despite the insistence of neighbors that the body not be brought into the courtyard during a wedding, Kanti insisted on moving her father-in-law's body from his *choopar* into the courtyard so that she could prepare it for cremation. Therefore, Suchet's body was in the courtyard, along with the displayed dowries, until his son and brothers took it to the cremation ground. The ceremony ending formal mourning, usually held 13 days after the death, was held after only 13 hours so that the *shadi*s could proceed. The custom of feeding a Brahmin every day during the period of mourning was altered to feeding 13 Brahmins during the single day of mourning.

The family women were distressed because, as one said, "We can neither be happy for the marriages, nor can we cry freely, because guests have come for the marriages. We have to cook sweets and *puri*s [fried, stuffed unleavened bread served at feasts] when we do not want to eat even a simple *chapati* [dry-roasted unleavened bread, eaten every day]." The brides were worried that their new in-laws would think they brought bad luck with them since they had "eaten their own grandfather, just before coming to their grooms' houses." The young wife of Rekha's son cried so profusely over the death of her father-in-law that she developed fits and, having refused medicine brought to her, was sent home to her parents' house a few days after the wedding, despite the suspicions of some neighbor women that she was faking her distress to obtain a visit home.

It is significant that the marriages of Harpyari and Lajwanti took precedence over the death of the male family head. Marriage and the birth of sons are the only times at which attention, time, effort, and expenditure are focused on women. Their role in the perpetuation of the patrilineage of their husbands mandated against any delay in their marriage ceremonies, even when the family was in mourning.

CONCLUSIONS

The Rajput dowry system places much of the responsibility for the support of an adult woman with her parents and brothers, while her labor benefits her husband's household. This arrangement places a lifelong drain on the finances of a daughter's family. In addition to paying for visits by a married daughter, her family bears the expense of visits by her husband and sometimes by her *soosar,* while they do not freely visit the villages of their sons-in-law, except when a brother or father brings a daughter home or returns her to her husband's house. Sons, on the other hand, farm the land, bring in dowries, and support their parents.

While the new land inheritance laws are a mark of economic progress for Indian women, they are not readily implemented within the context of existing social and economic structures. Few daughters would alienate their relatives to claim an inheritance which they cannot easily utilize. Furthermore, since the sons work the land throughout their lifetimes, and may well pay for improvements such as tube wells, tractors, or remodeled or electrified homes, it is somewhat unfair for sisters who have married and ceased to contribute any work to their parental households to claim land and houses upon the death of parents.

Women were generally clear in their realization that they could not claim land and receive dowries. Since the dowry goods are taken to their husbands' homes, dowry is far more useful for women than land inheritance, particularly since women are gaining increased control over their dowry property. While most women uphold the right of *sasus* to control dowry goods, support for greater control of a rightful portion of dowry by *bahus* is growing. Reports indicate that most women do retain ownership of much of their jewelry. Only three women reported that all of their dowry was gone, and for only one of these women had it been given away.

The comparison of the dowries of daughters-in-law and daughters shows that daughters' dowries are consistently larger than the dowries of daughters-in-law; the expenditure of cash is generally double the intake from sons' wives. When responding to the family planning interviews, several women said, "It is best to have two sons and one daughter, because then you will receive two dowries, but give only one." The comparison of the dowries of daughters and daughters-in-law (see Table 5.6) indicates that, if a family had the dowry goods of two daughters-in-law to supplement a daughter's dowry, they could marry one daughter without drawing from their capital.

Project this dowry difference throughout the Indian population and it becomes clear that, whereas men hold the land's wealth within the patrilineage, women serve as conduits of transportable wealth. The hypergamous marriage of women moves their dowry wealth up the status hierarchy, so that the wealthiest groups have the most to gain from the custom of giving large dowries. This conduction of wealth up the socioeconomic status ladder is the basis for persistence of the customs of female infanticide and suttee among wealthy families who would be most able to support daughters and widowed *bahus* were it not for the dowry drain. Female infanticide prevents daughters from taking wealth away from the patrilineage, and sati frees families from the necessity of supporting young widows, particularly those without sons. These archaic customs will be examined in more detail in later chapters.

Despite the long tradition of land for sons and dowry for daughters, attitudes of women about both these customs were changing. These changes are documented in chapter 6.

There is no doubt that the demand for large dowries has a negative effect on the welfare of Indian women. Families are reluctant to pay for daughters' higher education because the money is needed for their dowries. Poor *bahus* are often treated badly by their in-laws, and grooms' families may become increasingly demanding concerning long-term dowry payments.

The perception that daughters already get more than their fair share of the family estate is one justification for opposition to daughters' claiming land shares. However, the creation of enmity between brothers and sisters is the more important basis for such opposition. This concern is realistic, particularly since married brothers often face opposition from their wives concerning expenses involved in inviting sisters home. It is therefore understandable that most women think that daughters receive more in dowry inheritance than their sons do in land inheritance, particularly since daughters do nothing to earn their portion of the parental estate.

It is notable that no women mentioned the possibility of sisters without brothers in their evaluations of the justice of daughters' claims on land. It may be that this omission reflects a tacit approval of traditional land inheritance by brothers, when a man dies without sons, but it is more likely that the family without sons is so rare that this situation did not occur to them.

While it is understandable that most women oppose daughters' claiming land, it is more surprising that so many women who oppose land inheritance by daughters favor reduction or elimination of dowries, since this combination would deprive daughters of any inheritance. Apparently, this dilemma was not considered, or was outweighed by the drain on family finances and concern for the welfare of poor brides in their husbands' homes. Dhooli's plight shows dramatically that the concern expressed for poor brides is well-founded.

In my opinion, legal supports for the return of dowry in cases of wife abuse would do more to protect the property rights and safety of rural Indian women than land inheritance laws, particularly since women of most caste groups come from families that do not own land. The motivation for abusing or killing wives to obtain more money and goods from their parents would be removed if such actions were sanctioned by the return of dowry goods. This legal backing would further protect the rights to property that women in fact receive as their inheritance, rather than giving them access to property they cannot claim without serious family strife. Since efforts to reduce dowry have been unsuccessful, the best course of action would seem to be maximizing dowry protection.

A woman sits beside her lighted *chuula* patting flour balls into *chapatis*. A brass tray containing dough lies before her and other brass utensils are placed beside her (1975).

6

Domestic Economy: Chores, *Chuulas*, Cash, and Clothing

Now *bahus* only want to cook for their own husbands and children. They teach their husbands to ask for separation of the land and *chuulas*.

Now the *bahus* want to take all the money for themselves and do not even give the *sasu* any food.

Bughars are women's workplaces as well as women's quarters. Much of the grain is processed in the *bughars*. Traditionally *sasus* assigned work to *bahus* and exercised control over stored grain, unallocated dowry goods, money *bahus* brought from home, and income from spinning and loans. The control of *bahus* over the money and clothing they bring from home has increased in recent years, and some *bahus* have more autonomy over their work selection than was the case in former times. The increase in literate *bahus* in *bughars* with illiterate *sasus* has enhanced the financial autonomy of *bahus*, who buy products not previously available. Educated *bahus* may think they are more capable of handling financial matters than their illiterate *sasus*, and some *sasus* agree. As might be expected, these changes are a cause for concern for some *sasus*, but they are adjusting to them as they are adjusting to the other innovations sweeping the country.

CHORES

The daily routine of the families during our second visit had not changed much from that described in the earlier study. *Sasus* allocated chores to their *bahus*, and work assignments varied by *sasu* preferences, the number of *bahus* and children in the family, and the time of year.

The village day begins before dawn when the temple priest blows his horn. The signal calls the sleeping villagers from their cots to start the day's work. How soon the call is answered depends on the morning's division of labor. In the courtyard, the daughter-in-law who is to make breakfast emerges before her sisters-in-law. Grandmother may decide that grain needs to be ground. Perhaps there is a calf to feed or milk to churn. These early morning tasks bring some women from their beds while the daughters and children of the house are still sleeping soundly.

In summer the men must get to the fields early and do the morning's work before the blazing sun drives them to a noonday siesta in the shade. On cold winter mornings they enjoy lingering in the warm quilts, going to work after the chill has lifted and the dust of the roads has become warm for bare feet.

But winter or summer, one by one the villagers arise, and, taking a small brass pot filled with water (the Indian version of toilet paper), they take care of elimination. The younger daughters-in-law use the courtyard's drain or latrine, if there is one; the children may use the streets. For everyone else, the fields are the "facilities." The men may go alone, the older women always in groups; but every gray dawn finds the fields filled with silent, white-cloaked figures performing the first task of the day.

The toilet completed, the women return to the courtyard, wash, and begin the day's work in earnest. Grandmother may go to her churning or grinding, or she may decide to rest and smoke hookah while she waits for breakfast. The hearth must be given its first purifying coat of mud each morning before it can be used. If the family eats breakfast, then the fire must be laid and unleavened bread cooked for all members of the hungry household, and the daughters-in-law whose turn it is to make breakfast have a few busy hours.

Gradually the children emerge from their beds, stumble sleepily into the street or to the drain, and return to wash their faces and huddle, shivering, around the hearth fire waiting for breakfast. If it is winter, they may gather brush and build a bonfire in the courtyard for added warmth. Some people drink only milk to break their fast; others eat a good breakfast. The men finish feeding and milking the cattle before they come in to eat. Finally, when the men and children are out of the way, the women have their meal. Eating is a strictly private matter in the village. Each man eats either at his own hearth or men's quarters. Each woman takes her food into her room or into a corner of the courtyard where she can turn her back toward the other women. Children are fed when they demand food and may eat together or separately, depending on whether or not they get hungry at the same time. Since the family does not gather for a meal, the dining hour is not fixed but is a matter of individual convenience.

If an individual wishes to bathe, he uses water from a pot or pail. The women bathe in the courtyards behind screens of cots, placed on edge. The men bathe by the village wells. Both sexes remain clothed while bathing and, when finished, wrap clean dry clothes around themselves, dropping their wet clothes from underneath the fresh ones without ever exposing their bodies.

After breakfast the men leave for the fields or return to their quarters to smoke the hookah and talk. During the morning the women sweep the floor, gin cotton, spin or mend clothes. If there is a daughter to be married, they make things for the dowry. If a festival day is near, they may be busy plastering and whitewashing the house. There is always woman's work to do. The children go to the streets to play. The schoolboys collect their books, slates, and pencils, put them in bookbags or tie them in a rag, and start off in the general direction of school, where they will arrive sooner or later. The older boys who are not in school drive the village cattle across the bridge to the grove of trees by the side of the pond. Every morning several hundred cattle leave the village by this bridge, and every evening they return the same way.

By about 10 o'clock in the morning, when the school officially opens, most of the students have arrived. They settle themselves on the open sunny platform, and from then until noon they sit chanting their lessons, teasing the boys next to them, or just staring into space, to be jolted back to reality by a sharp reprimand from the master. The boys with the cattle have collected and quieted their herds and are playing hockey or *kabaddi* under the shade of the trees. The younger children are playing less organized games in the streets or on a vacant men's quarters. The women start cooking lunch about this time, and in every courtyard a pot bubbles on the hearth. The men are off working in the fields unless it is the slack winter season, when they may be away arranging for a marriage, fighting a court case, or visiting in the village, discussing local politics.

Around noon, the task of feeding the men of the household demands attention. When work in the fields is light, the men come home to lunch; but if it is harvest or planting time, they prefer to have lunch carried out to them by an older daughter or son. The women pack rice, pulses, and unleavened bread into pots or tiffen carriers, tie them with a cloth, and balance them carefully on the head of a child and send him or her off on the long walk to the fields. The older men may come to the courtyard for their lunch, or it may be brought to them at the men's quarters by a daughter or son. The boys come home from school, and the herders, leaving a few of their number in charge of the cattle, also return for their noon meal. When the women have fed everyone and forced their reluctant sons back to school, or at least out of the house, they again snatch enough time from the day's routine to eat their own lunches.

Now the day is at its hottest. The sun beats down relentlessly. The heat shimmers over the fields and is reflected from the mud walls of the courtyards. Shadows are scanty and everywhere the villagers seek shade. The women huddle with their spinning or mending along the narrow shadow of a wall, shifting as the sun shifts. The men pull their cots under a tree on the men's quarters or under the roof of the rear sleeping quarters. The schoolboys crowd for seats under the trees; the herders abandon their games for conversation; and when they must start their cattle on the long walk to the fields, their pace is slow. In the fields the men leave their plows and squat in groups under a lone tree or rest in a mango grove and eat their lunches. The small children return to their homes or seek the shade of a friendly tree for their play, and their voices are muted. Even the dogs look for a cot to sleep under. In the summer work ceases entirely during the middle of the day. The men work in the fields before the dawn and after dark, and everyone takes a siesta during the middle of the day.

Around 4 o'clock in the afternoon the pace of work quickens again. The children start returning from school; some have chores to do, others return home only to throw down their books and run out to play. The women start preparing the evening meal. In the fields the men get ready to go home. At dusk, around 5 o'clock, the road to the village is once again a crowded thoroughfare. Men and boys carrying loads of fodder on their heads, men driving plows or bullock carts, an occasional youth on a bicycle, and from all directions the lowing, slow-moving cattle—all must filter once again back across the narrow bridge and into the village. This is the time of day so often described by Indian poets, when the dust from the hooves of the returning cattle catches the light of the setting sun, and the ground dissolves into a yellow–red haze.

As night falls, the men and boys feed and water the cattle, the women prepare to feed their men again, and the children return from play to try teasing some dinners from busy mothers. The bats emerge from the rafters and become darting black shadows in the dying light. The cattle stamp restlessly and then become gradually quiet as they are fed.

Around 8, the men come into the courtyard for their evening meal. Once again the efforts of the women are concentrated on serving food to their men. Only when the men have left do the women eat their own dinners.

By now the oil or kerosene lanterns are lighted, making small yellow patches in the darkness of the courtyard. The women sit and gossip. If there is a good storyteller in the house, she may tell stories to the children or to the other women. The young daughters-in-law may play games or retire to corners to whisper about their husbands, their joys or disappointments in the home of their in-laws, or to reminisce about their own villages. In the men's quarters the men visit each other, smoke the hookah, and talk of farming or politics. Gradually the children drift off to bed, to be joined later by their mother or an older sibling or cousin. One by one, in courtyard and men's quarters, the villagers climb into their cots, cover themselves from head to foot with quilts or sheets, and at last the village sleeps—but never completely. All night a few are stirring. A man slips into the courtyard to call his wife quietly from their children to a separate cot and then returns as silently to the men's quarters, careful not to disturb the occupants of the still cocoons. Another man gets up in the night to check the cattle. A mother stirs in response to the crying of her baby. And if the crops are nearing harvest time, the fields are full of silent sentinels guarding them against the thieves who prowl in darkness. After harvest, farmers plow their fields and the tinkle of bullock bells may be heard far into the night, for the moonlight is bright and cooler than the rays of the sun. In the winter the night's stillness may be pierced by the barking of jackals, with an occasional answer from a vigilant watchdog. But these are only periodic interruptions of the silence—intermittent movements in the stillness—for it is night and the village may sleep until the horn of the priest calls us once again from slumber to meet the toil of a new day.

(Minturn & Hitchcock, 1966, pp. 37–40)

The performance of some household chores is prescribed by purdah restrictions, but generally *sasus* have the authority to assign household tasks to their *bahus*. In addition to the universal chores of cooking, cleaning, and child care, household chores in *bughars* include threshing, winnowing, and grinding grain, and feeding, watering, and milking the cattle. We interviewed women in several *bughars* about their chores. As might be expected, the general pattern of housework was the same throughout the families; in many respects housework is the same throughout the world.

Grain Processing

The processing of household grain, some of which needs to be shelled or cleaned, took up a lot of the women's time in 1975, as it did in 1955. The women were particularly busy during February and March, when peas are harvested. A mustard seed is still grown by some families for cooking oil but is time-consuming to shell and thresh. Seeds reserved for sowing must be sorted from the seeds of weeds so that the crop will not need weeding. One day Draupadi was angry with Dhooli because she had sent wheat seed out to the fields without cleaning it. Draupadi had a box frame with a screen bottom and was shifting the remaining wheat back and forth on the screen to sift out the smaller weed seeds.

Most grain is threshed by the men of the village in threshing fields at the village outskirts. The men spread grain in a circle on the ground around a horizontal wooden pole attached to a central fulcrum. A bullock is hitched to the end of the pole and led in circles around the fulcrum, threshing the grain with its hooves. The threshing field that had been just across the bridge in 1955 had buildings on it in 1975. Grain could also be taken to the village mill for threshing, and some *sasus* reported that *bahus* wanted to send all the grain to the mill and "be like Leigh and sit with Indira Gandhi." In fact, women in almost every *bughar* process some grain as it comes in from harvest or is needed for the family.

Women, working as they must in enclosed courtyards, thresh without the benefit of animals. Each *bughar* floor has a small pit lined in metal. Grain is put into this pit a few handfuls at a time. One or more women stand around the metal pit and pound the grain with heavy wooden poles tipped with metal sheaths. Sometimes as many as four or five women will surround the threshing pit, singing to keep time as each in turn strikes the grain with her threshing pole. Although the poles rebound from the impact with the grain and metal pit, threshing can be tiring work.

Once threshed, grain must be winnowed by placing it in flat winnowing baskets with a few inches of vertical basketry on three sides. The grain is bounced and shifted from side to side until the chaff is jarred out of the open side of the basket. The chaff must then be cleaned up from the *bughar* floor and the grain spread on *charpoys* to dry before being stored or ground.

Grinding was still done in some houses by feeding the grain into a shoot between two horizontal millstones and rotating the top stone with its handle as the flour came out of a spout. The millstone is heavy, and the grinder must extend her arm with each rotation, so grinding is by far the most physically demanding work. I tried it for a few minutes in 1955 and had a sore shoulder for a day or two. Because of the difficulty of hand grinding, families who could afford to pay took their grain to the village miller to be ground on the electric mill. Some families sent their corn, the hardest grain, to the mill but ground their own peas, wheat, and rice. Commercial cooking oil had replaced homegrown mustard oil in cooking, so few families grew or pressed mustard.

The amount of time spent on grinding varied from house to house. When women ground at home, they usually did it in the early morning before the other chores began, or in the evening after other chores were done. One woman ground her wheat each morning from 4 to 6 a.m. Two woman sharing a *chuula* said that one ground while the other cooked. They said they ground from 5 a.m. until noon, presumably taking turns, or for 2 to 3 hours in the evening. In a third *bughar,* women said they ground two to three times a month for 4 hours at a time.

As usual, some old women said that the younger generation was weaker than they were and could not grind as well:

> I am an old woman and I have pains in my arm. Even so, if I start to grind, I will grind 5 kilos of grain. Young women grind for one-half hour and they say that they have a headache or their arm is paining them. Old people are so energetic that they

can work even when they are about to die. Young women are not so healthy and cannot do the work.

Q. Why aren't the young women healthy?

A. Now when they get pregnant, they say that they have headaches and stomachaches and they get so many injections. These injections make the children weak. Previously we had no medicine when we were pregnant and our children were healthy.

Since the present generation of young *bahu*s were the children of women of the speaker's generation, this explanation was illogical, as well as inaccurate. However, it reflects a belief among some older Rajput men and women that they are stronger and healthier than their children.

Cooking

In 1975 cooking was still done on *chuula*s, and the diet remained essentially the same as that described in our earlier book:

In general, the handling of food occupies a good proportion of the women's time. The principal diet is rice with a potato or vegetable curry, eaten with *roti* and *ghi*. *Roti* is the generic term for several kinds of round, unleavened bread (not unlike tortillas). *Ghi* is clarified butter made from curd and is used both for frying and for pouring over food. Both the rice and the curry are cooked over the hearth in large brass pots. The "breads" are first cooked in small, slightly concave pans, then put directly into the side of the hearth to puff, and finally stacked in a dish by the side of the fireplace. Whole spices are ground by placing them on a flat stone or board and crushing and pulverizing them with another stone. Unrefined brown sugar, called *gur,* is also eaten and used in making various kinds of sweets. In the summertime, the women make vermicelli (thin spaghetti) from wheat flour by rolling it with their hands.

Milk, both from cows and buffaloes, is an important part of the diet. Men usually do the milking unless the cattle compound is within the women's quarters. The milk is boiled in large pots on a special hearth. Most of its goes into the making of *ghi* and curd, although boiled and sweetened milk is sometimes drunk.

Popcorn and sugar cane are popular between-meal snacks for both children and adults. Most of the children are very fond of popcorn, which they take themselves to one of the village shops to be popped. This is eaten without butter or salt. The children also eat quantities of sugar cane, particularly at the beginning of the cane season. We have seen children consume 6 feet of sugar cane during the course of a morning.

An interesting aspect of the division of labor between the sexes is caused by the fact that the women are vegetarians. Those Rajput men who like meat must get it and cook it themselves in the men's quarters because their women will neither touch it nor have it in the house. Some of the men keep chickens for eggs and meat.

(Minturn & Hitchcock, 1966, pp. 43–44)

The *chuula* is a sacred place within the *bughar*. If it is not purified, the food cannot be pure. Leather is polluting, so family members usually go barefoot within the *bughar* unless it is cold, and a person wearing shoes must remove them before coming near the *chuula*. Each morning the *chuula* must be cleaned, the ashes removed, and the *chuula* given a fresh coat of cow dung.

Rules of ritual pollution demand that only vegetables be cooked on the *chuula*. Some men eat meat occasionally, but they must cook it themselves in their *choopars*. One day when we went for lunch, we found that Amar Nath had caught a small fish and brought it to Draupadi to cook for us. When we arrived she had finished cooking the fish and was removing the mud from the inner side of the *chuula*. She threw out all of this mud and replaced it before cooking another meal. It was a generous gesture; some wives would have refused to have fish in the house. It happened that it was Thanksgiving Day, and I was particularly appreciative of this unexpected treat. This was the only time that I saw flesh being cooked in a *bughar chuula*.

Cooking was one of the most time-consuming chores. Meals are cooked on the *chuula,* and milk is boiled on the milk *chuula* to make yogurt. Cooking time includes churning the milk for butter and serving meals to family men and children. Women usually cooked from 5 to 10 or 11 a.m. and again from 5 to 8 p.m. During the day men were fed twice. When men were working in the fields, food was brought to them, usually by a child of the family.

In 1955 mothers did not teach their daughters to cook because of their status as guests. In 1975 some mothers were training daughters in the basics of cooking before marriage. One woman had an amusing account of her first attempts at cooking in her husband's home:

> When I had my *shadi,* I did not know how to cook. After 3 days my brother came for me and told them that I did not know how to cook, so please do not expect it of me. My in-laws said that I had already cooked *chapatis*. My brother was surprised and said that I did not cook at home. I did not know how to cook corn *chapatis* until my *soosar* brought me a lot of corn flour and told me to cook it. Then I knew how.

In traditional joint families, the food for all the family was cooked by a *bahu,* but men were served by their mothers or sisters. A wife did not serve her husband's meals unless he had no mother or sister in the *bughar*. Usually this did not occur until the *sasu* died and all the *nanad*s married. The purdah interviews with *sasu*s indicate that they often objected when *bahu*s fed their own husbands and children.

Washing

In 1975 most *bughar*s had hand pumps. The water-carrier women who, during our first visit, drew water from the wells and made daily rounds to bring it to *bughar*s were out of business. We were told that most of the water carriers had moved out of the village or bought land to farm. With pumps, water was more readily available, and washing had increased.

One *sasu* blamed the refusal of *bahu*s to grind on the increase in washing: "Before women had 2 sets of clothes, now they have 10 sets and there is more washing of clothes. Now women say that grinding is low-caste work."

This comment is interesting because washing clothes, which involves contact with dirt and bodily excretions, is low-caste work, while processing of vegetable food is not. The former is done by members of the Dhoobi caste, a lower caste of the Sudra group of castes. In 1975 some women said the Dhoobi charged too much, others complained about the cost of soap, and some no longer wanted their clothes washed at the village well because the water was not always as clean as water from their own pumps. Draupadi arranged for us to have our clothes washed by her family Dhoobi at the tube well in their fields so that the water would be clean. Most families still gave the Dhoobi their heavy cotton sheets and shawls worn by the family men, but a number of *bahu*s washed their clothes and their children's clothes because the Dhoobi took 8 to 10 days to return them, not fast enough to keep the children in clean clothes. Women claimed that, whereas men used to change clothes after 8 days, now educated people changed clothes daily.

The washing of men's clothes by family women is regulated by the status of the women, extensions of purdah and sex-avoidance rules. The avoidance of sexual contact with older men is extended to the washing of clothes men wear below the waist, and the status hierarchy and blood versus affinal kinship ties among women are extended to their washing customs. Thus, any woman may wash a man's shirts, but his pants, shorts, or dhotis, worn below the waist and in contact with the genitals, cannot be washed by a man's daughter or *derani*. These can be washed by his mother, sister, or *jethani*. In conservative joint families, wives avoid washing their husbands' pants, shorts, or dhotis, if a *nanad, sasu,* or *jethani* is available. A daughter or *bahu* can wash the clothes of a mother or *sasu*. A *sasu* may wash her daughters' clothes but will not wash the clothes of her *bahu*s.

Women wore their hair unoiled and in a single braid in 1975 and washed it more frequently than they had when strands of hair were cornrowed, woven into a final braid, and treated with mustard oil. Women washed their own hair more frequently with this simpler hairstyle, and only Draupadi and Sher's wife, Lakhpati, still had the barber's wife come weekly to wash and braid their hair.

Animal Husbandry

Animal husbandry and milking may be done by men, women, or children. Men usually tend the bullocks used for plowing and tether them beside their *choopar*. Men may milk, but milking is more likely to be done by women since they cook the milk. Most families have a milk cow and buffalo tethered in the entrance of the *bughar* during the winter months, and most *bughar*s have raised feeding bowls for these animals. With the multiple cropping of the new grains, cattle are no longer grazed, so their care by women has increased. One devout woman gave the first bread of the day to her sacred cattle. We arrived one morning when she was doing this, and all the cattle stood up as she approached. She laughed and told us that the cattle always stood to greet her as if she were a friend come for a visit, which indeed she is.

Water buffaloes must be bathed in the pond daily so that their skins do not dry out. This was usually done by children, who rode the large animals into the water and scrubbed their backs. In 1955 a girl of 3 walked the family buffalo to and from the pond and bathed it every day.

In 1955 most families had their cow dung cakes for cooking made by their Chamar women. In 1975 most women made their own dung cakes because they had more *chuulas* and because the Chamar women made the cakes too large and wasted dung. Increased cultivation had used up what little wood there had been, and women now relied exclusively on dung cakes for their cooking. In families with few cattle, the shortage of dung was beginning to be a problem.

Child Care

Women never mentioned child care when asked to list their chores. When we asked, however, they said that caring for children was time-consuming. When children get up in the morning their faces must be washed, and every time young children come in from playing they are dirty and have to be washed. One woman estimated that it took her 1½ hours to bathe her children. Nursing infants are usually held and fed on demand. Women complained that recently weaned children bother them for food before it is ready. Children also help with some of the work. Boys may help with the harvest, take food to the men in the fields, bring back fodder, and water the cattle. Girls help with cooking, sweeping floors, and cleaning utensils. Older girls spin and sometimes do the laundry.

Handicrafts

During both field trips women spent much of their leisure time making a variety of items for themselves or for wedding gifts. In 1955 they made padded jackets for babies and young children, but in 1975 they could afford yarn and preferred to knit sweaters. Knitting sweaters for members of a bridegroom's family had become a standard occupation of young women about to be married. They also made papier-mâché bowls, sitting mats with bright designs of close-cut knotted hemp or cotton, and some toys.

The only major changes in handicrafts were the switch from padded jackets to knitted sweaters and the use, by some *bahus,* of hand-operated sewing machines to make clothes for their children and sari blouses for themselves.

CHUULAS

According to most *sasus,* their *bahus* were more likely to demand separate *chuulas* than they did in former times. Concern for the loss of control over food and money was a common concern of *sasus* during both our visits. The decrease in observance of purdah customs had led more *bahus* to ask for separate *chuulas. Sasus* expressed concern about this problem more often on our second visit. The resistance to *chuula* separation was not based on the difficulty of construction. Separation of the *chuula* is the first step in separating food supplies and finances. When food supplies are

Table 6.1 Division of Household Food
Supplies

	N	%
Divided	4	13
Stored jointly	27	87
Total	31	100

Table 6.2 Number of *Chuula*s per Courtyard

	1955		1975		1955–1975
	N	%	N	%	%
1	30	78	36	63	−15
2	4	11	15	26	+15
3	3	8	4	7	−1
4+	1	3	2	4	−1
Total	38	100	57	100	

stored separately, *bahu*s may draw on their food to purchase small items at the village stores.

Table 6.1 indicates that 87% of the *bughar*s still stored their food supplies in a common bin in 1975, but Table 6.2 indicates a slight shift away from joint *chuula*s from 1955 to 1975. The number of *bughar*s with one *chuula* had decreased by 15%, while the number with two *chuula*s had increased by the same percentage. In most households, therefore, food was still cooked for the joint family on one hearth; when food was cooked on individual *chuula*s, separation had usually not gone beyond separate cooking arrangements to separate grain storage.

The concern of *sasu*s about this issue would seem to be exaggerated in light of the preponderance of joint-family functioning. Much of the indignation stemmed from the disrespect that failure to cook for a *sasu* symbolized. However, more careful analysis indicated that in *bughar*s where *chuula*s were separate, *sasu*s were sharing their *chuula*s with their youngest *bahu*. Apparently a *bahu* gets a separate *chuula* shortly after the *gauna* of her next *dewar*. Therefore, the concern of *sasu*s that they will have no one to cook for them in their declining years is understandable.

Some expressions of this concern are recorded in the following comments:

Now *sasu*s do not keep their *bahu*s as happy as they used to. Previously not all the sons were married. The household had only one or two *bahu*s. Now the house has so many *bahu*s and they have differences with each other. Previously if a woman had five or seven sons, one would marry and the *bahu* would cook for the whole family. One *bahu* used to cook and had no one to fight with. Now there are more *bahu*s and they fight more because there are too many of them. There are more people to cook for now so that the *bahu* does not want to cook for the whole family. She only wants to cook for her own husband and children.

Now the sons can say, "Why don't you get me married?" Nowadays all the men have to get married because they have no one to cook for them. Before *bahus* used to spend the whole of their lives cooking and serving the joint families. Nowadays most of them do not want to cook for the joint families. They only want to cook for their own husband and children.

In our house there is still only one *chuula* but in the adjoining house they have separate *chuula*s after only 5 years of marriage. In the village some *bahus* separate their *chuula*s after 2 to 4 years of marriage. They also want to get their land and their courtyard separated once they have a separate *chuula*. Previously not even a widow would ask for a separate *chuula*. Now *bahus* want a separate *chuula* so they don't have to cook for the *sasus*.

My six sons each have a separate *chuula*. Now the wife of my youngest son has come. If she is all right and serves me well I will share my *chuula* with her. If she is like the others I will have to have a separate *chuula* for myself.

In this house we have three *chuulas*. Each married son has one and I have one with my unmarried son. Earlier in the good old days when we had one *chuula* and I had control of it, I could have offered you food. Now you come to visit me and I have no food to offer you.

Nowadays immediately after marriage, if the *bahus* feel the least bit inconvenienced about their meals they teach their husbands to ask for separation of the land and *chuula*. Before that we did not even think of asking for a separate *chuula*. I have been beaten by my younger as well as my older brothers-in-law and my *sasu* as well. I lived 19 years in a joint family and in the presence of my husband my *taaya* used to beat me and my *dewar* used to go on abusing me, but my husband could not say anything.

The issue of *chuula* separation was so sensitive that none of the eight *bahus* who have joint *chuula*s would say when they expected to separate. Five *bahus* had separate *chuula*s. The oldest had been separated for 20 years and the youngest for only 2 months. The other three had been separated for 1, 3, and 5 years, respectively.

Since the fear of having no one to cook for them in old age was so pervasive among the *sasus*, we asked the *bahus* whether they expected to have their *bahus* cook for them. Eleven said yes, and four said no. One woman who expected to receive this service answered as follows:

I cook for my *sasu* and serve her, why should my *bahu* not cook for me? If she would not cook for me I would break her bones. As I have served my *sasu*, my *bahu* will have to serve me. Otherwise we would be separated.

Reactions to the possibility that *bahus* may not cook for them indicate that these young women saw this as an issue of simple practicality rather than status:

After all, there would be someone to cook for me. If I were too old and in bed, then anyone would give me a piece of bread to keep me alive. If my *bahus* will not give me two cooked meals a day, they will at least give me one.

One woman responded with some humor: "If one *bahu* will not cook for me the other will cook. At least there will be one who will serve me. Otherwise my husband will cook for me."

In view of the fact that 58% of the *bughar*s had only one *chuula,* and 87% stored their grain jointly, these answers seem exaggerated. Like other answers concerning changing customs, they reflect a real concern for potential alteration in the power balance between *sasu*s and *bahu*s.

DOWRY DISTRIBUTION

Table 6.3 shows the tabulated results of the interview on economic control, conducted with 31 women (see appendix D, questions 9, 10, and 10a). Answers to Questions 9, 10, and 10a show that jewelry is the dowry item most likely to be retained (41%), while clothes (37%) and utensils (30%) are most likely to be

Table 6.3 Dowry Distribution

How much of your dowry do you still have?		
	N	%
Jewelry, ornaments	22	41
Trunks	14	26
Clothes	5	9
Other	4	7
Everything	4	7
Nothing	5	9
Total	54	100

How much of your dowry has been given away?		
	N	%
Jewelry, ornaments	8	14
Clothes	21	37
Utensils	17	30
Other	2	4
Everything	5	9
Given	1	
Stolen	2	
Mortgaged	2	
Nothing	4	7
Total	54	100

When were your dowry items given away?		
	N	%
Shadi	11	23
Gauna	3	6
Chuchak	14	30
Female in-law marriage or *chuchak*	13	28
NA	6	13
Total	47	100

Table 6.4 Percentage of Dowry Goods Given at *Shadi* and *Gauna* for *Sasus* and *Bahus*

	Sasus						Bahus					
	Shadi		Gauna		Total		Shadi		Gauna		Total	
	N	%	N	%	N	%	N	%	N	%	N	%
Clothing and bedding	38	54	45	46	83	100	64	56	51	44	115	100
Utensils	30	77	9	23	39	100	55	68	25	31	80	100
Total	68	56	54	44	122	100	119	61	76	39	195	100

distributed. Four women still had all of their dowry, and five had nothing left. However, in only one case was all of the dowry given away. Two of these women had their dowries stolen, and two had their jewelry mortgaged by their husbands for loans. The interest on the loans was so high that they could not be repaid. Distribution of about one third of the dowry goods given away occurs at the bride's *shadi chuchak* (the birth of *nanads*' sons), and marriages of *nanads*.

Shadi and Gauna

The distribution of goods at *shadi* and *gauna* consists of gifts to the husband, gifts of clothing to members of the husband's household, and small gifts to members of the groom's party. These expenses are known beforehand, and the dowry goods include these gifts. Thus, the listings of clothing and bedding in Table 6.4 include sets of clothing for members of the husband's family.

Chuchak

A major drain on jewelry comes when sons are born to *bahus*. In wealthy families *chuchak* may also be celebrated at the birth of first daughters. At these times *nanads* come home and may demand any piece of their *bhabhi*'s jewelry they want; this gift is called *chuchak*. The custom was described in our first book:

> Before nursing begins, a sister of the husband washes the mother's breasts with Ganges water or milk. For this she receives a present of jewelry. Sometimes the sister-in-law clamors for a particular piece of expensive jewelry. If the child is a boy, particularly a first-born son, her request is usually granted. If no husband's sister is present, another woman acts as a substitute. She receives only a nominal gift.

(Minturn & Hitchcock, 1966, p. 101)

In practice, all *nanads* usually receive *chuchak* gifts, whether or not they are present when babies are born. When Succha's second son was born, during our visit, Succha insisted on presenting Swaran Kapoor and me with 50 rupees each for his *chuchak*, more than nominal gifts for classificatory sisters. Often *bhabhis* must melt down large jewelry pieces to provide presents for several *nanads*. Sometimes they may simply give money. Songs sung on this occasion express the reluctance of the young mother to give *chuchak* presents. The following are the lyrics to two *chuchak* songs:

> I am a young mother, do not drain my house.
>   Do not drain the inside and outside of my house.
> The gift for my mother-in-law should be given to my mother.
>   I am a young mother, do not drain my house.
> The gift for my sister-in-law should be given to my sister.
>   I am a young mother, do not drain my house.
> The gift for my aunt-in-law should be given to my sister.
>   I am a young mother, do not drain my house.

> Yashoda-jee has given birth to Lord Krishna.
> The midwife wants to take my gold necklace.
> Instead of my necklace, take *bindi* [colored powder] and *tikka*.
> I will not give you my necklace.
> Mother-in-law comes and gives a ring, Lord Krishna wants a necklace.
> Instead of my necklace I will give you earrings.
> I will not give you my necklace.
> Elder sister-in-law comes and makes the bed and wants my necklace.
> Instead of my necklace, I will give you my ring.
> I will not give you my necklace.

Contributions to *Nanads'* Wedding and *Bhat* Expenses

*Bhabhi*s must also give *nanad*s presents when the *nanad*s have their *shadi*s, *gauna*s, and *chuchak*s. Finally, older *bhabhi*s contribute to the marriages of their *nanads'* children through gifts called *bhat*. It is this lifelong drain of goods that leads to the proverb "A daughter grows old but the custom of giving to her never grows old."

CONTROL OF DOWRY GOODS

In answer to Question 8 of the economic control interview ("When you brought your dowry, who decided how it was distributed?"), all women reported that their *sasu*s distributed their dowries when they first entered their husbands' homes. As long as the *sasu* retains control of dowry goods, she controls the gifts, and often the *bahu* does not know how much of her dowry has been given away. However, when a *bahu* controls her own dowry goods, she is responsible for this gift giving. For this reason *bahu*s want control of their dowry goods as soon as possible.

Answers to Question 7 in the economic control interview ("When you bring presents from your parents, who distributes them?") describe examples of both *sasu* and *bahu* dowry control, the variety of husband's relatives who may claim dowry goods, and the occasions for mandatory gift giving.

Some answers from women whose goods were controlled by their *sasu*s are as follows:

> In the marriage of my *nanad,* my one sari was given to her and one of my small gold necklaces was sold to purchase another gold ornament for my *nanad.* At the time of *chuchak* and *gauna,* etcetera, my *sasu* gives, because we are still joint. Therefore, I do not know how much.
>
> My clothes, utensils, and other articles have been given away to the sisters of my father-in-law as I do not have any *nanad.* I do not know what was given at what occasion because mostly I used to live in my parents' house. I used to come here for 2 or 3 years and stay for a few months and again go there.
>
> Everything of my dowry is with my *sasu,* and she gives my *nanad,* when she comes, a few things like clothes and utensils, etcetera, but my jewelry is intact with her and my trunk as well.
>
> All the three *nanad*s were already married when I was married. Others already had *chuchak* before my marriage. At the time of the birth of my first son, one *nanad* came and I presented her a gold ring. The other two *nanad*s did not come. When they come I shall give one ring to each of them for the birth of my son. I do not know what was given by my *sasu* for *chuchak* to her daughter because at that time I was away at my parents' place. None of my jewelry has been given away.
>
> Neither I have any *nanad*s, nor any daughter. Therefore there has been no occasion to give anything to anybody. My *jaith* has two daughters. One is married and other is yet to be married. In her elder daughter's *gauna* my *sasu* might have given some clothes and utensils. I am living jointly, and have never given anything myself.
>
> I have my jewelry and trunk with me, but clothes, utensils, and other small things have been distributed by my *sasu.* We are still living in a joint family. Therefore, I do not give anything individually to anybody. In the marriage of my daughter my pair of anklets was given to her. Two sets of clothes, at the time of *gauna,* were also given to her.

One woman described the change from *sasu* control to self-control of dowry goods:

> My clothes, beddings, and utensils have been given away by my *sasu.* When my first son was born I gave 10 rupees to each of the three sisters of my *soosar* [father-in-law]. In the marriage of R [granddaughter of husband's elder brother] I gave one pair of bracelets, one pair of earrings, a big necklace, all gold, 101 clothes and one ring and a wristwatch for the groom. In *gauna* also there were 101 clothes and utensils and I do not remember the number; a pair of anklets of silver, etcetera.
>
> In the *chuchak* of R, I gave one wardrobe of wood. I do not remember how many clothes were there. Utensils, one ring for the bridegroom, another ring, one pair of anklets of silver, and one pair of earrings of gold were given to R.
>
> When my nephew was born I received one sari and some rupees. I do not remember the amount.

Women who controlled their own dowry giving described a variety of circumstances for mandatory gift giving:

> My ornaments are with me, but clothes and utensils were given in the marriages of my *nanad*s.

> Before my marriage my *nanad* was already married and her *gauna* had taken place. Therefore, nothing was given to her from my jewelry. At the birth of my daughter I did not give anything. Those who have enough may give at a daughter's birth but I did not do so.

> My parents gave me each and everything of household use. Buffaloes, calf, and all utensils for kitchen and even the things like scale and weights, etcetera, in my dowry. I have my jewelry, big boxes, etcetera, with me.

> My clothes and utensils were given to my younger *nanad* in her marriage, but before her *gauna* she died. The elder *nanad* was married before my marriage. No *chuchak*s were performed before me. On the birth of my sons I gave 50 rupees to each of the two *nanad*s and one good dress to each of them, and my *soosar* gave 100 rupees and clothes for their husbands. I gave my own clothes and the money I brought from my parents to my *nanad*s.

> On the birth of my son I presented a pair of anklets to my *nanad*. I gave a gold ring and a bicycle to the daughter of my *dewar* in her marriage, and two sets of clothes for the newly married couple. At *gauna* three sets of clothes for the newly married pair were given by us individually. When she went to her in-laws this time I gave two sets of clothes for her and her husband.

> I have my gold necklace and gold ring and silver anklets with me. My trunk is also here but my gold earrings and utensils and clothes were given to my youngest *nanad*, who was married after my marriage. The chairs and tables, etcetera, I brought in *gauna* were kept here in the house for my use. Only the youngest *nanad* was married after I came, and she was given the utensils and clothes I brought from my parents, and the pair of gold earrings which I brought.

> My jewelry is with me intact but clothes and utensils have been given away to others at various occasions. At the marriage of my husband's cousin's sister we gave many things. But nothing from my dowry, and at the time of births of my sons, we paid her cash and a suit piece for her husband.

One *bahu* expected to make a gift to her *nanad* when the *nanad*'s child was born:

> Earlier there has been no *chuchak* of any *nanad*s, but now when they come then they will get *chuchak* also. Now one of my *nanad*s is pregnant and if there is the birth of a son, then *nanad*s would be given whatever they demand.

Two descriptions of *bhat* payments (contributions to the weddings of *nanad*s' children) are as follows:

> My jewelry is with me. Utensils and clothes were given to *nanad*s. In my presence we gave *bhat* to my *nanad* in which we gave 202 rupees cash, 44 sets of clothes, 21 utensils, a pair of gold earrings, a pair of anklets, a pair of foot rings, and a decorative big key ring.

My *nanad* was married and *chuchak*s, etcetera, were given before my marriage. A couple of years ago my *nanad* expired and very recently her two daughters got married. We had to take *bhat* for them and gave the following items to each one of them: 51 sets of clothes, 21 utensils, one *tikka* of gold, one gold ring, one pair of anklets of silver, one pair of foot rings of silver. The families of my *nanad* were not happy with our gifts and have stopped relations with us now.

The descriptions of *chuchak* payments indicate that *nanad*s do not usually assert their right to demand the largest piece of jewelry at *chuchak* but settle for whatever gift they are offered. When the *nanad* is greedy, she incurs the resentment of her *bhabhi*s, particularly if they are poor and have little to give. When *bhabhi*s have a store of jewelry and cash to draw upon, they can have large gold pieces melted down and made into small jewelry items or can buy presents. One woman contrasted the situations of wealthy and poor wives: "A wealthy *bahu* is able to protect her dowry at *chuchak* by giving cash and buying presents, but a poor *bahu* is deprived of her meager possessions."

Generational Changes in Dowry Distribution

Table 6.5 shows the tabulation of goods in *chuchak* and *bhat* payments for *sasus* and *bahus*. The comparison of *sasu* and *bahu chuchak* payments indicates that all categories had increased except jewelry, which remained the same. Furthermore, one *bahu* gave furniture and another a bicycle for *chuchak,* items missing from *sasu* payments. Since *bhat* payments are given to *nanads*' children, all of the women making such payments were in the *sasu* generation. No one reported giving money for *bhat,* but jewelry, clothing, bedding, utensils, and occasionally furniture and appliances were given. The numbers in Table 6.5 indicate that, while the value of dowry goods had increased for the younger generation, the value of *chuchak* and *bhat* gifts had also increased. This is in line with the general principle that the wealthier the woman's family, the more she is expected to contribute to her husband's family.

Table 6.5 Classification of Dowry Items Given at *Chuchak* and *Bhat* by *Sasus* and *Bahus*

| | Chuchak | | | | Bhat | |
| | Sasus | | Bahus | | Sasus | Bahus |
	M	R	M	R	M	R
Rupees	40_2	15–65	70_3	10–150	—	—
Jewelry						
Number of items	4_8	3–6	4_4	2–6	7.2_5	$0–11$
Clothing and bedding	48_6	1–100	150_4	50–270	31_5	$0–101$
Utensils	4_4	1–11	9_2	5–81	18_2	$0–35$
Furniture and appliances	0	0	1_2	0	1_1	1
Bicycle	0	0	1_1	0	1_1	1
Other	1_1	0	1_3	0	—	—

Some women reported a recent trend to give more of the dowry goods at *gauna*, when the bride goes to live permanently in her in-laws' house, so that the *sasu* could not distribute them in the interim between the *shadi* and the *gauna*. Our records of the amounts given on these two occasions for *sasu*s and *bahu*s do not indicate a generational change in this direction (see Table 6.4). Instead, a somewhat higher proportion of dowry goods were given at the *shadi* for *bahu*s than for *sasu*s, (61% vs. 56%). If the reports of holding back on dowry goods until the *gauna* are correct, the trend may have been too recent to show up in our records.

CONTROL OF MONEY

The major source of cash throughout most of a woman's life is the money she receives when she returns from visits to her parents. *Bahu*s in 1975 still brought presents to members of their husbands' families but were more likely to keep undesignated goods, such as clothing, for themselves and their children. In previous generations such items might have been taken by *sasu*s for their own children. Draupadi's apparent wish to give Dhooli's shawls to her daughter, Luxmi, is an example of this prerogative.

Women were also interviewed about control of household money and sources of such funds. Answers indicate that there was no dominant pattern for control of household money (Table 6.6, question 1). Funds could be controlled by *bahu*s (23%), *sasu*s (23%), *soosar*s (13%), or *soosar*s and *sasu*s (13%). Other arrangements accounted for 16% of the answers, while husbands controlled the finances in 9% of the families (question 2). Only a minority of *bahu*s got money from either their husbands (32%) or their *sasu*s (16%) (question 3). *Bahu*s who did not keep money brought from home, therefore, were often without funds.

About one half of the women (58%) brought the majority of their clothing from their parents' houses. Only 12% bought most of their clothing in Khalapur, while 30% got clothes in both their parental and marital villages (question 3). If married women needed more clothes while in Khalapur they usually bought them locally (64%) rather than sending home for them (10%) (question 4).

Children's clothing must be purchased more often than adult clothing, so it is more likely to be financed with money from the husband or in-laws. Answers indicate that for children's clothing, 26% of the women interviewed got money from their husbands, 23% from their *sasu*s, 13% from *sasu*s and *soosar*s, and 16% from other sources, including their parents. Only 19% bought children's clothes with their own funds (question 5).

Older married women retain primary control over presents brought from their parents' homes and increasingly make their own decisions about gifts at weddings, *chuchak*s, and *bhat*s. Answers indicate that 55% of *bahu*s kept money they brought from their parents, whereas 45% gave their money to or shared it with their *sasu*s. Since presents are often designated for husbands' relatives, their distribution is less often controlled completely by *bahu*s; 32% kept presents for themselves, while 68% gave presents to or shared them with their *sasu*s (question 6).

Table 6.6 Control of Household Goods and Money

1. Who controls the money in this house?

	N	%
Self	7	23
Sasu	7	23
Soosar	4	13
Soosar and *sasu*	4	13
Other	5	16
Husband	3	9
NA	1	3
Total	31	100

2. Do you get money from:

	N	%
Husband		
Yes	10	32
No	20	65
NA	1	3
Total	31	100
Sasu		
Yes	5	16
No	23	74
NA	3	10
Total	31	100

3. Do you buy most of your clothes in Khalapur or do you bring them from your parents' house?

	N	%
Parents' village	18	58
Khalapur	4	12
Both places	9	30
Total	31	100

4. If you need more clothes, where do you get them?

	N	%
Khalapur	20	64
Parents' village	3	10
NA	8	126
Total	31	100

5. Where do you get the money to buy your clothes or your children's clothes, while living here?

	N	%
Husband	8	26
Sasu	7	23
Self	6	19
Soosar and *sasu*	4	13
Other	5	16
NA	1	3
Total	31	100

(continued)

Table 6.6–(Continued)

6. What do you do with money/property brought from parents' home?

	N	%
Money		
Keep for self	17	55
Give to *sasu*	11	35
Share with *sasu*	3	10
Total	31	100
Presents		
Keep for self	10	32
Give to *sasu*	6	19
Share with *sasu*	15	49
Total	31	100

Some *bahus*' descriptions of various degrees of control over money and property brought from parents are as follows:

> Neither my husband nor my mother-in-law gives me money, because whatever I need they either purchase or give money to their son to purchase. So there is no need for getting money from them. I bring 10 or 20 and sometimes 50 or 100 rupees from my parents and hand over to my mother-in-law. The clothes which are for me I keep them and those for others I give to my mother-in-law to distribute.

> My mother-in-law buys clothes for me and my children when I need them. Mostly I wear the clothes which I bring from my parents' house. The school fee and for books, etcetera, parents-in-law pay. They make clothes for children, because I seldom bring clothes for children from my parents' house. We earn money and hand over it to the parents-in-law; therefore, they bear all the expenses for us.

> When I used to go to my parents' place then only my mother-in-law used to give me 4 or 5 rupees, which I used to give her back on my return from the parents' home. For the last 3 years she does not give me any money. I also keep whatever I bring from my parents with me for the last 3 years. The clothes I bring for me and my children I keep them and which I bring for other members of my in-laws' family I hand over to my mother-in-law.

> Mother-in-law does not keep any money with her. I keep everything with me because my mother-in-law has shifted this responsibility to me for the last 2 to 3 years. I distribute everything myself, whatever I bring from my parents.

> When I bring money from my parents I keep it with myself because my mother-in-law never gives me any money. She asks me to give the money, which I give but she never returns that money to me. Whatever I bring for myself I keep and the rest I give to my mother-in-law.

ATTITUDES CONCERNING CONTROL
OF DOWRY GOODS AND MONEY

Sasus complained that *bahus* now kept this money for themselves, instead of giving it to them as had been customary. This was a particularly difficult problem for widows, who could not get money from their husbands and whose parents were dead. A few widows found themselves in the traditional position of *bahus*, with no spending money. Some *sasus* commented as follows:

> Previously no *bahu* kept money with herself. Whatever they brought from their mothers' homes or from any other source, they used to hand over to the *sasu* and the *sasu* would spend the money on the *bahu* or anybody else. When a *bahu* gave money to her *sasu* or sister-in-law then they were responsible for the expenses of the *bahu*. But now, the *bahus* keep the money with themselves. Before if the *sasu* or husband's sister gave the *bahu* a gold ring or bangles or saris they would wear them, otherwise not. Now they keep money for these things. They also keep some money which they get from their husbands.
>
> Also, previously the grain that was stored in the house belonged to the *sasu*. The *bahu* had no right to take it or give it even to a beggar. Now they send some grain to the shop and they get money for it on their own. The world has grown clever now. Whatever *bahus* bring from their parents they keep with themselves because sooner or later they will have to separate and then they will be in need of everything, while previously they used to hand everything over to their *sasus*.

> My *sasu* gave everything from my dowry to my *jethani*. There was not even a head cloth left for me. Now the *bahus* keep everything from their dowry under lock and key and they keep the key with themselves. They do not give a single article of their dowry to any *jethani*, whereas I used to wear only what my *sasu* gave to me. Now I have no control over money; I have no control over the families; I just wait to see if somebody will give me food. I have lost my good times. I am a widow. Now that I have married my sons, I cook for myself and my unmarried son. My married *bahus* will not cook for me and I have no money of my own. No one gives me money. Even the money by *bahus* get from spinning they keep.

> Previously if there were four *bahus* they gave all the money to the *sasu*. The *sasu* might spend it on her daughter or her *bahu*. Now if the *bahu* gives the money to the *sasu*, and the *sasu* spends it on her own daughter, the *bahu* will slap her *sasu*. They keep control of the money now because they have grown greedy. If their *sasus* do give the money, their *bahus* say, "My *sasu* does not give me anything." Now the *bahus* want to take all the money for themselves and do not even give the *sasu* any food. If the money is kept by the elders they will spend it wisely from experience. If the money is divided among younger women this is bad because it will be wasted.

Thirty-one *bahus* were interviewed concerning their control over money and presents brought from their homes and their sources of cash while in Khalapur. Table 6.7 shows the tabulated results of the interview on control of dowry goods. All women reported that their *sasus* distributed their dowries when they first entered their husbands' homes. Most women still supported the control of dowry goods by *sasus*. They said that they did not want more control over their dowries (81%) and did not think their daughters should have more control over their dowries than they had (78%). However, some comments indicate that changes were occurring. The following answers express varying degrees of support for control of dowries:

> I did not want to have more control over my dowry. It is only the right of parents-in-law on the dowry of their sons. My daughter should not have control over her dowry. Though her *sasu* is dead someone else should have the control over her dowry.

I should not have any control over my dowry. When my parents-in-law are bearing all expenses for me and my children, then they should have the control over the dowry and *gauna* presents.

No, it is not good if the parents-in-law have control over the money brought by the daughter-in-law. The control should be with the parents-in-law until she is in the joint family but when my daughter is separated then all property should be controlled by her.

Parents-in-law should control the dowry. My aunt-in-law did everything and therefore she controlled my dowry. I should not have more control over it. Whatever she gave me to wear, I wore. Nowadays times are changed and daughters do want their own control over at least their own clothes and ornaments so that they can wear whatever they wish. Moreover, we give everything of choice to our daughters and if they cannot use them it is bad. Therefore, daughters should have that much control.

During our times, all right was of in-laws to utilize the dowry and I do not think I should have more control over my dowry, but now people give most things in *gauna* in the name of their daughter, instead of at the *shadi,* so that the daughter has more control over the dowry.

In the village if a daughter-in-law keeps control over her dowry and other property, people criticize her badly. Therefore, we usually do not say anything to our *sasu*. She may give anything to anybody from the dowry, even our own clothes and jewelry.

Q. But what would you like?

A. Yes, there should be more control of the daughter-in-law on her property and there are many daughters-in-law who keep everything of their dowry with themselves and do not let the *sasu* give anything to her daughters. But I have not kept anything because people criticize.

I want my daughter to have more control. I will teach her to say no to her *sasu* when the *sasu* wants things from her dowry.

Table 6.7 Control of Dowry Goods

1. When you brought your dowry, who decided how it was distributed?

	N	%
Sasu	31	100

2. Do you think you should have more control over the property you bring from your parents?

	N	%
Yes	5	16
No	25	81
NA	1	3
Total	31	100

3. Would you like your daugther to have more control over her dowry than you have/had?

	N	%
Yes	6	19
No	24	78
Other	1	3
Total	31	100

CONTROL OF HOUSEHOLD FINANCES

Aside from money from *bahu*s, most of the women's disposable money comes from the sale of grain. Most women use the grain stored in *bughar* rooms as a source of petty cash. Some women utilize two additional means of getting extra money—money lending and spinning.

Grain Sale

When women want to buy small items such as spices, condiments, soap, or candy from a village store and have no cash on hand, they take a small quantity of grain to the store to use in lieu of money. Children are usually sent on such errands, and some children take grain to buy candy from the store. A woman must have some control over the grain supply in order to do this, so women prefer to have some grain stored in their room, which they can draw on for this purpose. If grain is stored in a common bin, the *sasu* controls such purchases.

Moneylending

Usury in India commands very high interest rates. We have already reported the problems of some families who owed money. Some women also lend money, usually to low-caste servants. Since they are often unable to pay off the loan, interest may be collected almost indefinitely. Women who can afford to lend money may show a considerable profit. On one occasion during the winter of 1975, we visited a *bughar* where a *sasu* was loudly berating a silent, sulky Chamar man for not paying off the principal on his loan from her.

Spinning

Most Khalapur Rajput families raise cotton. Women gin the cotton balls with a hand roller and take the ginned cotton to the mill to be fluffed. The fluffed cotton is rolled into long, loose skeins and spun. Rajput women do not weave but instead exchange their thread for cloth with a village weaver or at the Gandhi ashram. At the ashram—established as part of Gandhi's effort to increase production of homespun cloth and decrease reliance on imported cloth—they may also sell thread for cash. The ashram was in operation in 1955, when most women wore white homespun saris; in 1975 flimsy, commercial cotton saris had become fashionable and were worn by most *bahu*s. We were told that the number of women spinning for the ashram had decreased in recent years because its price for thread had decreased, while its price for cloth had increased, although the cloth was inferior to that available in markets. Nevertheless, we observed that quite a few women earned a little money by spinning cotton for the ashram, and a few women spent most of their time spinning. Nine of the 42 women we interviewed spun cotton from their own fields, or old cotton from the fillings of quilts, and exchanged the thread with village weavers for cloth. The more common practice was to weave for the village Gandhi ashram.

Until 1970, spinners received 2.5 rupees cash and 2.5 rupees credit for 1 kilo of

Table 6.8 Number of Kilos of Cotton Spun per
Month for Gandhi Ashram

Kilos	Women		Rupees
	N	%	
0	13	31	—
1–2	21	50	.75–1.5
3–6	8	19	2.26–1.5
Total	42	100	

thread. In 1975 this had decreased to 2 rupees per kilo, plus 1 kilo of cotton to spin. In 1974 the ashram had introduced colored thread, which sold for 18 rupees per kilo; however, none of the women were spinning it. If spinners chose to take their payment in credit for ashram cloth, they received 2 rupees of credit and 1.5 kilos of cotton.

Since cloth was the most common article purchased with spinning money, some women took their payment in credit and gained the extra half kilo of spinning cotton. Ashram cloth was available only twice a year at the festivals of Diivalii in the fall and Holi in the spring. However, even inferior cloth sold for 4 rupees per meter, an increase of 0.5 rupees over the past several years. Printed cotton sold for 6 rupees per meter. The decreased profit from spinning had discouraged some women from continuing to spin.

Table 6.8 indicates that 29 women spun for the ashram, with 21 spinning an average of 1 to 2 kilos per month and 8 spinning an average of 3 to 6 kilos per month. One *nanad* reportedly spun 8 kilos during the months she visited her parents. Some *bahus* spun for as much as 4 to 6 hours per day. The 13 women who did not spin reported that they had no time for spinning after their household duties were performed.

Women who took their payment in cash earned from 0.75 to 4.5 rupees per month. The domestic buying power of a rupee was roughly equivalent to that of a dollar, so spinning provided women with a source of petty cash. If two *bahus* shared a *chuula,* they might take turns cooking so that one could spend most of her time spinning. A *bahu* who had her own *chuula* and a small family had more leisure than one who must cook for a joint family. Therefore, the availability of leisure time for spinning was an additional motivation for wanting separate *chuulas.*

Most women bought cloth with their spinning money, either for cash or on credit. Usually cloth for quilt covers, men's shirting, or shawls was purchased, but some women reported buying cloth for their petticoats or for children's clothes. Toiletries, soap, and cosmetics were the second most common type of purchase. A few women spent the money on spices or vegetables, while a number of others bought sweets and school supplies for their children.

CONCLUSIONS

Women's work had not changed significantly from 1955 to 1975. In general, the *sasu*s still directed the work of their *bahu*s. Despite the contention of some *sasu*s that their new *bahus* wanted separate *chuulas* so they could cook only for their own husbands and children, food was still stored in a common bin and cooked on a joint *chuula* in most *bughars*. Where *bahus* had separate *chuulas*, *sasus* shared their *chuula* with their youngest *bahu*. *Sasus'* concern about having someone cook for them in their old age, while not entirely unfounded, seemed to stem more from a fear of loss of respect than a fear that they would not be fed. *Bahus* who did not cook for their *sasus* did not expect this service from their future *bahus*. This younger generation considered the issue of cooking in terms of food, not respect, and anticipated this situation with pragmatism and humor, rather than anxiety.

Most *bahus* supported the control of dowry goods by *sasus* and did not want extensive changes in these arrangements; however, some would like more control and were teaching their daughters to protect their dowries. *Bahus* were more likely to keep money and clothing brought from their parents' homes than had been the case in previous years. In a few houses the *sasus* did not have money, while their *bahus* did. These *sasus* were usually widows from poor families.

Bahus still brought most of their clothing from their parents, although the increased availability of commercial cloth and cash allowed them to purchase some goods in Khalapur when needed. Money lending, grain sale, and spinning remained the major sources of additional income.

The strains in *sasu–bahu* relations sometimes surfaced in work assignments and control of household goods, but custom still provided the major guidelines for *bughar* economy.

IV

RELIGION

Chapter 7 presents the main outlines of Hinduism, its historical development, and its variation by region and caste. The creation myths forming the basis of the *varna* divisions, the belief in reincarnation of souls and worlds, and the major deities are described. The legends most pertinent to Rajputs, notably that of Sita and Ram in the Ramayana, are also emphasized. The shrines of Khalapur, including ancestor shrines, and local religious fairs are described in this chapter. The text emphasizes the literature concerning the Great Mother goddesses who, according to recent feminist scholars, are still prevalent in the worship of Indian villagers in the form of local goddesses and goddesses of disease.

Scholarly descriptions of Hinduism (and other religions) are typically written "from the top down," not "from the bottom up." That is, they tend to concentrate on analysis of the sacred texts. This approach is misleading for Hinduism since most villagers, particularly women, are not only illiterate but do not understand the Sanskrit prayers their family Brahmin man chants during his blessings. Western scholars are often uninterested in village religious practices, or simply unaware of them. Indian scholars may also be embarrassed by villagers' inarticulate accounts of their beliefs and practices. Furthermore, village Hindu practices vary across region, *jati*, as well as sex. The variation of beliefs and practices across locales and *jati* groups severely limits the usefulness of the fieldwork reports of other scholars.

This "top-down" procedure renders many reports on the worship of village men incomplete or biased. The difficulty in understanding the religious practices and beliefs of village women is compounded by the reluctance of men to provide information about women's activities and the inaccessibility of women to male field-workers. These combined restrictions of information have, in my opinion, resulted in a number of distortions concerning reports about village religion.

Chapter 8 describes the frequent calendrical festivals and the life-cycle rites of boys' birth ceremonies, marriages, and funerals. In addition to their religious and familial functions, these events provide most of the recreation of

Rajput women. When both the secular and sacred functions of festivals are discussed, it becomes clear that there is little distinction between the sacred and the secular for these traditional women. They interpret their world largely in religious terms, and rituals are an integral part of daily life. Adults start each and every day with washing. Women purify the *chuula* with a new coat of dung before starting to cook the morning meal. Family cows are greeted as honored household members. In addition to daily rituals of cleanliness, frequent feasts and festivals punctuate the daily routine with celebrations. Irrespective of their origins, traditional celebrations are regularly and carefully observed.

Chapter 8 concludes with a section on media and politics. We conducted an informal interview with women on the frequency of exposure to movies or radio programs and their preferences for subject matter. Although we contacted about 60 women, the interview was done in groups and the frequency of "no answer" was high for individual women. This section describes women's accounts of their participation in the political process, the frequency of their exposure to radio and movies, and their preferences for types of movies.

Two women make offerings to the family ancestor shrine in a mango grove on the outskirts of Khalapur. Because they had to walk through part of the village and down a road to reach the shrine, they are doubly veiled, with *chaddar*s covering their heads (1955).

7

The Pantheon: One Divinity,
Many Names

I see thee, Mighty Lord of all, revealed in forms of infinite diversity.
Bhagavad Gita

The earth is a big Shakti

Sita-Ram, Sita-Ram

The Hindu religious tradition has its roots in the cultures of the tribal aboriginals, the Dravidians, who settled in the Indus valley, sometime before 2000 B.C., and the Aryans, who invaded and conquered North India about 1500 B.C. These traditions have become so inextricably blended that their historical origins are often difficult to determine. Religious beliefs and practices vary by locale and caste. In this chapter I will outline the main sources and components of Hindu theology and describe Khalapur shrines as background for the description of the worship of the Rajput women in Khalapur.

Probably the earliest tradition is the worship of Mother Earth and her attributes, such as rivers, trees, and the land itself. In villages throughout India, local goddesses are closer to the hearts of the people than the distant gods of the Vedas; the gods reign in mythology and theology, but the worship of the mother goddesses is the heart of Hinduism. The origins of this worship are lost in the mists of time. The great goddess whose origins have been traced to early Neolithic peoples is still an integral part of Hinduism.

Dravidians, who came from Asia Minor, lived in fortified cities, had a rich artistic tradition, used copper, silver, and some bronze, and domesticated dogs, cats, the humped cattle still used today, sheep, asses, horses, elephants, and some camels. Their skeletons are of a Mongoloid type. Only fragments of their writing have been found; thus, our knowledge of them comes from archaeological finds at Harappa and Mohenjo-Daro. There are many pottery figures of high quality at these sites, as well as utilitarian pots and bricks that were mass-produced. The Dravidians had a system of weights and measures, and the size of their bricks and utilitarian pots was standardized. The city planning and architecture indicate that the Harappa civilization was organized under a strong central government that controlled the production and distribution of goods. The presence of large granaries indicates that agricultural production was under central control. Undoubtedly there was a system of taxation.

Women were housed in separate quarters, and the presence of rows of identical small, two-room houses suggests a class of slaves or serfs. These features are similar to those of contemporary Indian society, and some scholars think that the Indian caste system had its origins in this Dravidian culture.

Figures of a snake god, and some phalluses, thought to be an early version of Siva, have also been found at these sites. Many figures of goddesses with short skirts and serpents have been found in the ancient Indus valley sites of Harappa and Mohenjo-Daro, indicating that goddess worship was practiced by Dravidians. The prevalence of these goddess figures in the ruins of Mohenjo-Daro led Marshall to conclude that the veneration of goddesses in modern India is of pre-Aryan origin. This opinion is substantiated by the fact that contemporary worship of mother goddesses is most prevalent among the Dravidians in South India, who were not conquered by the Aryan invaders. Marshall's comment on Indian goddess worship is as follows:

> In no country in the world has the worship of the Divine Mother been so deep and ubiquitous as in India. Her shrines are found in every town and hamlet throughout the land. . . . She is the prototype of the village Goddesses who one and all are the personifications of the same power like the Mother Goddesses of Western Asia they originated in a matriarchal state of society is a highly reasonable supposition.
>
> (Marshall, 1931, p. 111)

This reverence for the land, symbolized by an Earth Mother Goddess, presumably dates to pre-Vedic times and is also expressed in the Vedic texts. Reverence for an Earth Goddess is expressed poetically in the Atharvaveda in a passage that conveys the immanent aspect of Mother Goddesses noted earlier. Unlike the remote male sky god of Judaism and Christianity, the Great Earth Mother is omnipresent in all living things: "The earth has her hillsides and her uplands, hers is the wide plain, she is the bearer of plants of many uses: may she stretch out her hand and be bountiful to us." (Atharvaveda, XII, i).

The activities of Hindu goddesses are not confined to the domestic arts and child care. Like the muses and goddesses of ancient Greece, Hindu goddesses are associated with a variety of cultural endeavors, because their fertility is symbolic of all creative activity. As fertility deities they may be drawn or sculpted copulating or giving birth, but Madonna figures of a mother and dependent child are rare. Virtually all Hindu goddesses are called "mother" even when, like the disease goddesses, they do not have children. Unlike the Virgin Mary, who is called the mother of God but never God the Mother, the Hindu goddesses have the status of Goddess the Mother, equal in most ways to the status of their consorts. Like their male counterparts, the natures of the goddesses exhibit opposing traits; like real mothers, goddesses may be nurturing or punitive. This dual aspect of the goddesses recognizes the power of mothers over their children.

The invasions of Aryans, seminomadic horsemen from the Iranian plateau, began to come through the Hindu Kush about 1500 B.C. The Aryan invasion coincided with the end of the Harappa civilization, suggesting that the Indus valley people were conquered by these new invaders. These Aryans spread throughout North India and are the ancestors of most of its present population. They were a warlike people whose social structure comprised four major groups: priests, warriors and rulers, businessmen, and menial workers. This division of labor and status is characteristic of ancient societies of the Middle East and of Europe through the feudal period, and is still the basis of Indian social structure.

These Aryans spoke an Indo-European language, written in the Sanskrit alphabet, that is the basis of modern Hindu. They had a number of sacred texts, composed by different authors, at different times and places. The most important texts, forming the primary basis of Hindu theology, include the Vedas, the code of Manu, the Upanishads, the Puranas, the Ramayana, the Mahabharata, and the Bhagavad Gita. The core text—the Rg Veda—is presumed to be the oldest because all other texts presuppose its existence and often consist of commentary on it.

For centuries these sacred texts were passed from teacher to pupil by the Brahmin priests in an oral tradition that forbade writing them. Often teachers and pupils were illiterate. During these centuries of oral transmission, deities assumed new names, sometimes local, sometimes coming from post-Vedic writings. It is said that Siva and Vishnu each have 1,000 names, and the same is true of goddesses. In addition, multitudes of minor gods have grown out of the thousands of years of Hindu mythology. The Aryan gods were primarily male, and the earlier goddesses gradually became the consorts of these new gods, as they did in Greek mythology. However, all of the major Hindu deities are essentially androgynous in nature. Their portrayal as husbands and wives is an artistic device; they are ultimately a union of Purusha, the male principle, and Prakriti, the female principle. Furthermore, these Indic goddesses are usually the more active member of the couple and are not necessarily subservient to their "husbands."

Brubaker describes the historical process of goddess transformation as follows:

Originally seminomadic, the Aryans were an aggressive people. And as their sacred texts, the Vedas, show, the deities they invoked were overwhelmingly male. . . .

There were other peoples, many of them tribal, in India when the Aryans arrived, and the history of ensuing cultural interactions is complex and not fully understood. But there is increasing evidence of continuity, including linguistic continuity, between the Indus Valley civilization and the Dravidian culture of the South. The emergence of Goddesses as major figures in later Hinduism reflects an ongoing interaction between Aryan and non-Aryan elements. But the humbler folk Goddesses in regions outside the Aryan heartland seem to have been present, in one form or another, for millennia. . . .

In India, village Goddesses tend to be rare or of minor importance only in

regional strongholds of a vigorously male-oriented faith. And the same is broadly
true for other Goddesses as well, with the notable exception of those praised as
dutiful wives of their divine lords. Nor is India the only place where the female
aspect of the divine has suffered such a fate.

(Brubaker, 1988, p. 149)

Khalapur lies in the "Aryan heartland" where Brubaker says ancient goddesses
have been suppressed. Furthermore, Rajputs, who trace their mythical descent to
Ram, hero of the Vedic epic Ramayana, and who still maintain much of their
warrior tradition, emphasize the warrior Vedic gods. Nevertheless, I found that local
goddesses played an important part in the religious beliefs and ceremonies of Rajput
women. In my opinion, scholars have overestimated the diminution of goddess
worship by concentrating on sacred texts and the religious practices of men. Women
continue to worship female deities in Khalapur, and probably elsewhere. Kinsley
recognizes this bias in his book *The Goddesses' Mirror:*

The texts upon which we are usually forced to base our pictures of these religions
(especially in the case of dead cultures) are androcentric. The elite religion tends to
play down certain aspects of popular religion (which may include a strong emphasis
of Goddess worship) that challenge, or differ from its elitist (and male) biases. The
popular tradition (often nonliterate), on the other hand, is more revealing of the
religious experience of those who are excluded from the elite (usually women) and
therefore may be more centered in the worship of the Goddess, whose importance
may be central for women.

(Kinsley, 1989, p. xix)

Hindus also believe in the balancing of forces, including male and female. One
myth says that Prakriti, the eternal female principle, representing substance and
nature, and the source of the female energy Shakti, united with Purusha, the eternal
male principle, representing the spiritual realm. The entire universe, including the
gods, was created by their union. Sensual reality is thought to be Maya, or illusion;
the only true reality is the invisible spiritual realm. The ease with which the sex and
identity of deities move from one mode to another, and the enigmatic nature of these
descriptions, are exemplified in a reference to Bhagwan in the Bhagavad Gita: "I
see thee mighty Lord of all, revealed in forms of infinite diversity." These descriptions of the goddess and Brahma are poetic representations of the "infinite diversity." The diversity of representation of Hindu deities has led some Western scholars
to conclude that Hindus are polytheistic. It is more accurate to say they are worshipers of a manifold deity. All Hindu deities are manifold. Unlike the Olympian
and Norse deities, Hindu deities are not located in one place, nor do they have a
clearly described social structure. This essential difference from Western conceptions of the deity must be appreciated in order to comprehend Hindu thought.

The sacred texts represent the elite Hindu theology. Understandably, simple,
illiterate people require more concrete and comprehensible representations of their
deities. Artistic portrayals of deities, in painting and sculpture, abound throughout

India, and vary by time and location. Over the centuries, the iconography of deities proliferated, and the portrayal of Hindu deities as figures with many arms developed to enable the deity to hold all of the icons associated with the god or goddess.

Rajput women refer to the images of Kali in the local temples of Bhudana and Durga, at Shakumbrii, as the Bhudana and Shakumbrii goddesses, either because they do not know their more global name or because such accuracy of naming is not important to them. The women I knew usually referred to God as Ram. It was Ram's name they repeated the first thing in the morning and in saying one's prayers. When I told an inquiring woman that the English name for Ram was God, she took this to be a translation, explaining to another woman that the Muslim name for Ram was Allah, and the Christian name for Ram was God. In Hindu thought the names and identities of the gods and goddesses merge and separate; they are all manifestations of one supreme being, and their personified images are themselves Maya.

THE TRIMURTI

The Hindu religion has three major gods—Brahma, Vishnu, and Siva—known collectively as the *Trimurti*. Brahma is the god of creation, Vishnu the god of preservation, and Siva the god of destruction. The Trimurti is usually portrayed as one figure with three faces on one head.

Each of the major gods has a female consort who is worshiped in conjunction with or separately from the male god. The goddesses are typically the energetic aspects of the gods. It is the goddesses who possess Shakti, the primal energy of life. These consorts are known by several names but are always manifestations of the same entity. Brahma's consort is Sarasvati, the goddess of wisdom, or Maya, goddess of form and substance; Vishnu's consort is Lakshmi, goddess of wealth, and prosperity; and Siva's consort is Durga, or Kali, the warrior goddesses.

All of these major deities have animals or plants associated with them, and they are frequently depicted riding on their sacred animals. Brahma rides the goose, Sarasvati, the peacock, Vishnu the Garuda (half man, half bird), Lakshmi the elephant or cow, Siva the bull, Nandi the serpent, and Durga the lion or tiger. Vishnu, Brahma, and Lakshmi may also be depicted riding on lotus blossoms, the symbol of spiritual purity and power.

Although Siva is primarily the god of destruction, he is also the god of fertility and is typically represented in Siva temples by a statue of lingam (penis) rising out of the base of the yoni (womb, or vagina). Although this image is usually referred to simply as "the lingam," it always rests on a yoni base. The yoni is most frequently represented in the shape of an oil lamp, with four ridges in the pointed end, separated by three grooves. These ridges are described as the four heads of Siva's serpent or as the labia major and minor. When worshipers pour their offerings of milk or *ghi* over the lingam, the liquid flows through the yoni ridges into a basin surrounding the figure. The lingam–yoni represents the cosmic union; in its design the male principle rises out of the female principle. Sometimes Siva and Vishnu are portrayed as androgynous figures, half male and half female.

Vishnu is born to earthly form in 10 avatars, or lifetimes, sometimes as a man and sometimes as an animal. Lakshmi is born as his consort for each avatar. The two avatars most celebrated and most noted in mythology are Ram, the mythical ancestor of Rajputs, with his wife, Sita, and Krishna, with his mistress, Radha, and his wife, Rukmini. In mythology and iconography Krishna appears as a mischievous boy who steals butter from his mother, as a youth who is the lover of the Gopis (milkmaids), and Radha, and in the Mahabharata as the charioteer of Arjuna. Krishna's advice to Arjuna on the eve of a major battle is the text of the Bhagavad Gita, one of the most popular of the sacred texts.

Although the Trimurti is usually portrayed as the three male deities, Brahmin, Vishnu and Siva are androgynous, in that each has female consorts. These consorts are portrayed as wives or lovers in art and mythology, but all are ultimately the Prakriti that complements the Purusha of the deity. Contemporary descriptions of the Vedic goddesses usually classify them as consorts of either Siva or Vishnu. (Brahma sleeps between creations of successive worlds and, although important, is said to have only two temples in India.)

CREATION AND RE-CREATION

Hindu mythology gives conflicting accounts of the creation of the world. While some texts say that Brahma issued from an egg, the most frequent creation paintings show him sitting on a lotus that is growing out of Vishnu's navel. Vishnu is depicted, with his consort, Lakshmi, reclining on a tortoise that floats on a sea of milk, the life-giving fluid of the Great Mother. A great seven-headed serpent rises above them and shades them. A popular creation myth says that Vishnu and the other gods used this cosmic serpent to churn the sea of milk, resting it on the cosmic tortoise; their aim was to extract the nectar of immortality from the milky sea. Lakshmi emerges from their stirring and becomes Vishnu's consort. This myth recognizes that the source of life is maternal, in this case mother's milk.

The major *varna* divisions that form the basis of the caste system are set down in the origin myth of mankind. The four main *varna* divisions arose from four parts of the body of the cosmic man, Purusha. The Brahmins, the learned men, and the priests were formed from his head; the Kashatriyas, the rulers and soldiers, from his arms; the Vaish, the merchants, from his body; and the Sudras, or working class, from his feet. Outcaste groups are not mentioned in this myth. This omission is one basis for the scholarly assumption that outcastes descended from the indigenous tribal populations with whom the Aryan invaders had contact after these texts were written.

The conception of immortality is a second essential difference between Christianity and Hinduism. Hindus believe in one supreme world soul, present in all living things, into which all human souls will merge when freed from the cycle of rebirth. Whereas Christians desire eternal personal immortality, Hindus desire to lose themselves in union with this supreme world soul. Souls are reborn through successive lives, starting in the form of animals and working up to the highest of castes, the Brahmins.

Karma (fate) determines one's position in each lifetime. Karma is based on correct fulfillment of dharma (duties) in past lives. It is the duty of every Hindu to fulfill the obligations of whatever caste he is born into. Fulfilling these obligations earns good karma and results in rebirth into a better life; failure to fulfill obligations earns bad karma and results in regression in the cycle of rebirth. The ideas of karma and dharma are one with the fiber of the caste system. As one village man put it: "When there is no caste there will be no dharma and karma."

The village women I talked to conceived of reincarnation simply as successive endless rebirths without eventual release. Along with the belief in reincarnation was a conception of both a heaven and a hell as places through which the soul passes on the way to the next birth. Their ideas about the kind of life one would be born into, depending on one's present virtue, were varied. Some thought that they would be born up into higher castes; some merely thought that they would have a better, more comfortable, richer life in the next incarnation if they were virtuous in this one. One girl thought that the best thing that could happen would be to be born back into the same house that you had lived in previously. Some of the women thought that you could be reborn as animals, and others thought not. There seemed to be fairly general feeling that one's virtues and faults would be preserved in successive incarnations, that if one were a thief, for instance, one would continue to be a thief in the next life. The most amusing example of such a belief is the following story:

> Once there was a man and his wife who kept fighting with each other. When they were born again the husband was a donkey and his wife was a crow. The crow kept sitting on the donkey and pecking at it.

A third major difference between Western and Indian thought is the conception of time. Westerners, from the time of the Greeks, have conceived of time as linear; for Hindus it is circular. Hindus believe that the world, as well as people, is reincarnated endlessly, controlled by Kali, the goddess of time. Each world incarnation is divided into four stages, or yugas, with each stage less ideal and shorter than its predecessor. The first stage is the Golden Age, when Rama ruled. Whereas Hindus and ancient Greeks share a belief in a golden age, for Hindus that age will reappear in endless cycles of time.

Hindus believe that we are now living in the Kali Yuga, or Iron Age, ruled by the dread goddess Kali. Hindu fatalism and pessimism are sometimes expressed in statements that life in the Kali Yuga is destined to be hard. More optimistic views hold that the independence of India ushered in a second golden age. However, since the world was not destroyed in 1947, these views do not conform to Hindu theology.

The Golden Age lasts for 1,728,000 years; the Silver Age for 1,290,000 years; the Copper Age for 864,000 years; and the Iron Age for 36,000 human years, for a total of 432,000 years. A village song describes the horrors of the Kali Yuga in terms of some social ills that are embodied in modernization, including the break-down of the extended family and loyalty among brothers, the demise of the loyalty of servants under the *jajmani* system, the participation of daughters in marriage arrangements, and, worst of all, the decline of religion and the rule of women. It is understandable that women raised with a tradition that includes this song of Kali Yuga are anxious about changes in their traditional way of life.

> The daughter will say, "Find a bridegroom for me or I shall kill myself."
> The atmosphere will topple so much that religion will be untraceable.
> Oh, such bad things will happen that women will rule.
>
> Oh, such bad things will happen that brother will entrap his brother.
> Oh, there will be such a fight that brother will kill brother.
> The atmosphere will topple so much that religion will be untraceable.
> Oh, such bad things will happen that women will rule.
>
> The Kaliyuga will bring a time when workers will come only to make money.
> Hospitality will be given to the helpful one and he will be dashed after the
>   problem is solved.
> The atmosphere will topple so much that religion will be untraceable.
> Oh, such bad things will happen that women will rule.

In summary, there are three major differences between Hindu and Western thought, the manifold nature of their deities, the belief in the reincarnation of individual souls and worlds, and the ideal of final loss of personal identity. These three beliefs combine to produce values and ways of thought that give Hindu beliefs their distinctive character.

SIVA'S CONSORTS
Sati

An important version of the goddess is Sati, meaning chaste or virgin. Sati is the embodiment of Shakti and one with India itself. According to the myth, the goddess sets out to win Siva for her husband. She becomes an ascetic like Siva, and her devotion wins his love. Sati's father, Daksa, thinks that this unkempt hermit who lives in the forest is not a suitable husband for his daughter. Shortly after the marriage, Daksa holds an important sacrifice and invites all the notable divinities except Siva. Although Siva ignores his omission from the festival, Sati is furious. She goes to her father, and when he snubs her, kills herself to protest the insult to her husband. When Siva hears of her death he is so distraught that his grief threatens the world's stability. Vishnu is summoned to save the world. He does so by dismembering Sati's body and distributing it around India. When Siva finds that Sati's body is gone, he stops grieving and resumes his godly meditations. Sati's body becomes the Indian subcontinent and renders its land sacred. Sati was also reborn as the goddess Parvati, who may also transform herself into the goddesses Durga and Kali. Sati has given her name to those virtuous wives who practice self-immolation on their husbands' funeral pyres, and widows who practiced this custom do so in the belief that they are following her example.

Vina Mazumdar, whose family still preserves the story of the sati of her great-great-grandmother, comments on the importance of the sati tradition for the self-esteem of Indian women.

> Social scientists may seek anthropological origins for these myths in pre-Aryan rites and symbols, but this is the stuff on which traditional Hindu women are bred, from which they drew their strength to endure and overcome whatever life had in store for them. A woman's virtue lay in cleaving to one man, but the anticipated result was gain in strength and power to protect one's progeny, not the loss of one's personal freedom. Personal freedom, by Hindu logic, is impossible and unreal as long as one lives in society. To obtain personal freedom one must abandon communal living and all possessions and become a wandered, which is quite appropriate in old age, but not during one's youth or prime of life.
>
> (Mazumdar, 1978, p. 272)

Durga-Kali

Sati is reborn and reunited with Siva in the form of the warrior goddess Durga. Like Parvati, Durga dwells in the mountains. She represents the untamed aspect of Siva. Durga's origin seems to be non-Aryan, and in early texts she is described as independent of any god. She aids Brahma and Vishnu in fighting demons. Like Vishnu, she comes in several avatars and her identity sometimes merges with that of Vishnu. In painting and sculpture, Durga is usually depicted riding a lion or a tiger.

Durga assumes her fiercest aspect in the goddess Kali, who makes her first appearance around A.D. 600 during the early medieval period. Kali is sometimes described as Durga's helper and sometimes as Durga herself. Kali, "the dark one," probably has pre-Vedic origins. She is the personification of a wild tribal woman. Light skin, as we have seen, is the hallmark of beauty for Aryan Indians. Kali is always described as dark, but often as beautiful, suggesting that she comes from a Dravidian tradition. Kali is the goddess of time who reigns supreme in the Kaliyuga and finally causes the destruction of the world. Statues and pictures of Kali show her as a fearsome goddess. Indeed no major god is portrayed in as bloody and aggressive an aspect as Kali.

> Kali, whose name means "the Black One" is commonly described as being dark as night, naked and standing on a corpse in the cremation grounds, surrounded by jackals, snakes and ghosts. She has four arms; her four hands variously hold a bloody sword, a noose or goad, a freshly severed head, and a cup made from half of a human skull, filled with blood. From her neck hangs a garland of human or demon heads; newly cut arms dangle from her waistband; and two dead infants form her earrings. With sunken belly, sagging breasts, and disheveled hair, she stares forward with her three bloodshot eyes, a fitting complement to her gaping mouth with its large fangs, lolling tongue, and blood trickling out of the corner.
>
> (Mackenzie Brown, 1988, p. 111)

Despite her gruesome appearance, Kali protects the innocent and is usually addressed as "Mother." Kali represents Mother Nature in both her nurturing and destructive aspects. Just as nature's storms, drought, and diseases are unpredictable, so is the nature of Kali. Because she is all-powerful, worshipers must return to her, just as children return to their angry mothers.

VISHNU'S CONSORTS

Vishnu's divine consort is Lakshmi, goddess of wealth and prosperity. In some myths Lakshmi is paired with the god Dharma. She also dwells with demons in some stories and is associated with Kubera, lord of the demons. Her association with Vishnu comes in the story of the churning of the sea of milk. When Vishnu assumes an *avatara* (earthly manifestation), Lakshmi assumes an *avatara* as his wife. The *avatara*s of Lakshmi who figure most prominently in the contemporary worship of Rajput women in Khalapur are Sita and Radha.

Sita

The goddess of most importance to Rajput women is Sita, the wife of Ram, from whom they trace their mythical descent. Sita is an Earth Goddess who arises from the earth at birth and returns to the earth at her death. In the Ramayana, her father, King Janaka, says that Sita emerged from a furrow while he was ploughing the earth in a place where sacrifices were made. The king was childless and took Sita home and raised her as his daughter. She is sometimes called "furrow born" or "earth born."

The Ramayana epic tells the story of Sita and Rama. Rama is the son of King Devaratha, king of Ayodhya, and his wife, Kausalya. Rama and his brothers, Lakshmana, Bharata, and Shatrughna, are an *avatara* of Vishnu. In the beginning of the story, Rama wins Sita for his bride. His father retires and designates Rama as his regent. His wife, Kaikeyi, the mother of Bharata and Shatrughna, wants her son Bharata to have the throne, and she forces Devaratha to banish Rama to the forest for 14 years. Lakshmana and Sita go with him. The demon Ravena abducts Sita and takes her to his kingdom Lanka, said to be Sri Lanka. Rama and Lakshmana, assisted by millions of monkeys, notably the warrior god Hanuman, wage a great war to regain Sita.

Ravena has been cursed if he ever violently attacks a woman, so Sita is protected from him during her imprisonment. Nevertheless, when Rama reclaims her, he disowns her publicly to test her virtue, because he knows that his followers will mistrust her. When Rama bids Sita farewell, she defends her honor and demands to be tested by fire:

> "I came from the House of King Janaka. King Dasharatha was my father-in-law. You are my Lord and know me well. Knowing me as you do, how can you torture me like this? In my childhood, I played with children, but never touched a boy. Only here I have been touched by the sinful Ravena. Why do you take me to be a common woman? Why did you not disown me when you sent Hanuman? If you

had, I would have taken poison or entered fire. The monkey troops suffered much in bridging the ocean and you have suffered greatly in this battle. After having done this you disown me? Born of the race of Sages, I came to the Solar race and this was destined for me? Vain is my life. I am not a dancing girl that you should make a gift of me to others. You insult me in open court. Lakshmana, kindly do me a favor. Prepare a pit of fire for me and all slanders shall cease."

Lakshmana looked at Rama.

"Prepare the pit," said Rama. "Sita's life is not needed at all. Let her be burnt in the fire and her shame removed."

(Ramayana, bk. 11, pp. 184–185)

Sita speaks to the fire before entering it, saying:

"Listen, O Fire, thou knowest the sins and merits of mankind for long. If in body, mind and speech, I have been a true and virtuous wife, then O Fire, from thee I shall remain unharmed."

(Ramayana, bk. 11, p. 185)

Brahma summons Agni, the god of fire, who enters the fire, rescues Sita, and testifies in her behalf.

"I am the witness of good and evil. Nothing is concealed from me. No one can deceive me. But I see no sin in Sita. Rama, I glory today in having touched so virtuous a woman. Cause no grief to Sita for if she were to curse your kingdom, it would surely perish."

(Ramayana, bk. 11, pp. 186–187)

Rejoicing, Rama returns with Sita to Ayodhya, where they live in peace for many years. Then a rumor starts among the people that Rama should not have taken back a wife who had spent a year with another man. When Rama hears two washermen talking of this disgrace, he banishes Sita to the forest, where she gives birth to two sons, Lava and Kusa. When they are grown they decide to make war on Rama and kill him. Rama, restored to life, recalls Sita and his sons to Ayodhya.

However, Rama must again deal with the suspicions of the people. He decides to make Sita undergo a second fire test before the court of Ayodhya. This humiliation is too much for Sita's pride to bear, and her patience is exhausted. Finally, her honor means more to her than her beloved husband. She calls upon Mother Earth to claim her and leaves Rama to mourn, as Siva mourned Sati.

The chariot halted. Sita stepped down. Her loveliness was such that it lighted up the court. Approaching Rama, she bowed low before his feet.

Then Valmiki said to Rama:

"I am the son of Chabyan and am known by the name of Valmiki. Listen to me Rama, I pray. By the knowledge I have gained by penance and prayers, I know there is no sin in Sita. She is matchless in virtue, pure and excellent. Lava and Kusa are her sons. What trial do you intend to hold? Rama, do not disbelieve my words.

Take her to your home and give your two sons their rightful place." Valmiki trembled with emotion as he finished his speech.

Rama, with folded hands, replied:

"O Muni, full well I know of the excellence of Sita. She was tried by Fire in Lanka, and the Gods were witness. Speak no more O great Sage. Although I know there is no sin in Sita, yet I must try her once more before this court of Ayodhya, and my people. Sita, listen to me," said Rama, turning to the beloved figure before him, "your trial was first over the seas, my people did not see it. You must be tested once more before all."

At this, Sita with folded hands said slowly:

"O lord of the Raghu race, all know the place of gentlewomen is in the safety and privacy of their homes, and being one, yet am I thus brought forth before this assembly to stand another trial. I was tried once before, the Gods were present and you heard what they said. You gave me hopes, brought me home and then suddenly banished me. Although I am a high born lady, I lived in the forest, and in a hermitage passed my days in fasting and prayers. Now, you have commanded me to come to this open court and undergo a second ordeal by fire. You are said to possess every merit and to be wise in judgement. Consider how you insult me by ordering this second trial. Since I have no place in my husband's or father's home, I have no desire to live. I shall take myself away from your sight and thus do away with all your burdens. From today, may all your shame and grief be removed. You will never see the face of the Daughter of Janaka again. Farewell Lord, may I have thee as my husband again in my next birth, but do not treat me like this."

And Sita bowed low before Rama. All heard her speech.

"Mother Earth!" cried Sita in sorrow and shame, as she clasped her hands. "Mother mine, do a mother's duty. A daughter's shame is cast on her mother as well. I beg thee to grant me sanctuary at thy feet."

Sita's anguished cry reached Vasumati, the Goddess of the Earth, and she hastened to rescue her child. With a great rumble the ground before Rama's throne cracked and parted, and from beneath rose a jewelled throne held on the head of Ananta, the Thousand Headed Serpent. On the throne, in resplendent robes and dazzling jewels, was the regal figure of Mother Earth.

"Daughter!" called Vasumati once again, and Sita turned and cast herself in her mother's arms and buried her face in the bosom of the Shining One. Clasping Sita in her arms, Vasumati cried as she turned to Rama:

"For the sake of your people, you want to make my daughter undergo yet another trial! Be happy with your people. I take my child away with me."

Sita never looked at her sons, but only on Rama. . . .

Rama, who had been like one in a trance, now uttered a great cry and leaped forward with eager hands to snatch back his beloved, but alas, it was too late. With a mighty noise the Earth opened once more and the jewelled throne bearing Vasumati and Sita disappeared. In Rama's hand was left only a long silky lock of dark, scented hair.

(Mazumdar, 1953, pp. 265–267)

Sita, obedient, long-suffering, and above all honorable, is considered the ideal wife throughout India and is particularly cherished by the Rajput women who believe themselves to be descendants of this royal couple. Rama, in turn, is regarded as an ideal husband and ruler, who puts the concerns of his people before compassion for his beloved wife. The importance of sons is exemplified in Rama's acceptance of Sita after discovering that she had given birth to Lava and Kusa.

Radha

While Sita is the ideal wife, obedient to the customs of society, Radha, a married woman, defies custom to pursue her passionate affair with Krishna. Krishna is a dark-skinned tribal hero, associated with the Pandavas of the Mahabharata, themselves a tribal group.

> Radha, like Sita, is understood primarily in relation to a male consort. Throughout her history Radha has been inextricably associated with the God Krsna. Unlike Sita, however, Radha's relationship to Krsna is adulterous. Although she is married to another, she is passionately attracted to Krsna. Radha's illicit relationship with Krsna breaks all social norms and casts her in the role of one who willfully steps outside the realm of dharma to pursue her love. In contrast to Sita, who is the model of wifely devotion and loyalty, whose foremost concern is the reputation and well-being of her husband, Radha invests her whole being in an adulterous affair with the irresistibly beautiful Krsna.
>
> (Kinsley, 1986, p. 81)

This passionate affair was reinterpreted by later writers as a metaphor for devotion to God, a reinterpretation similar to that of the biblical Song of Solomon. In this revision Radha becomes an aspect of Krishna, just as Kali is an aspect of Siva.

The multiplicity of the nature of the Vedic deities is evident in their change of identities and associations as portrayed in different texts. The major deities are honored at major ceremonies, observed by most Hindus. In addition to honoring these deities, villagers worship local goddesses, saints, and ancestors.

SACRED PLACES, SACRED PLANTS, SACRED ANIMALS
Sacred Rivers

All rivers have a sacred status in Hinduism. They bear the water essential for agriculture, drinking, cooking, and cleanliness. Ashes of cremated bodies are put into a nearby river for final purification. Worshipers bathe in temple ponds before presenting their offerings, and make pilgrimages to holy cities on the banks of rivers to bathe in the cleansing waters and wash away their sins. The Ganges, the most sacred of India's rivers, is not far from Khalapur. Hardwar, the city where the Ganges, flowing from the mountains, enters the plains, is the holy city nearest to Khalapur and the one most frequently visited. The Ganges is thought to originate in heaven and is sometimes represented as a goddess.

Sacred Plants

Some plants are sacred to Hindus, especially the basil bush, which is grown in most of the courtyards. Basil is sacred to Vishnu, and the women have a song about the basil bush: "Where basil is standing, there Krishna was born. / Ghosts surround the courtyard where God is not and where the basil is not growing." Some women said that the basil bush was a Brahmin girl who had been miraculously turned into the bush while escaping a Muslim man who had kidnapped her. A fig tree, in one of the mango groves, thought to have been a Brahmin man, is worshiped on the festival of Ekadsi. Some of the fig trees are believed to be the abodes of ghosts.

Sacred Animals

The most important of the sacred animals is, of course, the cow. Women said that the cow was sacred because they could not live without it: They needed the bullocks to plow their fields and the cows to give them milk and cow dung for fuel. The practice of serving milk to guests arises from the fact that the cow, and hence the milk, is sacred. It is therefore considered to be an honor to serve milk to one's guests and a disgrace not to have milk or a cow in the house. Bulls also have a sacred status because of Siva's bull, Nandi.

The second most important sacred animal is the monkey, associated with the monkey god Hanuman, who assisted Ram in his many exploits of the Ramayana. There was a herd of rhesus monkeys in the mango groves near Khalapur, and the village women would sometimes scatter grain to the monkeys in these groves.

Snakes, associated with both Siva and Vishnu, are sacred and have their own festival called Naag Panchmi, which comes in September, about the same time as the Sanjii festival. The day honors snakes and protects the family from them. (Cobras are found in the Khalapur area, so concern for protection from snakes is serious.) Women shape dough into figures of a male and a female snake, then fry the figures and leave them in the bushes or fields. This is done so that the snakes will live with their figures and not come into the houses.

All of the animals associated with deities have a sacred status. Some, like the tiger and swan, are not indigenous to the Khalapur area. When such animals were in the vicinity they were treated with special reverence. Bulls, while not as sacred as cows, command reverence because of Siva's bull, Nandi. The peacocks nesting in the mango groves are never disturbed, although they eat some of the mangoes, because they are the steed of Sarasvati.

CONCLUSIONS

Formal religious training, which has been restricted to a few high-caste men throughout the centuries, has consisted largely of oral memorization. Few men and fewer women can read the ancient Sanskrit texts. The religious beliefs and practices of villagers stem from diverse sources and traditions. Hinduism provides more variety in mythological role models than does Christianity, Judaism, or Islam, and Hindus are not usually concerned with deviation from orthodoxy, which might be condemned as heresy in less tolerant religious traditions. Since they trace their mythical ancestry to Ram, Rajputs particularly cherish the stories of the Ramayana, but the entire Hindu pantheon is part of their heritage.

Like ordinary folk of most religions, village women do not know or care about the diverse personalities represented by their deities. All goddesses, mythical heroines, and Satis embody Shakti, the female energy that is the essence of woman's nature. Shakti, present in all women, unites them with their goddesses and heroines and sustains them in their subservient roles. They give Sita, the obedient wife, Radha, the passionate adulteress, and the untamed village goddesses (described in chapter 8) their due at their respective festivals. As Mazumdar says, these legends are indeed the stuff on which they are bred and from which their derive their strength.

Ultimately the identities of all of the manifold Hindu deities merge into one. Women refer to goddesses by the name of their temple town, much as Catholics might do for patron saints. This merging of identities is probably greater for goddesses—particularly local goddesses—than for the major gods, whose identities have been solidified in Vedic literature. Kurtz (1992) emphasizes this point for goddesses in his book *All of the Mothers Are One*, comparing the merging of mother goddesses with the merging of mother figures in extended households.

Women sit and talk before a Sanjii figure of their *bughar*. A milk *chuula* and two pots are in a corner of the courtyard (1955).

8

Ritual and Recreation

We cook halwar and puri.

Men and women are separated in their religious worship, as they are in their secular lives. When I arrived in Khalapur in 1955, I was immediately recruited by John Hitchcock, the project field director, who had found that many ceremonies are performed only by women, to record women's religious ceremonies and interview women about them. Purdah restrictions prevented him or other men from entering the *bughar* courtyards to observe these ceremonies, and the men he asked about them said they knew nothing about women's ceremonies. After I had participated in a few of the women's household ceremonies, it was obvious that boys under the age of 14 or 16, who had not yet shifted their residence to the *choopars* were usually present along with the women and the younger children. It seemed clear that the men must have remembered details of ceremonies from their own childhoods but simply would not talk about women's activities.

I was able to observe and participate in these ceremonies without difficulty, but interviewing women about them was almost impossible, then and again in 1975. Women had only the vaguest ideas about the origins of their ceremonies, and these varied from woman to woman. Even the Brahmin woman who painted the Hooii goddess on the bedroom walls could give only the briefest explanation of the meaning of her designs. Furthermore, women quickly became impatient with these questions if I probed for more than the habitual response—"We do this because our ancestors did it." In 1975 I had to abandon my inquiries about the meaning of Shakti after a few interviews, because these questions evoked outright hostility. Since 1955 a number of researchers have warned against asking abstract or hypothetical questions of illiterate people. A common response to questions women could not answer was that, since I could read and they could not, I should look up such matters in a book. Unfortunately, information on village worship is relatively rare in books.

Men usually worship at the Siva temple, whereas most women's ceremonies are held in their *bughars*. Both sexes observe the major festivals, but several women's ceremonies are intimately connected with family welfare. Women worship disease goddesses, and some women's ceremonies involve fasts to honor and ensure the health of sons and husbands. Men do not fast in honor of their wives or daughters.

As part of their warrior tradition, the obligation of Rajput men to protect their families is expressed in a ceremony in which men worship their weapons.

Early in the twentieth century, the Rajput men of Khalapur and elsewhere were influenced by a reform Hindu movement known as Arya Samaj. This movement, opposing idol worship, castes, and purdah, preceded the activities of Mahatma Gandhi, and many of its ideas were also expressed by Gandhi. As a result of Arya Samaj, a temple to the god Siva was built in the 1930s by devotees who thought that the absence of any Hindu shrine was a disgrace to their community. Arya Samaj men began a number of new religious practices, such as the singing of religious songs at the temple. In response to Arya Samaj doctrine and the teachings of Gandhi, some Rajput men became less conservative in their caste practices and, as reported in chapter 1, gave up the practice of untouchability while working with their field hands. The women, on the other hand, were more traditional and still excluded untouchables from the women's quarters, where food is cooked.

Khalapur, like most traditional rural communities, does not have secular recreational facilities. The high school athletic meets are the only formal sporting events. Bhudana, the railway town 4 miles away, has a few movie houses and holds professional performances for religious holidays that some village men attend. Married women's recreation consists primarily of the celebration of religious and family festivals, such as weddings of daughters or the birth and haircutting ceremonies of sons. Religious celebrations are not only occasions of worship but the primary recreation for cloistered women.

The frequency and importance of traditional festivals, and of home entertainments such as storytelling, must be appreciated for a balanced understanding of the lives of village women. The cloistered daily routines of Rajput women are frequently interrupted by festivals. Hardly a month goes by without some celebration, a calendrical holiday, a birth ceremony for a newborn boy, or a marriage, that breaks the routine of daily choirs and turns *bughars* into places of feasting, dancing, ceremonies, and visiting; thus, the *bughar* courtyards are places of festivity, as well as workplaces and living quarters.

WORSHIPING

Khalapur women's attitudes about their worship were somewhat varied. Some women said that worship would bring good luck; others said that the goddesses would be angry if one did not worship them, but the performance of the ceremony did not necessarily ensure good luck. Perhaps the clearest statement of the villagers' attitudes toward their worship is that of a young *bahu:*

> It is like being friends and remembering them when they go away. It is a proper form of respect, like keeping purdah for the living. The gods are happy when they are worshiped. They do not cause bad luck if not worshiped. Sometimes it helps to worship a god or goddess, but you cannot change your fate.

The women most frequently began the description of their ceremonies by saying: "We cook *halwar* [carrot candy] and *puri* [fried *chapatis* stuffed with vegetables] on this day." This description was so frequent that I teased the women by saying that they used their ceremonies as an excuse to eat special food. They laughingly agreed that this was partly true. Some said that the Brahmins invent festivals so that they will be given food. Rajputs and their servant families eat well on feast days. The giving of alms, usually food, is a feature of almost all ceremonial days. Every attendant family, from Brahmins to sweepers, sent a representative to the households where they worked to collect alms on feast days. In 1955 Rajput women were always busy cooking food to distribute to these servants; in 1975 the decreased dependence on servants was evidenced by the reduced amount of time the women spent in festival cooking.

We found that a number of festivals were celebrated by one family on one day and by other families on the following day. The Rajput women claimed that this was because the Brahmins divided the festivals into 2 days so that they could share the food over a 2-day period. The Brahmins, however, said that the Rajputs were inaccurate in the timing of their festivals and would not listen to their advice concerning the correct dates for performing festivals.

Some aspects of the villagers' worship follow much the same pattern throughout a number of ceremonies. Whether they be at the ancestral shrine, at one of the three village shrines, or to a particular goddess within the household, prayers and offerings are essential to most ceremonies. Offerings are *halwar, puris*, and small clay oil lamps. During some festivals water is offered to the sun, moon, and stars.

There were almost no festivals celebrated by all families. When a family member dies on a festival day, it is assumed that the deity was displeased and that another family member might die if the festival is celebrated. Therefore, the entire lineage of the deceased person stops celebrating that festival until either a son or a cat is born into the family on or near that festival day. (Few families keep cats, so the birth of a son is more likely to end the ban.) Women may visit the houses of neighbors to observe festivals not celebrated by their own families.

Children participate in most of the festivals. One woman told me that they kept festivals because the children enjoyed them. Girls are considered to be goddesses, or *devis*, since, like goddesses, they are virgins. In some ceremonies little girls receive small offerings of candy or money in honor of their *devi* status. Girls help make clay pieces for the Sanjii figure and other decorations. When they are not participating in the ceremonies, children watch and listen to the adults singing; the only time that children are expected to keep quiet and out of the way is when the Brahmin priest is in the *bughar* performing a ceremony.

FAIRS

Throughout the year religious fairs in honor of various deities are held in towns near Khalapur; the closest and most frequently attended annual fair takes place in Bhudana. Women may come out of purdah to attend these fairs. Wives often visit their parental homes to attend fairs held near their natal villages.

Fairs are crowded, hectic, noisy, dusty, festive, and colorful. They provide an occasion for festive, daylong outings and are welcome respites from the quiet routines of village life. The fairs are held at temples where worshipers, usually women, make offerings to the temple deity. Temples have pools where worshipers bathe to wash away their sins, and there is usually a large fairground in the vicinity of the temple. The activities of the fairgrounds resemble those of county fairs in Western nations. The fairgrounds are filled with booths where the villagers can purchase a variety of goods, ranging from household equipment such as furniture, trunks, pots, and pans, to luxuries such as candy, clothing, toys, soft drinks, baskets, and cosmetics. Vendors without booths display their wares on blankets or carry them through the crowds, hawking their goods. Village women do much of their shopping at fairs, bargaining vigorously for their purchases.

Fairgrounds also have a wide variety of amusements. *Sadhu*s, beggars, snake charmers, and marching bands move through the crowds shopping at booths and adding to the congestion. There are rides on ferris wheels and merry-go-rounds for the children, and performances by comics and dancers for adults. Carnival dancers are hermaphroditic female impersonators whose dance style resembles that of American hootchie-kootchie dancers. A circus is often held in the afternoon and evening.

Bhudana Fair

In spring the fair is held in honor of the goddess Baalsundrii, known by many of the villagers simply as the Bhudana goddess. As Bhudana is only 4 miles away, most of the people of Khalapur attend this fair. The women look forward to it for weeks ahead of time, and children busy themselves trying to earn a few annas to spend at the fair. Only families keeping the most strict purdah do not permit their women to attend this fair. In 1975 Dhooli and her daughters were left in the *bughar* while Draupadi went to the fair with the other wives, taking her grandsons with her.

The Rajput women are taken to the fair by their men in bullock carts, leaving Khalapur about 4 or 5 a.m. Women make their offerings at the temple, bathe in the temple pond, and then go shopping at the fairground stalls. At about 4 or 5 p.m. the men bring the women back to the village. The men often return to the fair in the evening to see the dances, circus, and movies.

Shakumbrii Fair

The Shakumbrii fair, which takes place at the end of September, is held a number of miles from Khalapur, and only a few of the villagers are able to go. The Shakumbrii *devi* is a representation of Durga. Some women offer the birth hair of their children to this goddess rather than to the Bhudana goddess.

Gher Fair

A few days after Ghas, on the full moon, the Gher fair is held at a town on the banks of the Ganges about 60 miles away from Khalapur. Unlike most fair sites, this one has no temple. People believe that the gods go to the Ganges on this sacred night to wash away their sins, so pilgrims go there to join their gods. Not many Khalapur women go to the fair, except for the *bahu*s who come from that region. These *bahu*s may take advantage of the fair to visit their parental homes.

VILLAGE GODDESSES

Local goddesses, usually called village goddesses, who do not appear in the Vedic texts are widely worshiped throughout much of India. Village goddesses are usually fierce, unmarried, and childless; nevertheless, they are addressed as "Mother." According to Kinsley, emphasis on the worship of local goddesses is characteristic of village religion throughout India. He describes the village goddesses as follows:

> [T]hese deities, Goddesses for the most part, capture the primary interest of the villagers and tend to be worshiped with more intensity than the great Gods of the Hindu pantheon. Although the great Gods are acknowledged to be in charge of distant, cosmic rhythms, they are only of limited interest to most villagers, many of whom traditionally were not allowed within the precincts of the temples of these deities in the first place. The village Goddess, in contrast, engages the villagers directly by being associated with their local, existential concerns. She is perceived to be *their* deity and to be concerned especially with *their* well-being and that of their village.
>
> Finally, these village deities are often directly associated with disease, sudden death, and catastrophe. When the village is threatened by disaster, particularly epidemics, the local Goddess is usually said to be manifesting herself. She erupts onto the village scene along with disasters that threaten the stability, and even the survival, of the village. Furthermore, her role vis-à-vis such epidemics or disasters is ambivalent. She is perceived both as inflicting these diseases and as protecting the village from them.
>
> (Kinsley, 1986, p. 198)

Kolenda classifies the local Khalapur goddesses into four types: those associated with Kali, those associated with smallpox and other epidemic diseases, those associated with calendrical festivals, and a benign Earth Goddess, Dharti Mata (Kolenda, 1982, p. 228). Some of these are worshiped only by particular castes. The disease goddesses and Dharti Mata figure most prominently in the worship of the women I knew.

In Khalapur Rajput women worship disease goddesses, particularly when a family member contracts an epidemic disease. Some goddesses are associated with particular sites, usually the location of their temple. The village women refer to Kali at Bhudana simply as the Bhudana goddess, and to Durga at Shakumbrii as the Shakumbrii goddess. Many women did not know that these temple images represented Kali and Durga. Although both are major deities, they are considered local goddesses, in the same way that major saints may be regarded as patron saints of the localities where they lived.

Sakut usually takes place during January. This day is devoted to the worship of the goddesses Baalsundrii (Kali), whose temple is in Bhudana, and Shakumbrii (Durga), whose temple is in Shakumbrii, a nearby town. Sanjii, a water goddess and deity of a major village celebration, may also be counted as a local goddess. Satis are also worshiped as local goddesses.

Some Rajput women's ceremonies center on the worship of disease goddesses. There are said to be 101 sister goddesses, but 7 of them, representing the major epidemic diseases, are the most important. Some disease goddesses have shrines in the fields; others are worshiped at the *bhumia* (village shrine). Most commonly, water and cooling food are offered to these goddesses to calm them. They are treated as honored guests and asked respectfully to move on and leave the family in good health. Despite their stern nature, the sister goddesses are believed to be concerned with the welfare of children. The Bara Mata, or Big Mother, is the name for the smallpox goddess and for the goddess who makes children.

During the months of June and July, with the unhealthy monsoon season imminent, many of the sister goddesses who bring disease are worshiped at the *bhumia* shrine. The dread Bara Mata is especially worshiped at this time. The beliefs that health depends on the bodily balance of hot and cold and that life is a cycle of rebirth are embodied in the nature of these deadly goddesses.

The disease goddesses, who intimately affect the health of family members, are of more immediate concern for women than the remote high gods of ancient myths. Women are careful not to complain when a family member has been stricken with a plague lest the goddess be offended. Modern medicine has diminished the epidemic diseases and fear of their goddesses, but it is not unusual for young parents to take their children for inoculations, while grandmother puts a bowl of water on the roof to cool the goddesses of plague.

It is clear from our description of the status of village women that the powerful goddesses of Hinduism do not confer power on Hindu women. This paradox has been noted by a number of authors. Gross comments as follows:

> I see no evidence that the past and current Goddesses promote equality as we think of it today—equal opportunity for all regardless of sex differences. Nor do I see any evidence for the theory that Goddesses indicated political and social power for women. Rather, it seems that male strength and the demands of female biology fostered male political and social dominance even in traditional societies that had a keen sense of the reality of the Goddess.
>
> However, on the positive side, clearly the Goddess does indicate a tremendous respect for the feminine side of humanity and experience—whatever that may mean. This dimension of the meaning of the Goddess is, I believe, the most powerful aspect of Her presence. . . .
>
> Furthermore, in Goddess religions, this respect and awe for the feminine are not confined to women. In fact, if anything, the Goddess seems to be as much a creation of men's projections and a recipient of male devotions as anything else, at least in those historical situations close enough for historical research.
>
> (Gross, 1988, pp. 271–272)

Gross goes on to point out that sex equality is an irrelevant concept in traditional societies, where all roles are largely inherited, but concludes that the goddesses are important for women's self-concepts.

> Traditional societies, which are extremely role-bound, in which sex roles are functional and necessary, cannot be compared to modern society in which sex roles have become obsolete. Equality, in the modern sense of not being subject to the limits of both male and female sex roles, is a very recent possibility. . . . It seems that even though power and equality are lacking, . . . the Goddess imparts to a woman a certain sense of dignity, self-worth, personal assertiveness and simple visibility.
>
> (Gross, 1988, p. 274)

I agree with these conclusions. Goddesses did not empower the women I knew in any practical or secular sense, but they did, in my opinion, contribute to the fortitude and pride that are so much a part of their character.

VILLAGE SHRINES

The actions of the Vedic gods are distant in both time and place, but the actions of the village deities are local and contemporary. Therefore, the worship of these local protectors has an urgency that is absent from the worship of the major divinities. Disease goddesses kill. Darga, the Muslim saint whose tomb is in the village, brings hailstorms. Local deities may also war with major ones. In Khalapur some local events are attributed to disputes between Darga and Siva.

The Sati Shrines

For a description of these shrines, see appendix E.

The Siva Temple

The Siva temple was built about 60 years ago by a leader of the village who felt that it was disgraceful that the village had no Hindu temple. Since its construction, the Siva temple has been the major center for the village Hindus. It is the primary place of worship for Hindu men, the oldest primary school is held on the temple platform, and the meeting rooms of the *panchayat* are adjacent to the temple.

Darga, the Piir

In a clearing in Khalapur stands the Piir, the Mogul tomb of a saint named Darga. Both Hindu and Muslim villagers believe that Darga protects the village. One legend says that during the Indian rebellion of 1857, Darga appeared on his horse, wielding a sword, and prevented the British troops from entering Khalapur.

In 1955 we were told by a local widow that Siva and Parvati had a fight with Darga, who, angered by the construction of the Siva temple, rode forth on his horse, struck the temple with his sword, and cracked the foundation of the temple wall. Further inquiry revealed that the cement mold for the wall had given way before the cement hardened so that the wall had to be reconstructed. The widow attributed this accident to Darga's wrath.

Darga is supposed to have blessed the village with a promise that the spring hailstorms would never ruin the villagers' crops. During the spring of 1955 the crops were badly damaged by hailstorms. Many of the village women attributed this to the wrath of Darga, claiming that he was angry because the villagers had switched their worship from his Piir to the Siva temple. Some of the women also claimed that the Piir was angry because some men had urinated on the wall of the tomb, but most thought the Piir was angry because the brick kiln had been built near his tomb and subsequently the villagers, for the first time in many years, had burned a holy fire at the Siva temple. The Piir was reputed to be too warm from the combined fires of the brick kiln and the holy fire.

Kalapur residents, both Hindu and Muslim, have great faith in their village saint. Sometimes they swear an oath in his name. Whenever a son is married, he is taken to the Piir and some offering is made. When a son-in-law comes to Khalapur, 1 rupee, 5 pice, and 2 candies are offered to the Piir. In addition to receiving offerings at weddings, the Piir has a special day to honor him sometime in July. On this day offerings are made to Darga at the Piir by both Muslim and Hindu families. In addition to the usual offerings of food and *devas*, some families offer cotton shawls. The offerings are taken by families living near the tomb.

The *Bhumia*

The *bhumia* is a small brick shrine consecrating the building of Khalapur. Such shrines are built when a new village is founded. No particular deity is associated with the *bhumia;* rather, it seems to function as a focus for local spirits, who may protect the village. Offerings are made at this shrine on various occasions. Bride-grooms ride on horseback to visit the Piir, the *bhumia,* and the Siva temple before leaving for their brides' villages.

ANCESTORS
Narayan

The god Narayan figures in some Hindu mythology. He is of particular importance to the Khalapur Rajputs because he is considered to be the god of Pundeers, the group (*gotra,* or exogamous patrician) of Rajputs to which the Khalapur Rajputs belong. As such he may be considered their primary ancestor.

Around November, Ghas, the birthday of the god Narayan, celebrates the awakening of Narayan, other deities, and ancestor spirits, who have been sleeping for the previous 4 months during the time of the fall harvest. While the gods are sleeping no marriages can take place, and daughters cannot travel to or from their parents' houses. Ghas used to mark the time that the villagers started eating sugar-cane. By 1955 the mills demanded delivery of sugarcane before Ghas, so most families began eating cane when it was harvested.

Women celebrate Ghas by making a painting on the floor of the courtyard to bring good luck to the family men and animals. The painting consists of circles representing hooves of animals owned by the family and crosses representing shoes of family members. One pregnant woman added a small cross to represent her unborn baby. The central figure is a square outline of the Narayan with two figures of people inside it. These two figures represent the god Narayan again and his wife. Some of the women also made designs of dripping dots of rice water on the house walls, the *choopars,* and the *ghers.*

When the Ghas painting is completed, the family Brahmin comes to the *bughar* and performs a ceremony to Narayan. When the ceremony is finished, the children light oil-soaked rags and go through the village waving them and finally throw them in the pond. In some families the children go from house to house and beg for grain, which they take to the shop to exchange for sweets. Following the ceremony family women sing a song to awaken the God.

Get up, Narayan, sit, Narayan
Go to the *ghram* field, Narayan
I will cut and you sort, Narayan
Get up, get up, oh god of Pundeers, Narayan.

The spirits of male ancestors figure prominently in the worship of villagers. Many prayers invoke the name of the family ancestors. Many families had ancestor shrines, built from cement or brick in a family field or mango grove. Ancestor shrines were usually built when a male ancestor either possessed a living member of the family or began to haunt the family by entering the house in the form of a snake. This was interpreted as the desire of the ancestor to have a place to live. The family would then build a shrine to the ancestor and ask him: "Live here and do not trouble us." Men who had died childless were particularly likely to come back in this manner since, being childless, they had no place to live in the house. Like childless goddesses, the spirits of childless men are considered potentially dangerous.

Although only male ancestors are worshiped, it is the family women who worship at the ancestor shrines, including wives, who are not directly related to the men the shrines honor. The women of most families worshiped at their shrines irregularly, but the women of one household worshiped at their family *pitar* every month at the dark of the moon.

FASTS

Although feasting is an important part of festivals, some of the women's ceremonies also involve fasting. A fast may require not eating any food throughout the day but is equally likely to be a prohibition against eating certain kinds of food. Fasts, which are usually broken with the ceremonial feast, tend to be mild. Sometimes the little girls of Khalapur fasted, particularly on Hooii and Shiv Ratrii. This was done in the spirit of fun, and the girls were sometimes teased about fasting for their future husbands. Less frequently, some boys kept the fast.

Some feasts are held in connection with festivals. Women fast from the evening of one day to midnight the next day before celebrating Janmashmii. During the Sanjii festival one of the family women is supposed to abstain from eating wheat and corn for 9 days. In most of the families no one keeps this lengthy fast; instead, one of the family women usually fasts for at least 1 day. We were told that this fast ought to be performed by an unmarried girl, since unmarried girls are considered to be *devi*s, or goddesses, themselves; however, in some cases a married woman fasted. The fasting was a matter of individual choice, and few of the families were able to tell us in advance which woman in the household would hold it.

Women have two occasions on which they may fast for their own welfare. A fast at the time of the full moon, known as Puuran Maashii (full moon), is held in honor of the god Narayan to purify the worshipers' souls. Some women keep this fast occasionally, and a few keep it regularly. Ekadsi, the thirteenth day of the lunar cycle is a fast day considered particularly auspicious for widows. Women worship a particular tree growing in a nearby mango grove by walking around the tree, considered to be the transformation of a Brahmin, several times, wrapping a white sacred thread around it. They then make the usual offerings of *halwar, puri,* and a *deva* light. When we observed this worship service in 1955, a Brahmin man was sitting about 20 feet away from the tree. He and the monkeys of the mango grove, sacred because they represent Hanuman, divided the *halwar* and *puri.* The monkeys, who snatched the food as soon as the women left, usually got the bigger share.

Bahai Duge

The most important fasts are those kept by women for family men—brothers, husbands, and sons. The most elaborate ceremonies of these fasts are those for brother's day.

The third day after Divalii is Bahai Duge, or brother's day, which celebrates the love between brothers and sisters. Sisters fast for their brothers and put marks made of yellow pigment on their brothers' foreheads. The brothers give their sisters money to thank them for their devotion. Ritual sisters celebrate Bahai Duge by exchanging presents in honor of their brothers.

Karwaa Chauth

Karwaa Chauth, in October, is a daylong fast kept by women for their husbands' health and longevity. Women also honor older family women on this day. Wives cook rice and legumes and feed the family Brahmin. Each fasting woman gives a pot containing water and 1 anna (a small coin) and 2 seers of raw rice to an older woman in the house. Each *bahu* gives this offering to a *jethani* (wife of husband's older brother), and the eldest brother's wife makes this offering to the *sasu.* The eldest woman in the *bughar* gives to an older woman from another house. In 1955 the eldest woman in the neighborhood received a number of visits from elderly *sasus* and a great deal of rice. When the fasting women see the moon rising, they throw offerings of water to it and then break their fasts.

Hooii

Several days after Karwaa Chauth there is a similar fast, called Hooii, for sons. On Hooii the family Brahmin woman goes to each house to begin the clay and rice-water paintings. Brahmin women make these paintings at a number of houses, so they do not complete them on the day of the Hooii festival. Hooii paintings must be finished within 22 days, when the Gher fair is held. A painting is usually placed in the room of each mother in the house who has a separate room. Sometimes the old Hooii painting of the year before is washed off and the new one is put in the same place. Sometimes the new painting is put in a different spot, so some rooms have two or three paintings.

The Hooii painting is a stylized picture of the goddess in the shape of a square with a head and limbs, similar in form to the outline of Narayan painted at Ghas. As usual, the identity of the goddess was not specific. Some of the women said it represented the goddess Hooii; some said it represented the Shakumbri goddess; others said it could represent any goddess. The square body of the goddess is solid white, and on it are painted red designs representing the sons and daughters-in-law of the house. A marriage cart with bride and groom is pictured to ensure that there will be marriages in the family. Underneath these are various designs, such as flowers, people, and horses. Some of the paintings also have pictures of women ascending staircases to throw water at a star. The painting varies somewhat with the Brahmin women who paint it; women in whose house it is placed do not ask for particular designs.

Round earthenware pots containing water are placed in front of the paintings; a silver necklace with a large silver pendant on which is portrayed the goddess Hooii and variable numbers of silver beads is hung around the neck of each pot. The women keep these necklaces and usually have them restrung for each festival. Some of the women said that they added a pair of beads for each son. Others, however, said that you could add a bead whenever you wanted. A necklace is sometimes passed down from generation to generation, so the number of beads does not always represent the number of sons of the woman who owns the necklace. In the evening the women pray to Hooii and wear their necklaces for about half an hour. (We were told that they used to wear them all year long, but this custom has died out.) When the worshipers see the first star, they throw water to it as an offering and break their fast.

FESTIVALS AND FEASTS
Divalii

Divalii, around the middle of November, celebrates the day on which Ram returned to the city of Ayodhya after 14 years of exile in the forest to reclaim his kingdom. Called the festival of lights, it is the loveliest of the Hindu festivals. For 2 nights small earthenware oil lights are lined up around the walls of the courtyards and *choopars*. On these nights Indian settlements glow with millions of flickering candles. A major festival throughout India, Divalii is particularly important to Rajputs who trace their mythical descent from Ram. For weeks before Divalii, Rajput women clean and whitewash their houses in preparation for this festival.

Divalii celebrations are 4 days long. The first day, called "little Divalii," is a day of preparation for the festival. On this day the women cook special food and in the evening they light the small oil lights. The next day, Divalii, is devoted to the worship of Hanuman, the monkey god, who helped Ram rescue Sita from the demon Ravena. Each house is again filled with small oil lights. The oldest woman of the house fasts in honor of Hanuman, and the family Brahmin is fed in his honor. Songs in honor of Ram and his faithful wife, Sita, are sung during Divalii as well as at other times. The lyrics to one of these songs follow:

Rama   Neither there is worry about going to the forest,
              nor there is worry about being a hermit.
              The worry is about the tyranny of Sita's going to the forest.
              Mother Kaykeyi's order is to go into the forest.
              We have to go soon.
              The great worry is about Sita's company.

Sita   You my respected husband, don't refuse.
       Your left side must not be unoccupied.
       I shall wear the saffron-colored dress like yours.
       And shall go to the forest with you.

Rama   The great worry is about Sita's going to the forest.
       There are many troubles in the jungle.
       There are snakes, lions and wild animals.
       Sita, you stay in the palace.
       Don't go with me.

Sita   O Ram, when you go from Ayodhya I will also be with you.
       I will not be happy in the palace with you.
       Your beloved Sita will go along with you.
       Respected husband do not order me to stay back.
       The blood in my body has blackened by such orders.

Ghoodhan Day

Divalii also honors Lakshmi, goddess of wealth and prosperity, who is tacitly represented in the worship of agricultural wealth. On the day after Divalii, known as Ghoodhan day, women worship a cattle god, Ghoodhan to honor wealth from cows and ensure the health of their herds. They make stylized figures of Ghoodhan out of cow dung on the *bughar* floor. The figures are decorated with small tufts of cotton, and barley is placed on the figures' ears. The women then throw sugarcane and berries on the figure and worship it. Some women said that this day was more important than Divalii because their herds are an important source of food, a statement that illustrates the merging of major and minor deities in village worship.

Shiv Ratrii

Shiv Ratrii, in February, is the only time that married women worship at the Siva temple. Siva is considered to be the ideal husband, and women celebrate Shiv Ratrii to honor their husbands, as well as the god. In the morning married women fast to honor Siva and so that their husbands may have long lives. Unmarried girls may fast on this day and pray to have husbands like Siva. Childless women pray for children.

In the afternoon, groups of *sasu*s and older *bahu*s go to the Siva temple, singing religious songs and carrying small brass pots, fruit, candy, and *deva* lights. When they reach the temple, they fill their pots with water from its well, enter the temple, and bathe temple idols with the water. When the idols have been cleansed, the women take the candy and touch it to the lips of each of the idols and put one *deva* light in each of the shrines and on the lingam (phallic representation of Siva). Their offerings completed, they sit in a circle around the lingam and sing religious songs.

After they have finished singing, the women come out and walk around the temple three times while sprinkling water in offering to Siva. They pour more water onto the corner of the temple platform as an offering to the sun and finally throw water on the roots of the sacred fig tree growing near the temple. They end their worship by putting marks of yellow pigment on their foreheads and on the foreheads of the children who accompany them, and then return home singing. At home they break their fast with milk and puffed sugar balls. In Khalapur most of the younger *bahus* did not go on to the temple but sent their offerings through someone else.

Flora Duge

Flora Duge (flower day) comes shortly after Shiv Ratrii and is one of the most colorful of the village festivals. On this day groups of young daughters of the village, dressed in their best and most colorful saris, walk to the fields, singing as they go. When they reach the fields, the younger girls gather flowers while the older girls form a circle to sing and dance. The children pick the blossoms off the flowers and put them in baskets; when finished, they return to the village, still singing, to distribute their blossoms.

Their first stop is the Siva temple, where the girls toss flowers inside, offering them to the temple gods. After visiting the temple, the girls go from house to house, singing and throwing flowers at the people in the courtyards. The custom, an imitation of throwing of colored water on Holi, is called playing Holi with flowers. This festival is performed again on the day before Holi.

Basant

This festival usually comes in February. To celebrate Basant one is supposed to put on yellow clothes and cook yellow, saffron-flavored food. Starting on Basant, a village official takes one cow dung cake to the Siva temple each day; the cakes are burned on the Holi pyre. Only a few Rajput families celebrated Basant, but this festival is recognized as the day on which many marriage and engagement letters are sent and received.

Holi

Holi, which occurs 1 month and 8 days after Basant, usually in March, celebrates the revels of Krishna and the Gopis (sacred milkmaids). On Holi women make garlands out of mud and cow dung. The garlands, consisting of a large center disk representing the moon and a number of small disks representing stars, are sometimes exchanged between families and hung in the courtyards, but most are used as offerings. Khalapur has no temple to Krishna or Vishnu, so women bring their Holi garlands to the clearing in front of the Siva temple where they are placed in a large pyre and worshiped. Women ring the pyre with white sacred threads and designs of white and colored powder and give offerings to it. In the afternoon the pyre of dung garlands is burned.

A meeting for singing religious songs is held at the temple on Holi for the men, who usually sing on the temple platform while the women worship at the pyre in front of the village temple. After the women return to their *bughars*, the men's dancing and singing continues all night long.

The day after Holi, called Phaag, is the bacchanalia of Hinduism. On Phaag many social restrictions are abandoned and people throw colored powder or water at each other. No one on the streets is safe from these attacks, and people are reluctant to travel. People usually throw color at others with whom they have a friendly joking relationship, but teenage boys often throw colored water at the new brides who have just returned to their in-laws' house. Women living in houses without latrines go to the fields for elimination at about 4 a.m. on Phaag to avoid attacks. On Phaag the sweeper men, some dressed as women, spend the afternoon going from one Rajput *choopar* to another, singing, dancing, and begging for money.

A drink called *baan,* made with a narcotic, is served on Phaag, and the men sometimes indulge in excessive drinking. When drunk, Rajput men may become aggressive, and old enmities are likely to break out. In 1955 one of the old blood feuds erupted in violence on Phaag, and a man was killed in the resulting fight.

Tiijoo

This festival, usually in August, is a festive occasion chiefly celebrated by unmarried girls and young wives. Tiijoo is the only time at which a wife receives presents from her in-laws. If *bahu*s are visiting their parental homes, these presents are sent to them, so many gifts are delivered from one village to another around this time.

Each *bughar* puts up a swing for Tiijoo, and groups of young girls swing and sing for a week before the festival. On the day of Tiijoo the girls are given new clothes, and they decorate their hands with henna pigment and put on new glass bangle bracelets. Then they get together and sing and swing for hours, showing off their new clothes. In the evening girls and young wives go to the fields and enact a wedding ceremony. One girl dresses like a bride, one like a bridegroom, and others take the parts of the various in-laws. The whole wedding is acted out as a drama, including a mock fight over the amount of the dowry. The wedding drama is accompanied by a singing contest between the people representing the bride's family and the groom's family. The women representing the families of the bride and groom engage in competitive singing, and whoever stops singing gets taunted by the other side. This contest represents the animosity between the in-laws and allows expression of the brides' anxieties about marriage and moving to the in-laws' villages.

One of the Tiijoo songs expresses the women's desire for sons. One singer, who represents a childless wife, asks her sister to lend her a son. When the sister refuses she asks her *jethani,* who offers to lend all seven of her sons to her *derani.* Such an offer is, of course, unrealistic, even if one assumes that the two wives are blood relatives. The song symbolizes a wish for harmony among sisters-in-law.

> Seven friends are wearing earrings, listen O my sister,
> Go fetch water, while swinging in the swing.
> The pitchers were kept there, listen O my sister,
> They started talking among themselves, while swinging in the swing.
>   Is your *sasu* bad? listen O my sister,
>   Is your husband away? While swinging in the swing.

My *sasu* is not bad, listen O my sister,
Nor is my husband away while swinging in the swing.
My worry is my being childless, listen O my sister,
It has lessened my honor, while swinging in the swing.
My elder sister has four sons, listen O my sister,
Lend one to me, while swinging in the swing.
   Wheat or rice can be lent, listen O my sister,
   Sons are not lent, while swinging in the swing.
Jethani, you have seven sons, listen O my sister,
Lend one to me, while swinging in the swing.
   Why are you asking for one? listen O my sister
   Take all seven on a loan, while swinging in the swing.
   For these 12 years my womb has been active, listen O my *Derani*
   I gave birth to sons like gems, while swinging in the swing.
   You wrote many letters to me, listen O my sister,
   Why don't you take my sons on loan now, while swinging in the swing.
If one son of mine dies your seven may die, listen O my sister,
You have insulted me, while swinging in the swing.
If one son of mine survives, your seven may survive, listen O my sister,
You have honored me, while swinging in the swing.

Janmashtmii

In August, Janmashtmii is celebrated in honor of Krishna's birthday. The women fast from the evening of one day until midnight the next day. The family Brahmin man constructs a swing in the *choopar;* the swing is decorated, and a statue of Krishna is placed on it. In the evening, daughters, *sasus*, and older *bahus* go to the *choopar* to pray, make offerings, and worship at the shrine until about midnight. The Brahmin receives the food offered during the celebration. This is the only occasion on which a women's family ceremony is held in the men's quarters. After Janmashtmii the gods sleep again until they are reawakened at the time of Ghas.

Sanjii

The Sanjii ceremony usually occurs during the latter part of September. Sanjii is described as a local representation of Durga, as the Shakumbrii goddess, and as one of the seven sister goddesses of disease. She brings riches, keeps away evil spirits, and protects the children's welfare. If a family member or animal is sick, money is set aside for Sanjii and is offered to her temple. For 16 days during the Sanjii festival the family Brahmins are fed in honor of the families' dead ancestors. If the Brahmins are unable to come for the food, it may be given to an unmarried girl or a cow, because both are sacred.

A figure representing the goddess Sanjii is made of clay and placed on the wall of the courtyard. In 1955 the Sanjii figure was made in a number of small parts, the body usually being represented by various designs indicating the clothes, and the arms and legs represented by several bracelets and anklets. In 1975 most of the new

*bahu*s were making Sanjii figures in a more simplified design, with large clay pieces
for the head, body, and limbs. We were told that women no longer had time to make
the more complex and time-consuming figures. One woman jokingly said that they
were economizing on clay.

A veil is placed over the goddess's face, and for 9 days a light is burned in front
of her image in the evenings. Barley seed is placed in a small pot in front of the
goddess and allowed to grow for about 7 days. The women worship the goddess and
offer prayers to her. Then the sisters in the house put this barley seed on their
brothers' ears to wish them good health.

On the ninth day the goddess is removed and the pieces are carried to the village
pond, where she is "drowned." The explanation for this is that she is connected
with water and is therefore returned to water. Water also cools the temper of the
disease goddess.

After the Sanjii figure is taken down, a small figure representing Sanjii's brother
Launkaria is put up in its place. He is sometimes pictured on a horse, but more often
is a crude human figure with some of the barley in its head. This figure, indicating
that sisters leave the house but brothers remain, is supposed to stay on the wall until
the following year. Usually the figure is washed away by the rain or plastered over
and not replaced until the next Sanjii festival.

SECULAR RECREATION

Most of the leisure time of adults of both sexes is spent smoking hookah and talking.
Women talk about lending and borrowing grain, about marriages and new brides,
and about the health of their cattle. They may also speculate about where their
husbands are and whether they have come home from the fields. They talk about
major ceremonies and fairs, and plan for them for weeks before the dates of their
celebration.

Two 1955 accounts by village women of the recreation of women in their homes
are as follows:

> The young daughters-in-law of the family visit in one room compound. While they
> talk, they work with their hands—knit, embroider, etcetera. They tell about what
> happens in their own homes in their mothers' villages. The three daughters-in-law
> play games before dark with the girls of T's family. They play hide-and-seek, dog
> and cat, and jacks with stones. R's wife sometimes tells stories in the evening, and
> D's wife sometimes reads stories to them. Mrs. K. plays cards in her own village.
> They bet in the family for money, but they never really take it.
>
> Mrs. R. C. and Mrs. A. tell stories about ancient kings and ghosts. They tell
> stories until about 10 or 11 p.m. They paint designs on the walls for marriages and
> they make up their own designs. They draw designs on cloth for their embroidery.
> They play drums and dance. Sometimes they go to S's house to hear the Victrola.

Occasionally traveling players come through the village and stage musical dra-
mas performed by female impersonators who sing and dance. The men attend such

plays, but the women generally do not because the plays are not considered quite proper.

Although the children do not formally participate in adult recreation, they are usually present. They may listen to adult conversation or play by themselves. Children also watch the athletic competitions of the high school. At one such competition, a group of smaller children had formed a play group and were having a track meet and jumping match of their own while similar activities were going on among the high school boys.

Storytelling is a favorite pastime for women. Traditional storytelling is a means of teaching important beliefs and values to the younger generation, embedded in entertaining tales they will remember. Like many European fairy tales, all of these stories are about kings and queens, and all emphasize traditional values. Preference for sons, the sacred nature of the brother-sister relationship, the husband-wife bond, and the dire consequences of failing to perform religious rituals are common themes. Several stories tell of the trials of faithful queens whose husbands are deceived about them—often by false queens. Justice triumphs in the end and all is set right. (See pp. 196–97 for a sampling of two such stories.)

Some women fear that these traditional values are being challenged in some of the modern stories in movie scripts. All popular Indian movies have several episodes of singing and dancing. Kissing is forbidden in movies, and the romantic involvement is depicted by seductive dances. The results of the interview are presented in Table 8.1.

Although India has the world's largest movie industry, movie attendance was

Table 8.1 Secular Recreation Interview

| | Movie attendance | |
	N	%
None	16	30
One	14	26
Two to five	15	28
More than five	9	16
Total	8	100

| | Attitudes toward movies | |
	N	%
Likes all	4	22
Dislikes all	8	45
Likes some	6	33
Total	45	100

| | Types of movies | | | |
| | Liked | | Disliked | |
	N	%	N	%
Religious	10	38	0	0
Social	3	12	4	23
Romantic	2	8	7	41
Songs	5	19	3	18
Dances	6	23	3	18
Total	46	100	49	100

understandably infrequent among Khalapur women. Women accustomed to seclusion and sex segregation and afraid of all strange men were uncomfortable about sitting in a darkened room with strangers. Nine *bahus* said that women who went to movies objected to purdah, but four denied that movies made a difference in attitudes towards purdah.

Thirty percent of the women had never been to a movie, while another 26% had seen only one; only nine women (16%) had seen more than five movies. Movies were not very popular with the women who had seen them: Only four women (22%) said they liked all movies, eight women (45%) said they disliked all of them, and six women (33%) said they liked some movies.

Reported preferences for types of movies clearly reflect women's religious predilections and their dislike of public displays of romance. Religious movies were the most popular (38%), and no one said they disliked them. Romantic movies were the most disliked (41%), and only two women said they liked them. Social themes were moderately popular, as were songs and dances.

Most women did not seem to feel that movies or radio were major influences in bringing about changes in traditional customs. One who did described the influence as follows:

> Boys go to see the movies and they want their wives to be with them hand in hand as they have seen it in the movies. Many boys and girls have run away because of the cinema. Whatever they see in the movie, they copy it and whatever they listen to on the radio, they do the same. So, because of the movies and radio purdah has almost finished.

CONCLUSIONS

Most women's recreation still revolves around traditional festivals and celebrations of births and weddings. Religious and family values are woven into the fabric of village life by sacred threads of feasts, festivals, and storytelling. Many of these traditions are local and different festivals are observed in different villages within the same geographical area. Because of the local nature of some festivals, wives may have observed religious rituals in their parental villages that are not observed in their husbands' communities. Such differences are respected by *sasus*. Wives may visit their parental villages to observe local festivals, or they may observe them in their husbands' homes. Religion seems to be a realm of self-expression for women; although cloistered and restricted to rigidly defined roles in their daily life, they may exercise choice in the festivals they observe and the manner in which they observe them.

Women's worship is directed to a wide variety of sacred entities, including major Hindu deities, local goddesses, saints, ancestors, sacred animals (e.g., monkeys and snakes), and celestial bodies (e.g., the moon, stars, and sun). Major gods are worshiped at festivals widely celebrated by Hindus. Narayan is worshiped at Ghas and Puuran Maashii, Ram at Divalii, Siva at Shiv Ratrii, Krishna at Holi, and Janmashtmii and Hanuman at Divalii. Local goddesses or local representations of major goddesses, are worshiped at Sakut, the Sanjii festival, at local fairs, and summer worship ceremonies to placate the disease goddesses. A cattle god, Ghoodhan, is worshiped the day after Divalii. The village Muslim saint and Jhinvar saint have their own ceremonial days.

Sacred trees and plants figure in several celebrations and are featured at Flora Duge and Ekadsi. Snakes are honored at Naag Panchmii, and monkeys usually eat the food offered at ancestor shrines. The sun is included in the offerings of Shiv Ratrii. The moon is worshiped during Karwaa Chauth, when women fast for their husbands, and the stars are worshiped during Hooii, when women fast for their sons.

Women are responsible for family welfare in their religious as well as their secular roles, and these traditional value and familial duties are expressed repeatedly in the calendric festivals. Most family ceremonies are concerned with other family members. Husbands are honored at Shiv Ratrii, Karwaa Chauth, and Sanjii; brothers at Bahai Duge and Sanjii; and sons at Hooii. Ancestors are worshiped at Ghas and Sanjii festivals, as well as at family ancestor shrines. Cattle, representing family wealth, are honored on Ghoodhan and Shiv Ratrii, when Shiva's bull, Nandi, is honored. The festival of Tiijoo concerns the welfare of brides. Sanjii, Hooii, and the 101 sister goddesses of disease are worshiped to ensure the welfare of children. Even the unlucky widows have their auspicious days.

Purdah restrictions limit communication between fathers and daughters, as well as between husbands and wives, to messages essential for daily routines. Perhaps for these reasons women have been able to retain the right to worship village goddesses without interference from their men. These goddesses are primarily the cause of disease, so their worship protects the family members from diseases and helps cure those who are afflicted. In any case, the importance of goddess worship by these Rajput women is greater than the published literature on the subject seems to indicate.

Cross-cultural investigations of associations between the importance of goddess worship and machismo might help explain goddess worship in societies where women's status is low. Religious scholars agree that goddess worship originated in the distant past, probably when women were relatively equal to men, and that it declined when men took on more secular control. Indian goddesses are usually wild, untamed, and a threat to social order. Like women, they embody *shakti*. It seems likely that the power of women is particularly threatening to men who live in societies that emphasize machismo. If this is the case, and if goddesses in other societies tend to be untamed, then one might expect strong controls on women to appear in societies where fear of women is projected onto the personas of female deities.

The attribution of the end of purdah to exposure to movies and radio represents the sort of exaggerated fear expressed so frequently in the purdah interviews. It is true that radio reaches into the cloistered *bughars* and brings news of the outside world to isolated women. Movies are relatively cheap and popular, as they are throughout the world, and their plots often reflect changing lifestyles in urban areas. Reactions to movies clearly shows that these women are selective, preferring religious movies with traditional themes and resisting films portraying "shamelessness." Village life has maintained its structure through invasions, independence movements, religious reforms, land reforms, Western-based education, and change

from subsistence to market economies. It seems unlikely that modern technology
will do more than contribute their share to the multiple forces of modernism imping-
ing on traditional people.

Stories

I

There was a Raja who had a kiln for firing earthen pots. Every time he fired his pots
he sacrificed someone by putting him into the kiln. The man sacrificed was the first
man who passed his house on the day of the firing.

On Sakut day the Raja was sitting in front of his house when the only son of a
widow came by. The Raja told the boy that he will be killed in the evening. The boy
went home to his mother, who was fasting for Sakut Devi and said that he had only
one day to live, so please give him good food. The mother cooked and was crying
while cooking.

Vishnu, disguised as a sadhu, came along and asked the mother why she was
crying. She said, "I have only one son who is to lose his life this evening. The
servant of the Raja will come to get him." Vishnu asked to share the food and the
mother fed him. After the sadhu and the son had taken their meals, the servant came
for the boy. Vishnu said that he would go in the boy's place, but the mother refused
to send a guest instead of her son. Vishnu insisted but the lady refused.

Vishnu gave the mother some mustard seeds and told her to give them to the son
and tell him to spread them around him when he was in difficulty. She gave them to
the son, saying, "Let us see if they will help you."

The boy went to the kiln and the mother followed, crying. The boy sat on the
floor of the kiln and sprinkled the seeds around him. The pots were put in and the
kiln fired. The pots usually took three days to fire, but when the Raja sent his
servants to put more wood on the kiln the next day, they found that the pots were
ready. They called the Raja to come and see. First he said they were foolish and he
would not go until the third day. However, after they insisted he went and saw the
boy was sitting unharmed with the green plants of the mustard seed protecting him.
He ordered the pots to be removed. When the servants started to do this, the boy
said, "Please take them out slowly." The servants were frightened. The Raja removed the pots and the boy stood up, saying, "Ram, Ram, Hari, Hari." The Raja
asked who had given him the seeds and he told the story. From that day on all started
observing the fast for Sakut Devi.

II

Once there was a king. He went hunting. He was killed. Someone telephoned the
queen that her husband was killed. She rushed to the jungle where he was. She sat
by his unburied body for 12 years. She stayed in the forest and never left him. She
did not move or bathe. The body was stinking and the insects on it were on her also.
She never ate.

After 12 years she saw a woman coming and called to her. She told her that her husband was killed 12 years ago and she had been there ever since. She said, "I have been praying to God to bring him back to life. I have not had a bath for 12 years because I am afraid to leave him. You wait here with him and I will go and bathe." She went and as soon as she left the husband got up. He asked the lady where he was and what was wrong. The lady said that he was killed while hunting and that she was his queen and had been sitting there for 12 years. She said, "Now at last God has heard my prayers and has given you life." Then the queen came back. As soon as she came the other woman said, "Who are you and why have you come here?" She said that she was the king's wife but the king thought that she was a madwoman. He did not recognize her because she had not eaten and her complexion was changed. The queen said, "All right, at least make me your maidservant. I will work for you." They agreed.

They went back to the palace. The woman became queen and the queen was a maid. One day the king was going to another town. He asked the queen what she wanted him to bring her. She asked for a necklace of red beads. He asked the maid what she wanted. She asked for a dancing doll. When he got to the town he found the necklace but could not find a dancing doll. Everyone asked him who wanted it. He said that his maid wanted it. They said, "You must be mistaken. The queen must have asked for the dancing doll and the maid for the necklace. Only the king's daughters play with dancing dolls." He went to many places and could not find a doll.

Finally he reached where there was a crowd of men. He told them he was looking for a dancing doll. When the king of that place heard that there was a visiting king in search of a doll, he called to the king. He said, "I have a dancing doll that my daughter used to play with when she was young. But her husband was killed and she went into the forest with him and now they are both dead. You take this doll. But I am sure that no maid would have asked for it. It must be some king's daughter."

The king went back with the doll. He gave the necklace to the queen and the doll to the maid. When he gave the maid the doll, she said, "Where did you get it? This doll belongs to me. I used to play with it when I was young." The king told her and she said, "He is my father." She told him the whole story about how he had died and she had looked after him and how the other woman had come. He took her to her father and she recognized him. They buried the false queen alive and the true queen became queen again.

V

WOMEN'S NATURE

This section is devoted to beliefs concerning women's nature, the roles of widows, and the problems that these beliefs pose for Rajput women. Chapter 9 describes the paradox between the importance of women's chastity and honor and the belief that women's female energy, *Shakti*, makes them highly sexual. The energy of Shakti is believed to be responsible both for women's sex drives and for their ability to reproduce. Men's attitudes about sex and women's honor, and their effect on marital relations, are described.

Case histories of two women are described in this chapter to illustrate the importance of women's honor. The first story, that of Radha, the shameless daughter, concerns an unmarried girl who died as a result of an illicit affair. The second story, that of Sita, the innocent wife, tells of a wife who fled to her father's home when wrongfully accused of infidelity by her husband. Reactions of neighbor women to both incidents are described and evaluated.

Chapter 10 describes the traditional roles of widows. Because of their high-caste status, Rajput widows are forbidden to remarry, even when they are still virgins. They are expected to live pious, celibate lives. Traditional mourning customs, which exclude widows from the formal mourning for their husbands, widow's dress, and widow's work, are described.

The honor of widows is often suspect, and they may be called *rand*, or whore, if rumors about them persist. The tradition of sati, although still an ideal for widows, has been illegal for over a century and is largely a custom of the past. Widows are expected to lead chaste, religious lives in the service of their husband's kinsmen. One Khalapur widow went beyond the usual expectation and became a *bhaktani*, or holy woman, with a congregation of local women. Her story is told in this chapter.

Chapter 10 ends with the tragic story of a household with three widows and no men. The sister of the deceased elder man left her husband and has spent her life in a vain effort to reclaim her brother's land from the men who stole it from him.

This wealthy, elderly widow is regarded as an honorable and respected community member. She wears an embroidered cashmere shawl over her homespun sari. Despite her widowed status, she still wears her gold nose plug and ring. Eyeglasses—even with the nosepiece mended—are a luxury and indicate that her family takes good care of her. Despite her age, she modestly pulls her sari and shawl across her face when facing the camera (1955).

9

Women's Nature: Honor and Shakti

Woman is reproducing and there cannot be an end to human life.
Woman is Shakti.

The honor of a woman is like the golden thread in a sari;
if that thread is spoiled, the whole cloth is ruined.

A woman of honor will not tolerate insults.

The secluded wives of Khalapur are women who possess both sexuality and honor.
The poetic epigraphs to this chapter embody their beliefs about virtue and sexuality.
Virgins are sacred, and prepubescent girls are often called *devi,* or goddess, and
given special food and gifts on some feast days. The reputations of their families
and community are elevated or dishonored by the virtue of their women. Rajput
women will defend their honor fiercely against immoral women who are traitors to
their golden thread, and against any blasphemer who wrongfully accuses a virtuous
keeper of this trust.

Western beliefs about human nature include the assumption that men have
stronger sex drives than women. In nineteenth-century Europe and America, the
belief that middle-class women, in particular, are honorable was accompanied by
the belief that respectable women were not interested in sex and, if truly proper,
were frigid. This tradition holds that men have stronger sex drives than women, a
belief that is still cited as a defense for greater promiscuity by men, and sometimes
for rape. The belief that a high sex drive in women is a characteristic of the lower
classes, and incompatible with refinement, is still present in Western thought.

Hindu beliefs about sexuality are similar to the general meaning of libido in
Freudian theory. Sexual strength is the core of psychic energy and associated with
strength of character. In contrast to Western belief, Hindus believe that it is women
who have more psychic energy and stronger sex drives then men because of their
ability to give birth. This power, called *Shakti,* is exclusive to women.

Not only do women have Shakti while men do not, but wealthy, high-caste, and
powerful women have more Shakti than do poor, low-caste, or weak women.
Therefore, this psychic strength surrounding sexual energy is a hallmark of upper-
class women rather than a sign of poor breeding. There seems to be no concept of

201

frigidity. High-status women should possess high standards for honor, so that their behavior will not disgrace them and their family. The combination of much Shakti and much honor is the ideal for Rajput women.

The belief that high-caste women have stronger sexual drives than men and would be unable to control their lust if not carefully guarded was usually the first reason given by men in 1955 to explain the necessity of purdah. Viewed in this context, the belief may be dismissed as a convenient fiction that serves as an excuse for keeping women cloistered. As with any central tenet about human nature, however, it is believed by both men and women. Perhaps the single most important difference between the self-image of Hindu and Christian women is their assessment of the strength of their sexuality and the centrality of this reproductive power to their entire character. It probably accounts for much of the pride and dignity of these seemingly oppressed women.

The disgrace of a woman's immorality falls not on her husband's family, as in many Western societies, but on her parental family, who are charged with the obligation of raising virtuous daughters. Therefore, if a husband finds that his wife is adulterous, he sends her home to her parents rather than punishing her himself. Traditionally, a woman's father and brothers are obliged to execute her if she loses her virtue and disgraces the family. Nothing enrages Rajputs more than a slight to the honor of their women, and nothing is punished more severely than dishonor in women.

One of my first tasks when I returned to the village in 1975 was to update the census. Therefore, I spent the first few weeks asking about deaths, births, and marriages. During one such interview, a mother describing the death of a young married daughter broke into silent tears and sat motionless and quiet, overcome by the sadness of her memories. She told us that while home on a visit, the girl had died of snakebite while in the fields with her brothers. It was the only report of death by snakebite, and an unusual demonstration of emotion, but certainly understandable. We expressed our sympathy and did not question this story of the daughter's death until we were told by others that she had, in fact, been murdered by her brothers. Her husband had found her to be pregnant when she arrived after the *gauna* and had sent her home. Since her brothers had done their duty and redeemed the family honor, the incident was closed.

Infractions of the premarital intercourse taboo are the most carefully guarded secrets because the virtue of an unmarried girl is essential to her prospects of marriage. Marriage between persons of the same khandhan (lineage) is an outcasting offense, and all Khalapur Rajputs belong to the same khandhan. In 1955 we heard that some of the unmarried girls had romances in the fields when they went there to work, and village songs describe affairs with cousins. The lack of chaperoning of the adolescents is the weak link in the severe chaperone system of the village. However, in view of the severity of the taboo, it is likely that most of the village girls are virgins when they are married.

Most of the illegitimate children in the village are probably the children of their uncles or grandfathers, and these cases go undetected. It is only the case of the unmarried girl, the widow, or the married woman who becomes pregnant in her parents' village that cannot be covered up. While we were in the village in 1955, one unmarried Rajput girl in another part of the village did have an illegitimate child. The father of the child was evidently a cousin of hers who was from the household. The girl's father delivered the child himself and killed it. All of the women with whom we talked were horrified by this scandal. One woman said: "Unmarried mothers should be strangled so that other girls will have some fear and not have affairs. Such girls spoil the name of the village."

The fear of premarital affairs is one of the reasons given for marrying girls at an early age and is a major deterrent to higher education for girls. While adultery is prevented by strict chaperonage, premarital affairs are prevented by marrying daughters young. Khalapur daughters are usually married by 16 or 17.

SHAKTI

Shakti not only enables women to reproduce, it is the essence of their strength of character. Shakti is associated with Sita, the Earth Goddess wife of Rama; its power enabled Sita to enter the earth at the end of her life. We asked several women about the concept of Shakti. All of them were familiar with the concept but were irritated by the question, saying that this was written in books and we, who were educated, should read about it. Shakti seemed too personal, too vague, and too important to put into words. It also seemed to be an unfit topic to discuss in front of unmarried girls, who are usually present in a *bughar*. In 1975 we obtained the best description from Maina, an elderly, educated daughter of the village, who was home on an extended visit to her brother and came to the project house to be interviewed:

Sita entered into the fire when Rama wanted to prove his wife's purity to his subjects after her return from Ravana's country, Sri Lanka. It is because of Sita's entrance into the fire that fire possesses so much Shakti. Fire reduces everything to ashes, it is so Shaktiful. Due to piety and purity Sita possessed divine Shakti. We women are also Shakti. When we have a child in our body, then we have Shakti. Women have Shakti so we can reproduce. Men have all talents, but they do not have Shakti.

Women have three Shaktis along with talents. The first Shakti woman possesses is that she reproduces and keeps the human life continuing. She keeps the lineage and name of the family alive through her offspring. The second Shakti is that when a woman puts on a beautiful red or yellow sari, dresses her hair in a good style and puts eyeliner on her eyes and color on her cheeks, and uses lipstick and other cosmetics, then she looks like a goddess. This is another Shakti. The third is that when a woman does not wear any good clothes and leaves her hair unbraided, and cries and starts fighting, she can look very bad. This is a bad Shakti, but it is still a Shakti.

The earth is bearing the weight of all of us and at the same time giving us food. If the earth does not give us food, how can we survive? Earth gives food to all living beings and all are satisfied with the food the earth grows for them. Therefore, the earth is a big Shakti.

Similarly, woman bears the weight of her unborn child, and while sitting at home, has the responsibility to feed each and every one at home and look after their welfare. She also gives alms to beggars and satisfies the hunger of the men and other household people, so she also has Shakti.

If there are 10 to 15 men in a building and no woman, the house is not attractive and warming. When all the men go out locking their house, the building looks as if nobody lives there. But if there is a woman in the house, she will keep it open all the day. Anyone can come and satisfy his thirst and hunger. A house without women looks dull.

It is women who improve the race by reproducing very healthy, strong, virtuous, and attractive children. This is due to her Shakti. But if a woman behaves differently and does not look after the welfare of her family, does not give food to the hungry, or alms to beggars, and does not welcome visitors, then she can ruin a family of wealth and good name.

All women do not have the same amount of Shakti. Each woman has as much Shakti as she has earned by her previous karma. There can be good and bad Shakti, virtues and vices always go together. If someone has an evil power, that is a bad Shakti.

Shakti can be lost, as well as earned. You lose some when you become proud of your Shakti.

Shakti decreases with age, because you divide it among your children. It gets divided when you reproduce, and when you give some teaching to your children, you lose some of your Shakti. Shakti gets divided among your children, but a woman with no children has no Shakti, because she is unable to continue the name of the family. A woman who has eight children will have less Shakti than a woman with two children, because she has divided it among her children. However, because all of her eight children will earn for her, she will acquire more Shakti than the woman with two children.

If there had been no women, men could have died fighting each other and there would have been rivers of blood. Woman reproduces so there cannot be an end of human life. She is Shakti. Brahma tried many times to start human life on earth, but he failed because he never consulted Siva and Parvati, so he produced only men from *mani,* the seed with which man can be reproduced. Men have no Shakti, but they have *mani.* There was a big fire and all the men started cutting each other, and there was a river of blood. Brahma produced only men, as if they were hundreds of thousands of pollen grains in a flower.

When Brahma had failed many times to create a continuous human life on earth, he decided to go to Lord Siva to find out the reason for this failure. Lord Siva told Brahma that the problem was that he had not asked permission from Shakti Parvati. "The seed of Shakti who can survive the human life on earth is only with Parvati, so you must go to her," said Siva. Brahma then went to Parvati and obtained three seeds from her. With these seeds he tried again, and this time he produced both men and women. Therefore, human life on earth has now been continuous for thousands and thousands of years.

In earlier yugas [mythical ages] women did not produce children the way women do in this yuga. One woman could produce thousands of sons during her lifetime. In this Kali Yuga (the last and worst age) women's Shakti has been lessened by the curse of a saint named Papparman Rishi.

This saint went away from his wife for 12 years, and his wife was most unhappy about this long separation. Before leaving the saint gave his wife a marigold in a small box and told her, "Whenever you remember me look at the flower. When the flower fades, I will also fade." The wife looked at the flower many times. When the saint had been gone for 11 years and 3 months, the flower began to fade.

The worried wife wrote to her husband, saying, "The flower you gave me is fading, please come home." She folded the letter and put it around the beak of a crow, who flew to the place where Papparman Rishi was meditating. After reading the letter, the saint put his sperm in the crow's mouth, and told it to give the sperm to his wife and tell her that he would return after 12 years.

On the return trip the crow met some friends. He thought that if he did not greet his friends, they would feel that he was very proud, also not greeting them went against his religion. Therefore, he opened his mouth to greet them, even though it meant losing the Rishi's sperm. The saint's *mani* fell out of his mouth and into the mouth of a fish, swimming in the sea below him. When he reached the wife he told her that her husband would return in 9 months, but did not tell her about the lost sperm.

When Papparman Rishi finally returned to his wife, she looked at the flower, which had faded, and reproached him, saying, "Your flower has faded. How can I continue the lineage?" Then Papparman Rishi became angry because his wife talked only of the flower when greeting him. He cursed her, saying, "Woman! You will not be able to speak because of your shamelessness. Your eyes must reveal whatever you want to say."

Shakti would do justice to a theologian. The complexity of this description of Shakti is primarily concerned with reproduction, but its power extends to many aspects of behavior. Since it is earned by good or bad karma, it can be good or bad in nature. It is embodied in the earth. Childless women have none, but mothers lose theirs by giving to children through the acts of birth or teaching. It can return from children from earnings, so it may be embodied in wealth and secular power. It can be lost through pride, and greatly diminished by a saint's curse.

HONOR

While Shakti is not talked about and is difficult to describe, honor is discussed openly and frequently. Any indiscretion evokes gossip and criticism from the guardians of the golden thread. The fragility of honor is evoked in the following myth:

Once there was a princess who was truthful and who was never seen by any man. The parents used to weigh her every morning and her weight used to be equal to the weight of seven flowers every time. One day she was alone at home cooking when a sweeper [a person of an untouchable group who cleans latrines] came in the house to remove the garbage and feces. He just saw the back of the cooking princess and thought, "Oh, how beautiful this woman is. How fortunate I would be if I could possess her as my wife."

He was a sweeper and the maiden was a princess and therefore he could not dare to talk to her even and went away. As the sweeper cast his lust upon the princess, she became heavier than the weight of all the flowers blooming in the garden that day.

The queen grew worried and informed the king, saying, "Our daughter is no longer as chaste now; she has grown heavier today." The king was also worried and grief stricken and asked his daughter the reason for her weight gain. She told him, "I have not even seen the shadow of a man, but yesterday the sweeper came in the house and he might have seen me."

The king consulted some learned Brahmin who suggested that the princess should go along with her brother to a temple on some auspicious day.

They did not walk on the road with other people, but through the jungles where nobody could see the princess. However, people on the road saw the princess and her brother from a distance and said, "Look, some vulgar and corrupt man and woman are going to the forest, hidden from others. Everybody is going on the road while these characterless man and woman are going through the bushes and trees." These people distributed the effects of the sweeper's lusty imagination on the princess among themselves by making bad remarks about them.

When the crowd reached the gate of the temple, everybody tried to open the doors, but the doors would not open for anybody. Everybody was disappointed at not being able to have the glimpse of the god inside the temple, for which they had come all the way from their homes. The princess and her brother were also standing and waiting, away from the general public. When everyone had tried and failed to open the doors, the princess, veiled from all sides, came along with her brother and touched the doors, which opened immediately. Then all the people had glimpses of the god. The princess offered the sacred *prashad* [food offered to a deity or Brahmin] and came back home following the same secluded route through the bushes in the jungle.

Her overweight from the lustful imagination of the sweeper was gone because of the people's wrong assumption about the chaste brother and sister walking through the forest. Therefore, on reaching home, the princess again was equal to the weight of seven flowers as before.

Therefore, my child, the older people believed in such purdah and they were pious and truthful. They never allowed any outside person to cast his sight on any part of the body of their married or unmarried women. They would not even consume the food on which some outsider had cast his sight.

The myth does much to explain why the older women of Khalapur were so concerned with covering their entire face, and some even their hands, and why they crouched to make themselves as inconspicuous as possible when men entered the *bughar*. These women believe than an evil eye can kill young children, and a lustful eye can weigh down a woman's honor.

It should be noted that our storyteller relates myths which justify and explain purdah at the same time that she is describing the two most essential traits of women. The saint's curse seems to be a rationale for the silence imposed on women by purdah customs. The evil effects of lustful glances are cited as a justification for extreme cloistering. The theme of an innocent, long-suffering woman, wrongfully accused by her husband or father, is typical of women's stories.

MEN'S VIEWS OF SEX

The prevailing attitude of the village men toward sex seemed to be that it was an unfortunate and troublesome human failing. The ideal of the virtuous man is that of the aesthetic, the pious *sadhuu,* who has managed to divorce himself from all earthly desires. The following quotation of an elderly village man, recorded in 1955, illustrates this attitude:

> The best kind of love is "pious love" between two men. You should always have your friend in mind. This kind of love is very rare between a man and woman in India. I do not know about America. The love of a man for a woman always has "sinful sexual love" present. It is selfish. It is just like bringing fire and straw together. Even if such love [pious love] existed between a man and a woman, people would always be suspicious of it. It is possible to have such love between a husband and a wife when they are old, in the fourth (oldest) stage of life. The fourth stage of life (the oldest stage, when one gives up earthly desires and retires to a holy life) is the best stage. There are three kinds of love, pious love of men, love of a man and a wife, and the love of those who are not married. The first is the best and the last is the worst.

Another village man said: "Women are just like a disease, but one that cannot be cured." This attitude that women are an incurable disease and a barrier to a man's virtue seems to be founded on the belief that sex is harmful to men. Statements by village men that too much intercourse is injurious to a man's health appear so frequently in the notes of John Hitchcock that it seems to be a major theory of disease. The following statements, taken from Hitchcock's notes, illustrate this attitude:

> In the beginning men had more sex desire and then the women had more.

> Men are losing their vitality because they work too hard. Women are gaining more because they are in purdah. They have eight times as much as men. Purdah makes women more attractive and men have illicit relations through curiosity. Men should have intercourse once a month. Twice a month is all right and four times is the maximum. After marriage and in the winter, people want to "put the wood in" twice a day.

> My son is going to see his wife too often and is getting sick. He will not stop so his father is going to send the girl home. A woman's nature is fire and a man's is *ghi* [clarified butter]. When *ghi* comes in contact with fire it is damaged so it should be kept away from fire.

> My father lived to be 98 because he would stay in the fields for months on end and not see his wife.

> D is sick because he has two wives. It is necessary to check the semen to make one healthy.

> After marriage I went to see my wife every night. My brother noticed me looking pulled down and had his wife put my wife in a room and lock the door. I waited 4 or 5 days and then I broke down the door.

Coming as they do from men who consider themselves to be rulers and warriors, and who expect their wives to be totally submissive, these statements may surprise Western readers.

Beliefs that sexual activity saps the strength of males are widely held throughout the world. They should not be interpreted as representative of deviant anxieties about sexuality but as expressions of a generally accepted belief system, grounded in Hinduism, just as Western beliefs are grounded in Judaism and Christianity. While the young husbands of 1975 might express less concern about loss of strength through sexual activity, these beliefs are part of their paternal heritage.

The quotations show that the men regard their sex drive as an unfortunate failing and women, the source of this failing, are regarded with distrust. There seems to be no comparable belief that the woman's health was injured by too much intercourse, except when she was pregnant. Instead it is women's Shakti that drains men of their strength. Some quotations indicate that whereas the sex act is considered to be injurious to the health of men, it is actually considered to be beneficial to the health of women:

> People have extramarital affairs because the men cannot satisfy their women.

> If the man discharges first then the woman will not discharge and is unsatisfied. An unsatisfied woman is quarrelsome and she may become weak. She will say there is no difference if I am here or with my parents.

The ideal of asexual pious love is one reason why the brother–sister relationship is sacred, while the husband–wife relationship is profane. Sisterly love is pious, and a sister's fidelity can prolong her brothers' lives. Wifely lust, on the other hand, saps men's energy and injures their health. Bennett describes the distinction between a man's love for his sister and his wife in her book *Dangerous Wives and Sacred Sisters*. She argues that the reification of brother–sister love is a custom designed to increase the loyalty of men to their patrilineal kin and distance men from the wives who threaten this loyalty. Clearly her analysis may also be applied to the families I studied. Beliefs about the danger of sex for men are one of the complex of beliefs and customs contributing to the aloofness between Rajput husbands and wives.

MARITAL RELATIONS

In 1955 the women of Khalapur were often shy with their husbands, particularly during the early years of marriage, and said that though young girls were often afraid of the initial phases of intercourse they did not express any of the deep-seated anxieties apparent in the quotations of the men. It may well be that after the first few years of marriage the sex anxiety of the women is lower than it is for the men of the village. It was not possible for us to do extensive interviewing with the women on the topics of sex or reproduction because the men objected to us discussing these topics with their wives. It is interesting that most of these objections came from the men, who seemed alarmed at the possibility that their wives might criticize them. Men expressed none of these objections in 1975. Some of the older women were quite free in discussing their relations with their husbands in front of us, although there was usually a certain amount of shyness attached to this subject.

In 1955 an older woman remembered her experiences as a young bride in the following account of her wedding night:

> When I was married at 14 I knew nothing. I was very frightened of men. When I came after my *shadi* I stayed for 6 days in my husband's house and slept with my *jethani*. On the second night I woke up and my *jethani* was gone. I heard her tell my husband to take me in the room. I ran to my *sasu*'s bed and slept with her. My husband was too shy to approach me when I was with his mother. The third night I woke up and found my husband asleep beside me. I again went to my *sasu*. The next 3 nights I slept with my *sasu*, then I went back home to my parents.
>
> I came back to live when I was 17. By this time I knew everything and thus I was not much scared. I slept with my *sasu*. The door was unlatched and I would go and bolt it. My husband with the help of friends scaled the courtyard wall. I found that my *sasu* had slipped away. My husband came and sat beside me. I said that I was hot and needed a fan. Then I went and slept with my *sasu*. The next night the same thing happened. This time I pretended to be thirsty and escaped. The third night I tried again, but he caught me firmly by the arm. He said: "I have had enough of your deceitful excuses." Then he took me into the room and then we both became fond of each other and I began to love. At the time of marriage a girl has no love for her husband. It is only after the *gauna* when she lives with him that she develops affection for him. Now I do everything for him.

This account illustrates both the anxieties of the bride and the shyness of the groom. A 1955 quotation from an educated woman, the second wife of an educated man, describes her initial meeting with a more poised husband:

> When I was first married my mother-in-law told me to sleep in the room with my dowry so it would be safe. After lying for some time I heard the door crack and my husband came in. I stood up, he sat on the bed and asked me to sit. I sat on a stool and he teased me saying I was sitting too close. Why did I not move farther away? Then he asked me about my interest in study and I told him what books I had brought. I stayed for 6 days and every night he came and talked. Not until after the *gauna* did we have relations. My husband believes that a man should not go to his wife unless they desire a child.

This woman was pregnant at the time of the interview. When we asked if she wanted a child, she replied, "I knew that my husband wanted me, and since in life husband and wife should agree with each other's wishes, I fulfilled his desire." Despite the belief in Shakti, women are expected to be, or appear to be, relatively passive in sexual relations. This woman's passivity is illustrated by the fact that she explained her pregnancy by saying that she had fulfilled her husband's desire.

Under the rules of strict purdah the sex life of a young couple was under the constant surveillance and control of the *sasu*. One woman described this situation:

> The husband comes like a thief in the night to his wife's room. She leaves the door unlocked. He whispers to her during the day. The chances of meeting are slim when there are many women in the house. It is not good manners to speak to each other before other members of the family.

However, despite the controls, the marital relationship of young couples usually developed into ones of enthusiasm and affection. Many of the young men in our families slept with their wives rather than in the *choopar*. The young educated woman whose account of her first days as a bride has just been given said of her husband, "Some time ago he had a guest so he had to stay in the *choopar* with him for 1 night and he found it very difficult." This woman was pregnant in 1955 when this second statement was made. Her husband had evidently so far abandoned the idea of going to his wife only when a child was desired that he went to her even when she was pregnant, which was considered to be a dangerous habit.

In 1955 the young *bahu*s often came in for teasing by their *sasu*s because of their sexual relations with their husbands. For instance, in one household, two of the older women were teasing a young girl who had a headache and a cold by telling her that she had caught them from sleeping in the courtyard with her husband.

Of course, marital relations are not always good. The control of the bedroom and the kitchen and refuge in her parents' home are a wife's means of influencing her husband: She can go home and refuse to return for some time; she may refuse to feed her husband or cook badly for him; she may also lock him out of the bedroom. Here are two 1955 accounts of village women that describe such incidents:

> I fight with my husband more than other women. I write my parents and someone comes and takes me home. For two or three times, he comes to take me back and I send him back just to teach him a lesson. Then my parents force me to come and then I go reluctantly. When I go I do not take anything from the house except something to eat on the way. I do this just to show my anger. When I get angry and he comes in the evening and lies on my bed, when anyone is present I do not say anything. If we are alone then we wrestle with each other, and I say that you have no right to be here, go away. Then he wrestles with me and goes. When I go to my parents I miss my husband. No woman can forget her husband. You cannot talk about your husband to your parents, only to your friends you can talk. In our house we always remember our husbands. My husband is exceptionally happy with me.

> Once when I would not put some onions away, my husband hit me and we had a fight. He was so angry that he would not come at night for 1 year, and then I would not let him come for 3½ years. He would come every third night. He was so shy of all the ladies that he would take off his shoes and come, and then I would shout "See, he has come again," and the women would wake up and say, "Why are you keeping us awake?" and then he would go away. So there is 6 years difference between S and P [her first and her second sons]. Now my husband and I do not fight. I talk too much but he does not say anything. I told him straight after that incident that I will do my work, I will cook and do the work at home, and you earn and that is all. If you don't want me to stay, I will go home. I told him this after 1 year when he wanted to come back. I told him, "You've not bought me, you've not paid a single *pie*" [the smallest denomination of coin]. The old ladies used to scold me for keeping him out and I never felt bad when they scolded me. I don't know what happened to me. Now so many times we do not agree, but we never fight and he never hits me. I do not know what happened to us then.
>   Q. Did any of the other women do this?
>   A. Yes. I slept in a room next to S's mother, and there was a half wall between

us. Once he came and she would not open the door. She shouted, "Go away, dog," and he said, "It is not the dog, it is me," and she would not let him in. Three dogs started barking at him and he was too shy to chase them. I had to go and chase them out of the house so that he could leave. The women who have mothers-in-law, the husband is too shy to wake the mother, but if they live alone, then the husband will beat her.

Q. Is he not afraid to waken the children?

A. Yes. He will not beat her at night, he will come back the next day and do it.

Evidently the barring of the husband from the bedroom works best if there are other women in the house. If a woman's husband is fond of her she can use the threat of not returning from her parents' home or of barring him from the bedroom to obtain what she wants from him. However, if the husband does not care for his wife, her position becomes one of great helplessness since divorce, while legal, is effectively impossible in village society. There were two women in one of our families who claimed that their husbands had not slept with them in some 16 years, claims confirmed by other women in the house and the fact that each of these women had only one child, aged about 16 or 17.

Once a couple has married children they are expected to curb their own sexual desires. It was considered shameful for a woman to have a child when her daughter-in-law is present in the house. There is also the expectation that at this age the sex urge of the couple will have been finished. In 1975, I saw no evidence that this attitude had changed. When answering questions about modern methods of birth control, several women said that older men still preferred celibacy. This attitude is expressed by the following quotations from a man who said that his wife wants no more children:

I am not using birth control, but self-control. I am over 40 and the desire is almost finished. Also my daughter-in-law is in the house, and I should not go there while she is there. There is much talk in the village if both mother and daughter-in-law have babies. If a wife has her own room then they can go there, but still there is some feeling of guilt. Mother and father should not procreate while their sons are doing so. Not everyone follows this. Some people are just like dogs and go to their wives anyway.

The extreme shame that is felt by an older woman when she finds herself pregnant is illustrated in the following quotation from the same woman who had the extended disagreement with her husband over the onions. In 1955 she thought she had had a miscarriage and several months later discovered that she was pregnant.

I fell very shy and that people will say that I have just had a miscarriage and now I am having a baby again. I am so angry that when I was young I did not have children and now I am having two in 1 year. The other day I was sitting and feeling very lazy. My husband said that I did not work. I was always lying here and there. I said how could I work when I was having two babies in 1 year. He said, "All right, don't talk too much." I have not told my daughter that I am pregnant. She might know about it. I do not go out at all because I am so shy, having just said that I had a miscarriage.

This woman was one of the most dominant and least shy of the women we knew. Nevertheless, both she and her husband were so embarrassed about the oncoming child that they had not even told her own daughter about it, and the wife refused to leave the house for fear that someone would see that she was pregnant.

THE SHAMELESS DAUGHTER

My 1955 field notes record the prediction that since the age of marriage was rising in the village due to an increased desire for education, chaperoning might present more problems in the future. When I returned, this prediction was tragically confirmed when an unmarried girl died mysteriously after an unsuccessful suicide attempt.

In the spring of 1975, the village was shocked by a scandal. Radha, daughter of one of the village's wealthiest and most prominent families, became pregnant by a fellow student at the intercollege. The lovers came from the same khandhan and were therefore distant cousins, so marriage was impossible. Discovered by teachers in a room at the college, they took poison. Both survived, but 2 days later Radha was dead amid rumors of pregnancy, suicide, and murder. Some women thought that she had taken a second dose of poison, others that the family had killed her. We did not determine the cause of death, but the following account of the events leading up to it are well-established:

> The boy and girl were seen together in a room of the college by some teachers. One of the teachers went to the boy's house to tell his father, the other went to the girl's house to tell her uncle. Since Radha and Krishna knew they had been seen by the teachers, they decided to kill themselves by taking poison. Consequently, the boy did not come home all night. The next morning he was caught in the fields. He had taken some liquid poison, and had some in two vials in his pockets. He was brought home where he vomited and came out of danger.

Radha was the only child of a widow. Her father had committed suicide when Radha was an infant because his father, mother, and brothers refused to avenge the family honor by killing his sister Mara for her immorality. The young man had jumped into a well, a traditionally female method of suicide, to take his sister's place and redeem the family honor. The tragedy of the widowed mother, who lost both husband and child for the honor of her husband's relatives, was keenly felt, and Radha's death renewed this older scandal. Several women criticized the family men, saying that if they had killed their wayward daughter as they should have done a generation back, they would not have raised a granddaughter who also lost her honor. Some went so far as to say that Radha had died, like her father, to cleanse the honor of the family.

The intensity of ire that this event brought forth was expressed by one indignant woman, who blamed Radha's grandmother for the young woman's death:

> Radha's mother was cheated by this family. We heard that Radha was pregnant and took poison at home. Her mother immediately came out of the house and asked people to send for the doctor because her daughter had taken poison. She did not depend on the mercy of the household people. The doctor gave Radha an injection and took care of her, and after 2 days she was all right. She washed her hair and took solid food.
>
> But at night the old woman, in consultation with her sons, sent for the dispensary compounder and secretly gave Radha a medicine for abortion. The compounder is not a qualified doctor, therefore the medicine killed Radha, rather than killing the embryo. Radha started bleeding and her mother wanted to call the local doctor, but the old woman refused, saying, "Let the abortion be complete." The mother became afraid and helpless; had she been determined to call the doctor again, only then could Radha have been saved. But her uncles and the old woman might have been behind bars for poisoning and murdering Radha like this.
>
> This is a family of butchers, I tell you, especially the old woman. She did not kill her own daughter, who gave birth to a full-fledged son before marriage. Her son wanted to kill his sister, and had to kill himself because he could not tolerate the insult to the prestige of the family, let down by his sister's shameless deeds. Mara was the daughter of this *sasu,* and Radha is the unfortunate daughter of her *bahu.* Therefore, this woman, who would not kill her own daughter, played with the life of the innocent fatherless granddaughter and killed her.
>
> She never liked Radha's mother after the death of her son. She always wanted her to die whenever she was sick. The old woman might have succeeded in murdering Radha's mother long ago, had her parents not been actively watching the welfare of their widowed daughter and grandchild. They did not let their daughter live here long with this family, and came frequently to fetch her for a change either in Delhi or in their own village. They are very wealthy and the old woman is afraid of them.

The pathos was heightened by the receipt of a parcel of gifts for Radha's dowry from a maternal uncle in America. Many village Rajput families have relatives in the cities of India, but it is rare to have a relative abroad. The *jethanis* and *deranis* of Radha's mother wanted her to give them Radha's dowry goods for their own daughters, an unrealistic expectation even if the death had been a natural one. The bitter widow said that she planned to return to the home of her brothers and give Radha's dowry to her brothers' daughters.

The brothers arrived promptly to take Radha's mother home. Before leaving, she threatened to ask for her widow's share of her husband's family property. The demand of a childless widow for a share of the family land enraged her *taaya,* the senior man of the family, who furiously defended traditional inheritance customs. Another family wife described this reaction:

> She should have considered her brothers-in-law as her own people, but she thinks of them as enemies. If she wants to take a share of our land to give to others, we

will consider her as our enemy. If she comes here to live with us, then she is a member of the family, but if she lives with her brothers, then she is no longer a member of this family. She has taken everything, even her brass utensils which she bought for her marriage. One locked steel box is here, which she will take away when she comes next. She may take everything she likes. What can we do about it?

Radha's mother always talked so high and boasted about her parental family and their riches. Then why did her brothers come here for begging? If they are rich enough, why cannot they feed their sister when she comes to live with them? Does she need more than two meals a day and one pair of clothes a year at this stage of life? What has she to do with landed property when she has not a child of her own alive? She should have stayed here with us and taken what she required for herself. If she wants to live with her brothers and nephews, then she should not take anything from this family. No one will let her take a share of land and hand it over to her nephews.

When our *taaya* [father's elder brother] heard that Radha's mother was talking about her share of the property in this house, he got furious and shook his staff and shouted at his sons, saying, "I am not going to distribute my property between all of you, what to say of Radha's mother, as long as I am alive. After my death you do whatever you want to do, but I will be very bad if I hear anybody asking to divide my property, or anything else, before me!"

Radha's mother accused our old *sasu* of murdering Radha. I say, how could this poor old women kill the girl. Did she tell Radha to take poison? Radha's mother forgets the character of her own daughter. She was talented, educated, and rich. Was there a scarcity of good marriages for her? Her mother knew everything. She should have asked her brothers to get her daughter married if Radha was getting out of her control. She could have asked her rich brothers to arrange a marriage, but she was foolish and got Radha educated instead of getting her married.

The responsibility for marriage arrangements always falls to the husbands' families; therefore, the suggestion that the maternal uncles should have arranged a marriage for Radha is contrary to custom and a denial of the responsibility of Radha's father's kinsmen. Radha's mother denied that she had any knowledge of her daughter's affair, and blamed Krishna's mother for not telling her about the affair and her husband's family for Radha's death:

The fault of Krishna's mother was not to inform me, instead of defaming my girl. When she came to know of the affair she could easily have told me. I, poor woman, knew nothing. Had I known, I would have sent Radha to my brother's place. Now I have lost my child and she is telling people different stories, blaming my daughter who is no more in this world and defending her son who is a big rogue.

Radha's mother agreed that her *sasu* was against her and Radha:

Once I was sick and used to get treatment of a doctor at Bhudana. My *sasu* accompanied me to Bhudana. The doctor gave me an injection, and I started feeling very weak and sleepy. The doctor told my *sasu* that I was very weak. She replied, "Let her die, it is good if she dies." I know because the doctor told this to my brother. So I am living among the people who are not my well-wishers. I depend on those who perhaps killed Radha, what to say of saving her. Thus they have saved a lot of money which might have been spent on Radha's marriage. They always criticized her for going in for higher education. I do not want to live with them, but this I am telling to everybody, even to my *sasu*. I will not sit idle. I will claim my share of land, even if I have to go to court.

At this point her *sasu,* who was listening, broke in angrily, saying, "It is very bad to give our land to your brothers and nephews." Radha's mother was furious at this accusation:

Why do you name my brothers and nephews? They cannot look after their own big lands, which are more then enough for them. Should they set fire to your land? It is I who need it, because as long as I can work here I will get two meals a day, but when I am unable to work, then who will feed me and look after me? Then I will be helpless and miserable and at the mercy of people who wish that I will also die and let them enjoy my share of the property.

The tragedy of Radha's death had strained the bonds of respect and deference between *bahu* and *sasu* to the breaking point. A widow without sons burdens her husband's family with her support, but a widow with a daughter and no sons incurs the expense of a dowry without the compensatory dowry of an incoming *bahu.* Radha's mother was correct in saying that the family had been saved a large expense through Radha's death.

The widow's threat to cause a new expense alarmed her *sasu,* who had other sons with wives and grandsons. The *sasu* did not want this childless widow in her household. The widow, alienated from her husband's family, faced the prospect of mistreatment in old age, so frequently mentioned by senior women in the purdah interviews. Tragedies that bring scandal into the family strain traditional decorum to the breaking point. Then the constraints on communication are breached, and angry words are spoken.

The comments of Krishna's mother showed the anguished conflict of a woman torn between the defense of her son and sympathy for Radha and her parents:

Radha was a very darling child. She was beautiful, educated, talented, and she belonged to a very rich family. Her maternal uncles were rich and her mother had collected articles from India and abroad for her dowry. She was intelligent and very good in her studies. She got first division in her examination. But her taking poison to end her life proves her to be very stupid.

We have other children, and had our son died it would not have been so difficult to bear his loss. But Radha was the only child of her late father and the only hope of her poor mother. She should not have died. My husband and I have deep sympathy for her mother, but we cannot think of anything to do to solace her. We are preparing to do anything, even if the life of our son can give her any peace of mind, we shall be happy for that also. It would have been better if our son had died. He took poison three or four times but it could not affect him. Please, if you see Radha's mother try to soothe her and express our feelings.

When my son got over taking the poison, I said to him, "None of your grandparents from both sides of the family were like you. Your uncles from both sides of the family were not like you. How did you become without character?" He replied, with tears in his eyes, "Dear mother, I am not characterless, but Radha was after me badly. She had developed a mad love for me. Many times I told her to stop this, but she could not restrain herself. I told her not to try to meet me, but she said that she could not stop herself from doing so."

Radha was not a girl of loose character, as some people say. She never talked to another boy except my son. She was a godly, pious girl, having no one in mind but my son. Once she came to the house with Krishna's notebook, saying that he had forgotten it. The notebook had a letter and her photograph in it. My son cried when I scolded him and said that Radha demanded his notebook at the college. After that she never came to our house.

Once Radha's aunt came to visit her parents' home, and I invited her to my house, and clearly told her about the affair between Radha and my son. I clearly told her to stop these things, but they could not check her. Had Radha been my daughter, I am sure I could have stopped these things and there would not have been this death. I am sure you will agree that it is difficult to control or check the outings of a son, but not very difficult to check the outings of a daughter. They have been careless in this matter.

The last could be the comment of a mother in most countries. It is the mothers of the daughters who are the keepers of the golden thread.

The burdensome responsibility of raising daughters led several women, in the course of gossip about this tragedy, to comment that daughters will disgrace the family, particularly when educated. The death tore wide the gap between tradition and the modern world. It was a case where the transition from the cloistering of purdah to the freedom of education had borne tragic fruit. One women, forgetting that both Swaran Kapoor and I were educated, told us that all the college girls of the city are immoral and have babies before they graduate. Another thanked God for her scarcity of daughters:

> Once my daughter danced at a wedding and her breasts showed, but nobody ever saw my daughter standing outside the house or talking to any person. She died in her in-laws' house. I had two daughters who died. Thank God that now I have only one daughter, who is already married, and I do not have any granddaughters.
>
> Daughters disgrace the family. These days are very bad, and the college in this village is the main cause of girls becoming corrupt because they study with boys. When the college closes, girls and boys come out together laughing and walking shoulder-to-shoulder with each other.

The intercollege principal, sensitive to both village morality and the need for educated women, responded to the scandal by expelling Krishna from the college. He was sent to his mother's village to continue his education, a move that protected him from the danger of reprisal from Radha's relatives.

The scandal of Radha and Krishna will haunt their families for many years to come, but there is another side to the defense of virtue. This brighter luster of the golden thread shone brightly when a village couple acted out a parody of the final tragedy of Rama and Sita.

THE INNOCENT WIFE

At the end of the Ramayana saga, Sita, rescued from Ravana an
rightful position as wife and queen, is slandered by the washerman
does not believe the accusations, he cannot tolerate the scandal
wife a second time. Sita, daughter of the earth, returns to her n
opens and receives her virtuous daughter.

The Sita of Khalapur was a wife from a poor family who had been purchased as
a second wife by a wealthy Rajput man, whose first wife was barren. The practice,
called by villagers "buying a wife," refers to marriages where the groom's family
finances the dowry. This arrangement is made most frequently by poor men who
cannot arrange marriages with families who can afford a dowry. Second marriages
of wealthy older men are probably the only circumstance in which "purchased"
wives enter a wealthy household. Such wives have lower status than women from
traditional marriages. Therefore, far from being a princess, this Sita was a woman
of humble origins, but she was a woman of honor.

Her husband, visiting outside of Khalapur, met a man who had tried to marry
Sita's sister and been rejected by her father. Out of spite he said that Sita was
immoral. The husband believed him and, returning home, berated his young wife.
When she defended her virtue, he added to the insult by reminding her, "I bought
you."

The next day Sita was missing. Her good clothes and gold earrings, without
which no woman would leave her husband's house, were in her room. The family
assumed that she had returned to Mother Earth by jumping down a village well. For
several days a dozen or more men took time off from their harvesting to drag the
village wells, without result. Then her husband received a letter from his absent
wife saying that she had returned to her father's home and intended to remain there.
She demanded that her sons be sent to her to raise until they were grown and able to
protect her. Only then would she consent to return to her husband's home.

Although poor, Sita could read and write, and she had carried out an escape
that would have been impossible for an illiterate woman who had been transported
to her husband's home shrouded in a bullock cart. Disguised in old clothes, she
had left Khalapur and returned home to her father's house by rail. Although she
had never before traveled alone, she bought a ticket, boarded the train, and was
able to read the railway station sign or recognize the station nearest to her village.
At the railway station of her village she had met a policeman, who had escorted
her at her request safely to her house. She wrote demanding that her young son be
sent to her, saying that she would not return until he was old enough to defend her
from her husband.

Father have the obligation to execute immoral daughters, and affairs prior to
marriage can occur only in the parental village, where the scandal would be known.
Therefore, Sita's return to her parental home proved her innocence. The senior wife
was not only deprived of her co-wife servant but was forced to care for Sita's son
and two young daughters. The women of the courtyard and the neighborhood were
righteously indignant at this unjust slander of a virtuous wife. When tradition says
that women must be killed for immorality, there must be an implicit norm that

ents men from accusing their wives unjustly. Sita's husband had violated his
sponsibility with his unjust accusation.

He went at once to Sita's home with a *panchayat* of five men to make his
apology and retrieve her. Sita refused to return, repeating the demand that her sons
be sent to her. Her father, poor but proud, refused to send her back. The village
Rama and his five prestigious friends returned to Khalapur. It was not until he
returned again to Sita's home, in the company of Khalapur's Mayor as a formal
witness and an official representative of Khalapur, and apologized publicly to Sita's
father, male relatives, and representatives of her village that Sita agreed to return.

We asked Draupadi, who told us of the golden thread, whether she thought Sita
had acted correctly in refusing to return to her husband. Her answer was immediate
and definite: "Of course. A person of bad character can tolerate such insults, but a
woman of good character cannot tolerate them." Draupadi emphasized the strict
criterion for a woman of good character by commenting: "I do not even like a
woman who laughs with full teeth showing. I am very bad that way."

CONCLUSIONS

Like beliefs about human nature and sexuality in most societies, Hindu beliefs
contain contradictions and paradoxes. Women are thought to have more sexual
energy than men, but are expected to control it and be passive in their sexual
relations. They bless their husbands with the sons necessary for men's secular and
spiritual well-being, but sap their strength in the process. Their virginity is sacred,
but their motherhood is essential. They are expected to be obedient daughters,
nurturing mothers, sacred sisters, and faithful wives. Like most women in all
societies, they live with these contradictions and fulfill their roles.

Cultural differences in beliefs about human nature are frequently founded in
religion. The essential difference between the Judeo-Christian tradition and Hinduism is the importance of a remote male sky god for the Western tradition and an
omnipresent Earth Mother for the Indian tradition. All life comes from the earth, so
it is the biggest Shakti. Since the earth is female, women derive more strength from
her than do men.

Reproduction, then, is considered to be the primary reason for sexual activity.
This view, and the centrality of the sexual nature to the entire character, imposes the
necessity of responsible sexual activity, particularly by women. Immoral women
dishonor their entire family and community, and sexual indiscretions cannot be
isolated from the overall code of honor that defines a woman's obligations to her
parental and her husband's families. Immoral women are generally without honor.
If their dishonor becomes public through the birth of illegitimate children, the
penalty is death. However, if they are wrongly accused, the sisterhood of the golden
thread rises as one to their defense.

The tales of Radha and Sita tell much about the values and affiliations that
regulate Rajput life. A wife is never fully at home in her husband's village; when
trouble strikes, haven is always in the village of her parents. Therefore, both Sita

and Radha's mother looked to their parental families for support when trouble struck them in their husband's homes.

The traditional concern for family honor was expressed in the critique of the *sasu* who did not do her duty when she opposed the execution of her daughter, and was therefore too late to rectify this sin by killing her granddaughter; in the words that Krishna's mother spoke to him, invoking the honor of the family men for two generations to berate her son; in the flight of Sita to the haven of her father's home to seek his vindication of her virtue.

The values of money, prestige, and power are never far below the surface of the Rajput mind. The quarrel of Radha's mother with her in-laws quickly revolved around her share of the land and the distribution of dowry goods. The reminder of poverty in Sita's husband's insult, "I bought you for my wife," was the final indignity that sent her fleeing from the village. But the wealth and power and prestige of Radha's family were no shield from criticism when the honor of their women was sullied. The wealth and power of Sita's husband and the five "big men" he brought with him could not stand against injured virtue and the stain upon her family honor. Despite her wealth and education, Radha could not survive the scandal of her pregnancy. Indeed, the prestige of her family made her sacrifice more vital. The poverty of Sita's family did not prevent her triumphant return to her husband's home. Indeed, her husband's wealth and power made his abuse of them more subject to atonement. The British did not teach Hindus the concept of noblesse oblige; it is basic to the fabric of their society.

Any married man has to deal with his wife's wrath, no matter how low her status. In the joint family, a man who has wronged the honor of the women faces their united anger. Women's quarrels among themselves may be quickly set aside when their honor is attacked. When this happens, the wrath of these righteously indignant women is fearsome to behold. Such is the power of the golden thread.

The concerns of the old woman for the shamelessness that comes with the end of strict purdah take on validation when the consequences of this change are considered. Mothers raised with cloistering cannot teach daughters how to resist seducers. Mothers of these educated girls were reared under strict purdah; they cannot teach their daughters how to deal with an outside world they never knew. The fathers of this generation's boys were raised with cloistered, uneducated women. They have no rules to teach their sons for dealing with these new girls "with two braids" who change their world. The boys and girls themselves are caught between the gossip of the village and the demands of modern India. The dicta of their parents do not apply to their new situation. They make their way unguided, and when they slip, the golden thread is spoiled. The problem of preserving traditional values, while moving with *bhagwan* into the modern world, is found throughout traditional societies. With this change come many who, like the women described here, either withstand or are destroyed by the changes that surround them.

A widow with shorn hair and a white, borderless sari uses a string of prayer beads and a brass pot of water in her personal worship service (1955).

10

Widows: Sati, *Rand, Bhaktani*

When the husband dies, then the crown is gone.

When my husband died a woman came and embraced me and said,
"The joy of your life is gone." I went into my room and I did not cry.

You are crying over my plight, but my heart has become a stone.
I have no more tears.

Widows are unlucky, so unlucky that they are frequently underreported in census figures, because other family members are reluctant to admit that a widow, particularly a young widow, lives in the household. Hindus believe that misfortune is the result of bad karma earned by sins of previous lives, and widows may be blamed for their husbands' deaths. They are an unwelcome burden on their husbands' families, particularly if they do not have grown sons. Although the general improvement in women's status by 1975 had lessened the stigma of widows, their basic situation was the same as I described it in 1955. Rajput widows were still forbidden to remarry but remained in their husbands' homes as financial burdens and potential sources of scandal.

Because it is believed that women are virtuous as a result of external, not internal controls, and must live under the authoritarian control of fathers and husbands to ensure their proper behavior, a widow's virtue is suspect. Widows' roles are constrained by three stereotypes: *sati,* the saintly suicide; *rand,* the immoral woman; and *bhaktani,* the holy woman. While all of these roles are, to some extent, abstractions, they influence beliefs and expectations concerning the behavior of widows.

Several Rajput customs make the social position of widows particularly difficult. The traditional constraints on them have a religious basis. The custom of female infanticide persisted into this century despite the 1795 British law against it. Northwestern Indian census figures still show an excess of men. Indirect female infanticide resulting from the greater medical neglect of girls has been recently documented (Miller, 1981). This direct and indirect infanticide alters the natural sex ratio, resulting in an acute shortage of women. This shortage of available wives is

221

further increased by the prohibition against widow remarriage. Widows are expected to remain unmarried and celibate in their husbands' households, under the protection of the *soosar* and *jaith*s.

> Prescriptions, often reiterated, for the proper conduct of widowhood included instructions that she should not eat more than one very plain meal a day, that she should perform the most menial tasks, never sleep on a bed, leave the house only to go to the temple, keep out of sight at festivals (since she was inauspicious to everyone but her own children), wear nothing but the drabbest clothes, and, of course, no jewelry. Perhaps the most humiliating of all for a high-born lady was having her head shaved monthly by an untouchable male barber. All this was held to be necessary for the sake of her husband's soul and to keep herself from being reborn as a female animal. (Stein, 1978, p. 255)

A widow could escape this miserable life by dying with her husband on his funeral pyre. This custom, called *sati,* was regularly practiced by Rajputs and other castes into the nineteenth century despite British laws prohibiting it.

The prohibition against remarriage of widows means that even virgin widows must remain unmarried if their husband dies between the *shadi* and *gauna.* Reformers have opposed the custom of not remarrying widows since the middle of the nineteenth century. Much of this opposition has been based not on concern for widows' welfare but on concern that widows will be seduced and damage their families' reputations. Gandhi called virgin widows "a source of corruption and a dangerous infection to society" and used this judgment as the basis of his campaign for the remarriage of virgin widows (Stein, 1978, p. 263).

Despite these reform movements, the prohibition still exists. The patrilineal kinship system of Hindus assigns children to the patrilineage. Therefore, a widow with children would have to abandon them or marry one of her husband's kinsmen. Among Hindus the nonremarriage of widows, including virgin widows, is widely accepted as a status symbol. For this reason the custom is often adopted by upwardly mobile caste groups whose members wish to increase their social status.

Whatever a widow's age, her status is never as secure as that of women whose husbands are alive, but the widowed *sasu,* whose husband lived out his life and who has married sons and *bahu*s, is much better off than the young, widowed *bahu,* who must be supported by her husband's kinsmen. When we asked about mourning for husbands, several women mentioned that it is much worse to be widowed when the sons are young and still unmarried than when one is already a *sasu.* The worst fate is to be widowed before one has borne sons for the patrilineage.

The degree to which widowed *sasu*s lose their position of authority depends on the amount of wealth they control and the loyalty of their sons. Most widows maintain some degree of authority in their *bughar*s, by virtue of their control over their husbands' property, their sons, and their *bahu*s. The control of the husband's property passes to his widow for her lifetime. Widows usually do not relinquish this control to their sons, since it represents their primary source of power. Disputes between mothers and grown sons may arise over decisions regarding land. Conflict with sons presents a difficult dilemma for some widows, since control of their sons' loyalty is another important factor in their status and treatment. As one widow put it: "When a woman has her husband, her *bahu*s will have some respect for her and fear her. When the husband dies, then the crown is gone and the *sasu*s will not respect her." This fear is probably the most important basis for the concern expressed by older women about husband–wife intimacy. If a mother cannot keep the loyalty of her sons in disputes with her *bahu*s, she may be mistreated by them after her husband dies.

A young widow remains under the direction of her *sasu*. The husband's kinsmen have the responsibility of looking after her and her children and arranging the children's marriages. Although they may go there on visits, few widows return to the homes of their parents permanently. Returning permanently to one's parental home would indicate that the husband's family was negligent in its responsibility. If the widow has sons, they are part of their father's lineage, and his relatives want them to grow up as part of their paternal kin group. If they are young, their mother is needed to take care of them.

Widows' rights to their husbands' property give them economic control of their sons' families, and they generally resist efforts by their sons to legally divide the land among them. If a widow's sons are grown when their father dies, they usually respect their mother's wishes, although they may farm their sections of the land separately. The holdings of a widow with young children are usually managed by her husband's kinsmen, and this situation sometimes results in conflict. Control of land by widows with sons too young to work it is a matter of concern to men of the patrilineage, particularly if a widow insists on managing the cultivation and sale of crops herself. Some widows do insist on managing their own property because they fear, sometimes with justification, that their husbands' relatives may cheat them and divide their land among their own sons.

Such efforts are fiercely resisted by her husband's relatives. If a widow's sons are still too young for fieldwork, she must get others to farm the land for her, usually on a sharecrop basis. This means that she herself often must leave the seclusion of purdah and go about the village alone. Even if she is a fairly old woman, this always stimulates gossip, damages the family reputation, and annoys her affinal relatives. More serious, however, is the fear that she may allow herself to be duped and lose or sell some of the land. If a widow has only daughters, the suspicion that she may sell land is even more intense. Traditionally widows without sons could not control land, even by regency. One Khalapur widow with an only daughter who insisted on managing her own estate and let it out on shares was severely beaten by her husband's kinsmen. The worst situation is that of a widow with no children, like Radha's mother. Land is basic to Rajput economy; therefore, it is not surprising that Radha's grandparents reacted so strongly to the threat that Radha's mother would claim her share of their property.

There is strong feeling among Khalapur Rajputs that a wife's lifelong loyalty should be to her husband's family, although her affection may remain with her blood kin. Since a widow's place is in her husband's home, and the obligation to support her rests with the husband's family, she may not be welcome in her natal home, particularly if her parents are already dead. As we have seen, relations between *nanad*s and *bahu*s are often strained, and few *bahu*s would welcome a widowed *nanad* and her children as a permanent addition to their household.

The status of widows, like the status of all married women, is usually better if her family and her husband's family are relatively wealthy. A widow is expected to give presents to her husband's relatives, just as she did when he was alive. If a widow comes from a wealthy family, the value of these presents offsets the cost of supporting her. However, if she comes from a poor family and is seldom called home by her parents, her work is the only compensation she can give for her support.

There is considerable variation in the treatment of widows by their husbands' families, and this is an important consideration for most families in their selection of husbands for their daughters. A number of village families have well-founded reputations for dealing justly with their widows and for taking good care of them and their children. In one family of the sample there was an elderly widow who was treated with great deference and who had become something of a matriarch in a large *bughar*.

In some houses widows are mistreated; in others they are tyrants. Mamta and her sister, Durga, had married two brothers. The two sisters had entirely different temperaments: While Mamta was kind and gentle, Durga was ill tempered. Mamta's widowed *sasu* lived with Durga, and Mamta said that Durga beat her. This was the only unkind remark we heard Mamta make, so there was no reason to doubt it. In some families where widows do have problems, the fault lies partially with them. One widow was known to beat herself with bricks and then run from the house accusing others of beating her. One elderly lady became so angry when a busy *bahu* asked her to wait to have her hookah filled that she then refused the hookah and caused a family upset. The most disruptive action of a widow that we heard of was that of a cantankerous elderly grandmother who accused a new bride of immorality. Fortunately, the girl had a maternal great grandaunt living in a neighboring household who was so concerned about the treatment of this bride that she wrote to her brother-in-law to come and bring his daughter home. The aunt's account of the situation is as follows:

> This old woman has a bad nature. She always finds fault with everyone. Now, suppose I tell you in the presence of everyone that my *bahu* is of loose character, then everybody will also say so, even if the *bahu* is not at fault. You know this bride is the granddaughter of my real sister. She got pregnant in the very beginning, when she came to this house for *gauna*, 3 months ago. Since that time the poor girl has not taken a piece of bread and has grown very weak. She kept lying on her bed in such hot weather in May and June.
>
> The *soosar* asked "Why does the new bride not come out into the open air? Is she sick?" The girl told her *soosar*, through a young *nanad*, that she felt very weak and could not get up from her bed. The *soosar* felt pity and sent her some fruit. Similarly, her *jaith* also sent some fruits to her.
>
> On this the old grandmother started telling everybody that the bride is entangled with her *jaith* and *soosar*, who sends fruits to her. How sad it was! What might the poor girl have felt? She was very healthy and is now reduced to a skeleton in this house, in these 3 months. Another *jaith* was shouting at me, saying why should I interfere in their household affair. I said that the girl would die under such unhealthy conditions.
>
> I asked my brother-in-law to come and fetch his daughter for a while. So she is

not here now. Now her husband has joined the service out of the village, and the girl need not come here. She will join her husband and live there peacefully. The boy is good, educated, and healthy and of good nature. We are satisfied. I think that the groom for a girl should be energetic so as to be able to earn with hard work, and educated and of matching age. For the rest, I do not care. A woman cannot be unhappy with such a man.

That old woman killed her own *bahu* like this. In her eyes every woman is of loose character.

In general widows are respected, although not as much as women whose husbands are still living. In a few houses where poor *sasu*s were mistreated by their *bahu*s, a facade of respect was always maintained.

MOURNING CUSTOMS

When a married man died, his widow's glass bangles were broken and her gold jewelry and toe rings were removed. Her head was shaved, and she was dressed in a plain white cotton sari. At the end of the 20-day mourning period, family members took the widow to Hardwar, a holy city on the Ganges. There, she discarded the clothes she was wearing when her husband died and threw them into the Ganges. Until this was done, she was unclean and could not cook or use cooking utensils. This ritual cleansing of widows is still practiced, with varying degrees of exactitude.

The separation of husbands and wives, enforced by customs of purdah during their lifetimes, is maintained even at death by excluding widows from the funeral rituals and forbidding them to cry for their husbands. The exclusion of widows from mourning is the final act that dilutes the bonds of marriage. At death, the primacy of the blood relatives is emphasized. While exclusion from the ritual wailing emphasizes the peripheral status of widows, it also serves to give them privacy at a time of grief. Whereas ritual wailing is expected to be loud, women weep in silence when they are genuinely upset. My description of the death of a *sasu* in 1955 illustrates the contrast:

> When married women of the deceased's lineage receive news of the death, they come to help prepare the body and express their regrets. Together with the women of the household, they beat their foreheads, breasts, and thighs and raise their voices in the high-pitched tones of ritual wailing. A family will be criticized by neighbors if the women's wails are not long and loud, and one woman said that when women mourned properly, their bodies should show the bruises of their self-inflicted beatings. The wailing reaches a peak when the men of the family arrive to remove the body to the cremation grounds, usually not more than two or three hours after death. In marked contrast to ritual wailing, grief, when wailing is not required, is expressed in complete silence. As the body of a mother-in-law was carried away, a daughter-in-law beat her head against the courtyard wall and had to be restrained by the other women, but the dead woman's teenaged, unmarried daughter stood on the sidelines, holding the baby of her wailing aunt, with silent tears coursing down her face.

(Minturn & Hitchcock, 1966, p. 81)

Khalapur widows used to remain alone in their rooms while the other women of the family engaged in ritual mourning. Several of the older widows remember being thus secluded when their husbands died. Some women said that their home villages also had this custom, while others reported it absent in their parental homes. Most reports indicated that the widow was simply isolated from the formal ritual wailing. However, one woman reported that a particularly vindictive *jethani* looked under her *gungat* to see if she was crying.

Women gave various explanations for this custom. Some women said that a widow's crying was interpreted to mean that she was shamelessly sexual and could not bear to live without a husband, an ominous validation of the belief that her Shakti was uncontrollable. Widows who cried were reportedly rebuked for their lust by phrases such as, "Can the man come again through your weeping?" or "If you are so fond of your husband, nail him to the wall, or dry the body and keep it with you. Do you want a corpse with you?" According to this interpretation, the prohibition against mourning for spouses also applied to widowers, who were forbidden to come near the bodies of their wives. If a widower approaches his wife's corpse, people said, "Even now he has come to her breast." Although there was no fear that a married man would return as a ghost if his widow cried, some women feared that the man's spirit would not rest quietly. Others denied the sexual explanation, attributing the custom to the greater closeness between blood versus relatives. Some women reported that a widow does not participate in public mourning when her *sasu* and *nanad*s are alive to mourn the death but may do so if they are dead.

The absence of financial support for widows without sons of working age was a third explanation for the custom. Reportedly, weeping widows may be told, "Your widowhood is a burden for us, not for you, since we must now support you." Since the expense of supporting orphaned children and arranging for their marriages falls on their parental uncles, and the orphans' share of the family land diminishes the shares of their cousins, the support of widows and orphans is a burden to the husbands' families. An older woman said that older widows whose husbands have lived out their lives should not mourn, and will be ridiculed for doing so, but that widows of young husbands cry because they are unlucky and have no one to support their children.

Women vigorously denied that the absence of open crying means that they did not mourn their husbands. Several women emphasized their denial by saying that one cries for the loss of an animal, so one will certainly cry for a husband. Some reported having spells of unconsciousness, because of this prohibition. Others said they cried alone. One said that a widow may mourn all of her life, if she does it alone. One woman utilized the traditional closeness of the brother–sister relationship to participate in the mourning of her husband by crying and chanting the names of two recently deceased brothers during the ritual mourning for her husband.

WIDOW'S WORK

The work of widows is no longer confined to "the most menial tasks." It does not differ greatly from the work of other women of their age and family status. The degree to which they maintain the desirable qualities of widows and avoid scandals is a subtle determinant of the respect they are accorded. *Bahus* do most of the hard labor in the *bughar,* but their contributions to the household economy are downgraded. This denigration of women's work is often more acute if the woman is widowed, particularly if her sons are young and her *sasu* is still alive. Although widows may work hard, their labor is often not appreciated.

Young widows who are still *bahus* are considered to be particularly unlucky since their husbands died prematurely. *Sasus* and family women may blame them for their husbands' deaths and make them scapegoats in the *bughar.* They are often burdened with most of the household and treated like servants, particularly if they do not have wealthy parents to support them. Radha's mother was able to maintain her own household within her *bughar* because of the wealth of her father's family.

Older widows are better off, particularly if their sons are married and they have attained the status of *sasu. Sasus* may move about the village and surroundings with ease, and this mobility is often an advantage to other women of the *bughar.* Widowed *sasus* often leave the responsibility of running the household to their *bahus,* thus avoiding conflict, and take on tasks that require leaving the *bughar.*

In one family, when a buffalo was stolen, their widowed *sasu* walked for days throughout the village, going into the neighborhoods of low-caste residents, which she ordinarily would not enter, to search for it. Once we were visiting the *bughar* when she set out to search for the missing animal. She was obviously exhausted and asked two grandsons to come with her. They both refused, saying, "Can't you go alone?" Without arguing, the old woman got up and left to search alone. She finally found the animal in the courtyard of a Sudra family. Without calling on any of her family men for assistance, she went into the *bughar,* claimed the animal, untied it, and led it home. Since farmers know their individual cattle, and the cattle know the roads to their home compounds, the thieves could only excuse themselves by saying that they had found the buffalo wandering in the fields and were keeping it until it was claimed. Although the buffalo was valuable property, the young women and boys teased the widow; one brash young daughter of the household, back from her *shadi* and puffed up with her newly married status, was particularly rude, saying sarcastically, "The most energetic person in the house has found our buffalo." The distraught widow finally became so angry with her insolent tormentor that she called the girl a co-wife, an insult which not only silenced the young bride but sent her crying to her room, refusing to come out.

Each day the widow Mamta, the *sasu* of Bala, the child bride, took her spinning wheel to her grove of four guava trees; there she spun and guarded the ripening fruit from thieves and parrots while her sons worked the family fields. Her fields and guava trees were next to the land of Bahai, a widow (described at the end of this chapter), and the two women were good friends. They often sat chatting in the shade of the trees, away from the smoke and noise of the *bughars,* Bahai smoking her hookah and Mamta spinning. Their quiet conversation was interrupted only by Mamta's periodic forays to shoo away hungry parrots.

Some *sasus,* particularly widows, act as peacemakers. When women quarrel, their shouting can easily be heard in neighboring houses. Senior women from the neighborhood come to the *bughar* when arguments occur. They separate the quarrelers, and each is talked to quietly by one or two women, who listen to their stories, calm them down, and mediate the dispute. I noticed, after seeing several of these incidents, that the same women usually appear, even when they are not the closest neighbors. Their intervention is quiet, informal, and usually successful. This seems to be a self-selected role that *sasu*s may assume. These peacemakers are not overtly praised or rewarded for their efforts, but they are always welcome in the homes they enter, no matter how bitter the dispute they interrupt. Other older women are typically the bearers of bad gossip. When Radha died, one *sasu* of a poor family appeared in several houses, repeating the scandal, praising the virtues of her own daughters, and obviously relishing the opportunity to criticize a wealthy family.

While older women do not visit their parental homes as often as they did when they were young, they still return for family festivals. Widows are often freer to return for visits in their parents' homes than are women who must still care for living husbands. As senior daughters of the village, older women have the most freedom. One elderly woman, Maina, stayed for several weeks in her brother's house. Maina usually wore widow's white, immaculately clean, but dressed in tunic and pants rather than the sari usually worn by married women. She was the gayest and most humorous of the women that we knew. She danced for us and talked freely about marital relations, assuring us that purdah was not kept in the bedroom. Maina was the only woman who openly admitted the danger of seduction of *bahu*s by senior men. Like many older people she had lost most of her teeth. Most toothless Rajput women cover their mouths with their saris when talking, but Maina simply smiled and laughed without embarrassment. She came to see us unexpectedly one day, and we thoughtlessly served her the usual company food of peanuts and seeds. She joked about her inability to eat them, saying, "The hut of the cow dung cakes is empty." We offered her an orange, which she ate with relish. While Maina seemed to be a particularly happy and outgoing woman, her vacation in her childhood home no doubt enhanced her relaxed demeanor. Evaluation of the lives of widows, as of married women, must include the recognition that they do, throughout their lives, spend time in their parents' havens.

WIDOW'S ROLES
The Sati Tradition

The custom of sati probably characterizes, in the Western mind, the mystery and cruelty of India better than any other aspect of it. Sati seems to have originated as a custom among the Rajputs and other warrior castes, but it became a fairly popular prestige symbol for other caste groups as well. Banias and other low-caste groups did not practice sati until the nineteenth century, when the custom became so popular that low-caste groups often adopted it. Although widow murder is associated with India in modern times, the custom is not unique to that culture.

> The practice of burning or burying women alive with their deceased husbands, even as an expression of an underlying view of women as property, is not as bizarre and

exotic a custom as its identification with Hindu India has made it seem. Although Greek visitors to North India wrote accounts of sati as early as the fourth century B.C., there are accounts of widow sacrifice among Scandinavians, Slavs, Greeks, Egyptians, Chinese, Finns, Maoris, and some American Indians. The practice apparently originated among warriors who probably also elaborated the mythology attached to it. The heroism of the *sati* (the sacrificed woman) was in fact equated with that of the warrior. The connection of sati with the warrior and ruler (Kasatriya) caste endowed it with a social prestige which it never lost. In the fourteenth to sixteenth centuries, it became usual to make a clean sweep of the women's quarters of a dead ruler before installing his successor. Sometimes even ministers were included, and the total could amount to the burning of several thousand persons, including queens, concubines, and servants of both sexes.

The practice was said to have been forbidden, at least originally, to Brahmans, the highest caste in terms of social rank, but the associations with honor which sati acquired proved too strong. Eventually, Brahman women were burning as liberally as Ksatriyas, or even in greater numbers as the power and retinues of the princes declined. The Brahman association with sati was probably responsible for the form of the ceremony and its assimilation to the scriptural and sacrificial tradition.

The most usual form that sati took was that of burning the wife alive in or on the funeral pyre that consumed the husband's body. There were scriptural rules prohibiting the ceremony while the woman was menstruating (which was equated with uncleanliness or unchastity), pregnant, or could not be spared from the care of her young children. In such cases, or when the husband's death occurred during his absence from home, some women burned themselves along with an article of clothing or personal effect of the dead man. This "following after" was forbidden to some castes, including Brahmans. In those castes where the dead were disposed of by burial rather than cremation, the widow could be buried alive.

(Stein, 1978, pp. 253–254)

The ideal of voluntary sati is a religiously sanctified suicide or martyrdom. The act of sati confers salvation not only on the martyr but on her relatives as well; it also confers economic benefits on her husband's relatives. It is believed that through the Sati, her husband, her husband's family, her mother's family, and her father's family would be in paradise for 35 million years, no matter how sinful they all had been.

Economic as well as spiritual rewards were bestowed through the act of Sati:

Over and beyond these scriptural inducements given, custom conferred prestige on the surviving families in this world as well as the next. For families of high rank and some affluence there were also tangible benefits. When a Hindu girl marries, she is officially transferred from her father's patrilineage to that of her husband; at the same time, her family is relieved of any moral responsibility for her future maintenance. Once widowed, she is of no further value to her in-laws as a potential bearer of sons; indeed, their worst fear is that she should chance to become pregnant, casting a possible shadow on the legitimacy of any previous children. In such a fanatically patrilineal tradition, the widow's death assured guardianship and

undisputed influence over her children to her husband's family. It also kept her
from enjoying in her lifetime rights in her husband's estate.

(Stein, 1978, p. 2)

This magnificent spiritual reward, contrasted with the abuse faced by widows,
makes their willingness to accept the custom of sati more understandable. The sati
tradition makes the contemporary conflicts between widows and their husbands'
relatives over management of property more comprehensible.

The rationalization for the custom was twofold. First, the assumption that wom-
en possess powerful Shakti and weak wills led to the conclusion that they must be
married before menstruation, and that they would be incapable of leading chaste
lives if their husbands died while they were young. Second, women were not
expected to outlive their husbands. (India, today, is one of the few countries where
the life expectancy of women is less than that of men.) Therefore, widows' sins in
past lives were the presumed cause of their husband's deaths. The younger the
husband at the time of his death, the greater the blame attributed to his widow. Sati
expiated this bad karma and ensured an extended period in paradise and a "clean
karma slate" in future lives. Widows who chose sati went to their deaths gloriously
and proved their virtue by their choice.

In order to understand the reverence for such a cruel custom, one must appreci-
ate the values of piety and loyalty that sati embodies. When Rajputs ruled Rajasthan, and some surrounding states, as feudal lords, they commanded the service
and devotion of wives and vassals. This time holds the same romantic appeal for
Rajputs that the age of knightly chivalry holds for Westerners. However, in India the
feudal system ended in this century. The Zamindar Abolition Act was not passed
until 1952. Older Rajputs in families like that of Amar Nath and his brothers and
cousins were the Zamindars.

The burning of wives became more frequent during the Middle Ages, when
Rajputs frequently fought with Muslims. When defeat was inevitable, wives were
burned to avoid capture. The custom is called *joher*. Probably the most famous
immolation of women was the *johar,* or mass suicide, at Fort Chittor in the thirteenth century, when the Rajput women in the fort were burned to avoid being
captured by a licentious Mogul invader. The story, cloaked in myth and legend, is
still very much a part of the Rajput heritage. The newspaper report of the Lohars'
return to Chittor includes a brief history of the mass sati and the final defeat of the
Rajput rulers of the fort:

> The annals of Chittor throw up from history the story of man when he either lived
> by the sword or died by it, when kings and princes, soldiers and generals defied
> death for love, for freedom and the glory of conquest.
>
> Pappa Rawul, according to history, took Fort Chittor sometime in the fifth
> century and from then till the middle of the 16th century 59 princes, his lineal
> descendants, ruled it. Twice the fort was stormed and ransacked. The first attack
> was in the 13th century. Allauddin Khiji, history reveals, ordered the massacre of
> men and destruction of property for a woman he could not get. He wanted to

possess Padmini, a celebrated beauty of the time and wife of the Rana Bhimsingh, ruler of Chittor.

When the marauding troops of Khiji were about to take the fort, the defenders preferred death to dishonor and slavery. Women folk, led by Rani Padmini, whose reported beauty had incensed Khiji, entered the funeral pyre set alight in the subterranean retreat within the fort. In chambers impervious to the light of day the Rajput women were sealed off, allowing them to be devoured by fire rather than dishonored by aliens.

No human eye has peeped into the dark cavern so far and legend has it that a serpent, probably multi-hooded, keeps watch over the place warding off intruders.

Shortly after, however, Rajputs retook the fort and ruled over it until Akbar reached his commanding hand into the interior of Rajasthan. Udai Singh, the last of the Rajputs to rule from Chittor, fled the fort when it fell to the Moghuls in 1568. With a handful of followers and Prince Pratap, he scoured the jungles chased by Akbar's soldiers and agents. Four years later, Pratap became the Rana and took the vow to be a nomad until Rajput glory was revived at Chittor. He shunned all earthly pleasures and died without fulfilling his pledge.

The faithful Rajputs and Lohars, who had followed their monarch, were bound by the pledge and for generations it has remained. Their descendants have been roaming about the plains and plateaus of India living in carts and abstaining from comforts.

(*The Hindustani Times,* April 6, 1955)

The long shadow of this event became apparent in the spring of 1955. Prime Minister Nehru led about 2,000 Lohars—descendants of those who served the last Rajput Rana of Chittor—back into the ruins of Fort Chittor to encourage them to abandon their nomadic life and become settled citizens of modern India.

The Indian government took this action in order to relieve the Lohars of a vow they took when Fort Chittor fell, for the last time, to the troops of Akbar, the greatest of the Mogul emperors, in February 1568. The following account is taken from a newspaper report of the story on the occasion of the return of the Lohars. Centuries after the events described, the newspaper report reads like a legend.

When they left the fort after its fall to the Moghuls, they [the Lohars] took a fivefold vow—not to rest until the fort is recaptured, not to live under a roof, not to draw water from a well with ropes, not to lit [*sic*] any lamp, and not to sleep on a cot. . . .

The pledge was taken by the Gadi Lohars four centuries ago in February 1568, when the fort fell to the Moghuls. Lohars, who made arms for the Rajputs and the Ranas, left Chittor along with the Rajput defenders, taking a vow not to return until the fort was liberated. With Rana Pratap, who refused to bend the knee to the mighty Akbar, they resolved never to rest or seek a life of ease and pleasure until the honour of Chittor and all it stood for was vindicated.

Another legend says when the Moghul troops took Chittor, thousands of Brahmin priests—whose safety was the first duty of the Rajput king—were done to death by the invaders. The slaughter was so great that the weight of the sacred threads of Brahmins, who fell to the sword, was estimated at 600 lb. Rage and

remorse caught the Lohars, the legend records, and they pledged not to rest until
the sacrilege was avenged.

(*The Hindustani Times,* April 6, 1955)

A band of Lohars camped in Khalapur in the winter of 1954–55, on their way to
Fort Chittor. The men wore *dhootis* and turbans and women wore the full red cotton
skirts and head clothes characteristic of Rajasthan dress. Their carts were handmade
and elaborately carved. They were poor, proud, dusty, and colorful. For 400 years
they had been nomads in Rajasthan and surrounding states. They were not included
in census reports and were not on the voters' roll of any of the states in which they
roamed. They maintained their own system of justice with their own *panchayat*s.
They still forged tools and sold them to Rajput families.

The legends of Fort Chittor incorporate several themes central to Rajput values.
One theme is the purity of the Rajput bloodline and the chastity of the Rajput
women on whom the bloodline purity depends. The sanctity of the bloodline and the
belief in ritual pollution are the basis for the permanent exclusion of women who
have been raped or seduced by alien men. Whereas a high-caste Hindu man may
remove the pollution of sexual intercourse with a low-caste or non-Hindu woman by
a ritual bath, the pollution of high-caste women from comparable sexual contact is
permanent. The biological rationale for this belief is that a man's pollution is
external, while a woman's is internal.

Another theme is the irresistible and fatal appeal of a woman's beauty. History
records land and power as the causes of wars, but in legend men fight for beauty.
Like Troy's Helen and Camelot's Guinevere, Chittor's Padmini is the legendary
cause of the attack that destroyed her husband's rule. Unlike Helen and Guinevere,
however, Padmini was a blameless, faithful wife. Whether Khiji saw Padmini in her
cloistered harem or had only heard of her beauty is not clear. The legend is one of
many stories that place the blame for the seclusion of women on the lust of alien
Muslim invaders.

Finally, there was the ultimate seclusion of Padmini and her attendants, said to
number 300. The funeral pyre was "in chambers impervious to the light of day,"
which have never been unsealed. Already sanctified, their ashes were never scattered on the sacred Ganges but remain entombed in their subterranean pyre. For
1600 years the privacy of these royal Satis has been sealed with their mortal
remains, guarded by the multi-headed serpent of Siva. It no longer matters whether
they were 300 or 30, whether they went bravely to their satis, led by their Rani, or
were dragged screaming to their death chamber by their husbands, or the Rana's
soldiers. They are holy Satis, sanctified by time and tradition. The *johar* tradition
drove hundreds of Hindu women to suicide during the partition riots of 1947. Many
village wells were filled with the bodies of women who had jumped in to avoid
capture by Muslim troops. Reportedly women who were captured by Muslims
during these riots still reside in Pakistan because their families would not take back
their permanently polluted relatives.

This is the heritage of the daughters who keep the golden thread of honor pure. It
is a heritage they cherish still and will for generations yet unborn. Just as Christians

who would not suffer martyrdom, worship at the shrines of martyrs, Hindu women worship at the shrines of their Satis.

The continued worship at village sati shrines and the pride of women relating the stories of these local saints indicates that this ancient custom still represents ideal values for widows. Women who want to join their husbands in death may still kill themselves in private. A Khalapur woman says that her sister-in-law became a Sati by this method around 1960.

> She locked herself in her room after her husband's death when no one allowed her to enter his funeral pyre. The family had built a sacred fire in a large iron can because of the death. The wife sat on the fire, behind locked doors. When her relatives saw smoke they tried to open the doors, and when this failed they put a hole in the roof and took her out. They wanted to take her to the hospital, but the wife said, "Why have you taken me out of the fire? That was bad on your part, and you should not have done so." With these words she died and her husband's family built a large shrine for her.

Sati is still an ideal for some Khalapur men. In 1955 Amar Nath said that he would be pleased if Draupadi, his third wife, committed sati when he died. In 1975 Draupadi commented jokingly, "That old man has made chutney out of two wives. Now I will make chutney out of him." Clearly Amar Nath's wish is a nostalgic dream that he does not expect to have realized.

Religion Versus Law

The Portuguese, French, and Dutch colonial governments outlawed sati before the nineteenth century. Encouraged by the success of these efforts, the British colonial government began abolishing sati state by state in 1829. The last legal sati reportedly occurred in Udaipur in 1861 (Stein, 1978). However, newspaper accounts of satis appeared about every six weeks during the winter of 1954–55, usually with the comment that it was unclear whether the widow had climbed onto the pyre voluntarily or been forced by relatives. Despite the reported lack of clarity, papers never reported any police investigation of these satis. Most of them occurred in the sacred city of Banares, where many devout Hindus go to die. The newspapers reported that as many as 100,000 people came to worship at Banares sati sites. In 1974–75 I did not see sati reports in the newspapers, but some Rajputs in Rajasthan have tried to revive the custom in recent years. A sati in Rajasthan in August 1980, in a village about 70 kilometers from Jaipur, received little national attention, but the sati of a young bride Roop Kanwar in 1987, in a village close to the main Delhi-Jaipur highway and reputedly witnessed by 10,000 people, was reported in the national press and caused widespread protests and government intervention was necessary to stem the revival of this ancient custom. The newspaper account of this event is as follows.

> The ancient Hindu rite of sati, requiring a woman to immolate herself on the funeral pyre of her husband, was abolished in British India in 1829. But early this month,

when her young husband died suddenly of gastroenteritis, Roop Kanwar, 18, a bride of just eight months, declared her intention to revive the grim custom. By that afternoon thousands of people had gathered to witness her immolation. After taking a ritual bath, the woman dressed once more in her bright red bridal finery. Sitting atop the funeral pyre with her husband's corpse, his head on her lap, she asked her teenage brother-in-law to light the fire. Within moments, as the crowd's cries reached a climax, she was consumed by flames.

The Indian press and public reacted in horror. Said the national daily *Indian Express:* "A barbarous and primitive act." Women's groups protested, and the Rajasthan high court banned further ceremonies at the site. But to some people, Kanwar had become a goddess. Pilgrims thronged to the village of Deorala, 47 miles northeast of Jaipur, to pay homage. Last week hundreds of thousands of people converged on the site for ceremonies marking the end of the 13-day mourning period. The pyre, which had been kept smoldering with ghee (clarified butter) and coconuts, was decorated with a flower-bedecked silk canopy. Kanwar's four brothers spread a stole embroidered with gold thread over the pyre. As Brahman priests chanted mantras, the stole was burned. The pyre was then extinguished with holy water from the Ganges and milk.

Despite the high-court ban on the ceremony, police, fearful of provoking a riot, did not interfere. They did, however, arrest Pushpendra Singh, the youth who lit the pyre, and four other in-laws, charging them with murder. The maximum penalty: life in prison. Authorities were investigating whether the bride's in-laws, who by tradition would have been required to care for her the rest of her life, had pressured her into the act. Kanwar's father, saying he believed that she acted under "divine orders," took consolation from the fact that his daughter had become a devi (goddess). A shrine commemorating the widow will be built at the sati site. More than $160,000 has already been contributed by devotees.

(Time, September 1987, p. 41)

The history of sati from its ancient origins to the events following Roop Kanwar's sati are recorded in S. Narasimhan's excellent book *Sati: Widow Burning in India* (1990). Narasimhan reports the failure of the government to stop the thirteenth-day sainthood ceremony, reputedly attended by 100,000 people, and the first-year anniversary celebration, attended by 4,000 people. She describes the formation of a permanent shrine and the money it earns. She notes that although the men responsible for the burning had commited nonbailable offenses, they were let out on bail and have not been tried.

Narasimhan compares the contemporary reaction to the government's attempts to stop sati with similar reactions to the British anti-sati law of 1829. Widespread protests occurred both times. Government action was seen by traditional people as an attack on their religion, caste, and tradition by outside forces. In the nineteenth century this force was the British colonial government; now it is the modern, Westernized Indian government. Rajputs resisted British efforts to stop sati, and at the second anniversary of Roop Kanwar's death a convener of the anniversary celebration is quoted as saying, "This government wants to finish off Hinduism and Rajputs in the name of this anti-sati law" (Narasimhan, 1990, p. 146).

At both times some religious leaders invoked scripture as sanctified justification for this custom. In 1988 a religious leader in Rajasthan attributed natural disasters in the years following these government actions to divine wrath, saying, "You will notice that ever since this anti-sati law was enacted, nature has been revolting. Today, when we should be feeling the heat of summer, it is cold. The monsoons bring no rain. And the untimely rainfall has been destroying crops ready for harvest. . . . All because sati has been insulted" (Narasimhan, 1990, p. 132). The ban against sati became impossible for the British to enforce and is proving resistant to contemporary government actions.

There was evidence that Roop Kanwar and the widow who had been consumed in 1980 were coerced. One Rajput widow interviewed after Roop Kanwar's sati said, "I am a widow. I know what it is to lose a husband. You go insane. It is cruel to term an act of insanity as an act of voluntary bravery. It is the womenfolk of the household who use a moment of weakness and madness to encourage you to die." This suspicion was also voiced in earlier times. In 1818 a British magistrate wrote that "ninety-nine out of a hundred women sacrificed themselves under the influence of the infatuation poured into their ears . . . than from any conviction of their own minds" (Narasimhan, 1990, pp. 86–87).

Narasimhan also discusses the relationship between sati and the recent burning of brides for their dowries. Since the husbands of these brides are still alive and their deaths were clearly involuntary, bride burning is as far from sati as murder is from martyrdom. However, Narasimhan argues that these bride burnings, along with female feticide, are a manifestation of the low value placed on women's lives in Indian society.

Rand

Hindu scriptures say that women cannot control their Shakti when they do not have husbands to satisfy their lust. Widows, particularly young widows, may tempt their male relatives and bring disgrace upon the household. The Hindu word for widow, *rand,* also means prostitute, and "immoral widow" is one of the most frequent insults hurled by angry women. Some families may avoid the burden of supporting widows by selling them into prostitution. Such action would bring disgrace upon a Khalapur Rajput family. Nevertheless, in 1955 a woman told me about one family who had reputedly sold a widow into this degraded occupation.

Village society has no place for spinsters; all daughters marry. However, the excess of men, brought about through female infanticide, and prohibition on marriage outside of acceptable *jatis* meant that in the past a number of men remained bachelors, a situation that still exists in some families. Many families could not afford to arrange good marriages for all their sons. The work of adult sons increases the family income, and in poor families the work of the eldest brothers was often necessary to build up enough capital to arrange marriages. Sons are married in order of their birth, and it is virtually impossible for a man to marry after a younger brother has been married. Furthermore, these elder brothers were often past marriageable age by the time they had earned enough to arrange good marriages for their younger brothers. Therefore, it was the younger brothers who usually married, while elder brothers, who had authority over them, remained bachelors. The separation of *choopars* from *bughars* and the custom of bringing food to men in their *choopars*, so that they did not have to enter the *bughar*, functioned to separate bachelor brothers from the vulnerable *bahus*.

The concern for the virtue of family wives is increased when there are widows, particularly young widows, in the *bughar*. The presumed seductiveness of widows is the primary rationale behind their traditional lifelong mourning dress and shaved heads. This traditional mourning dress, like other purdah customs, was no longer strictly enforced in 1975. Some widows no longer cut their hair and continued to wear colored saris, or the homespun saris with colored borders, worn by many older women. Since toe rings were no longer worn by married women, this mark of widowhood was no longer present, and a few widows continued to wear gold jewelry. In 1975 widows could be reliably identified only the absence of glass bangle bracelets.

Although mourning dress had been abandoned, and, in most families, all men married, concern for widows' morality persisted. When a woman of 50 years lost her husband in the fall of 1974, leaving her *jaith*, aged 65, as the only senior man in the house, rumors that they were having sexual relations surfaced within 2 months of the husband's death.

Bhaktani

When sati was abandoned, high-caste widows faced lives of austerity so bleak that some English reformers thought that a return to sati would be preferable to their miserable existences. Widows no longer face these severe restrictions, but they are expected to live celibate and holy lives, so as not to disgrace themselves and their families. Widows are particularly likely to visit holy shrines and make offerings to deities. One childless Khalapur widow had gone beyond the expected degree of religiosity and become a *bhaktani*, the feminine version of *bhaktana*, or religious leader. The Khalapur *bhaktani* was a commanding woman, standing about 5 feet 8 inches and towering over most village women. She was about 50 years of age when we met her in 1975.

The *bhaktani*'s husband was a student of Urdu who used to teach his wife 1 hour each day, imparting his religious lessons to her. He lived for 4 years after their marriage. Three days before his death, he gave his wife three orders, "Lead a religious life as a *bhaktani*, obey my father, and look after my younger sisters and take the responsibility of getting my two younger sisters married with they grow up."

The widow took a Punjabi teacher, who lectured in Khalapur, as her guru. This guru taught that women should obey their parents-in-law, not trouble anyone with their actions, obey Almighty God, and refrain from, and teach others to refrain from, bad actions. She worshiped Lord Rama, Siva, Narian, and her now-deceased guru.

In 1975, she had been practicing this life for 14 years, since her husband's death. She had a following of about 40 women, who met with her regularly, 22 of whom lived in Khalapur and 18 in surrounding villages. Most of her followers were Rajput, but a few were from other castes, including one low-caste barber woman. About one half of her followers were widows themselves. Throughout the year these women had regular meetings during which they prayed and sang religious songs. During the months of July and August they had a 1-month fast from cereals and gathered for 3 hours a day to read a religious book.

Hindus believe that the temporal world is Maya, or illusion, and the spiritual represents the true reality. The songs sung by the *bhaktani* and her followers speak to the false illusion of worldly trials and the promise of better lives hereafter. The first song says that cares of the world "will soon be cleared" if the worshiper sings "the songs of God." The second compares the body to a rented house soon to be vacated and reminds worshipers that immortal souls travel from body to body.

Sing the songs of the God with full devotion, O friend.
    Your sins committed in all births will be washed away
And clouds of distress will soon be cleared
    Your mind will be purified with the soap of devotion.
Sings the songs of the God with full devotion, O friend.
    Distress from all directions has come to surround me.
In distress nobody comes near to you when you are in trouble,
    The world is full of falsehood. You can try and find it false
Sing the songs of God of the God with full devotion, O friend.
Mother, father and the whole family.
    All these relatives are just a fabricated system of the world
All the worldly love is a falsehood I can play on the beat of drums.
Sing the songs of God with full devotion, O friend.
O my soul, you have to travel.
    You have been granted this body
So you have to complete the journey.

This body is like a rented house, why to bother about it much.
    One day, the house owner
    will ask you to vacate it.
    You have to pay the rent as well as
    to vacate the house.
O my soul, you have to travel.
    You shall have to pay the rent and
    vacate the house.
    If you do not listen to my suggestion
    The messenger of Death [Yamraj] will make you obey him.
    You will get the treatment according to
    your own good or bad karma.
    You shall have to burn in the fire of sins
    and vacate the house.
O my soul, you have to travel.
    You shall have to face the court of Yamraj
    How shall you convince him in your case?
    You shall have to clear the account there,
    and vacate the house.

The *bhaktani*'s husband was an only child, so the household had no other *bahus* to do the housework. Therefore, after her husband's death, the *bhaktani* asked her own younger married sister to move in, along with the sister's husband and children. The sister kept house so that the widow was free to pursue her religious life.

The *bhaktani*'s *soosar* still lived in the house. He was happy with the devotion of his widowed *bahu* and supported her religious life. The *bhaktani* spent whatever money she got on alms and religious gatherings, and her *soosar* never objected to her expenditures. She helped other widows lead religious lives by attending *kirtan*s within the confines of her *bughar*.

Like a sati, a *bhaktani* can acquire Shakti through her religious life. Maina, the widow who described Shakti to us, said this of the village *bhaktani:*

> She has no Shakti. During her previous life she might not have done any worship and had no prayers and consequently she remained devoid of Shakti. Now, if she does not pray to God and have devoted worship, how can she get Shakti in her future lives?

THE HOUSE OF THREE WIDOWS
The Orphans

Bahai is an elderly virgin widow who returned to her parental village to fight for the land of her brother, Takadwar. After the death of her brother and the tragic death of his newly married son, Hoshiyar, Bahai stayed to continue the struggle for her dead brother's wife and Hoshiyar's virgin widow. Takadwar's two married daughters sometimes stay with their mother while their husbands are working in cities, increasing the household to five women.

The tragedy of this household began when Takadwar and his older sister, now called Bahai, lost their parents. Their father, the last surviving man of his lineage, had inherited a large landholding of about 900 *bighas*. Their mother was already dead, and there were no paternal uncles to care for the children. Therefore, their father, on his deathbed, entrusted their care and guardianship to a neighbor, the senior man of one of Khalapur's most powerful lineages, and the responsibility for their marriage arrangements to a cousin of this neighbor, a man who was himself wealthy and politically powerful. The brother and sister were raised in this neighbor's household across the street from their parental home.

Apparently, the men of their guardian's families and other wealthy families bribed officials to change the land records and list much of the children's land in the guardian's names. The children were too young to know how much land they had inherited, and most of their property was stolen in this manner before they reached maturity.

The girl Bahai was the first to marry. Although her inheritance was sufficient to supply a generous dowry, her guardian married her as a second wife to the wealthy husband of his own dead sister. Her husband was considerably older than Bahai and already had a half-grown son and two daughters by his first wife. It is customary for a widower with children to seek a second wife from his first wife's household, on the assumption that a blood relative of the children will make a kindly stepmother. The custom also saves extensive negotiations with a new set of in-laws. Since the bridegroom has already received a dowry from his first wife, and the bride's family is giving him a replacement, the dowry of a second wife is customarily small. The guardians, therefore, cheated the orphaned girl out of a youthful husband and her rightful share of her inheritance.

Meanwhile, Takadwar, less shrewd than his sister, worked as a servant for the family of his guardian, completely unaware that his birthright was being gradually stolen from him by the men of his adoptive family. In time he too was married. His wife, dissatisfied with life in the joint household, asked for a separate house, and the division of her husband's land. One of the several houses owned by the bridegroom's father was repaired and given to the young couple, along with 150 *bighas* of land. The young bridegroom apparently accepted this as his rightful inheritance; his sister, however, was certain that their landholdings were much larger than 150 *bighas*. She left her husband and returned to live with her brother for most of her adult life to fight for their inheritance, giving up a life of luxury for one of poverty and fieldwork.

Bahai, the *Nanad*

Bahai said that she had never wanted to marry, have children, and be burdened with housekeeping and purdah restrictions. She liked her husband but did not want to be his wife. Circumstances allowed her to make a most unusual arrangement. Before the marriage had been consummated, her husband ran a high fever and became delirious. While delirious he called the young wife "sister." After he was well she told him that since he had called her his sister, she wanted to live with him as his sister and consider him to be her older brother rather than her husband. If he had been a young man without children, he would no doubt have refused, but since he already had a son, he agreed to her request. The marriage was never consummated, and Bahai remained a virgin. It was several years before her husband's family were aware of their arrangement. When they found out, they accepted it and praised the bride for her virtue in wishing to lead a celibate life.

The decision to remain a virgin relieved her of the burdens of childbearing. Her husband's family was wealthy enough to have servants and even elephants, the ultimate symbol of conspicuous consumption. Her husband's wealth relieved her of many of the household chores commonly performed by Rajput wives. Since she had no children of her own to contribute to the patrilineage and her labor was not needed in the house, she received the approval of her husband and his relatives when she asked to return to Khalapur to help her brother. When her husband died, she went to mourn him. She was offered a share of his land, for the duration of her life, but gave it to her stepson and relinquished all claim to her husband's fortune. She continued to visit her husband's home for weddings, births, and funerals. She also did not claim her share of her father's land but fought only for her brother's rights to his inheritance. In 1954 she had already been fighting this land case for several years.

The brother–sister bond is traditionally close and sacred in Indian families. This was particularly true for Takadwar and his sister. The loss of both their parents had brought them close together. Takadwar reportedly would not eat his food until his sister was in the house. Throughout his life Takadwar was closer to his sister than to his wife.

As a daughter of the village, Bahai did not have to keep purdah and soon began to help her brother and their field hands with the farming. She rented time on a tube well with another farmer and sometimes had to go to the fields at night, when much of the irrigation is done. It was this unusual role that led to her being called "Bahai" (brother). Her hired hands, unused to working with a woman, made her, in effect, an honorary man. They called her "Bahai" and she, in turn, addressed them as "Bahai."

They shared their hookah with her, after she promised she would not smoke hookah with other women. The sharing of a hookah is one of several customs by which women are treated like low-caste men. Men will not smoke hookah with men of castes ranked lower than theirs, nor with any women, even those of their own family. In order to maintain good working relationships with her field hands, and to avoid gossip, Bahai de-emphasized her sex as much as possible by her dress and manner. She always wore the loose shirt and *sutan,* a form of dress that had been worn by women of older generations. In winter she wore her sweater under her shirt so that it would not cling to her figure.

While Takadwar and Bahai worked their fields and fought the futile battle to obtain more of their land, Takadwar's wife kept house and gave birth to four children, three daughters and the long-awaited son who, like his father before him, was the last surviving male of his lineage. All hopes for the survival of the family rested on the fate of this single son.

Once in her brother's home Bahai assumed the role of a *sasu* and directed the activities of Mrs. Takadwar. Since Bahai usurped the rightful place of Takadwar's wife, friction soon developed between the two women. In 1954 Bahai complained about Mrs. Takadwar:

> She is a perfect fool. She is very dainty. If she steps on a sugar candy it will not break. She takes 6 hours for work that should be done in 1 hour. She takes 6 hours to bathe. The spinning and cooking also takes ages. I get tired of this, because she is so lazy. She is fond of embroidery and knitting. No one else in the village is as good at it as she is. She has taught all the girls to knit and embroider and make hooked mats. I get angry and say, "Why are you wasting your time doing this? Do something else."
>
> She is educated and very intelligent. She wants to consult her husband on everything. My brother is simple and shy and does not care. She is not responsible and does not care about the children. Otherwise she is very good.

Bahai's concern for the way the children were being raised led her to separate them from their mother on more than one occasion. When Takadwar's son was 2 years old, Bahai took him to her husband's house and did not return with him for several years. In 1954 Takadwar's wife was living at her parents' house with her son and two daughters, because Bahai had sent her there after they had quarreled. The youngest daughter, 9 years old, stayed with her and Takadwar. This girl, one of the children in my first study, was a child of fragile beauty and a most gentle disposition. When Bahai talked about her future she often added, "If she lives." She did in fact die when she was 10 years old, just after I had left the village. Her aunt still spoke of her with fondness when I returned. Her death brought sadness to the family, but the truly tragic deaths were yet to come.

The Death of the Men

The only son, Hoshiyar, lived up to his name, which means wisdom. Despite the family's poverty, he pursued his education through college and went on to study for his master's degree at a nearby city, a most unusual achievement for a village boy. Hoshiyar was not only intelligent but a young man of exceptionally fine character. He was deeply religious, did not smoke or drink, and sometimes tried to reform the habits of the village men. On one occasion he pleaded with the elder men of Khalapur to stop some illegal practices that resulted in police intervention. He argued, with unusual skill for one so young, that the intervention of the police impoverished all concerned, since the police took bribes from both the accuser and the accused and seldom settled the disputes. In 1975 Hoshiyar was still remembered and praised by those who knew him.

Hoshiyar's marriage was arranged while he was still in residence at school, working on his master's degree. A few weeks after his marriage he came home from college sick, was taken to a hospital, and died suddenly in his mother's arms. His death was so abrupt and unexpected that Bahai suspected he was poisoned by the family of their faithless guardian. By this time his parents were too old to have children, and their last hope for a son to farm their land and perpetuate their lineage was lost.

After Hoshiyar's death, his father failed fast. Several times he took his sister and started to leave the village, saying nothing remained to keep them there, a vivid indication of the low status of wives and daughters. Each time they were stopped by friends and neighbors at the village edge. He died a few years after his son, leaving the family of five women: his sister, his wife, two surviving daughters, and Hoshiyar's virgin bride.

Mrs. Hoshiyar, the Devoted *Bahu*

Hoshiyar's young bride was staying with her parents when her husband died. Since students are traditionally celibate in India, her idealistic young husband had chosen not to consummate his marriage until he had finished his studies and could live at home permanently, rather than visiting on weekends. When news of the death reached the bride's family, her father wanted to remarry his daughter. She refused, arguing that if widowhood was her fate her second husband might also die. She said she had grown fond of her *sasu* and felt that if the mother had lost a son, she should share her fate and accept the loss of her husband. She chose, therefore, to live out her life in service to her husband's family. She wore a widow's dress and no jewelry, and believed herself to be a burden on the family, despite her lifelong service to them. She had no relatives in Khalapur but did not seek a ritual sister because she believed herself unlucky.

Bahai has high regard for Hoshiyar's illiterate widow. She does the family cooking and is greatly praised for this by Bahai, who says that it is only because of this *bahu* that food is in the house when she returns home from the fields. Bahai told us about the sacrifice and hard work of Hoshiyar's widow on our first visit to the house:

She thinks nothing of herself. She does not want to dress in pretty saris or wear
jewelry. She thinks of herself as no better than mud and has given her life to help
our family with our work. She thinks she is unlucky.

Unfortunately, Hoshiyar's widow is not treated well by her *sasu*. She would like
to learn to read and complains that although both her *nanad*s and her *sasu* are
educated no one will teach her to read. She needs eyeglasses, but when we suggested that she ask Mrs. Takadwar to buy them for her, she replied, "Oh no, who
will get me glasses?"

Mrs. Takadwar, the Cunning *Sasu*

Mrs. Takadwar had none of the courage and unselfishness of Bahai. She had a
reputation for being cunning and played on her helplessness by wheedling, begging,
and occasionally lying. She showed little gratitude to either woman for their sacrifices and work, although Mrs. Hoshiyar did all the cooking and most of the housework, and Bahai's fieldwork formed the financial basis for the funds Mrs. Takadwar
saved to educate both her daughters and provide them with substantial dowries.
While she had some reason to resent Bahai's assumption of the *sasu* role during the
early years of her marriage, she had no justification for abandoning her faithful
bahu.

The Land Dispute

Since the death of both father and son, the women must rely entirely on hired help to
farm their land, which is now reduced to 90 *bigha*s, despite all the efforts of Bahai
to defend the family inheritance. At present their field hand is a Muslim man,
probably because few Rajput or low-caste men would dare to help a family of
women who challenged the honesty of some of Khalapur's most powerful men.

At the time of our second visit, Takadwar's eldest daughter had been married for
several years. Like her brother she had a master's degree and taught at the village
school rather than living with her husband's family. Her husband was not a farmer
but was employed in an office job. He visited his wife frequently. The younger
daughter was also married to a man employed in an office.

On the surface these five women seemed to get along unusually well. The
bickering one often sees among women in a Rajput household was absent.
Hoshiyar's wife cared for the family women with unusual affection. The women of
this household helped each other quickly and without comment. The second sister
gave up her own college education to care for the daughter of her elder sister, when
the young mother was working for her master's degree. (Unfortunately, this child
also died.) The women presented a united front against the village families who
oppress them.

This unity was threatened, however, by the demand of the elder sister for
separation of her landholdings while her mother was still alive. Not only did she
want her inheritance then, but she wanted the land divided between herself and her
sister, with no provision for her brother's widow, whom she would have liked to see

sent back to her parental home. Reportedly, she often fought with her mother about this issue, took meals separately, and would not speak to Hoshiyar's widow.

Bahai's status as an honorary man did not extend beyond the field hands, and so because of purdah customs, she could not bring herself to testify in court, even to save the land that she had spent her life trying to regain. The family could not afford a lawyer, and without a male heir their traditional claim to the land was weakened. In 1975, Bahai wanted the land to be divided among her two nieces and her dead nephew's wife. While revised laws permit women to inherit land, village men and many village women feel strongly that since women cannot farm the land, they should not inherit it.

A family of sisters without brothers, and in this case without male cousins, are the only legal heirs to their father's property. Their situation is the circumstance that women did not consider in our interviews on dowry. Neither husband of Takadwar's daughters was eager to leave his job and face the hostility of the village men in order to farm the family's meager holdings. When they inherited the land they would probably sell it, an action abhorred by Khalapur men. According to law, the land should be divided into thirds, with each sister and the brother's widow receiving an equal portion. By custom all the land should go to Hoshiyar's widow while she lives and pass on to the family's nearest male relatives upon her death. These male relatives are the men who cheated Takadwar and Bahai while they were children.

Bahai never claimed her own share of Takadwar's land after his death; Mrs. Takadwar is now the legal owner of all the remaining landholdings. Mrs. Takadwar could not be forced to divide the land before her death, and it was unlikely that she would do so, since control of the land and money was her main source of power.

Whether this young widow would have the strength to press her claim against her sisters-in-law remained to be seen. Without the help of her urban brothers-in-law she would have to continue to rely on hired help to farm the land. Unlike Bahai, Mrs. Hoshiyar was meek and unassertive; furthermore, she was not a daughter of the village and, by tradition, had to maintain purdah in her husband's village. If both sisters-in-law desert her after her *sasu* dies, she may be defenseless. One hopes that Mrs. Hoshiyar's virtuous life will lead to her acceptance, if she must return to her home village.

Mrs. Hoshiyar said her mother died of grief because of her sufferings. She had no brothers, so when her widowed father died, she would have no male relatives to support her. She said that Mrs. Takadwar had promised to divide the land evenly between her and her two daughters. When asked what she might do after the two older women die she said, "I do not know what my future will be. If my *nanads* treat me well, it will be all right. Otherwise, I will have to go to my parents' house." Without the education to fight for her share of the land against her well-educated sisters-in-law, she would be helpless unless Mrs. Takadwar kept her promise to leave her one third of the land, and she would find some way to farm it.

It is disgraceful for a Rajput family to abandon a widow in such a fashion, but such fine points of honor injure the reputation of men, since it is men who are responsible for the support of the family women. A household of women has no traditional responsibility for their sister-in-law and no prestige to lose.

In 1955 Bahai was still cautiously optimistic about the family's chances of winning back their land. Her brother and nephew were alive and healthy. Although Takadwar failed to live up to his name, which means "strong," he borrowed his sister's strength by following her orders. He appeared in court to fight his case when hearings on the land dispute came up. At that time Bahai was also mistress of the household because she had sent Takadwar's wife to her parental home. She prepared food, managed the household budget, and raised her favorite niece. All this changed with the death of the two men. Mrs. Takadwar was now mistress of the house and in control of the household budget. Bahai directed the work in the fields but had no authority within the house. Her clothes were old and torn, and she had no money of her own to replace them. In 1975 she complained bitterly about Mrs. Takadwar's ingratitude:

> She buys clothes for both her daughters and herself, but I have mended my clothes so often that I see now that I was foolish to have left my husband's house and my share of land to help my brother. I spent the prime of my youth to fight for my brother's land. It is because of my effort that this family is living in this house and still has a small patch of land. I gave whatever I brought from my husband's house to these people. My nephew was not thankless. Now my brother and nephew are no more, but even so I am still working in the fields my whole life for these people, but they are thankless. This family, for whom I have spoiled my life, look strange to me. They are not my own. I have grown so old and weak now that I cannot work in the field, so I am barefooted and in torn clothes. I am much worried about my future. I cannot return to my husband's house nor am I given proper treatment in this house.
>
> Mrs. Hoshiyar is also at the mercy of this woman. Her future is worse then mine. So long as she is young and able to work like a slave for them, they give her two meals a day, but when she grows old or becomes incapable of doing anything, she will, perhaps, be treated badly by this mother and her daughters. Perhaps she will be given some land, but nothing is guaranteed.

The guardian of Takadwar and Bahai, and his family members, had apparently expected Takadwar, along with his wife and children, to live with them throughout their lifetime, leaving them their land in exchange for support. While this expectation was not particularly logical, considering the wealth of Takadwar's family, their conviction that the land should be left to the men of the guardian's family was strengthened when Takadwar and his son died, leaving only female heirs.

In the fall of 1974, the alienation between the two families led to further trouble. The guardian's son, now a prominent man in his own right, began construction of a large cattle compound and men's quarters in front of Takadwar's house. Part of the construction was on the land owned by Mrs. Takadwar. Furthermore, the wall of the cattle compound blocked their door, leaving them barely enough room to pull their bullock cart up to the door to unload their grain. The women protested this action, claiming that, in addition to the encroachment on their land, it was illegal to block the doorway to another house. However, the construction was not stopped, and the family had resigned itself to the loss of another piece of property. Neighbors agreed that some of the land under construction belonged to Mrs. Takadwar, but no one would help them to oppose the powerful man who had appropriated it. On one occasion we were moved to tears by Bahai's account of her failures to keep control of the family land. When she saw our distress, Bahai's only comment was: "You are crying over my plight, but my heart has become a stone. I have no more tears."

CONCLUSIONS

Widows are considered to be unlucky, both for themselves and for others, because a husband's early death is blamed on bad karma acquired by his wife in previous incarnations; therefore, a widow's fate is essentially thought to be self-inflicted. In 1955 I used a census based on Hitchcock's interviews with family men. I found several widows living in these families who were missing from the census, because the men had not reported them.

The stigma of this belief is attached primarily to young widows whose husbands' deaths were premature, but any woman who outlives her husband is considered to be somewhat unlucky. Children belong to their father's lineage and must remain attached to his home, so finding an acceptable second husband for a widow with children is virtually impossible. Although rules against widow remarriage are being abandoned in more urban areas of India, Khalapur widows still do not remarry. In order to avoid gossip and the stigma of *rand,* widows must lead lives of piety and celibacy. Devotion to this holy life has replaced the custom of sati as a means of earning good karma for subsequent lives, but local suttee shrines are still places of worship for women.

The roles described in this chapter are carried out singly or in combination by most Khalapur widows. Widows retain ownership of their husbands' land during their lifetimes. This gives them a degree of financial control over their sons and *bahu*s, which most guard jealously.

The women of Takadwar's family epitomize the problems of village Rajput women without men to support them. Although their legal claims were just, they had no means of endorsing them. Bahai had had to deny her sex by dressing like a man, assuming the male role to carry out her work, and not smoking hookah with her women friends. It was only her lifelong virginity and her devotion to her brother's family that saved Bahai from slander. Mrs. Takadwar, anxious about the family's fate, had assured the future of her daughters with education and good marriages. However, she was not committed to the support of her husband's sister and her son's wife. Relationships between *bahu*s and their *sasu*s and *nanad*s are frequently strained. The problems of coping with a patriarchal society in the absence of men has enhanced this friction, rather than reducing it.

VI

HEALTH AND EDUCATION

Chapter 11 describes changes in health and family planning. Like many people in developing countries, Khalapur women have abandoned their traditional birth control practices but have been slow to adopt modern methods. The historical practice of female infanticide and the persistence of indirect female infanticide are discussed in this part. The demise of the postpartum sex taboo, already disappearing in 1955, by 1975 had reduced the amount of time between pregnancies. The preference for sons continued to be a deterrent to birth control among women who had given birth to daughters.

The salience of government planned-parenthood programs presented problems for family planning interviews. Radio broadcasts included daily messages for extolling the government policy of encouraging families to have only two children. The village nurse visited families to persuade women to use birth control. Because Rajput women were reluctant to express opinions contrary to those of more educated persons, including the planners of government policy, it would have been useless to ask them how many children they wanted or thought they should have. Therefore, we asked questions concerning family planning in the context of the limitation of economic resources for the support of present and future children (see appendix F).

A second problem for the family planning interview stemmed from the opposition to birth control by some mothers-in-law, and their belief that birth control was an improper topic of conversation. Because of this opposition, it was not possible to interview daughters-in-law individually on this sensitive subject. We conducted interviews as open-group discussions of all women in the *bughar*. For this reason, answers to the questions are not independent, and the number of individual answers varies from question to question. Nevertheless, the results of the interview are clear enough to draw some conclusions concerning the government's family planning efforts.

We repeated our 1955 census on child health and documented substantial decreases in the incidence of children's diseases. The results of these comparisons are presented in the second half of chapter 12.

Chapter 12 describes changes in socialization. Son preference is discussed in the context of sex differences in socialization and illustrated by descriptions of birth ceremonies, accounts of Drapaudi's co-opting of the loyalties of her grandsons, and the return of a prodigal son who had run away from home for 7 years.

We excerpted parts of the socialization interview done in 1955 and gave them to a new sample of women to assess the degree of change in socialization. A new and more detailed coding system was developed for the 1975 interviews, and the 1955 interviews were recoded using the new system. Spot-checks consistently revealed reliabilities to be above 90%. After the analysis of the 1975 interviews was completed, questions that seemed to have been redundant or unclear to the respondents were eliminated. The resultant analysis is based on 26 questions concerning the identity of caretakers, disciplinary techniques, and training in obedience, expressiveness, leadership, aggression, and sex.

The age range of the children was from 3 to 12 years for both samples. In 1955, 12 mothers of boys and 12 mothers of girls were interviewed, for a total sample size of 24. The 1975 sample of children was selected from the same families we had studied before; we interviewed 24 mothers of girls and 14 mothers of boys, for a total sample size of 38. The larger sample of girls was selected to compare the socialization of daughters of mothers with separate versus joint *chuulas*. No differences were found between these two subsamples, and the data were combined.

A number of differences were found between the responses of women interviewed in 1955 and 1975, indicating that the changes in mothers' lives were reflected in changes in their socialization practices. We describe these changes and conclude that they have arisen from the greater education and autonomy of the recent generation of wives.

Chapter 13 reports on changes in education. With the exception that literate mothers sent all their children to school, the reported socialization practices of the mothers did not differ as a function of literacy in either the 1955 or the 1975 sample, so the data of these two groups were also combined. It seems likely that the reason for the absence of any difference in socialization practices between literate and illiterate mothers is that the minority of literate mothers of 1955 were being influenced by the norms of their illiterate *sasus* and *jethanis*, while the majority of educated mothers in 1975 were setting the norms for the less educated *bahus* in their *bughars*.

We also interviewed teachers in the primary schools and intercollege concerning enrollment, school terms, school funding, government control of schools, curriculum, discipline, and children's school behavior. The increased enrollment of girls in both elementary schools and the intercollege is documented.

An educated husband and wife pose with their six children. Despite the government family planning program, which encourages families to have only two children, most rural couples have large families.

11

Health and Family Planning

All illness comes from God.

One son is no son.

It is best to have two sons and one daughter.
Then one can get two dowries, but give only one.

Hindu beliefs about cleanliness are based on ritual pollution, as defined by caste rules, not on sanitary beliefs based on the germ theory of disease. Traditional Hindu medicine is based on proper diet and the use of medicinal herbs. Because of beliefs about blood pollution, surgery is not included. Minor surgery is done by village barbers, a low-caste group. The village women we interviewed had little knowledge of anatomy, including the anatomy of their reproductive organs, and no knowledge of methods of sterilization.

The Indian government has tried to institute family planning since independence in 1949, and its efforts to encourage two-child families increased during the sixties. Government workers may be fired if they have more than two children; men are paid for having vasectomies; billboards advertise the virtues of the two-child family; government programs encouraging two-child families are broadcast several times a day. In Khalapur a village-level worker visits homes to encourage family planning and discuss birth control methods. Among rural families, resistance to these efforts stems from the economic necessity of having sons to farm, and from ignorance and anxiety about modern birth control methods.

Population control and adequate medical care for mothers and children are essential goals of government policy in most developing countries. This chapter describes the improvement in birth control and medical care from 1955 to 1975, and the impediments that ignorance and traditional norms create to progress in modern health care.

NEW MEDICAL FACILITIES

A dispensary and small hospital had been built after my first visit, in memory of village boys killed in a train accident in 1954. These young men were on their way to work on a government service project when their bus was hit by a train while crossing the tracks. The government offered to pay families for the loss of their sons, but most families refused. The government then arranged to build a dispensary in their memory. Some village families also contributed to its construction.

A resident nurse and pharmacist worked out of this building, and it served as the base of operation for visiting physicians. These facilities had improved access to medicine for Khalapur residents. Unfortunately, their effectiveness was marred by suspicions about the honesty and ethics of their operation. The most common complaint was that the pharmacist sold medicine he was supposed to dispense free of charge. The practice is widespread throughout much of India. Because of this graft, poor families did not get medicine and many families preferred to go to private village doctors, even though their charges were no less than those of the government workers. Despite these problems, health care facilities had improved since 1955.

HEALTH
Beliefs

Some of the obvious improvements in health (e.g., the absence of smallpox and malaria) have already been noted in chapter 1. Hindu beliefs concerning illness and some changes in health that affect women and girls are described in this chapter.

Beliefs about health and illness are based on ancient lore and are embedded in Hindu religious beliefs. As we have seen, sexual activity is considered to be debilitating for men. Epidemic diseases are believed to be caused by disease goddesses. One important theory of health involves the proper balance of heat-producing and cold-producing foods. A balance between these two types of foods is thought to be important for health maintenance. Informants generally agreed that meat was heat producing, but classifications of other types of food varied from person to person.

In addition to hot and cold foods, Hindus distinguish between *pukka* and *kaccha* foods. *Pukka* food is cooked in *ghi*, or clarified butter. Since the cow is sacred, food cooked in *ghi* is pure enough to be taken from a low-caste person. *Kaccha*, food cooked in water, must be cooked and served by a member of one's own caste or a higher caste. Water itself may not be taken from a person of lower caste. Rajput families call on their Brahmin women to cook for feasts where large numbers of guests are fed.

Rajput women are vegetarians. Rajput men, whose warrior status exempts them from a purely vegetarian diet, on rare occasions feast on pork, chicken, or fish. The portions of meat on such occasions are meager, usually just enough to flavor a stew. The men cook meat in their *choopar*s, since no woman will cook meat on the *chuula*. *Chuula*s, which must be pure to cook the vegetarian meals, are replastered each morning, using a mixture of dirt and cow dung. Because the cow is sacred, its dung and urine are considered pure and are sometimes also used in medicines.

In understanding some of the Hindu practices of cleanliness, it is important to realize that in Hindu thought cleanliness is defined as absence of ritual pollution, not absence of germs. Pollution is defined in terms of religious beliefs concerning the ranking of caste groups, the uncleanliness of occupations involving contact with feces or blood, and abstaining from the eating of meat, particularly beef and pork. The differences between my definition of dirt and that of my Hindu colleagues was illustrated in a dispute over the appropriate time of day to bathe. Because clothing is thought to be soiled after being slept in, Hindus are required to bathe each morning before eating breakfast. Bathing after contact with dirt is not required unless the dirt is defined as polluting.

The region of Khalapur has fine dusty soil and frequent dust storms. We were covered with dust after a day's work. Furthermore, the hostelry bathroom was crowded each morning with Hindus performing their morning ablutions, and the water was cold from the night's chill. Therefore, during both of my visits, I usually bathed when I returned from the day's work in the village. I was dusty, the bathrooms empty, and the water tank warmed by the sun. Our Hindu colleagues expressed surprise, and some concern, at the uncleanliness of this practice. When I explained to one of them that my religion mandated bathing when dirty, and I was dusty when returning from the village, I received the surprised reply, "But you have only been in Rajput homes."

The primary source of pollution is contact with low-caste persons or their possessions. Members of untouchable groups are particularly polluting. With the exception of the midwife, Chamar servants do not enter the *bughar*. When my interpreter and I went for a walk in the Chamar neighborhood in 1955, we faced worried inquiries from Rajput women about whether or not we had bathed and changed our clothes before entering their houses.

The belief that contact with blood, feces, and leather is polluting affects diverse customs. Traditional Hindu medicine lacks any surgical procedures, and knowledge of internal anatomy is meager. The blood of childbirth is polluting, so midwives are from untouchable groups. Hindus will not touch leather shoes with their hands. Sandals have no back strap, so that their wearer may step in and out of them without adjusting any straps. In 1975 plastic shoes had been introduced and were becoming popular.

Cow dung is the fuel used for cooking, and dung ash is used for cleaning the brass plates on which food is served. China tableware is considered foreign and generally unclean, since it cannot be scoured with ash without scratching. When many guests are present, they are served on banana leaves. The cleanliness of the food is determined by the caste of the cook and the material of the plates on which it is served. Germ sources such as flies, dirt, or the proximity of open latrines are ignored during cooking. Guests may be given fans to wave over their food, to discourage the many flies who descend on any unguarded dish of food.

Some ritual eating practices have sanitary outcomes. Hindus use their left hands to wash themselves after elimination and their right hands to eat. They rinse their hands before every meal and eat with their fingers, without the use of utensils. Food should not go beyond the second knuckle, so it does not come into contact with the palm. Except for ceremonial feasts, meals are taken individually; all meals are eaten quickly, without conversation, a custom that minimizes the chances of germs getting on food after it is served.

Feces are polluting and are removed daily by the family sweeper. Family women sweep refuse out of the house into open sewers. Once polluting refuse is removed from the immediate vicinity of the house, people are unconcerned about it. Most Indian cities, as well as villages, have open sewers. Their stench can be overwhelming, and they are breeding grounds for vermin.

Beliefs concerning ritual pollution are, of course, worldwide and far more ancient than the germ theory of disease. Both sanitary practices and ritual pollution rituals are embedded in customary behavior. When the two conflict, the traditional practices tend to prevail. While some ritual customs have sanitary benefits, others present serious barriers to modern sanitation and medicine. The ritual pollution practices of Hinduism contribute to making India a highly unsanitary country.

Probably because of the caste rules limiting the taking of food from persons of lower caste, villagers favor injections rather than oral medicine. Villagers' faith in injections has eased their acceptance of this modern medical technique but has also led to the overuse of injections, including placebo injections.

Finally, villagers attribute some illnesses to sorcery, the evil eye, or ghost and goddess possession. Infants are more susceptible to the evil eye, while newly married women are most likely to become possessed. Persons suspected of having these illnesses are taken to the local shaman rather than to a doctor. Shamans, locally called *siana*s, are men trained to identify possessing spirits and remove them, and to identify persons practicing sorcery. While the practice of sorcery is deliberate, the evil eye may be caste unintentionally by someone who is envious.

Women's Stress Reactions

Young brides are at risk for stress-related health problems. Some of the most common are coma, spirit possession, and depression. Case studies of possession and depression are contained in chapter 2. A temporary coma, usually lasting 24 to 36 hours, is one typical response to stress. During this time a woman goes to bed and loses consciousness. Usually no doctor is summoned for such comas. The woman is allowed to simply "sleep it off" and is not disturbed unless the coma lasts longer than 36 hours. In 1955 one wife was particularly likely to take to her bed after a fight with the *bahu* with whom she shared her *bughar*. In 1975 we found no reported cases of coma during our stay. Probably the educated *bahu*s of this new generation are able to deal with conflict more directly.

The new *bahu* who becomes possessed by a goddess moves temporarily from the bottom to the top of the status hierarchy of family women. The possessing goddess typically not only refuses to work but orders the *sasu* and other family women to worship her and bring her special food. Rituals to remove the goddess put the possessed woman at the center of attention.

Children's Health

Mothers were interviewed during both field trips about the illnesses that had affected their children, living and dead. No large sex difference in type of disease contracted appeared in either time period. The overall health of the children had improved from the fifties to the seventies. The decline of important ailments is recorded in Table 11.1.

Three afflictions—smallpox, boils, and sore eyes—had virtually disappeared by

Table 11.1 Incidence of Children's Disease, 1955 and 1975

Ailment	1955 %	1975 %
Smallpox or chicken pox	52	10
Boils	52	8
Sore eyes	83	8
Malaria	72	42
Colds	20	11
Measles	21	20
Typhoid	22	50

1975. In 1955, 52% of the children had *mata,* referring to either smallpox or chicken pox. Both diseases, like other epidemic diseases, are believed to be caused by one of 101 disease goddesses, all of whom are called *mata* (mother). Villagers clearly recognized the difference between the blisters of smallpox or chicken pox and the bumps indicative of measles. However, because a light case of smallpox and a heavy case of chicken pox look much the same, these two diseases were sometimes confused. There was general recognition that smallpox was the more serious disease. It was called big *mata,* while chicken pox was called little *mata.*

In 1955 vaccination programs were relatively new and not always accepted. The confusion between big and little *mata* contributed to this lack of faith in vaccination because children who contracted chicken pox after their smallpox vaccinations were sometimes cited as evidence that the vaccination had not been effective. In 1975, 91% of the children (85% of the girls and 100% of the boys) had been vaccinated; the difference indicates greater concern for the safety of boys. However, the incidence of both diseases had been drastically reduced. Although there was a major smallpox epidemic in India early in 1974, no village children had smallpox and only 16% had contracted chicken pox.

Boils and eye infections had also become rare. Boils were reported for 52% of the children in 1955 versus 8% in 1975, and sore eyes for 83% in 1955 versus 8% in 1975. I attribute the absence of boils to better nutrition and cleanliness. The absence of sore eyes was undoubtedly due to the cessation of the practice of putting kohl, taken from a common pot, under babies' eyes. In 1975 we seldom saw babies with kohl under their eyes, and when it was used, the kohl pot was not widely shared, as it had been in the past. The reported incidence of malaria had dropped from 72% to 42%, and common colds from 20% to 11%. The frequency of measles had remained virtually the same: 21% in 1955 and 20% in 1975. The only major disease with a reported increase was typhoid, cited as an illness for 22% of the children in 1955 and 50% in 1975.

Because it is customary to feed the family men before the women and children, poor nutrition adversely affects the health of women and children in many Indian families. However, Rajput women reported that they always had enough to eat, although the variety of food might be small in the months before a harvest. Some also said that they gave children first priority in receiving milk. In fact, young children often pestered their mothers for food long before it had finished cooking and were therefore fed as soon as possible.

The custom of feeding men first has been cited by a number of Western scholars as evidence of mistreatment of women and children. In defense of this practice it should be recognized that the survival of the entire family depends on the health of the men, since it is the men who farm. A sick woman can rest, because her duties are easily assumed by other household women, and a sick child can rest with even less drain on the family resources. But if a man is ill, particularly during planting or harvest season, his work is sorely missed, even in a joint family. A nuclear family may need to call on the help of relatives or hire someone to replace the work of a sick father or senior son.

On one occasion, when a family did not have enough milk to prepare sweets for a family wedding, one of the family men became angry and accused the women of drinking milk. The women denied the charge and explained that they did not have enough milk. In response, one of the family men refused to take any milk, except in his tea, prompting one elder woman to advise the *bahu*s not to talk of food shortages in front of the family men so that the men would not stop eating.

The overall improvement in children's health may be linked to better nutrition, vaccination, malaria control, the replacement of open village wells which bred cholera with tube wells, and the presence of a government-sponsored village health center with a resident nurse. The improvement in the health of daughters is one indication of the recent rise in the status of females. Although avoidable health problems certainly remain for children, considerable progress has been made in the past 20 years.

Preferential Treatment for Sons

In the past, the expense of dowry payments led to female infanticide throughout high-caste groups in northwestern India. The British government outlawed female infanticide in the latter half of the nineteenth century, although the practice persisted in Khalapur until the turn of the century. A government official sent to Khalapur in about 1900 to enforce the law was reputedly murdered by Gopal, the patriarch of Amar Nath's family, because he violated purdah restrictions by entering the women's quarters in order to identify pregnant women. A combination of government pressure and the Arya Samaj religious influence brought an end to the custom of female infanticide in the early decades of this century. However, the ratio of males to females is still unnaturally high throughout northwestern India, and this country is one of a few where the life expectancy of women is less than that of men (Miller, 1981, 1984). While female infanticide may still occur, this difference is largely due to better health care for boys than for girls, a practice that has been called indirect infanticide, and, in middle-class city families with access to amniocentesis, to female feticide.

In 1955 the neglect of girls, particularly those suffering from long-term illness, resulted in a striking preponderance of boys. Of the 128 children in the sample of families studied at that time, 37% were girls and 63% were boys. In 1975 the number of children in the original families sampled had increased from 128 to 250; a rise of 277% in the total number of living offspring. In the 1975 sample 55% of the children were boys and 45% were girls. The ratio of 37% versus 63% recorded in 1955 was significant at the 10% level. The 45% versus 55% ratio found in 1975 was not significantly different from chance.

The unbalanced sex ratio observed in 1955 led me to question 35 mothers about the sex of children who had died after full-term births. I found that the mortality rate for 61 deceased children reported deceased after full-term births was 25% for boys and 41% for girls. A comparison of the number of living versus dead children as a function of sex was significant at the .01 level in 1955. The child mortality rate was high from birth to 3 years and then declined sharply. In 1955 there were four very sick babies in our sample, all girls, who were receiving little or no medical aid during my first field trip. No comparable cases were observed in 1975. I did repeat the interview about differential death rates for boys and girls because the decreased sex ratio indicates that childhood death rates must have been relatively comparable for both sexes in 1975.

The proverb "One son is no son" expresses the fear that one son may die, leaving the parents with none. Families are reluctant to stop having children until they have at least two sons. Therefore, if their first children are daughters, they continue having children until this goal is reached. Despite the cultural norm for son preference, I found, in 1955, that some women did want daughters:

> There does seem to be some compensatory status for girls. When asked whether they would wish for a girl or a boy when pregnant, the women either expressed no preference, saying that it was in the hands of Rama or that they wished for a boy. But when asked whether they *liked* boys better than girls, the women were as likely as not to express a preference for their own sex. They said they were fonder of girls because girls go away to their husband's homes, while boys stay with their parents. This attitude seems to reflect a sentimentality about girls which is not accorded to boys.

> (Minturn & Hitchcock, 1966, p. 97)

Several indications of the preference for sons in our 1975 sample of women— sex differences in type of midwife, vaccination, and incidence of disease—appear in Table 11.2. Sons are more likely to be attended by the trained midwife rather than by the untrained sweeper midwife (Midwives are frequently not summoned until the

Table 11.2 Incidence of Disease and Identity of Midwife for Daughters and Sons

	No. of Cases	%	No. of Cases	%	No. of Cases	%
Delivery by trained midwife	5	21	4	29	9	24
Delivery by untrained midwife	16	67	8	57	24	63
Vaccination	21	88	14	100	34	92
Evil eye	14	58	12	86	26	68
Malaria	10	42	6	43	16	42
Typhoid	13	54	6	43	19	50
Measles	5	21	3	21	8	21
Chicken pox	6	25	0	0	6	16
Cough/cold	4	17	0	0	4	11
Sore eyes	3	13	0	0	3	8
Fever	4	17	0	0	4	11

Daughters = 24.
Sons   = 14.
Total   = 38.

Table 11.3 Preference for Sons or Daughters

| | Sons | | | | Daughters | | | |
| | Wife | | Husband | | Wife | | Husband | |
	N	%	N	%	N	%	N	%
Not many	2	4.5	2	5.5	2	4	2	5
Present number	2	4.5	2	5.5	2	4	2	5
What God gives	2	4.5	0	0	2	2	0	0
As many as possible	0	0	4	11	0	0	3	8
Husband has no opinion	0	0	1	3	1	2	1	3
One	2	4.5	2	5.5	33	73	15	42
Two	30	68	12	33	4	9	3	8
Three	1	2	4	11	1	2	0	0
Four or more	5	11	2	5.5	0	0	1	3
NA/DK	0	0	7	19	1	2	7	19
Total	44	101	36	99	45	98	36	100

Table 11.4 Preference for Sons

| | Wife* | | Husband† | |
Number wanted	Sons	Daughters	Sons	Daughters
One	2	33	2	15
Two or more	36	6	25	11

*$\chi^2 = 48.88$; $p < .001$.

†$\chi^2 = 15.54$; $p < .01$.

infant has been born and its sex is known). Sons are more likely to be vaccinated. Sons are more likely to contract the evil eye, an ailment thought to be caused by envious persons looking at babies; girls, on the other hand, are more likely to contract typhoid, chicken pox, coughs and colds, sore eyes, and fevers. While the number of cases recorded is too small for the figures to be stable, they do indicate a trend towards better health care for sons.

In 1975 we systematically interviewed a sample of women about family planning. Table 11.3 summarizes the answers to four questions: "How many sons/daughters do you want?" and "How many sons/daughters does your husband want?" We did not interview husbands, so all answers concerning their preference are based on their wives' responses. A number of women were reluctant to give numerical answers but stated their preferences as "not many," "as many as we have now," or "as many as God gives us." No women said they wanted as many children as possible, but four women said their husbands wanted as many sons as possible and three said their husbands wanted as many daughters as possible. Three women said their husbands had no opinions on family size.

Both sets of answers shows marked preferences for fewer daughters than sons. The significance of these differences is shown in Table 11.4, where the numerical answers are condensed into two categories—one, and two or more. The significance of son preference is less than .001 for both wives and wives' estimates of husbands' preferences. It is interesting that women's reported son preference is larger than their estimates of their husbands' son preference.

Some women quoted a proverb favoring three sons and one daughter: "I like four sons, one for bringing green fodder from the fields for the animals, one to keep the animals, one working in the fields, and one to be sent for getting a higher education. One daughter is sufficient." Several women cited the need for dowry as a reason for preferring more sons:

> I like two sons and one daughter because one can give a dowry to one daughter as big as one could give to two daughters. Then the daughter has good respect in her in-laws' family. This is easy only when you receive two dowries in the marriage of your two sons.

> I like two sons and two daughters. Every woman wants to have two sons and one daughter because they want to get dowries twice and give a dowry only once. This is being selfish. One should give as much as one gets in marriages of sons and daughters.

FAMILY PLANNING
Traditional Birth Control

Khalapur Rajputs had traditionally controlled family size and birth rates by observing a postpartum sex taboo on intercourse for 2 years after the birth of each child. Intercourse was resumed when the infant was weaned. The traditional taboo had largely been abandoned by younger mothers in 1955, at which time I found a significant increase in the number of children born less than 2 years apart. In 1975 the postpartum sex taboo had been completely abandoned by young couples, and several couples used a rhythm method of birth control. The belief that couples with married children should stop sexual activity was still present. I was told that older men preferred abstinence to vasectomies or tubal ligations.

In 1955 women frequently said that they had heard that American women had methods of not having children, and asked what they were. At that time abstinence was the only birth control method they knew. I reported this situation as follows:

> Although the Indian government sponsors a birth-control program, knowledge of birth control had not yet reached the village women. No contraceptive methods are used in the village, although some of the women asked about American practices. They realized that "medicine" was available for this purpose but were vague about its nature. Education, expense, and the high child-mortality rate are probably the three most important factors standing in the way of an adequately planned parentage program.

> Certain methods for abortion are known to the villagers. One elderly lady was reputed to perform abortions, and some informants mentioned the use of a medicine which is inserted in the vagina to dilate the cervix. Abortion was certainly not frequently practiced, however. Probably it was practiced only for cases of illegitimacy.

(Minturn & Hitchcock, 1966, p. 97)

Government Family Planning

One of the most important changes in the knowledge of Rajput women occurring between my two visits was the increased knowledge about modern birth control methods, although confusion about the effects of these methods was still prevalent. Some Rajput women thought that vasectomies caused impotence, and several said that the operation made men sick. An amusing instance of such a belief came from Draupadi, who assured me that a vasectomy had killed a man who had died between my visits. When I asked his wife about her husband's death, she told me he had died in a tractor accident 5 years after his vasectomy. I reported this discrepancy to Draupadi, who assured me that the man had been sickly since the operation and would have died from it if the tractor had not killed him first.

In 1975 most Rajput families were aware of government population control policy. Most also realized that their landholdings were no longer large enough to provide for the families of their sons. However, women's status and power still depended heavily on bearing children, particularly sons, who are essential for the continuance of the patrilineage, the cultivation of the land, and the support of female and elderly family members. In the judgment of most women, who reasoned that their sons could earn enough money to buy more land, the income derived from sons's work took precedence over the diminishing landholdings. Therefore, the traditional proverb "One son is no son" carried more weight than the government slogan "The tiger has only one cub but rules the forest. The pig has litters but they only follow."

The presence of a government dispensary and resident nurse in 1975 made access to health care easier for all Khalapur residents, although many families preferred a local doctor to the government dispensary. In 1955 Rajput families seldom sought medical help for daughters outside the villages, whereas boys with prolonged illnesses might be taken to Delhi. In 1975 many families still might have been reluctant to take girls to Delhi for treatment, but the greater availability of local medicine had improved medical treatment, particularly for girls.

Because norms of modesty prevent large numbers of Indian women from being examined by a male physician, even when they do not keep purdah, and because India has a shortage of doctors, particularly women doctors, who are willing to work in villages, the government has concentrated its birth control efforts on vasectomies. In addition to coming to villages, government workers worked out of railway stations, encouraging men waiting for their trains to have the operation and paying those who did. In 1975 the unethical padding of vasectomy rolls had been going on for years: It was rumored that the operation was performed on old men, that some men had it repeatedly to get paid, and, most seriously, that it was sometimes performed on unmarried or newly married men who did not understand its effect. Public concern about government administration of vasectomies finally caused a scandal that contributed to the challenge to Indira Gandhi's government in the summer of 1975.

The Family Planning Interview

Because of the government propaganda encouraging families to have only two children, our 1975 family planning interview began by asking women whether they had enough land to support their sons and grandchildren. When women answered no to this question, we asked about their plans for dealing with the situation. Family planning interviews had to be conducted in groups of women because *sasus* were reluctant to let us interview *bahus* individually on this sensitive issue. The text of the family planning interview is reproduced in appendix F; results of the interview are presented in Table 11.5.

Table 11.5 Tabulation of Answers to Family Planning Interview

1. Do you think you have enough land to support the children of this house and their families when they are grown?

	N	%
Yes	2	4
No	37	70
Maybe	4	7
NA/DK	10	19
Total	53	100

1a. What are your plans for supplementing your income to support your children and their families?

	N	%
Buy more land	40	32
Improve production	33	27
Start other work	20	16
Take out loans	18	14
Save money	7	6
NA/DK	6	5
Total	124	100

2. Do you think there will be enough money to give good dowries for the daughters of this family?

	N	%
Hope to have enough	11	26
No	13	30
Depends on God, luck	13	30
NA/DK	6	14
Total	43	100

2a. What will you do to obtain money for dowries?

	N	%
Give what we have	5	12
Take out loans	13	32
Sell land	11	28
Earn extra money	5	12
Get money from family	3	8
NA/DK	3	8
Total	40	100

3. The government thinks that people should have fewer children.

	Yes		No			
	N	%	N	%	T	%
Have you heard radio/seen literature	28	78	8	22	36	100
Has the family planning worker come to visit?	20	77	6	23	26	100

(continued)

Table 11.5–(Continued)

4. Do the men in your family object to family planning?

	N	%
No	18	61
Maybe	4	13
Depends upon method	3	10
Not after a son is born	1	3
NA/DK	4	13
Total	30	100

5. What do you think of the government program to encourage fewer children? Is it good or bad to limit the number of children?

	N	%
Yes	33	78
No	4	10
Yes and no	5	12
NA/DK	0	
Total	42	100

5a. Reasons for family planning:

	N	%
Economic	65	81
Health	11	14
Better child care	4	5
Total	80	100

5b. Reasons against family planning:

	N	%
Need children	9	70
Promotes immorality	2	15
Government motives bad	2	15
Total	13	100

6. Why do you think the government is trying to make people have fever children?

	N	%
Better standard of living	18	38
Increased population	14	29
More happiness	6	13
Better health	5	10
Government wants land/cannot provide jobs	2	4
NA/DK	3	6
Total	48	100

7. What family planning methods have you used?

	N	%
None	25	78
Pills	2	—
Operation	2	—
Loop	1	—
Rhythm	1	—
Abstinence	1	—
Total	32	

(*continued*)

Table 11.5–(Continued)

8. What family planning methods do you like least?

	N	%
All are bad	7	20
None are bad	3	9
Loop	12	36
Operation	3	9
Pills	1	3
Abortion	1	3
Condoms	1	3
Don't use so don't know	6	17
Total	34	100

9. Are there any family planning methods you would use if they were available?

	N	%
Pills	19	76
Other	2	8
NA/DK	4	16
Total	25	100

The interview began by asking whether the family lands were sufficient to support present children and their present and future grandchildren. Nineteen percent of the women did not know the extent of their husbands' landholdings; nevertheless, all the women were able to answer the questions, basing their answers on the amount of grain produced. Answers indicated that 70% of the women thought they did not have enough land for this purpose (Question 1). We then asked about their plans for supplementing family income. The most frequent response (32%) was that they would buy more land. The second most common response (27%) was that they would improve production on their present land. Starting other work was cited by 16% and taking out loans by 14%. Only 6% envisioned saving money. Some typical answers are as follows:

> The land is not sufficient even now, not to talk of when the children grow up. Then, if God is merciful, we can purchase more land. People whose luck is not bad like ours take a loan, purchase land, and pay back the loan after the next crop.

> We have 300 *bigha*s of land in my husband's name and we have six sons. Thus each son gets 50 *bigha*s, which can be increased to 500 *bigha*s if the sons work hard. Five *bigha*s of sugarcane earn 5,000 rupees and, if we spend 1,000 rupees on fertilizer and other expenses, we can save 4,000 rupees net, with which one can do whatever one likes. One can get a house built or get a daughter married, get sons educated or purchase more land.

> Fifty to 60 *bigha*s of land is sufficient for one adult worker, and according to that we should have sufficient land, but as the children grow up it will go on decreasing unless we add to it some more patches of land.

> At least 100 *bigha*s for one son is sufficient. I have three sons, so we should have 300 *bigha*s of land, while we do not have even that.

> We have not enough land, but it is not easy to purchase it. Land costs 5–6,000 rupees per *bigha*.

Some women were fatalists about their prospects:

> You know, the income of a cultivator is very uncertain. Now we have put seeds in
> the earth and if God is favorable and gives enough rain, so that the earth is saturated
> with water, and our plants start growing, then we have hope of getting a crop ready,
> otherwise, whatever we spend on seeds even goes to waste, if there are no rains.
> Therefore, sometimes even when we have sufficient land, our food production
> depends on God and the weather.

Most women saw the land as their only source of income:

> We earn only from our land, and our produce depends on the hard work we put into
> it. We have only the fields for meeting our expenses. Extra money comes from our
> land only. We cannot think of other sources of income.

Some planned alternate ways to earn money:

> Somebody goes in for service and the rest work hard in the field. In our house my
> husband is in service and all the sons are being educated to be able to get into
> service. When two or three sons get employment and one looks after the fields, we
> shall have no difficulty and we can purchase more land then.

> If the land is not sufficient for a family, they can work on a sharecrop basis and thus
> can increase their income to improve production and educate their children.

> There are many other works that one can do if the land is not sufficient to meet the
> needs of a big family. One can open a shop, or work on the land of others, or in
> some factory, or other work. This way one can bring up the family and educate the
> children and also purchase more land. If one does not want to do this, than one can
> get a loan from the government and purchase land. The loan can be paid back in
> small amounts every year.

One woman blamed the demise of the joint family for the land shortage:

> In earlier days many families could live in one house together, but nowadays brides
> come in marriage and ask their husbands for getting separated from the joint family,
> before she comes in *gauna*. Thus everyone wants to live in a separate house. The
> land is not increasing as the population is increasing. Therefore, it becomes a big
> problem for the government to feed and provide housing for all. During earlier days
> women used to have three or four children and they could live in a big joint family,
> but now everyone wants a separate house where men and women sit together and
> enjoy. Thus there are more children.

The shortage of land on the market probably makes the option of buying more
land unrealistic for all of the persons who mentioned it as a possible solution.
Improving production is a more realistic possibility for many farmers. Taking out
loans may involve assuming debts of massive interest. However, the government
backs low-interest loans for family machinery, and the village bank gives loans at
reasonable interest rates.

The next pair of questions, concerning dowries, followed the format of the land questions, that is, "Do you think there will be enough money to give good dowries to the daughters of this family?" "If not, what will you do?" We found that 26% of the women thought or hoped that they had enough money for their daughters' dowries, while 30% said they did not have enough and 30% fell back on the ambiguous answer "It depends on God, luck, or fate."

Only 12% of the women who did not think they had enough for daughters' dowries planned to reduce the wedding plans to fit their means. In response to the pressures to provide large dowries, 32% planned to take out loans, 28% planned to sell land, 12% planned to earn extra money, and 8% planned to get money from their parents to augment their daughters' dowries. The following are typical answers:

> Daughters are a liability. They have to be married at the appropriate time, and one has to perform this marriage even by selling his land sometime, if he has no other source of money. Marriages of sons can be postponed for a year or two, but marriages of daughters cannot be postponed, whether you have money or not. One performs the marriage even by taking out loans or by selling land.

> Men have to work hard on the land for the dowries and education of their children. Now we have one daughter who has had her *shadi* and *gauna,* and now our second daughter is mature enough to get married. What we do is that my husband works hard on his land as well as on the sharecrop basis for his elder brother, who has no children to help him with his land. The yield is divided in two equal parts, one for the brother and one for us. My husband thus accumulates money and does not spend it on merrymaking, drinking, etcetera. So we are happy and meet our extra expenses by working hard on the land.

> It all depends upon the luck of the daughter whether she gets a big dowry or not. If, at the time of her marriage, there is enough money, well and good. If not, then she will get a small dowry.

> Whatever is in her fate, my daughter will get. Some people put aside something for the daughter every year and when she is grown there is enough to give a reasonable dowry. Others get loans from moneylenders to get their daughters married, and pay the loan slowly in installments.

> I can bring some money from my parents for the dowry of my daughter. Whatever I get in the marriage of my sons, I can give to my single daughter. Therefore, I can say that I have sufficient funds for the dowry of my only daughter.

These answers are striking confirmation of the financial burden created by large dowries. It is notable that 28% of the women said they planned to sell land, since this is strongly opposed by tradition. It seemed unlikely that so large a number would actually obtain their husbands' consent to land sales that would permanently decrease the family's economic base.

Question 3 asked whether the women were aware of government family planning efforts. We found that 78% of the women had heard government broadcasts and 77% had been visited at least once by a family planning worker. One woman's answer was representative: "I have heard the family planning program on the radio. In this village I have not seen any literature. The family planning workers in the village come to see us."

A few *sasu*s resisted family planning efforts:

> I do not allow this nurse to enter our house. Why does she want to teach these bad things to my *bahu*s? She says to stop reproducing by undergoing an operation, but I scold her saying, "You go away. We do not want to stop the reproduction of my *bahu*s. I am not afraid of the nurse or anybody else. I do not like these dirty things. Why should she come and suggest to us to interfere in the godly system of reproduction?

> Twice daily we hear the radio broadcast on family planning, though I do not like it. That is why I do not want to listen to the radio, but the children play it. I do not let the nurse talk on this topic. She might be talking to my *bahu*s in my absence.

> I neither used myself nor do I want my *bahu* to use these things. Whatever God has written in our fate, that we shall have to get. I do not want any sort of interference in the natural process of reproduction.

When asked whether or not men of the family objected to family planning (Question 4), 61% of the women said no, 13% said maybe, 10% said it depended on the method used, and 3% said husbands did not object after the birth of a son. A few women reported that their husbands did not use condoms because it decreased their sexual pleasure:

> My husband is not clever. He is innocent and does not know anything about family planning methods.

> My husband and I have daily discussions on family planning. He wants to undergo an operation, while I wish to get myself operated on, not him.

> I have not considered using any family planning methods, including the ones for males. I have never used any. Once I talked to my husband about using the method for males. He was angry and answered, "I come here once in a while from my place of posting, and you want me to use them? I will not use them!"

When asked whether they thought it was good to limit the number of children (Question 5), 78% of the women answered yes. The reasons given in favor of family planning are overwhelmingly economic (81%), with health (14%) and better child care (5%) being mentioned much less often (Question 5a).

> The government is running these programs because the land produce is not increasing but the population is increasing very fast and the food will not be enough for all.

> In the village people think it is good to have more and more children to work the land. They think it is not difficult to feed as many children as possible. But they do not take into consideration the good living, education, and dowry for so many children.

> A big family gives displeasure and a small family brings happiness and comfort. Every woman should try to limit her family because with more children life is like hell. Health is maintained with fewer children.

There are some women who have eight or nine children. These newcomers eat their mother's skin. [She becomes very thin.] Every woman should try to have a big gap between the births of two children. There should be a gap of at least 5 to 7 years. It will help in maintaining the health of the mother and the child. If there is a new child every year, then you can only hear the cries of the children. A child who still wants his mother's attention is deprived of it when the new one is born. The life of the family becomes like hell.

The government wants people to have fewer children so that they can be well looked after. Previously people used to make one set of clothes for the children, when the earlier one was torn. Thus they used to have 1 dress at a time. But nowadays every child wants to have at least 10 dresses at a time. Moreover there is more fashion now and the children cannot do without *terricot* [a type of napped cotton]. Previously, handwoven clothes were acceptable to the children. Now even bedding of handwoven cloth is not liked by children. Their bedding also needs to be costly and fine. These children also want to be brought up nicely, which is only possible with fewer children in the family. That is why the government is asking us to have fewer children, so they can be well educated and well fed.

The primary reason for opposing family planning (Question 5b) was the need for children (70%). One woman's answer was particularly dramatic: "I had 10 sons and only 3 survived. Now supposing I had had only 3 sons? Then I would be left with none."

A few women (15%) pointed out that preventing pregnancy would increase immorality, and some (15%) questioned the government's motives. Some women said that the government was trying to increase the population of Harijans (the untouchable groups) and decrease the population of high castes:

The program is not good because now married and unmarried, all can go and use these methods and one cannot even judge that a particular woman is married or not or widowed. Any woman can now go to the hospital and get an abortion, and nobody even comes to know of these dirty deeds. Previously, when there was no family planning, if an unmarried girl had an illegitimate child, then the prestige of her family used to be spoiled. Now, with the help of this program, any girl can do anything and can get rid of the trouble in the hospital and the family's prestige is saved, as nobody comes to know about it.

The program is not good because, when there is a war with other countries, then where will we get the young men to fight? The low-caste people do not get these operations, and therefore their population will increase. The government is encouraging them and giving them high posts, and the landlords are not getting anything.

The government is taking land away from us and giving it to the Harijans. In the daily newspaper there was news that the government had given so much land to the Harijans. We will be left with no land and get food from the government.

The government should make the Muslims have fewer children. They are having dozens.

This suspicion of official motives is not widespread. When asked specifically about why they thought the government was trying to encourage people to have fewer children (Question 6), only 4% of the answers expressed the opinion that the government wanted more land or could not supply enough jobs for people. Most answers reflected the government's motives with considerable accuracy since 29% cited increased population, 38% cited a better standard of living, 13% cited more happiness, and 10% cited better health as official reasons for encouraging family planning.

Despite the reported recognition of the advisability of family planning, 78% of the women interviewed said they had never used any family planning method (Question 7). The number of women reporting the use of any method is too small to draw conclusions about method preferences. When asked what method they liked least (Question 8), 20% said that all were bad, 9% said that none were bad, and 36% disliked the intrauterine loop, making it the least preferred method by a considerable margin. The "operation," referring to vasectomy, was cited as the second least popular birth control method by 9% of the women interviewed. Since loops and vasectomies were the most common methods in Khalapur, it may be that these answers simply reflected a dislike of available birth control methods.

Two reasons most frequently cited for disliking the intrauterine loop—that it may hurt or kill the man, and that it may wander around the body cavity and get caught on the heart or liver—reflect the women's ignorance of anatomy. Some women thought the loop would give them cancer. However, most reasons were realistic: The loop causes bleeding and pain, it may be bad for the women's health, sometimes it is ineffective or it may come out and the woman may still become pregnant.

> The loop is dangerous because it is made of wire and can harm the husband. I have heard of a woman who had a loop inserted in her body and when she slept with her husband, the loop hurt him so much that doctors could not save his life. Not only this, the loop gives much heat to the body, which is very difficult.
>
> I am afraid of the loop, because when the husband comes to sleep, then the loop goes high up into the liver of the woman.
>
> The loop is worst because it may come out and there is bleeding also.
>
> The loop is best. One can stop births for some time and again can have children after getting it removed.

Suspicion of intrauterine loops and vasectomies was not entirely unjustified. The procedures of inserting loops and performing vasectomies were done by teams of visiting doctors, who traveled from village to village where medical teams were not in residence. Medical teams also performed tubal ligations, using a technique that did not require an incision. While this practice was effective in supplying birth control to large groups of people who would not otherwise have access to it, it meant that physicians were not always on hand to treat infections or complications arising from these procedures. The Khalapur doctor supplied medicine for 4 days of bleeding after loop insertion, and made at least one follow-up visit. If women had long-term pain the doctor might remove the loop and encourage the use of condoms.

An additional problem was the misuse of the procedures by some medical personnel. The village nurse told us of one such instance, apparently with no concern for the ethicality of her actions. The case involved a *nanad,* home for a visit, who had three daughters and badly wanted a son. She had gone to see the nurse to treat light and irregular periods, a condition common to these women who often become pregnant shortly after their youngest child is weaned. The nurse arranged for the insertion of a loop, which did, of course, increase bleeding, leading her patient to assume that her problem had been alleviated. The nurse explained that she would remove the loop before the *nanad* returned to her husband, so that she could get pregnant again.

The motivation for such unethical behavior lay in the government practice of assigning a fixed number of loop insertions and vasectomies as a goal for each village-level medical worker. Failure to meet the government goals reflected poorly on the worker's record. The bureaucratic loophole in loop insertions was that, while the nurse was not allowed to insert loops, she could remove them without recording the removal. She was therefore able to add this *nanad* to her count of the number of loops inserted.

Some women feared an operation or said that their husbands opposed operations. The most frequent concerns were infection and loss of strength. The answers reflect a lack of understanding about surgical methods and postoperative symptoms:

> I dislike the operation. For one thing the tummy is opened, and then if the stitches dissolve it may cause a very bad condition in the woman.

> All women say the operation is worst because its stitches get septic and then the woman's life is in danger. Many women have lost their lives by operations.

> I like operation the least because after that neither a man nor a woman can put in hard labor, neither the man in the field nor the woman at home. We cultivators cannot do without putting hard labor in everywhere.

> Last time when we had the birth of our daughter, my husband got himself listed for the vasectomy. But the doctor refused because we have only one son, and our daughter died after 6 days. I am afraid of the operation and loop because I do not have anybody who may cook for me if I am sick in bed.

Finally, women were asked what additional methods they would use if available (Question 9). In answer to this question, 76% of the women said birth control pills. Several women pointed out that the loop and vasectomy did nothing to space children, and they wanted the pill for that purpose. The dispensary nurse explained that birth control pills for uneducated women were being discouraged by the government, because of their misuse by women who were not accustomed to taking medicine regularly. A common problem was the sharing of pills by *bahus*, who would take them only when they thought their husbands were coming that night. This practice sometimes made the pills ineffective and produced an irregular menstrual cycle, making it difficult to determine when a baby was due. The latter concern was unimportant to women unaccustomed to prenatal care.

The nurse naively assumed that village women had not heard about the pill, although many houses had *bahus* who came from areas where pills were available. Even if this were not the case, it seems most unlikely that women who knew about the existence of birth control methods in 1955 in a country on the other side of the globe would not know of methods being distributed by their own government.

CHILDBIRTH

Hindu beliefs concerning ritual cleanliness and the pollution of blood severely hamper efforts to institute prenatal care and sanitary childbirth. Paradoxically, in a land where the mother is the most sacred religious symbol, midwifery is the most unclean of occupations. Traditionally children were delivered by the untrained midwife. Midwives washed the infant, cut the umbilical cord, and changed the mother's bandages, work that is considered particularly unclean. Midwives are the untouchables' untouchables, often considered unclean even by members of their own families, some of whom refuse to eat or smoke hookah with them.

Unfortunately, maternity care was no better in 1975 than in 1955. The techniques of delivery were the same as the ones reported in our previous account:

> When the labor starts, the mother retires to her room, and the family sends for a midwife. They are often not very prompt about calling the midwife. Since blood is considered to be unclean, the Rajput women will not deliver children, clean up after a birth, or change bandages on the mother, and midwifery is traditionally the profession of Untouchable women. In Khalapur the wives were usually of the Bhangi or sweeper caste. Although there is a government-trained midwife resident in the village, most of the sample families would not use her, for she refused to return after the birth to change bandages, a service which the Rajputs consider as important as aid in the delivery of a baby. Furthermore, the government midwife brings an Untouchable woman to cut the cord and clean up, necessitating the payment of two persons.
>
> While the mother is in labor, a sickle, knife, and plowshare are placed near her bed or under it. Many women procure a paper with prayers on it from a village Brahmin, which they look at to aid the delivery.
>
> After finishing with the birth, the midwife buries the afterbirth by a rubbish heap. She bathes the baby and sometimes the mother. She comes daily to the household and cleans the cot, washes the soiled clothes of the mother and baby, throws away the mother's bandages, and cleans the room with cow dung. She also removes the excrement of the mother and the baby. The mother is not allowed to go outside the room to eliminate until the ceremony of Jasutan. Until then the midwife must come into the house to remove her excrement. The length of time that a

woman is in confinement varies with her age, how she feels, and how many other women there are in the household to take over her tasks. She should remain in bed for 10 to 14 days and do no work for 12 days after that. She cannot start cooking until she stops bleeding because until then she is unclean. The mother, except for the Bahari ceremony, does not change her clothes for from 14 to 22 days. At the end of this time she puts on new clothes, and her old clothes are given to the sweepers. During her confinement no one may touch her eating plate and glass, which are also unclean. When the mother's confinement is over, the family cleans the room and purifies the mother's eating utensils by burning coals in them and washing them in Ganges water. After this the midwife cannot enter the house.

On the day that the baby is born, the mother eats sweets, a special corn dish, and a dish of pulse. The mother is fed as much *ghi* as she can consume, and many of the women eat a great deal after their babies are born. She may also be fed a dish which is a mixture of sugar, water, *ghi,* almonds, coconut, and dry ginger powder. This diet is considered to be healthy for the new mother and is continued for 20 days. The mother is not supposed to drink milk for some time after the baby is born. Again the length of time reported for this taboo varied from 15 days to one and one quarter months. The baby is fed sugar and water when it is first born and is given mother's milk from one to three days after its birth. The baby may also be fed a dish consisting of about one cup boiling water, caraway seed, two puffed sugar candies and a pinch of ashes.

(Minturn & Hitchcock, 1966, pp. 99–101)

In 1955 Khalapur had a government midwife in residence. Rajput families seldom made use of her services because she refused to return to change the mother's bandages. Older Rajput women were willing to deliver babies themselves but required the services of a *dai* to cut the cord and clean up blood. The government midwife usually was called only for difficult pregnancies, after the mother had been in labor for hours. Therefore, she was often faced with medical emergencies beyond her capabilities. When this occurred, her only recourse was to have the mother taken to the hospital in Bhudana in the family bullock cart, an uncomfortable and bumpy ride for anyone. These unfortunate circumstances led to an unusually high number of infant and mother deaths for those under the midwife's care, and decreased her credibility.

In 1975 the village had acquired a semiskilled midwife. A woman from the beggar caste who had learned midwifery working at the dispensary for three years, delivered babies for a few families who would call her. She would cut the cord and remove the afterbirth, but refused to wash the mother of the baby. She did this work because her husband was a drunkard and she needed money, but she did not want her family to know about her polluting service.

The older women of the household still delivered most of the babies in 1975. Mothers' reports indicated that 21% of girls and 29% of boys were attended by a trained midwife, whereas 67% of girls and 57% of boys were attended by the untouchable midwife. The remaining children were delivered by family women. Thus, there was a 10% difference in use of the more highly paid midwife to attend the delivery of boys. (The mothers were referring to the use of the *dai* in cleaning up the afterbirth and changing the mother's bandages.)

Hindu beliefs about cleanliness are so strongly defined by the idea of ritual purity that sanitary practices are difficult to explain, let alone institute, particularly when these contradict religious beliefs. A common cause of infant and mother mortality is tetanus caused by cutting the umbilical cord with an unsterile knife. When I asked women in one household about cord cutting, I was met with a striking example of such a contradiction. I found that the umbilical cord is usually cut with one of the household vegetable knives, since these are usually the only sharp knives in the *bughar*. When I asked whether the women washed the knife, I was greeted with a horrified chorus of "Of course, we are vegetarians. We cannot cut our vegetables with a bloody knife." When I tried to explain that the knife should be washed before cutting the cord, it was clear from their expressions that this advice seemed so absurd that they considered me to be slightly demented. The necessity of cleaning a knife that had only come into contact with the pure vegetables used for food, before polluting it with blood, made absolutely no sense in terms of their religious beliefs concerning cleanliness.

CONCLUSIONS

All women were aware of the government messages encouraging family planning. However, the pressure to produce sons to farm the land still led to relatively large families. Increased availability of local medical help and access to a local bus line had increased the probability that sick children of both sexes will be taken to a doctor. Increased education of mothers had made them more sophisticated about good health habits. Despite the obvious improvement in the treatment of girls, some evidence of differential neglect persisted. Boys were more likely than girls to be attended by the trained midwife and later to be vaccinated. The 10% difference in the 1975 sex ratios indicates that the death rate of girls was still somewhat higher than that of boys.

Nevertheless, the Khalapur information allows more optimism than the statistics quoted in the Indian Government Status of Women Report (1974) and the historical picture presented at length by Miller (1981). Both the government report and Miller's book indicate that, nationwide, Indian sex ratios and the relative life expectancy of women versus men have become less equal during this century. National data indicate that improved medical facilities have affected men's health more than women's. Purdah cloistering and unclean childbirth still take a high toll on women's lives.

Khalapur is a relatively modern village, and the Khalapur Rajputs are wealthier and more educated than most of their fellow countrymen. Young *bahus* are able to seek medical treatment at the village dispensary and seem less vulnerable to stress symptoms than their predecessors. For this group the overall picture is one of optimism.

In view of the extensive literature on the practice of female infanticide, it is somewhat surprising that indirect female infanticide from medical and nutritional neglect of girls, which is probably more widespread and frequent than direct infanticide, has received little attention. If indirect infanticide is an extension of direct infanticide, just as infanticide is an extension of abortion, then the same cultural conditions should be antecedent to both practices. That is, neglect of girls should occur in societies with a history of female infanticide, where daughters are an economic liability and where women are regarded as the property of men and are not accorded the same legal and social protection as males. The murder of brides and the neglect of women's health are other aspects of this total picture.

A daughter practices sewing on her mother's machine. Small, hand-operated sewing machines were a common dowry item in 1975.

12

Socialization

Everything that is going to happen to a child in its lifetime is written
on its forehead at birth.

When we interviewed mothers about their childrearing practices in 1955, the
proverb that a child's fate is written on its forehead at birth was one of the most
frequently stated beliefs. Mothers of that time were very reluctant to express any
long-term expectations for their children's future, and, if they did answer questions
concerning such expectations, such as how much schooling they wanted their children to have, they usually qualified their nervous answers with "if it is in his/her
fate." In 1975 no mother quoted this proverb, and they readily answered questions
concerning their plans for their children's futures. Clearly, the mothers of 1975
thought that they had control over their children's future. The 1975 mothers also had
more control over their own lives than the mothers of 1955. They practiced less
purdah, controlled more of their money, had more autonomy, and were less subservient to their *sasus* than the mothers of 1955. The increased education and autonomy of mothers was accompanied by changes in their treatment of their children.
These were documented by repeating the socialization interview given in 1955 with
a sample of mothers in 1975.

PREFERENCE FOR SONS

The preference for sons, the traditional practice of female infanticide, and the
greater concern for the health of boys, already discussed, are all part of the social
milieu in which children are raised. Boys soon learn that they are more-valued and
girls that they are less-valued members of their families. Son preference is evident
as soon as the sex of the newborn is determined. The birth of a son is heralded by the
family sweepers, who are summoned to drum outside of the *bughar* for several
days. The difference in the elaborate celebrations for the births of sons and the
private ceremonies for newborn daughters is observed by all children. The description of this evidence of son preference, published in 1966, remains unaltered:

> The differential status of boys and girls is apparent from birth. The midwife is paid
> twice as much for delivering a boy as for delivering a girl. The birth of a girl

273

occasions no public ceremony. One informant, in fact, declared that when a girl is born the mother hides, although this is an overstatement. When a boy is born, on the other hand, a sweeper is called to beat on a drum before the door of the happy household, announcing to the village the advent of a son. The Brahmin women are summoned to sing special songs, and the branch of a nim tree is put over the door of the mother's room for good luck and to keep ghosts away. This singing and drumming are repeated every day for ten days. A yellow cord is placed around the waist of male babies.

The first ceremony in a boy's life, the Bahari, may find him anywhere from 1 to 6 days old. The Bahari is usually held only for boys. It takes place in the late afternoon of his first Sunday, and to it are invited all the women from the family lineage and any other close female friends of the family.

Preparations for this ceremony are elaborate. The Brahmin women who serve the family make abstract designs of cow dung decorated with green and yellow dots. These are "painted" on the courtyard wall on each side of the mother's room and represent all of the Gods and Goddesses. The Brahmin women say that these designs are in honor of the ancestors. On the floor in front of the door to the mother's room is placed a square design made out of rice-water paint. This pattern is a sign of respect for the baby and mother.

Since the birth, the mother and child have remained in bed in the mother's room. She is still considered unclean. Now, however, she is bathed, her hair is washed, and she dresses in new clothes. Outside in the street, the sweeper man is drumming; in the courtyard the Brahmin women sing. Both Brahmin and low-caste women bring contributions of dub grass, for which they are given money. The grass symbolizes that they wish the family to prosper, as the grass prospers. A low wooden stool is placed beside the design at the mother's door and before it two or three bowls of food and a bowl of water.

When everything is ready, the mother comes out of the room and sits on the low stool, holding her baby. She greets the guests and they bless her. A woman, usually an elderly one, sits beside the mother and gives her water from a bowl. The mother sprinkles this water onto the food, and then the food is given to the Brahmin women. Each member of the family and each guest offer money and a handful of grain to the "ancestor" designs, and these gifts also are given subsequently to the Brahmins. Sometimes the wife of the family barber is present and touches the fingernails and toenails of the new baby to indicate that she will cut the child's nails when he gets older. After this brief ceremony, the mother again greets her guests and returns to her room. There she is permitted to break the fast which she has kept all day by eating a paste of sugar and ghi. She resumes her soiled clothes and remains in them until she completes her period of seclusion and returns to her normal working life.

(Minturn & Hitchcock, 1966, p. 102)

All infants have a Chotili ceremony, at which they are given their first set of clothes by their mother. Family women from other *bughars* may gather to celebrate the festival for sons, but for daughters it is performed with only the household women to note the event. The following description of an elaborate Chotili ceremony, published in 1966, applies only to sons:

The second ceremony, called the Chotili, is held on the fifth day of a baby girls' life and on the sixth day of a boy's. For this rite, a red sacred thread is tied around one leg of the mother's cot, and a small figure is made out of cow dung to represent the Goddess Bara Mata, maker of children. This Goddess is one of the 101 sisters concerned with disease; she receives homage only at the Chotili ceremony. The family women offer whey, grain, and a tiny oil lamp; they invoke the names of the ancestors, of Mata the smallpox Goddess, and the Goddesses Balsundri and Bahamata. The family may invoke the names of 5, 7, or 9 such deities, including local Gods, Goddesses such as the Bhumia and Darga, the Moslem saint, and ancestors. The baby receives its first costume, which may be either a cloth to go around his stomach, a shirt and cap, or both. These clothes are called Chotili. These are colored for girls and white for boys. Women from other houses in the lineage present gifts of grain to the mother, and the ceremony is over. Afterward, they hide the figure of Bahamata in a room of the house for good luck.

(Minturn & Hitchcock, 1966, p. 104)

The Jasutan festival, held 10 days after the birth of a son, marks the end of the family's celebration. Again, our earlier description is still accurate:

Jasutan, the third festival, occurring ten days after the birth of a boy, terminates the family's rejoicing over a new son. On this day the boy's yellow cord is exchanged for a black one. It is the last day that the sweeper drums and the Brahmin women sing. It is the end of the holiday from spinning, observed by the women of the lineage out of affection for the new son of the house. Apparently in some cases the Chotili ceremony is performed on Jasutan, although it is more common to clothe the child on its fifth or sixth day.

According to some accounts, a wealthy family gives a feast on Jasutan for one unmarried girl from each Rajput family in the patti. In the sample studied here, there were no families which observed this custom, but the family of Brahmins are fed and sweets distributed to the other houses in the lineage. It was stated that at least one Brahmin must be fed on this day in order to ensure the cleanliness of the kitchen. . . .

After Jasutan, the cow dung designs placed on each side of the mother's room are taken down and sometimes replaced with hand prints made of rice water, which are good luck symbols.

(Minturn & Hitchcock, 1966 p. 103)

The custom of small, private birth ceremonies for girls, in contrast to the large birth ceremonies for boys, and the absence of the Bahari and Jasutan rites for girls had not changed in 1975.

The final birth ceremony is the haircutting ceremony, designed to ensure the infant's health by protecting it from sorcery. Although this ceremony may be held for both boys and girls, it is more common for boys, and is more elaborate and includes more relatives when the infant is a boy:

The first hair-cutting ceremony usually takes place during the child's first year of life. This, like the Chotili ceremony, is performed for both boys and girls, and there are three occasions on which it may be done. The first and most usual occasion is the spring religious festival for Balsundri, held in Bhudana. A second possibility is the Shakumbri religious festival, held in the fall in a town about 80 miles distant from the village. Because it is so far away, the villagers do not often get to the fair;

but some manage it and may perform the hair-cutting ceremony at that time. A third and fairly common practice is simply to go to the family shrine and offer the hair to the ancestors. According to report, the ceremony follows the same general pattern wherever it is performed. The birth hair, cut any time from 12 days to a year after the child is born, is offered to the Goddess as a gesture of consecration. This hair is material which can be used for sorcery purposes. Offering it to the ancestors or to a Goddess, therefore, presumably consecrates the child and protects him from harm.

When the hair-cutting ceremony is performed at the family ancestor's shrine, a Brahmin and a barber are called. They go to the shrine with the family. The family barber cuts the child's hair, and it is placed between pieces of unleavened fried bread and left there. We asked what happened to the hair and were told that the dogs eat the bread and the hair blows away. But since the hair has been offered to the ancestors, it cannot be used for sorcery.

(Minturn & Hitchcock, 1966, p. 104)

The work and education of children become differentiated by the time they are 5 or 6 years old. Boys go to the fields to help their fathers and other family men with the farm work, while girls learn to help their mothers with household chores. While daughters may go to the fields to bring food to the men or to help harvest some of the crops, older girls are warned to guard their virtue and avoid even casual intimacy with men. Because of the concern for daughters' virtue, boys are much more likely to attend high school.

Patrilocal residence means that the men remain permanently in their parental homes; they do not leave the domination of their parents until the latter die. Their mothers regulate their sexual contact with wives, and their mothers, not themselves, are the principal controllers of wives' activities. Since boys remain at home, their faults are tolerated by their relatives. Their mothers favor them and, to some extent, they remain mother dominated, and mother coddled, throughout most of their lives. Their status in their family is determined by their birth order and remains static unless an older brother dies. Some families specifically train their eldest sons for their future leadership positions, but most make little or no differentiation between the treatment of their first son and other boys.

Girls are guests in their parents' homes, but as adults they must live among strangers. Girls are instructed in manners more carefully than boys so that they will be polite in their husbands' homes and not reflect poorly on their parental homes. Herein lies the paradox of the male-dominated patrilocal family. It is daughters who are taught the traits of stamina necessary to allow them to leave their parents' haven, move to a strange village, and survive the low status and often hostile atmosphere of their husbands' families. It is sons who remain at home, work with their brothers and cousins, and do not break their parental ties until their parents die.

The strength of these subordinate women may come from their change of residence. In her cross-cultural study of female initiation ceremonies, Brown (1963) notes that a change of residence that moves the adolescent out of the paternal home functions in the same way as an initiation ceremony in instilling adult behavior. She also notes that it is usually brides who change residence at marriage, and suggests that this residential change instills independence and responsibility in young women. Brown goes on to contrast the situations of women in matrilocal societies, where daughters remain at home, in endogamous societies, where brides move to another house within their own community, and in exogamous societies, where brides move out of their communities, and makes the point that the break with parents is greatest for exogamous societies. As we have seen, Rajput brides move not only to strange villages but into homes they have never seen, as brides of men they have never met.

Male initiation for Rajputs takes the form of conferring the sacred thread, worn by all men of the "twice-born" *varnas*. This initiation does not have the characteristics of male initiation in societies where the separation of boys from their mothers is emphasized (e.g., separation from the community; moving to another community, such as the mother's parental village; hazing; or extensive religious training). In Khalapur the sacred thread ceremony has been incorporated into the marriage ceremony, further minimizing its dramatic import. The only change of residence for boys is from their *bughar* to the family *choopar*. Boys are more likely than girls to play on the *choopars,* and listen to the men's conversations, but continue to live in the *bughars* and sleep with their mothers until adolescence. In 1955 mothers said that boys should move to the family *choopar* by age 9, but all boys under the age of 12 still lived in their *bughars*. In 1975 the greater crowding of *bughars* increased the pressure to move boys to the less crowded *choopars*. Mother–son ties are difficult to break in most societies. Sons are the basis of the Rajput mothers' power, and mothers are the women to whom men have the closest emotional ties. The minor move to the family *choopar* is not equivalent to moving to another village, and the mother–son bond is particularly close among these families.

Men and women are quite different in their expressions of aggression. Both sexes agree that women are more quarrelsome, but the women correctly observe that their fights usually amount to nothing, while disputes among the men may result in violence. It is the sons who inherit family feuds along with family land and prestige; like the latter, the feuds endure for generations. Our observation of 1955, that mothers did not perpetuate their quarrels through their children but fathers instructed their sons to carry on family feuds, was still valid in 1975:

> We were impressed by the fact that the women did not take their own quarrels out on the children. Men's quarrels, on the other hand, result in blood feuds which may go on for generations. Probably for this reason men are most concerned with impressing upon their sons that they should know their enemies. Fathers stated that they told their children not to be friendly with people with whom their fathers did not talk but to speak politely to their father's friends.
>
> The difference in training of boys and girls is reflected in the child interviews. When asked how they would react if a strange child tried to be friendly with them, 8 of the 10 girls said they would be friendly, whereas 5 of the 9 boys said they would not be friendly.
>
> (Minturn & Hitchcock, 1966, pp. 126–127)

Draupadi's Grandchildren

The quarrels of Draupadi did involve the children. Draupadi had successfully alienated Dhooli's eldest son, and the eldest son of Ganga, Amar Nath, son by his second wife. Draupadi refused to pay any attention to Dhooli's two young daughters, saying, "Since Dhooli does not like my daughter, I do not like her daughters." The daughters were left out of gift giving on ceremonial occasions and were clothed only in old-fashioned shirts. When I bought them dresses, Dhooli saved them for Holi, a festival for which children usually receive new clothes, explaining that she had no other clothes to give them and no money to buy them.

Draupadi showed the most extreme example of a *sasu*'s differential reactions to grandsons and granddaughters. When Draupadi arrived, as Amar Nath's third wife, his son Ganga was still a child. Amar Nath's mother thought that Draupadi would not be good to Ganga and called her Kaykeyi, the stepmother of Rama who exiled Rama and Sita into the forest. The accusation, while cruel, proved to have some validity.

When Ganga's wife, Sarvasati, had her first son, Kiran, she was unable to lactate and could not nurse him. Draupadi, who was about 40 years old when Kiran was born, had had no children since the birth of Luxmi, 12 years earlier. Nevertheless, Draupadi nursed Kiran, lactated, and breast-fed him for 2 years. She then claimed Kiran as her own son, saying that since she had nursed him, Kiran belonged to her. She and Amar Nath supported Kiran and paid for his education. The alienation of Ganga from his firstborn son made the rift between Ganga and Amar Nath irreconcilable. The subsequent birth of three sons and three daughters to Ganga and his wife had not healed it. In order to ensure his claim to his share of the house upon his father's death, Ganga still shared his father's *choopar* and kept his wife and children in the family's crowded *bughar;* however, he had built a new house across the street from the joint courtyard. He went about his business around the household without speaking to his father. Therefore, Draupadi not only co-opted the services and loyalty of the firstborn grandson by claiming him, but ensured that her son Succha was his father's favorite by alienating Amar Nath from his firstborn son.

When Succha's wife, Dhooli, was pregnant with her first child, she went home to her father's house, although it is customary for *bahus* to remain in their husbands' homes for the birth of the first child. Dhooli says that throughout her pregnancy, no one from Amar Nath's house wrote to ask about her. When her son, Ajab, was born, she refused to write to her husband's family and tell them of the birth because no one had asked about her health. Her father wrote to Amar Nath, who, upon hearing of the birth of a grandson, came to bring Dhooli back when Ajab was about 12 days old. Her father refused to send her so soon after the birth, and Amar Nath had to return when Ajab was 3 months old to bring Dhooli and her son back to Khalapur.

Dhooli remained with her husband for 2 years after Ajab's birth and then insisted on returning to her own home because Draupadi repeatedly blamed her for Succha's psychosis. When her father came for her, Draupadi refused to send Ajab with her and arranged to hide him. The two women disagreed on how the child was hidden. Dhooli said that Luxmi took Ajab and hid in the cattle compound, while Draupadi said that Succha took his son to the fields to hide him. Dhooli was so desperate to get away from Draupadi's accusations that she left her son behind and remained with her parents for 2 years. Amar Nath came once, without Ajab, to bring her back, but she refused to return until her son has been brought to her.

Unable to retrieve her son, Dhooli finally returned to Succha's house after an absence of 2 years.

Draupadi made good use of her time with Ajab. Remarkably, she lactated again and nursed the baby for most of the 2-year period of his mother's absence. In 1975 Ajab was 9 years old and refused to pose with his mother for a picture, insisting that he would pose only with his grandmother, Draupadi. Once he had torn up a photo of himself and Dhooli saying, "Now I am dead to you and you are dead to me." Dhooli fed and cared for Ajab as a servant might, but his loyalty and affection were clearly with Draupadi.

Draupadi had also turned Succha against his wife and ensured his loyalty to her and Luxmi. Dhooli told us that Succha beat her, but had not beaten her when he was mad. She said that if she asked Succha for anything when they are alone, he became irritated and threatened to beat her with his shoe. If Luxmi accused her of anything, even falsely, Succha came and beat her.

Dhooli's two daughters were born after Ajab, and a second son was born during our visit. As soon as Dhooli's confinement ended, Drapaudi put her to work cooking and keeping house. She sat with her new grandson on her lap (whenever Dhooli was not nursing him, ignoring her grandaughters' attempts to see the baby). Clearly this clever woman was intent on acquiring the affections of this grandson, as she had those of Kiran and Ajab.

The Prodigal Son

Despite their preferential treatment, or perhaps because of it, sons do quarrel with their fathers, and occasionally run away from home. If the son returns, his rebellion does not injure his chances of marriage. His defiance shows that he is proud, a trait much admired by Rajputs, and his return indicates that he is also responsible. While running away does not change a son's reputation, the loss of a son's labor and his bride's dowry can be a heavy financial blow to a family.

In 1975 Tara, the eldest son of a poor family, had recently returned to his father's house after a 7-year absence. His tearful mother told us about her suffering during Tara's absence and the celebration when the prodigal son returned:

> Tara had a fight with his father. His father is a man of angry nature and Tara took his bicycle and went away. He supported himself working in a thread mill. For those 7 years we did not celebrate any religious festivals, not Divali, nor Holi, nothing.
>
> I lost my eyesight with weeping. I nearly went mad. I used to sit on the doorstop of my house waiting for my son to return. I could not sleep at night nor rest during the day. All of these years I worried. I had raised my son and now he was lost to me. May no woman ever lose her son. A mother suffers from this.
>
> When he returned, all the neighbor women came to celebrate. We distributed *prashad* to all the women and celebrated my son's return. We also offered a man's shawl at the temple. When Tara returned, he told his father that he was sorry he had gone away and would not do it again. Now he works well in the fields. He works from morning to night.

Now that Tara has returned, we have received two or three marriage offers, which we have refused. The father refused them because we are waiting for a better offer.

The devotion of the mother to her son and of women to sons in general is indicated by the celebration of Tara's return by the women of his lineage. While his father and other male relatives were no doubt glad to see him, they did not participate in his celebration. The phrase of an old Irish folk song—"For men will go and women will weep"—is true for the families of many societies.

THE SOCIALIZATION INTERVIEW

Sasus reported that mothers were now the primary caretakers of their grandchildren and that they had less influence over the rearing of grandchildren than their sasus had over the rearing of their children. One sasu was particularly adamant about this change:

> No *bahu* depends upon her *sasu* for bringing up the children nowadays. They themselves bathe the children, feed them properly, and do everything concerning their children. Previously parents did not bother about their own children, now, *bahus* take care of the children themselves. Grandparents decided on whether or not to send their children to school, now the parents may decide. The husband gives the seed, the wife receives it, and after the birth the *bahu* looks after the children herself. Now they think that the *sasus* may not behave well toward the children so they do everything regarding the children themselves. They think that nobody else can have affection for the children than the parents themselves. If the mothers do not ask the *sasu* or *nanad* to take the child then why should a *sasu* or *nanad* touch the small child which is obviously dirty?
>
> My *sasu* used to beat me if I beat my own children for being disobedient to me. My *soosar* would come and say to her, "Why are you beating your *bahu* daily?" and my *sasu* would say, "Why is she beating my two grandsons?"

The comparison of the socialization interview results obtained in 1955 and 1975 is shown in Table 12.1. Differences in child care practices for boys and girls were usually minimal, and the tabular results are presented for the average response of boys and girls combined. When significant sex differences in reported practices do appear, they are discussed in the text. The significant time differences, based on chi-square analysis, are presented in Table 12.1. As expected, a number of changes have occurred.

Caretakers

In view of the finding that mothers no longer believe that their children's fate is predetermined, and because mothers are more autonomous, one might expect them to be more involved in child training and more particular about socialization practices than their predecessors. Indeed, mothers in 1975 more often reported being the

Table 12.1 Maternal Response Frequencies to Socialization Interviews, 1955 and 1975

	1955 %	1975 %	χ^2	P
Caretakers				
1. Who takes care of C?				
Mother	33	50	—	N.S.
Both parents	17	8	—	N.S.
Grandmother	0	16	—	N.S.
Other	57	34	—	N.S.
2. Who took care of C when C was a baby?				
Mother	52	82	4.95	.05
Grandmother	9	8	—	N.S.
Mother and grandmother	0	5	—	N.S.
Both parents	13	0	—	N.S.
3. Does your husband ever take care of C?				
Yes and sometimes	59	53	—	N.S.
4. Do others in the household see that C behaves well?				
Yes	58	92	3.31	.10
5. Who sees that C behaves well?				
Mother	30	50	3.31	.10
Both parents	17	10	—	N.S.
All elders, and mother and elders	43	39	—	N.S.
6. Do C's elder siblings ever see that she/he behaves well?				
Yes	72	71	—	N.S.
Discipline				
7. Do you beat C?				
Yes and sometimes	75	100	5.12	.05
8. Do you forbid C to have something she/he wants?				
Yes	75	81	—	N.S.
9. Do you make fun of C?				
Yes	50	45	—	N.S.
10. Do you stop speaking to C?				
Yes	48	5	13.08	.01
11. Do you frighten C?				
Yes and sometimes	29	53	21.27	.01
12. What do you do when C does something well?				
Praise, caress, etcetera	96	84	—	N.S.
13. Do you give C special presents?				
Yes	42	32	—	N.S.
14. Do you let C do any special things?				
Yes and sometimes	43	66	—	N.S.
15. Do you praise C?				
Yes	87	82	—	N.S.
16. What do other household members do to see that C behaves?				
Beat	39	34	—	N.S.
Scold, threaten	90	45		
No one else punishes C	5	18	—	N.S.

(continued)

Table 12.1–(Continued)

	1955 %	1975 %	χ^2	P
Expressiveness				
17. Is it a good thing when C tells other children what to do?				
Yes	66	77		
18. Should C help younger children in trouble?				
Yes	58	100	14.27	.01
19. When children fight do you ever tell C to fight back?				
Yes	13	27	—	N.S.
20. What do you do when C gets angry with you?				
Does not get angry	12	3	—	N.S.
Consoles (and ignores rewards, punishes)	54	35	—	N.S.
Reasons with	0	19	—	N.S.
Threatens, punishes	29	43	—	N.S.
21. What do you do if C hits or kicks you?				
Beats	25	76	5.12	.05
Scolds, threatens	10	2	—	N.S.
Has not, could not happen	57	21	—	N.S.
22. Do you allow C to cry?				
Yes and sometimes	0	37	6.87	.01
23. Do you allow C to show anger?				
Yes	0	2	—	N.S.
Responsibility				
24. Number of chores	1.5	3.4	6.55	.01
25. Frequency of chores	3.9	5.1	2.76	.01
26. Does C usually do his/her work well?				
Yes	65	63	—	N.S.

Note: Frequency of chores was coded on a 7-point scale, ranging from "never" to "several times a day." Four indicates that children do chores weekly and 5 indicates that they do them several times a week.

primary caretakers of both older children and babies than they did in 1955 (Questions 1 and 2). The difference in the increase in maternal care of babies is significant.

This result is substantiated by our observation that babies were less likely to be left on cots covered with quilts than they were during our previous visit. They were more likely to be held even while the mothers were working, and young mothers, free from the more severe constraints on behavior in the presence of the *sasu,* played with their babies much more freely than they did on our first visit. However, there are no significant differences in the amount of time that grandmothers and other household members spent caring for babies or older children (Questions 1–3).

Answers to Question 4 indicate that in 1975 mothers reported a tendency for other adults to see that children behaved well more frequently than they did in 1955. However, there is no significant reported increase in the disciplinary function of any particular category of relative; for example, the amount of discipline exerted by older siblings and other adults in the courtyard reportedly remained unchanged (Questions 5 and 6). The greater crowding of the courtyards probably accounts for the reported trend. There were fewer nuclear courtyards in 1975 than in 1955, and extended families were larger. Since more women were likely to be living in *bughars* in 1975, there were more women present to reprimand children.

One of the most appealing changes we observed in the care of infant girls was that grandfathers, who used to care only for infant grandsons, now performed this service for granddaughters as well. Infant boys often played with grandfathers on the men's platforms, relieving the mothers for housework. In the fifties such men usually reached for their fighting staffs when posing for pictures. In the seventies they often picked up a granddaughter.

Praise and Punishment

Our previous analysis had shown that mothers who raise their children in the same households as other nuclear families are less warm and more unstable than are mothers living in nuclear families. *Mothers of Six Cultures* described this situation as follows:

> The absence of praise is the result of a deliberate policy, designed to train the compliant personality required in an extended family. The parents believe that if children are praised too much they will become spoiled because they will think that the parents "love them too much." The concern here seems to be that the child who is "loved too much" will not only be grudging in obedience, which, like minor bickering, is tolerable but will be openly rebellious and recalcitrant. This policy is emphasized so strongly that, although we almost never heard a woman praise a child, the men complained that women lost control of children because of too much praise.
>
> . . .
>
> The larger number of siblings tends to mute the mother's warmth in a manner analogous to the way the larger number of cousins does. The mother must avoid the problems that can arise from any show of favoritism or special treatment in front of the host of little witnesses within her immediate family or outside of this close kin group.
>
> (Minturn & Lambert, 1964, pp. 232, 261)

The population of children between the ages of 3 and 10 had doubled since 1955. Twice as many children created noticeable difference. Courtyards were even more crowded, noisy, and confused than they had been. I often had the impression that I was knee-deep in children. The courtyard congestion was relieved somewhat by the fact that children in 1975 were more likely to be in school or working in their family fields than they were in 1955. Nevertheless, the increased congestion in the *bughars* was noticeable. Therefore, one might expect the 1975 mothers to exhibit less warmth and more instability.

The disciplinary techniques used by mothers had, as predicted, become more severe. In 1975 mothers were more likely to beat and frighten children than they were in 1955 (Question 7; 75% vs. 100%; and Question 11; 29% vs. 53%). The increase in the probability of beating is greater for boys than it is for girls. In line with the shift to direct methods of discipline, mothers were much less likely to use the indirect technique of not speaking to naughty children (Question 10; 48% vs. 5%); again, this trend was particularly significant for boys. The decrease in the incidence with which other household members scold and threaten children, while not significant, might be regarded as further evidence of increased maternal status. However, there was no decrease in the frequency with which other household members beat children (Question 16). The use of positive incentives had not changed significantly. Praise was the most common response to good behavior for both time periods, and there was no change in the frequency of use of praise rewards or privileges over time (Questions 12–15).

The measure of maternal warmth used in the 1955 analysis was a combination of the use of positive discipline, particularly praise, and punishment. Since the beating and frightening had increased, and the use of praise, privilege, and presents had remained unchanged, the finding that mothers with many children and mothers raising their children in extended families exhibit less warmth than mothers with fewer children and mothers in nuclear families is again confirmed.

The effect on children of the relative lack of warmth from mothers living in extended families cannot be equated with maternal warmth deprivation for children in nuclear families. In joint families there are several women present to nurture children. There was agreement among women in a *bughar* that more than one adult should not scold a child at the same time. When a child was upset from being scolded, he or she usually sought comfort from another woman. Most grandmothers were nurturant to small children on such occasions. Therefore, although individual mothers were relatively controlled in their expressions of praise, children did not suffer from an overall lack of warmth.

Obedience Training

During both periods mothers were more likely to be responsible for seeing that daughters behaved well than they were for the good behavior of their sons (Question 5). In 1955 this difference was 17% for boys and 45% for girls. In 1975 it was significant: 14% for boys and 71% for girls). One reason for this increased supervision of girls is that boys spent more time out of the courtyard, at school or working in the fields. However, the more important reason was the decreased importance of the belief that daughters are guests of the house and should not be expected to work because they will have to work so hard after marriage.

In 1975 mothers did exert their authority more directly than they did in 1955. They were more likely to see that children behaved well, although this trend was not strong (Question 5; 30% vs. 50%).

Expressiveness Training

Mothers were more likely to allow children to cry than they were in 1955 (Question 22; 0% vs. 37%). Previously, because of disapproval of individual demands for attention, children who cried were scolded or ignored. The increased permissiveness for crying was probably due to the greater involvement of mothers in the care of their own children.

Leadership Training

The increased assertiveness of mothers in 1975 was also reflected in their expectations for children's behavior. They were significantly more likely to think that their children should help younger children and that it was a good idea for their children to tell other children what to do (Question 18; 58% vs. 100%; and Question 17; 66% vs. 77%); this change was reflected primarily in an increase in their expectations for boys (58% vs. 78%).

Some of the mothers encouraged their children to direct other children:

> Telling other children how to work or play is not a bad thing, but I would neither encourage nor discourage him.

> There is nothing wrong if he tells other children how to play, what to do, and how to do it while playing with them, but he is not leaderlike. He is fearful and hesitant and weak physically.

Other mothers still discouraged such leadership:

> If he orders other children to play this way or that way, then there would be a quarrel among the children. This quarrel among children may lead to a quarrel among the elders, which is very bad. Therefore, I discourage this from the very beginning.

Aggression Training

In 1975 mothers were more punitive than in 1955, when their children become angry with them. In answer to Question 20 ("What do you do when your child gets angry with you?"), fewer mothers in 1975 reported that they did not get angry with (12% vs. 3%) or console (54% vs. 35%) their children, while more reported that they reasoned with their children (0% vs. 19%) or threatened to punish (29% vs. 43%) them. In 1975 mothers were more likely to beat children who hit or kicked them (Question 21; 25% vs. 75%) and less likely to say that such an occurrence could not happen (Question 21; 57% vs. 21%). This latter finding may reflect greater honesty in the responses but it probably reflects the greater assertiveness of the mothers and their lessened concern for intervention by *sasus*.

Some mothers in 1975 said that their children would not dare to become angry with them:

> She has no guts to kick me. She would be afraid of getting beaten. Of course, I would beat her if she hit me intentionally with something. I do not allow her to get angry with me and I threaten her, then she is all right.

One mother reported that she never gave in to her daughter's anger:

> If you have control over the children from the very beginning, and give them good teaching, then how can they kick or hit you? If any child behaves like this, it is due to the fault of his parents who could not control him right from the beginning. Our children never do that. When she wants something and is refused, and shows anger, then I never give her that thing because this will spoil her.   .

Our previous findings indicated that mothers with large numbers of children to contend with were more likely to prohibit fights among children than were mothers with relatively few children. Since courtyards usually had more children in 1955, one would expect that fights would continue to be prohibited. This prediction was confirmed. There was no change in the virtually unanimous disapproval of children showing anger (Question 23).

Chores

Girls seldom did household chores in 1955 but were likely to help their mothers with cooking and other household chores in 1975; therefore, there was more need for supervision of daughters. Despite the fact that children in 1975 spent more time in school, they also did more chores (Question 24; 1.5 vs. 3.4) and did them more frequently (Question 25; 3.9 vs. 5.1) than they did in 1955. There was no change in the percentage of mothers who thought that their children do their work well (Question 26). Women gave several explanations for this increase in children's work. The most salient was that life as not as bad for *bahus* since purdah restrictions had diminished; therefore, it was no longer necessary to shield daughters from work before their marriages. Some women said that whereas in former times *sasus* expected to train *bahus* themselves, they now expected incoming *bahus* to know how to cook and clean and may have abused them if they are unskilled.

Some older women said that these new educated *bahus* were lazy and therefore made their daughters share the work, an opinion not supported by our interview, which indicated that uneducated mothers were more likely to want their daughters to help with the housework than were educated mothers. The increase in separate *chuulas* made daughters' participation in cooking more probable. In the days when the youngest *bahu* was expected to cook for the entire family, her children were usually too young to help.

In 1955 only one 10-year-old girl from a poor family had regular work. Her mother had died, and she was being raised by her *taaya* (wife of father's elder brother), a circumstance that often leads to some exploitation. Her *taaya* described her niece's work as follows:

> Devi is the steady baby carrier for her infant cousin, and when she goes on visits in the village, he is almost always on her hip. She also takes food to her hardworking uncles in the fields. She sometimes sweeps the floor, cleans the hearth, and if the family exhausts their daily supply of water delivered by the water-carrying girls, she brings an extra pot or two from the nearby well.

In 1975 we found that three girls aged 10 to 15 had regular chores. They swept the floor daily, cleaned the kitchen utensils, and sometimes cooked the evening meal. An additional two made dung cakes, one washed clothes, and one cared for her younger sister. Seven girls aged 4 to 9 did not have regular chores. Two 8-year-old girls did no work, but the other five occasionally helped their mothers by sweeping, cleaning utensils, or putting a mud coating on the *chuula*. One 7-year-old girl took care of her younger brother, and one 5-year-old took her mother's spun thread to the Gandhi ashram and exchanged it for money. The work reported was relatively light, but it did represent an increase in responsibility training for girls.

One mother in 1975 said her daughter did not work well, but she was reluctant to punish her:

> She does not work happily. I have to shout at her to get the work done. I threaten her and then she does the work. I usually give her some time, but if she does not want to do it even then, I do it myself. I can chide her but I cannot beat her, because then her father gets angry. She does not keep her mind on her work. When she makes fresh mint chutney, one half of it is wasted. She is the darling child of this house. Therefore, if she says the work is difficult for her I usually help her.
>
> At her age, I could do all the cooking, because my mother died very young. I wish that she could learn every household chore soon, but it does not seem likely.

Another mother was happy with the work done by her daughter and attributed the change in chore requirements to a change in the age of marriage, although in fact the average age of marriage for girls was 20 years in 1955 and 21 in 1975:

> Usually she does not neglect her work. I praise her and she gets encouraged and finishes the work. She does her work very nicely. I encourage her and say, "You are a very good girl," then she tries to improve her work in the future. I help her when needed and always reassure her of my help. When she finds the work difficult, I encourage her to keep trying, but if she is really unable to do it, then I help, but first I encourage her to finish her work without anybody's help. In earlier days girls used to get married at a young age. Therefore, mothers considered them to be guests in their own homes and did not let them do any household work. But now girls are grown-up at the time of marriage. I also want my girls to learn everything sooner than I did.

Sex Training

Children were given no specific training about sex, and the topic was too sensitive to include in the standard interview during both field trips. We obtained information about sex training from some casual interviews and observations. One of the women said that they did not teach their children anything about sex, that God taught them. This may be a way of expressing learning by observation. The children were certainly under no delusion about the source of infants of all species. They witnessed the birth of both human and animal babies, and saw the sexual behavior of the cattle and the dogs with whom they were constantly surrounded.

When a husband comes to his wife, he calls her to another cot or a separate place in the room or courtyard. We were told that the couple would not have intercourse in the same bed with the children. However, it seemed unlikely that the children would, throughout childhood, be so sound asleep that they would not witness the sex act of some adults in the family. The women said that by the time the young couple got married they knew all about the "facts of life" although they never stated specifically how they learned. We sometimes saw children listening to women's conversations about sexual matters while feigning disinterest in what was being said.

CONCLUSIONS

The changes in socialization and education in Rajput families have come about because of greater affluence and increased education for *bahus*. The reported differences in socialization practices are probably a consequence of the overall increase in the power of *bahus* that has occurred in the intervening 20 years between my two visits. Increased literacy is the most important factor influencing this change in perceived empowerment. Other factors influencing empowerment reported by the women are government policy to discourage purdah and increase women's status; increased prosperity; the role model of Indira Gandhi as prime minister; exposure to movies, books, and magazines; and pressure from young husbands.

These changes have, in turn, been brought about by the increased education of women, modernization of social norms regarding purdah restrictions, and the prosperity resulting from high-yield grains and increased emphasis on profitably marketable agriculture. The new grains require more intensive cultivation, and the surplus is readily marketable; therefore, children, particularly boys, were more likely to work in the fields in 1975 than they were in 1955. In addition to their schoolwork, girls did more chores around the house in 1975 than in 1955.

Mothers, more autonomous in their control of household resources and the management of their children and relieved of the necessity to be passive and silent in the presence of their *sasus,* disciplined their children, particularly boys, more firmly than they did 20 years earlier. However, mothers were less likely to report being responsible for boys' good behavior. The increased number of women in the courtyards had resulted in a greater probability that other household members would assist in disciplining children; such discipline was used to back up the mothers' norms, whereas formerly mothers were more likely to follow the norms set by their *sasus*. In keeping with their own increased assertiveness, mothers in 1975 trained their children to be more assertive. They were more likely to approve of their children directing other children and helping younger children than they were in 1955. They were also more likely to allow their children to indulge in the emotional release of crying.

One of the findings of our previous study was that children in stem families and in families with a relatively large number of children were more likely to be punished for fighting with other children than were those in nuclear families or families with a small number of children. Rajput households were more crowded in 1975 than they were in 1955. The unaltered prohibition against fighting was consistent with these findings. The prohibition against fighting is integral to a primary aim of the socialization of children in an extended family: their training to be group members rather than selfish individuals. Kurtz (1992), drawing heavily on my 1955 account of socialization, correctly identifies and describes the importance of socialization for group identity.

The teacher sits on a chair in this girls' school, while her students sit on floor mats. In the center one girl writes on her wooden board while the others read papers (1955).

13

Education

Those with two braids have come.

In traditional societies, where children do not go to school, the primary method of socialization is usually apprenticeship. Whereas school teaches rote learning and the manipulation of abstract concepts, apprenticeship is on-the-job training that teaches skills. Fathers teach their sons farming skills, and mothers teach their daughters household skills by letting them help with simple tasks, gradually introducing them to more difficult chores. Children are always present: They listen to adult conversation and quarrels, participate in celebrations, observe births, deaths, and marriages, and the comings and goings of neighbors and family servants. The women we interviewed did not teach their children about caste differences; instead, children learned about expected behavior by observing the adults. Observation and practice, rather than reading and memory, are the methods of learning in apprenticeship.

Increased prosperity by 1975 had enabled Rajput families to educate virtually all of their sons and most of their daughters. The government had encouraged education and facilitated the education of girls by not requiring them to pay tuition in elementary school. Sons frequently attended the local high school. As we have said, the education of girls often did not extend beyond grade school (fifth grade). However, the number of girls enrolled in the intercollege (high school) had increased from 4 in 1955 to 86 in 1975. The intercollege girls often wore their hair plaited into the city style of two braids, rather than the single braid typical of village women. Because of their modern hairstyle, they were sometimes called "those with two braids" by uneducated women wary of their new ways.

In 1955 the goal of education for girls was simply to acquire the ability to read and write letters. Parental opinion on even this modest goal was divided. Those in favor argued that a literate daughter could write home to her parents after her marriage. Those opposed said that daughters would only complain about their husbands' families, so that it was better if they could not write. As we have seen, minimal literacy also enables women to travel on trains by themselves. This basic skill allowed Sita to flee to her father's house and vindicate her honor when it was questioned by her husband. In 1975, parents generally agreed that elementary school education was advisable for girls as well as for boys.

291

The greater education of Khalapur women seems to have emerged from the increased education of men. Educated men prefer literate wives. Therefore, education becomes an asset in arranging a good marriage for daughters. Similarly, Khalapur Rajputs educate their own sons in order to arrange good marriages for them. Some high school students, both boys and girls, are withdrawn from school when their engagements are arranged.

ADULT LITERACY

Between 1955 and 1975 there was a marked increase in the number of educated parents, particularly mothers, in the Rajput families of our studies. In 1955 the literacy statistics showed that education, particularly for girls, was a recent development for Rajputs (see Table 13.1). The literacy rate increased from 24% to 32% for men over 40, from 38% to 68% for men from 20 to 39, and from 70% to 88% for males from 6 to 20 years. The literacy rate increased from 7% to 9% for women over 40, from 5% to 38% for women from 20 to 39, and from 14% to 79% for females from 6 to 20. Since 70% of the Rajput boys in the families studied were in school in 1955, the increase in literacy for males was the 30% increase for men in the 20- to 39-year age range. Only 14% of the Rajput girls were in school in 1955; therefore, the greatest increase for females was the dramatic 63% rise for females in the 6- to 20-year age range.

Because married women move in from other villages, the slightly greater literacy rate for the younger group might have reflected greater education for Khalapur daughters. Literacy of *bahus* was not recorded in 1954–55, but this omission was corrected in 1975 (see Table 13.2). All of the older women were wives of Khalapur men and therefore were born in other villages. In the 20- to 40-year age range, 40% of daughters and 32% of daughters-in-law were literate. The higher educational levels of Khalapur daughters, as opposed to Khalapur wives, probably reflected the upward mobility of women resulting from hypergamous marriages.

As a result of this recent increase in female literacy, in 1975 most *sasus* were

Table 13.1 Percentage of Literate Males and Females, 1955 and 1975

	Age 40+		Age 20–39		Age 6–20	
	1955	1975	1955	1975	1955	1975
Male	24	32	38	68	70	88
Female	7	9	5	38	14	79

Table 13.2 Comparison of Literacy Rates for Married Daughters and Daughters-in-Law

	Literate		Illiterate		
	N	%	N	%	Total
Daughters	25	40	37	60	62
Daughters-in-law	30	32	63	68	93

illiterate, while most *bahus* were literate. Educated *bahus* have higher status in the households than do illiterate *bahus*. Educated women tend to come from wealthier families and bring larger dowries. Both their wealth and education contribute to their high status, and they tend to set the standards for the other *bahus* in their *bughars*.

CHILDREN'S EDUCATION

In 1955 we reported that the most common answer to the question of how long mothers wanted their children to attend school was "It is in his fate, no matter what I want" (Minturn & Hitchcock, 1966, p. 92). This answer was not repeated in 1975, when both educated and uneducated mothers wanted their children to go through primary school and apparently thought control of their children's education rested in their planning, not their children's predetermined fate.

All educated mothers send daughters, as well as sons, to school. Therefore, education of mothers appears to be a determining factor in children's education. In 1975 there was general support for primary school education. Some *sasus* had prevented their granddaughters from attending high school, but there was no reported opposition to primary school attendance, even from the grandparental generation. The following are typical answers to the question "Who decides whether the children will go to school?"

> Everyone wants that one's child should get some education.
>
> Parents as well as grandparents wish that their children should be properly looked after.
>
> In my house it is up to the elders to decide though the parents can also send their children to school.
>
> In our house it is the grandparents who decide when to send the children to school.
>
> Since it is the grandparents who pay for the child's education, they are the ones who decide whether or not the children should go to school.

Because there was a difference in school attendance between the children of literate and illiterate mothers, we interviewed a small sample of seven literate and seven illiterate mothers about issues that might affect their children's education. Few differences were found between the two groups, but these few reflect important differences in the goals that literate versus illiterate mothers have for their children's education. For both groups the decision to send children to school may be made by the parents and grandparents. Both groups reported that they and their husbands were happy that their children were in school. There was no difference between the groups in strictness about truancy. Both groups wanted their children to read and write and have good manners. Most mothers of both groups were content to give their daughters a primary education but wanted their sons to complete high school training or go on to earn a bachelor's or master's degree at a nearby college.

Twelve of the 14 mothers cited making good marriages as an important reason for wanting both sons and daughters to go to school. Twelve mothers wanted educated sons to be able to get jobs rather than become farmers, but eight women cited learning to be a good farmer as a reason for schooling. All mothers wanted their daughters to learn to be good wives and mothers, and 9 cited reading and writing letters as a school goal. Five literate and 3 illiterate mothers wanted their daughters to get jobs, an impressive goal for women who were traditionally forbidden to leave their *bughars,* let alone work.

The increased support for education is apparent in the following comment, recorded in 1975:

> Sometimes her uncle makes fun of her saying, "Since she does not study well, I will get her married to a herd boy, and she will have to cut grass and look after other peoples animals." He does not say this in the presence of others.

When asked why they wanted their sons to stay in school longer than their daughters, three mothers of each group said that they feared coeducation for postpubescent daughters. Illiterate mothers were more likely to say that sons will earn money so their education is worth the expense and to say that they needed daughters to help them with the housework.

The most important differences between the two groups of mothers were in some of their reports about what they wanted their daughters to learn in school. The illiterate mothers wanted their daughters to be able to read railway signs addresses, so that they could travel by themselves after they were married. Literate mothers said they wanted their daughters to become independent, a goal that would include the ability to travel, but added that they wanted their daughters to know about their bodies. Presumably, they wanted daughters to understand reproduction and birth control.

PRIMARY SCHOOLS
Enrollment

In 1954 Khalapur had two primary schools—the boys' school, located on a temple platform, with an enrollment of 200 students, and a girls' school with an enrollment of 40 students. In 1974 the village had four schools with a total enrollment of 579 boys and 342 girls (see Table 13.3). The total number of children in elementary school had risen from 140 to 921.

Primary School One, with 266 children and five teachers, was moved from its old location on the temple platform to the road between the project house and the village. Primary School Two, with 217 children and four teachers, was in the center of the village, near the Piir. The building had been previously used for the Sanskrit school, now closed for several years. Primary School Three had replaced the small private school that used to be in Keriputti in 1955; it had 204 students and four teachers. Primary School Four, the girls' school, had five teachers and an enrollment of 234 students. Two new buildings had been added to Primary School Four, financed with government funds and contributions from Khalapur residents.

Table 13.3 Comparison of School Enrollment by Sex and Caste

	Elementary School		Intercollege	
	N	%	N	%
Males	579	63	1,022	93
Females	342	37	82	7
Rajput	652	71	493	45
Brahmin and Vaish	49	5	273	25
Sudras	108	12	146	13
Harijans	83	9	145	13
Muslims	29	3	47	4
Total	921	100	1,104	100

Table 13.4 Total Enrollment in Elementary School for Rajput Boys and Girls

	Boys		Girls		
Grade	N	%	N	%	Total
1	142	58	104	42	246
2	55	50	56	50	111
3	71	58	52	42	123
4	43	50	43	50	86
5	56	65	30	35	86
Total	367	56	285	44	652

All four schools, including the former girls' school, were coeducational. Children usually went to the school nearest their homes. Parents also preferred to send all of their children to the same school. For this reason the girls' school had, for the past 7 years, enrolled boys whose sisters were already attending that school. In 1975 the girls' school had 43 boys.

The percentage of children in schools varied considerably by caste: 71% of the total elementary school enrollment consisted of Rajput children, 5% Brahmin, 3% Muslims, 12% Sudras, and 9% Harijans (see Table 13.3). The excess of Rajput children reflected both the large population in the village and their greater prosperity. The majority of the Harijan (untouchable) children, 63%, went to Primary School Three in Keriputti.

For all schools and all castes, 63% of the schoolchildren were boys and 37% were girls. The ratio for Rajputs was 56% boys and 44% girls (see Table 13.4). In 1954 only 40 girls attended the elementary girls' school, while 200 boys attended the boys' primary school. The 1975 school enrollments showed 367 Rajput boys and 285 Rajput girls enrolled in elementary schools from the first through the fifth grades. Therefore, the sex ratio of elementary school Rajput students had risen from 70% male versus 14% female in 1955 to 56% male versus 44% female in 1975, an increase of 30%.

Enrollment in Grade 1 was higher than the enrollment in any of the other grades (see Table 13.4). Admission to Grade 1 was open throughout the course of the year,

Table 13.5 Total Enrollment in Elementary Schools for Boys
and Girls of all Castes

Grade	Boys		Girls		Total
	N	%	N	%	
1	219	63	129	37	348
2	95	58	68	42	163
3	108	65	59	35	167
4	70	58	51	42	121
5	87	71	35	29	122
Total	579	63	342	37	921

whereas admission to the other grades was allowed only at the beginning of the school term on July 1. Therefore, a number of children who had begun the first year late were held back. In Primary School Three, for instance, 63 out of 94 students in Grade 1 had been held back. In Primary School Three, for instance, 63 out of 94 students in Grade 1 had been held over from the last year. In the girls's school, 60 of the 110 students in Grade 1 had been held from the last year.

The second reason for the excess of students in Grade 1 was that children of this age were too young to be of any use at home and a number of parents sent them to school to get them out of the house. Therefore, the schools acted as baby-sitters for the first-grade children, some of whom may drop out after Grade 1. Children may be held back at any grade on the basis of the final examination. Therefore, the number of children per grade tended to decrease for the higher grades.

Enrollment in Grades 2 through 5 remained fairly constant for boys but dropped for girls, particularly in Grade 5. The sex ratio for all castes dropped from 58-42 in Grade 4 to 71-29 in Grade 5 (see Table 13.5). For Rajputs the sex ratio dropped from 50-50 in Grade 4 to 65-35 in Grade five.

The headmistress of the girls' school in 1975 was the same woman who had held the position in 1955. She had complained in 1955 that families removed their girls after the fourth grade, when they had learned to read and write; she repeated this complaint in 1975, saying that the girls dropped out in the fourth grade because parents only wanted them to learn to read and write letters and because they were needed at home for housework. The enrollment statistics confirmed her complaint.

School Term

The school term began on July 1. The semiannual examinations were held in December, and final examinations were held the first week of May. Final grades were announced by the end of May. There was 1 month's vacation in June. During the winter, from October 1 to March 30, the school day ran from 10 a.m. to 4 p.m. The lunch period varied from 30 minutes to 1 hour, depending on the school. During the summer session, from April 1 to September 30, the school day ran from 7 a.m. to 12 noon.

Curriculum

Previously agriculture was taught as a separate subject, but in 1975 it was included as a portion of other science courses. Art and science had been added to the primary school curriculum. The examination system had been changed, and final examination booklets were now sent to an examiner in Bhudana who checked the grades. Language and arithmetic were taught through all five grades. In Grade 2 social studies (including history, geography, and civics), science (including botany and anatomy), and art were added. In addition to these official subjects, the girls' school taught home economics, including cooking, laundry, knitting, and tailoring. Dance was not taught as a regular subject, but occasionally the girls were asked to put on a dance performance and were taught whatever dances are needed for their projects.

Although prizes were given for athletics and dramatic competitions in most of the schools, no prizes were given for academic excellence as such. In all schools, grades—simply pass or fail for most students—were announced at the end of May. The names of the best students in each class were announced at the end of each term. None of the schools sent grades home to the parents; instead, the children copied their grades in each subject and were expected to take them to their parents themselves.

Friendships

Reports of children's friendship varied. Previously we noted that children tended to stay with their own relatives, and certainly with members of their own caste, when they were in school. Some teachers in 1975 confirmed that this was still the case, although others say that children may make friends with other children who have similar interests. Some teachers reported that children may sit with children of another caste. As with children in most countries, girls and boys tended to segregate themselves into separate seating groups.

Children were encouraged to help each other with their lessons as long as they did not cheat. Children could go to other children for help with their lessons, and dull children sometimes made friends with brighter children in order to engage their assistance. Older children usually helped younger children, but younger children also helped older children if they were bright or more advanced. All of the teachers reported encouraging this helpful behavior.

Teachers reported that the children did not fight in the school but sometimes fought going to or coming from school. The teachers insisted that there were no problems of fighting between castes and that there were no problems of boys bullying girls in the primary schools, but some parents reported that they did not like their children to go to school because they got beaten.

Truancy

Although truancy in 1975 was not as frequent as it had been 20 years earlier, it continued to be a problem. The girls' school reported that, of its total enrollment of 226, about 180 girls came in the morning and about 150 in the afternoon. Other schools also reported irregular school attendance and lower attendance in the afternoon session. The exception to this was the school in Keripatti, which had only a half-hour lunch period.

During both visits we noted a lack of commitment among parents regarding their children's school attendance. In one family, for instance, one of the three children was sick on a particular day, and all three children had failed to go to the school. Another mother told her son not to go to school because the school pump was broken and teachers were requiring the children to draw water. On another day this boy refused to go to the school although his mother told him to, because he preferred to work in the fields.

INTERCOLLEGE
Female Enrollment

Customs of seclusion of women and concern for daughters' virtue still made most families reluctant to send postadolescent girls to coeducational schools. A liquor store on the road to the school had been closed at the insistence of the high school principal because drunks were harassing girls on their way to school. A few girls were reading at home for college degrees, but none had been sent away to college. Norms for early marriage present strong barriers for college education of women. Most Rajput girls marry at 18 to 20 years, while men marry in their early 20s. These ages are comparable to the marital ages for the population of the state of Uttar Pradesh as a whole.

Nevertheless, the number of girls enrolled in the local high school had increased from 4 in 1955 to 82 in 1975. The total enrollment of the intercollege had doubled in size during the same time period, from 500 to 1,000. Therefore, the percentage of high school girls, mostly Rajput, had risen from .8% in 1954 to 8% of the high school population in 1974.

Female Participation

Sometimes high schools in the district had exhibitions in which students performed individually and in teams. Competitions among schools at the block and district level were not confined to athletics but also encompassed drama, speech, debates, recitation, and singing. Some prizes were received for performances during these competitions. Because school teams sometimes traveled for interschool competition, parents had to be willing to have their child leave the village in order for the child to be selected as a captain. The girls' school did not regularly participate in these interschool competitions.

CONCLUSIONS

The presence of four new schools and the increased enrollment at the intercollege indicate that more children were attending school in 1975 than were in 1955.

Seventy percent of Rajput boys were in school in 1955, and this figure had not risen significantly from 1955 to 1975, although more boys went on to the intercollege and to college in 1975. However, there had been a dramatic increase in the educational level of Rajput girls from 1955 to 1975. While the number of children tripled during this interim, the number of Rajput girls in school had risen to 7 times the 1955 level in the elementary school and 20 times the 1955 level at the intercollege.

The attitudes of mothers concerning education for their children had changed from one of fatalism to a general expectation that children should go to school. Mothers generally wanted their sons to have more education than their daughters, but whereas literacy for daughters was a debatable issue in 1955, it was a generally accepted goal in 1975. The new literacy for Rajput women is surely one of the most important guarantees that their progress toward modernization will continue.

VII

SUM AND SUBSTANCE

This final part presents the conclusions of the book and their significance in the context of other scholarship. Chapter 14 summarizes the roles and values of the women of our study and attempts to explain their strength and resilience in the face of their subservient status. The essential characteristics of the roles of daughters, virgin goddesses, sacred sisters, privileged guests, dangerous wives, domineering mothers, executive mothers-in-law, and unlucky widows are described. Women's major values—honor, traditionalism, obedience, family harmony, and avarice—and their functional value are summarized.

Chapter 15 is organized around comparisons of the Khalapur data with the national survey *Towards Equality* and with Whyte's cross-cultural study of the status of women in preindustrial societies. Scholarly analysis, including references to the work of other authors and the interpretation of the information from this study, as well as some speculations and suggestions for future research, are included in this final chapter.

An elderly widowed daughter, on a visit to her brother's home, sits behind her hooka and spinning wheel while enjoying the festival of the world (1975).

14

Sita's Daughters: A Profile

We are put on this earth to observe the festival of the world. It is foolish to go back to God too soon.

It was a dreary winter morning, the skies were gray, and a cold drizzle turned the streets into slippery mud when Chand, a middle-aged, childless wife commenting on Radha's suicide, described her drab existence as "the festival of the world." Chand had been married over 20 years, so her hopes for children had long since passed. Her husband was still attached to a particularly dominating widowed mother. Once Chand said that she was waiting for her husband, already in his 40s, to "grow up" and assert his authority in household affairs. Because of her sterility, Chand was one of the most unfortunate women we knew, yet she was hearty, humorous, and cheerful.

What gives these cloistered women such strength and resilience? They lack control over most of the important choices in their lives. Their parents select their husbands, and that choice determines women's place of residence throughout their adult lives. They marry men whom they have never seen and enter households of suspicious strangers. They usually spend the first decades of their marriages controlled by *sasus*. Their husbands, whose loyalties are centered in their natal family, are expected to side against them in disputes with *sasus* or *nanads*. They lead cloistered lives under conditions defined in most countries as house arrest. Yet they are typically strong, proud, and able to enjoy the festival of their world.

While adversity may build strength of character, excessive "coddling" inhibits the development of mature personalities. Paradoxically, while men are expected to be strong, it is sons who reside with parents and remain under parental domination and support while their parents live, while the subservient daughters move at marriage into villages of strangers. Rama's precious sons are catered to, while Sita's daughters learn that they must serve. Bad manners and unruly behavior are tolerated in sons because sons remain within their natal family, but daughters must be taught to be responsible and polite because their behavior in their husbands' homes will reflect on the reputation of their parents.

Men are coddled throughout their lives, particularly by family women, whose power in the *bughar* may depend on their sons's support. Mothers, dependent on sons in their old age, both dominate and cater to them, isolating them from the rival wives whenever possible. Sisters, dependent in later life on brothers for expensive invitations home, utilize the sacred status of the brother–sister bond and the affections of shared childhoods to renew their sibling bonds whenever they come home. Wives, dependent on husbands for children, love, and support, utilize their sexuality to win their husbands' backing in their new and alien abodes. Men's status increases with age; when their sons are married and they become *soosar*s, they are accorded deferential respect from *bahu*s and grandchildren, as well as from their wives.

Men and boys are also supported by their male kinsmen. Even the architecture of the elevated platforms of the men's *choopar*s proclaims their exalted and public status, in contrast to the enclosed, private *bughar*s that hide the family women. Boys are taught that they are born into an elite group of rulers and warriors. As with any elite group, expectations are high and standards of conduct are strict. However, barring the disaster of a serious family rift or the loss of parental land, men need never be alone.

The men are inevitably caught in the middle of "eternal triangles" of mothers, sisters, and wives. The exclusion of men from the *bughar*s is explained in terms of deferential avoidance and the interruption of the women's work that male presence brings, but this custom also serves to buffer the men from women and their quarrels. Men do not enter the *bughar*s without purpose. They come to eat or deliver messages and leave promptly when they have finished. When women quarrel, their angry voices can be heard in the family *choopar* and beyond. In neither of my visits did I see a man enter his *bughar* when the women of his family were embroiled in a quarrel.

According to the religious law of Manu, females should always be controlled by men: girls by their fathers, wives by their husbands, and widows by their sons. Village society has no place for spinsters. Shakti, the primordial female energy, is believed to endow women with stronger sexuality than men and render them unable to control it. Embodied in childhood in the virgin *devi* and in adulthood as the mother, Shakti is the entity that both ennobles and exploits women. As the manifestation of goddesses, women are revered; as the bearers of sons, they are essential; as the possessors of unbridled sexuality, they are married early as maidens, cloistered as wives, and suspect as widows. Always they are the troublesome responsibility of Rama's sons. This chapter focuses on the values and characteristics of these women, using the material described in previous chapters as the background for a profile of their salient roles and values.

WOMEN'S ROLES

The interface of the traditions, honor, and wealth of their elite group molds the roles of Rajput women. None of the women we knew held jobs or political positions. Purdah restricted their mobility, and aside from ritual sisters, they had few friends outside of their kin group. Only the *bhaktani* had an important role that extended her influence beyond her family, and that role was prescribed by traditions concerning widowhood. The lives of these village women were lived in the context of their kinship roles of daughters, sisters, wives, and mothers.

Diminished Daughters

The preference for sons is vested in the importance of the patrilineage and the value of the male work force. Female infanticide is a custom that many still remember. In 1955 the proverb "One son is no son" expressed anxieties about sons' mortality. In 1975 a family of two boys and one girl was described as best because the family would be able to receive two dowries but give only one. Women's reports indicated that they and their husbands preferred boys to girls by an overwhelming majority.

Boys are given preferential treatment from the moment of their birth. Chamars are called to beat their drums and proclaim the birth of every son. Their Bahari and Jasutan ceremonies are attended by many women of the lineage and family servants, while for girls these ceremonies are performed in private. Sons' health is guarded more carefully than the health of daughters. Boys are given necklaces of charms to ward off the evil eye and are taken to doctors more promptly than their sisters.

Each time a senior man enters the courtyard, his superior status is recognized by women in their sudden silence, squatting and pulling down their *gungat*s. Men are fed before women eat. Men sit higher than women on occasions when they sit together. Men can travel freely, while women's movements are restricted. Mothers fast for the health of their sons and husbands, but men do not fast for the health of wives or daughters. The superiority of men is evident in songs, stories, and religious observances. While growing up, girls are taught that men are superior and see this male superiority of status demonstrated every day. By both word and deed girls learn that they and others of their sex are inferior to males.

Sacred Sisters

Unlike mothers, who live with sons throughout their lives, sisters leave their natal homes and move into their husbands' villages. Perhaps because of this separation, the bonds between sisters and brothers are held to be sacred and remain strong despite their separation. These sacred bonds are celebrated yearly when sisters fast on Bahai Duge (brother's day). A village story tells of an exiled king who berated his sister for failing to extend customary hospitality to him and his wife.

Brothers and sisters in Rajput families are usually very close. Succha's breakdown when his sister Luxmi married stemmed from the strength of this brother–sister bond. The marriage of sisters is an emotional loss for brothers as well as for the brides. When telling us of Succha's madness, Draupadi echoed the values of the story of the exiled king by saying the Succha behaved so badly that Luxmi's husband's family would not take him in. In her letters to Draupadi, Luxmi repeatedly asked that her brothers and male cousins be sent to bring her back to her parental home. After his son's death, Thakadar tried to lead his sister, Bahai, out of Khalapur, saying that there was nothing to keep them in the village, although he had a wife and three daughters. The suicide of Radha's father to redeem the dishonor of his sister's infidelity was accepted as a substitute for his sister's death.

Sibling bonds are the kinship ties that hold the natal kin together after the parents die. The family landholdings can be reassigned with the death of parents. If brothers quarrel and divide their holdings, like Ganga and Succha, they increase the expense of cultivation and may have to remodel their *bughar* or build new houses for their families. If sisters claim their legal share of land, property may be lost from the patrilineage. Therefore, the bonds among brothers and between brothers and sisters have practical as well as emotional value. Land claims by daughters are opposed primarily because such claims would sever these bonds and make *nanad*s unwelcome guests in the homes of their brothers. Ranjeet gave up his plans to cede a portion of his lands to Maya when his irate son, Ranbhool, set fire to himself in protest.

Devis

The importance of chastity is impressed on girls long before puberty. Their virginity is honored by calling them *devi*s. *Devi* is often added to girls' names to form a double name (e.g., Kamla-Devi); after marriage the term is usually dropped. At festivals girls may be honored as *devi*s with *prashad* (offerings of food). The status of *devi* encompasses the paradoxical characteristics of goddesses—purity and Shakti. Because of their enchantress powers, women are often held responsible for men's transgressions as well as their own. Women's beauty is believed to attract men with irresistible force. The guilt for Krishna's affair with Radha falls on the faithless wife, not the bachelor god. Sita is banished by Ram, because his people believe she could not avoid the lustful advances of the enamored Ravana. In Rajput history the fall of Fort Chittor is attributed to the passion of a Muslim invader for the Rani.

These stories support and justify the pervasive suspicion of women and their sexuality that characterizes Rajput thought and shapes their concern for women's honor. The Khalapur Krishna justified his affair to his mother by saying that Radha would not let him alone. His mother, in berating Krishna, called on two generations of honorable family men but concluded that the responsibility for chaperoning rightly fell to Radha's mother. After the death of Radha, some mothers said that daughters bring disgrace upon their families. One mother rejoiced that she only had sons, and another that her daughter was safely married. Anxieties about coeducation surfaced in condemnation of higher education for girls as a source of immorality. The value of early marriages to ensure brides' chastity was reiterated.

This *devi* role confers sacred status on girls while teaching them that this sacred status is lost if their behavior becomes "shameless." Girls are taught, through this association of the sacred and chaste, to guard their honor as a holy trust.

Bartered Brides

The system of hypergamous marriage, mandating that women marry into families ranked higher in the kinship system than their own, has two important functions. It ensures that the social standing of a wife and her relatives will be lower than the social standing of her husband and his relatives, and it serves as a conduit that moves wealth up the social status hierarchy. The hypergamous marriage system extends throughout the *jati,* and the kin groups from whom families may take wives are proscribed, so although the social standing of wives' families is lower than that of their husbands, it is usually only one round down on the ladder of social rank. Therefore, the inferior social standing of wives' families in relation to their husbands' families is usually a constant factor, applying equally to all wives.

Variation in the status of wives is based almost exclusively on the size of their dowries. It is this dependence of the brides' status on their families' wealth that makes daughters and their dowries so expensive. The financial negotiations between families for dowry goods are a major consideration in marriage arrangements, but only the initial dowry, paid at the time of *shadi* and *gauna,* can be determined. The frequency and number of subsequent gifts depend on factors such as the number of sons *nanad*s will bear who must have *chuchak* payments, and the number of daughters *nanad*s will bear who will need marriage contributions. The failure of brides' families to meet these later obligations may lead to mistreatment, or even murder, of brides by their in-laws. Relations between Draupadi and her poor *bahu* Dhooli became strained when Succha's illness decreased the family income and made gifts to Luxmi's wealthy family unexpectedly difficult.

Privileged Guests

As children and adolescents, daughters are treated as guests in their own homes, because their lot will be difficult in their husbands' homes. In 1955, girls were not taught to cook or do household chores. Increased expectations concerning skill in cooking and household chores from prospective *sasu*s, and decreased anxiety over marriage, had reduced this prohibition and, in 1975, several mothers were teaching their daughters to cook. Nevertheless, the belief that daughters are guests persists. Teenage girls, in the years before their marriage and the periods between their *shadi*s and their *gauna*s, are excused from household chores and are free to wander throughout their neighborhoods with their friends.

*Nanad*s are given many items from the dowries of their brothers' wives. When possible, brothers are married before their sisters, and their brides are called for their *gauna*s so that their dowry goods may be given to *nanad*s. Thus, Ranbhool's wife returned for her *gauna* so that a portion of her dowry goods could be transferred to Maya's *gauna*. *Bahu*s are called back from visits to parental homes when *nanad*s are getting married and must bring presents for their *nanad*s' dowries. When *bahu*s bear sons, they must give up precious golden jewelry to *nanad*s. *Bahu*s must also contribute to the wedding expenses of *nanad*s' children and give presents to their *nanad*s' grandsons. Because these gifts continue throughout a woman's lifetime, it is said that the custom of giving to daughters never ends.

After marriage, young wives visit their parental homes as frequently as circumstances and their parents' fortunes will allow. *Nanad*s always outrank *bhabhi*s as kin because of their sacred status, by household status because of the primacy of blood relatives, and by clan because of hypergamy. Married *nanad*s welcome their extended visits to parental homes and are treated as guests throughout their stays. They usually bring their children and must care for them but are free from cooking and housekeeping. During these visits they renew their lifelong ties with parents, brothers, and friends. They may roam freely in their neighborhoods as they did when they were young. *Nanads*' visits make extra work for their *bhabhis*, who must cook for them and share crowded *bughar* space with them. Their return to their husbands' homes, laden with many gifts, brings extra expense that may tax the finances of brothers. Dhooli's reluctance to invite Luxmi for a visit after the birth of her second son was supported by Succha's concern for the expense of his sister's visit.

When *bhabhis* are poor and *nanads* are greedy, friction between them may develop, as it has between Dhooli and Luxmi. However, the *bhabhi* of one village is the *nanad* of another. *Nanads* must have the cooperation of their *bhabhis* to visit after their parents are dead, so relations between *nanads* and *bhabhis* are usually cordial.

Dangerous Wives

New brides are always a potential threat to the solidarity of the patrilineage. Wives are alien to the patrilineage until they have borne sons. Brides may co-opt their husbands' loyalties and tempt family men into illicit affairs. The elaborate network of customs of deference and avoidance that constitute the purdah complex is designed to guard against this threat. Basic separation begins with the construction of separate houses for men and women in each family and extends to customs of ritualized avoidance.

Separation of husbands and wives protects the loyalty of sons to the women of their natal families. The denial of the sexual bond between husbands and wives was enforced by several customs. Traditionally wives cooked the food and gave it to their *sasus*, who served it to the family men before feeding themselves and their *bahus*. Men were not served by their wives while their mothers or sisters lived in the *bughar*. Women did not wash the clothes their husbands wore below the waist. Mothers did not hold their own babies or play with them. Deceased family men were mourned by mothers, aunts, and sisters; widows did not participate in the formal mourning of their husbands. By 1975 the observance of these customs had greatly decreased.

The separation of *bahus* from senior family men that serves to guard *bahus* from seduction and men from temptation had not decreased from 1955 to 1975. The accusation of an ill-tempered widow that a young *bahu* was having affairs with her *soosar* and *jaith* was based solely on the gift of fruit from them to the sickly bride. In some families, senior men never enter the *bughar;* daughters or granddaughters bring their food to the *choopars*. When families constructed two-story *choopars*, senior men remained on the ground floor. Nevertheless, some neighbors constructed purdah walls on the roofs of their *bughars* to guard their women's privacy.

Some of the deferential customs accorded family men had given way to more practical observance. In 1955, when senior men entered the *bughars* to eat, women said that they would crouch and stay immobile until the men had left, even if they sat in filth or the cooking pot boiled over. In 1975 women continued with their work but remained silent and crouched when senior men were present.

In 1955 we reported that actions seriously threatening the patrilineage would not be tolerated, even by the strongest families; this prohibition remained in 1975. A marriage between Kirshna and Radha was impossible because the union was held to be incestuous. Great care is taken in arranging marriages to ensure that the groom comes from an appropriate clan. It is for this reason that most wives come from select locations, and wives from strange villages are suspect. Big men like Mussadi might keep a mistress openly but had to select a wife from the correct clan. Honorable women come from honorable families, so the family background of a potential bride is her initial screening. Illegitimate offspring are, of course, the ultimate threat to the patrilineage, and are killed to protect the bloodline.

Domineering Mothers

Maternal reliance on sons appears in legend and reality. Sita's sons defend her and kill their father, who must be magically revived. Stories told by women to their children relate the misadventures of queens saved by the actions of their sons. Sita and Dhooli refused to return to their husbands' homes until their sons were brought to them. Bahai took the baby Hoshiyar to her husband's home for 2 years and later sent Thakadar's wife back to her parents for several years while keeping the children with her. Draupadi was amazingly adept at co-opting the affection of grandsons. Twelve years after bearing Luxmi, she lactated to nurse her step-grandson, Kiran and then, claiming to be his real mother, adopted him. Later, she hid Ajab when his mother, Dhooli, returned to her parents, and alienated him from Dhooli during her 2-year absence. In 1975 she cared for Dhooli's newborn son while Dhooli did the housework.

The balance of power between *bahu* and *sasu* is changing as modern innovations affect women's lives. With decreased purdah comes increased husband–wife intimacy. Wives have more influence on their husbands and are more likely to enlist their support in *bahu–sasu* disputes than they were in previous generations.

Executive *Sasus*

*Sasu*s hold executive positions, directing the work of their *bahu*s as their husbands direct the work of the sons. The harmony among the women and the efficiency of their work are heavily dependent on the executive skills of the senior women. Competent *sasu*s divide the living space, supplies, and work loads of their *bahu*s equitably; organize celebrations; mediate disputes; soothe tempers; and run peaceful and efficient households. Mamta and her two *bahu*s were outstanding in the amiable delegation of work roles among women. Nakali's *sasu* ran a contentious and inefficient *bughar*. If she had been more astute and tactful, her *bahu*'s suicide and the resultant scandal would not have occurred.

In 1955 some men opposed education for girls on the grounds that an educated wife would not do housework or cook well for her husband or his guests. That fear has proved to be unfounded. Although they had fewer low-caste servants in 1975, women fulfilled their responsibilities as wives and mothers as well as they had in times gone by. Whether the *chuula* was shared or separate, the cooks illiterate or educated, dinner was always ready when the men returned from the fields. Family women cooperated to cook for small groups of guests and called in their Brahmin women for large feasts, so guests were fed as they had been in past times. Clothes and houses were kept clean, children were bathed and sent off to school or to work with their fathers. Despite *sasus'* complaints about *bahus'* control of money, household funds were allocated to meet family expenses ranging from spices and cooking oil to school supplies and clothing.

The executive skills of *sasus* will continue to be important as long as joint families share common residences. The diminution of *sasu* authority may have made their diplomatic skills more important to household harmony, but the essential parameters of this role are not significantly altered.

Unlucky Widows

Women who are widowed, particularly when they are still young and childless, may be blamed for their husbands' deaths on the assumption that their bad karma from previous lives had earned them the misfortune of their husbands' deaths. In the past, this belief sustained the custom of suttee. The act of voluntary death by fire was believed to redeem widows' bad karma and convey release from millions of rebirths on the *Satis* and their families. While suttee has not been practiced in Khalapur for many years, it is still revered, and women still worship at local Sati shrines.

In present times, the belief in widows' bad karma sustains the expectation that they should lead pious and above all celibate lives. The Khalapur *bhaktani,* by carrying her austerities beyond expectations, had become a religious leader and acquired the status of guru with her following of local women.

WOMEN'S TRAITS
Fortitude

Fortitude characterized most of the women we knew. Women managed to maintain their fortitude even when they were childless like Chand, poor like Dhooli, dark like Maya, widowed like Mamta, or trapped into deviant roles like Bhaktani or Bahai. Rajput women define themselves as the daughters, wives, and mothers of martial rulers who were the Zamindars, and who still control the majority of village land and wealth. Many Rajput men served in the British army, and this martial tradition lives on in the choice of military careers by many Rajput sons. Their cloistering and emphasis on honor are traits they share with women of warrior groups in other cultures.

As role models for their fortitude, the women draw from a rich tradition of religion and mythology. Their goddesses are fierce and independent. Durga and Kali, worshiped in the nearest temples at Bhudana and Shakumbri, are goddesses of death and war. Their favorite stories tell of the tribulations of regal, legendary wives, most notably the beloved Sita, whose name always precedes that of her husband in their most frequent mantra, "Sita-Ram, Sita-Ram."

Nurtured as guests in their parental homes and treated as little goddesses during their formative years, they are prepared for their inevitable separation with secure and stable childhoods. They are trained for their adults roles by attention to their manners, training in household skills, advice on how to please *sasu*s and husbands, and strategies for protecting their precious dowry goods. Their parents choose their husbands' families carefully, relying on the reports of married *nanad*s for information concerning scandals, the potential bridegrooms' reputations, and the treatment of the families' wives. The transition of young wives is eased by frequent and extended visits to their parental havens. Brides usually have natal relatives living in their husbands' villages, and when they do not, may adopt a ritual sister as a confidante and friend. The aunt's rescue of the bride accused of infidelity by her evil-minded *taayi* attests to the importance of these female alliances.

All wives experience the pain of separation, and to some extent adversity, as they move from the position of honored guests to servants in their husbands' homes. Always a threat to the bonds of the patrilineage, they must win themselves a place within their new kin group. This pain of this separation is written in every line of Luxmi's anguished letters to Draupadi. Repeatedly she lists the names of household members, particularly her brother and male cousins, saying how much she misses them and asking her mother to convey her *namistee*s.

Answers to the purdah interviews, particularly from *sasu*s, contain expressions of the value of fortitude, usually in the form of derogatory comparisons between their generation and the younger generation of *bahu*s. Older women recall that they arose early in the morning to begin their work, that they ground grain with the heavy grinding wheel, that they fasted if they needed to eliminate because they could go to the fields only after dark, that they were fed only the leftover food, and so on. Stoic endurance was expected of them, and they still expected it of their *bahu*s.

An aspect of female fortitude often neglected in descriptions of Indian village women is humor. Despite the emphasis on propriety, women's humor is robust and often bawdy. Women's deference to men does not prevent older women from caricaturing men with bad reputations in explicit, often hilarious mockery. Like healthy people everywhere, Sita's daughters laugh at their troubles.

Honor

For these women honor is the cardinal virtue and a central concern. Women's honor is like the golden thread, which, when soiled, spoils the entire cloth. When a woman is immoral, she disgraces herself, her family, and her village. Honor is the only value that may take precedence over obedience to one's husband. Sita, the ideal, faithful wife, finally disobeys her beloved Ram when he insults her honor publicly. Preferring death to public humiliation, she returns to Mother Earth.

For men, beliefs concerning Shakti and the importance of women's honor are rationales for marrying daughters young and confining wives. Beliefs about "human nature" inevitably embody cultural values and serve as both explanations and justifications for customary practices. When the threat of rape by Muslim rulers vanished, Shakti became a more important explanation for cloistering the family wives. The lack of logic in the Shakti rationale for control of female sexuality is seen in the freedom given adolescent girls, who roam the village lands unchaperoned; in the absence of concern for wives' behavior during their long visits to parental homes; in the ban on the remarriage of widows; and in the expectation that men with married sons should stop marital visits to their wives even when their wives are young. Women share these views, however illogical. Most women accept their cloistering as necessary to protect their honor. They believe that cloistering protects them not only from seduction or attack but from intrusive pollution. One village story tells of a maiden who weighed only as much as a flower but became heavier when weighted down by the leer of a lustful Chamar.

Women teach their daughters to guard their virtue and are quick to condemn a woman who arouses suspicions of immorality. Few point out that faithless women can find ways of circumventing the strictest of supervision; fewer still admit that senior men, who should protect them, may pose their greatest danger. The consequences of lapses in honor are indeed disastrous and persist for many years. In 1955 a *sasu* said that a girl who gave birth to a bastard should have been killed by her father because she had disgraced the village. One daughter had been killed by her brothers when her husband found her pregnant. The failure of Radha's grandmother to agree to the execution of her own daughter was seen as the reason for her son's suicide and the precursor to Radha's tragedy.

Women defend honor in others as well as in themselves. *Sasu*s not only enforce the purdah of *bahu*s, they protect them from the family men, as Draupadi did when she ordered the drunken Om Prakash out of the *bughar* for propositioning his *bahu*. Women rose to the defense of Sita, even though she was a purchased wife and her husband was rich and powerful. True to their regal tradition, women hold their golden thread to be a sacred trust. They guard it with great care and will defend it fiercely.

Traditionalism

Important changes in tradition had come to Khalapur in the years before our first visit in 1955. The most important of these was the Zamindar Abolition Act of 1952. When we arrived 2 years after this massive land reallocation, many Rajput families were engaged in court disputes over their landholdings. The Arya Samaj movement had brought some religious reform, and Indian independence had brought legal reforms. Some dowry reform legislation and the law enabling daughters to claim land had been passed before 1955, but the illiterate women who did not know their legal rights were not affected by these legal changes.

In 1955 the most usual explanation for any custom was "Because our ancestors did it that way." In those days the glory of a wealthy, powerful past made tradition a sufficient reason for perpetuating almost any custom. Rajput men with bristling moustaches and regal red turbans still saw themselves as rulers and warriors. In Hitchcock's words, they had "a touch of the princely and the medieval." Deprived of land, most were "nouveau pauvre" in both income and status. In 1955 the legends and realities of their regal past seemed far more satisfying than their future as subsistence farmers on reduced landholdings, so they clung to their legendary descent from Sita-Ram, to tales of wars and victories, and to the sacrifices of their ancestors at Fort Chittor.

The prosperity of the green revolution swept away this nostalgia for past glory. By 1975 young Rajput men had the air of the successful and the modern. The prosperity brought by hybrid seeds, irrigation, and oil-based fertilizers had moved Rajput farmers from subsistence agriculture into the market economy. Sons of men who disdained plows and left their farming to their low-caste field hands drove tractors and ran irrigation pumping stations. Amar Nath had forgotten the location of his fields, but Succha farmed regularly, installed an irrigation pump, and successfully defended it from his cousin's attempt to sink it.

The move to modern agriculture required constant contact with the outside world to keep up with information about new strains of hybrid seeds and new developments in farming methods and market prices. Government agricultural extension workers, ignored in 1955, became essential advisors during this transition. The sons of men who did not trust a stranger listened regularly to government broadcasts and followed the advice given by anonymous voices coming from their radios. As men traveled more widely, they came in contact with more people from marriageable clans. Wives were taken from more urban environments and brought new customs and ideas with them, accelerating the change in ideas and customs. Increasingly, the ways of the ancestors were made to stand the tests of modern times.

By 1975 old-fashioned clothing had been replaced with commercial clothes, old adobe houses with cement block structures, household grinding wheels with commercial grinding, village wells with hand pumps, village doctors with the government dispensary, the family bullock cart with regular bus service. Old-fashioned customs, such as the immediate crouch-freeze position of women when men entered the *bughar,* the dispensing of food and dowry goods by the *sasu,* the silence of *bahu*s within the *bughar,* and the control of marital visits by *sasu*s, were diminishing.

The most important traditional value change was the attitude concerning education for girls. As young men moved from farming to urban employment, and as farming moved from subsistence to market agriculture, the education of men became essential. By 1975 a high school education for sons and a grade school education for daughters had become the minimal educational level for arranging a good marriage. The ability to travel without escorts is achieved with minimal literacy, and, as we saw in the flight of Sita to the haven of her father's home, this ability can be crucial to a woman's welfare. For a growing number of girls, education went beyond minimal levels: The number of girls attending the intercollege had increased from 4 to more than 100, and a few graduates were reading for college degrees. All the children of literate mothers were in school, and literate *bahu*s set the standards of education for all the children in their *bughar*s, so this trend towards higher education is probably irreversible.

The fear that attending coeducational schools increases immorality is balanced by the belief that educated women can take care of themselves and do not need the strict protection that illiterate women required. The anxieties about coeducation for postpubescent girls is not limited to villages. Sex-segregated schools are common in Indian cities. I would expect the people of Khalapur to organize a girls' high school rather than reverse the trend toward higher education for their daughters.

While the move to greater education of children was not opposed by most *sasu*s, they were adverse to the attrition of their power and the demise of the traditional respect accorded to the *sasu*s they had served. In 1975 these deferential customs of traditional purdah were giving way to greater autonomy for *bahu*s and greater intimacy between husbands and wives. Educated wives refused to limit their vision with veiling that impeded their activity, so the *gungat* had shrunk to practical proportions and the *chaddar* had been abandoned. The curse of silence had been lifted, and while *bahu*s usually spoke respectfully to their *sasu*s, they did speak. The changes that most concerned *sasu*s were the increased intimacy and communication between husbands and wives, and the desire of *bahu*s to cook only for their husbands and children.

The sharpest critique of *sasu*s was directed at the shameless displays of sexuality between young couples. "They spread their legs before their elders" was a repeated comment. In fact, the new prosperity had enabled most families to provide rooms for each married couple; therefore, married couples had more privacy in 1975 than in 1955, when couples had often shared the *sasu*'s bedroom. This privacy was a threat to *sasu* power because it enabled young husbands to stay with their wives all night instead of making short and surreptitious marital visits, and gave wives opportunities to co-opt the loyalty of their essential sons. Despite the assault of these changes on the values of traditional asexuality, most *sasu*s accepted them with composure and often with some humor, as in the description of husbands coming "cloppity-clop" like horses into the *bughar*s at night and waking everybody up.

Religion still embodied traditional values and customs. Women's recreation still revolved around the feasts and festivals of the religious holidays, sons' birth ceremonies, and weddings. The *puja*s (family worship services), deference to deities and ancestors, and fasts for family men were still important responsibilities for Rajput women.

Practices of ritual purification and ceremonial activities remained essentially unchanged, as women cared for the physical welfare of their husbands' families in their daily chores and for their spiritual welfare in their fasts and ceremonials. The observance of ceremonial fasts for the welfare of family members had not decreased. Ceremonies honoring the family ancestors were still performed. When Maya was possessed, the family women conducted the traditional worship and finally started to construct an ancestor shrine, despite Drapaudi's suspicions about the reality of Maya's trances.

Dirt was still defined as pollution, not as lack of sanitation. Feces, blood, meat, leather, and persons whose occupations bring them into contact with these substances were still considered polluting. When the Chamar midwife has made her last visit to change the bandages of a new mother, the family women still purify themselves and the *bughar* from the pollution of birth and the midwife's intrusion. The Chamar women came to clean latrines but were not admitted into the *bughar* proper. The taboos of ritual pollution, particularly from members of low castes, are basic in the social structure and are unlikely to disappear.

Obedience

Rajputs tolerate, and even tacitly encourage, expressions of rebellion in sons, because they are evidence of the warrior traits valued in men. Tara's 7-year absence from his father's house did not injure his marriage prospects when he finally returned. However, obedience is important for the guarded girls and women. Rebellion in unwed daughters brings immediate anxiety about their chastity. Girls should be taught that *bahus* are expected to obey their *sasus* and not disgrace their families by quarreling with their in-laws. They know that husbands and *sasus* may send rebellious *bahus* back to their parental families, sometimes keeping the children and threatening to remarry the groom. Sita is held to be the model of the ideal wife, and ideally girls are taught to obey their husbands as Sita obeyed Ram.

In fact, girls receive mixed messages concerning obedience, especially to *sasus*. The subservient *bahu* is likely to be overburdened with work and neglected by her *sasu,* while the *bahu* who stands up for herself with occasional complaints receives better treatment. The wealth of complaints from *sasus* about the demands of *bahus* indicates the latter are not totally obedient. In answering the questions of our dowry interview, some mothers said that they were teaching their daughters to protect their dowry goods from excessive demands of in-laws. Servile obedience insults the pride of these highborn women; however, disobedience should not seriously disrupt the harmony so necessary among closely confined co-workers.

Harmony

As custodians of the family welfare, women try to maintain harmony within their work groups. Women avoid conflicts with their family men by taking pains to make the best meals possible from supplies at hand and avoid burdening the men with complaints about food shortages. The stage for harmony and friendly cooperation among *bahus* is set by their *sasu.*

Most illiterate *sasus* had willingly ceded purchasing to literate *bahus*, who understood the new commercial goods better than they did, but were reluctant to abandon the tradition of the family *chuula* and the common storage bin for grain. The control of food storage, cooking, and distribution had been a vital source of power for *sasus*. The increase in separate *chuulas*, and the trend for wives to cook only for themselves and their own children, was seen by some *sasus* as a threat to household harmony and joint family cooperation. Most families still had joint *chuulas* in 1975, but change was evident. Bahus claimed separate *chuulas* when their next *dewar* was married, and *sasus* shared *chuulas* with their youngest *bahus*. Some *sasus* wondered who would cook for them in their declining years, a concern not shared by their *bahus*. However, despite this trend, most women cooperate in threshing, processing, and storing grain and in cooking for the many family festivals.

The necessity for harmony within the close confines of the *bughar* makes the settlement of quarrels more important than the issues involved in them. Women in *bughars* with frequent quarrels are criticized for their contentiousness, irrespective of the issues that precipitate these quarrels. Therefore, while *bahus* who complain occasionally are likely to get what they want in order to avoid confrontation, chronic complainers like Dhooli are ignored by the women of their *bughar*.

Some *sasus*, particularly those with good diplomatic skills, take on the role of peacemakers for neighbor women. Widows, as well as older women whose husbands are still alive, may act as peacemakers. When intense quarrels break out, they intervene, separate the distraught women, talk and listen to them, and restore harmony. The peacemaker is an informal voluntary role but one that is important to group harmony.

Avarice

Rajputs of both sexes share skills that enable them to be covetous and canny husbanders of their resources. Educated women understood their legal rights much better than their forebears, particularly those that were important to them. While many Rajput women in 1975 did not know that women could serve on village *panchayats*, all knew that daughters could claim land and that their ownership of dowry goods was legally protected.

Land, basic to their agricultural production, is the most important source of Rajput wealth. In 1955 Hitchcock taught some of his Rajput friends to play the game Monopoly. He found that they mastered the rules with ease but refused to sell any of their property even when they were close to being bankrupt. Rajputs farm their land; they do not trade in real estate. The realization of the expectation, expressed by several women, that they could increase their family land through purchases will probably depend on the availability of land owned by low-caste families. The conspicuous display and dispersal of goods and money remain necessary attributes of Rajput families who aspire to be strong in village politics. The defense of landholdings was very much in evidence.

The fierce defense of land appeared often in our interviews. Most women opposed land claims by their daughters, and few daughters had dared to make them. The announcement by Radha's mother that she intended to claim her widow's portion infuriated her *sasu* and *jaith*. One family had a pregnant daughter who was murdered by her covetous *taayi* to prevent the possible birth of a son who would claim family land. Kela refused to fulfill his responsibility to arrange his nephews' marriages, hoping to keep them unmarried and childless and pass their land on to his sons. Even when women have no close male relatives, men think that they should not inherit land. Bahai had spent most of her adult life trying to regain the lost landholdings of her brother and was convinced that her nephew had been murdered so that he could not claim family land.

As men husband land, so do women husband dowry. A *bahu*'s status depends on the goods and money she brings with her at her marriage and contributes throughout her lifetime. When interviewed, all women could tell us exactly how much they had brought in dowry goods. In 1975 *bahus* controlled their dowries more than they had in previous generations. While the transfer of dowry goods from *bahu* to *nanad* was still the norm in 1975, it was no longer done as openly as it had been 20 years earlier. Dowries of daughters were still displayed in open courtyards before being taken to bridegroom's homes, but dowries of incoming *bahus* were hidden in dark bedrooms where neighbors could not examine them with ease.

Jewelry is the core of a woman's wealth. Gold and silver jewelry were hoarded and hidden. Gold jewelry is a mark of status and a matter of pride among Rajput women, who wear gold earrings regularly and take their jewelry with them when they travel to their parents' homes to prevent its theft. Ranbhool's wife was distressed and weeping when her earrings were stolen. The discovery of Sita's earrings in her room was the deception that delayed pursuit and allowed her to escape to her father's home. Luxmi's disdainful acceptance of Dhooli's *tikka* caused permanent resentment in her poor *bhabhi*. Dhooli's pride led her to refuse to take earrings given in poor spirit by her estranged *sasu*.

This concern for wealth is understandable. Many of these Rajput families lost landholdings with the Zamindar Abolition Act. In 1955 they were often involved in lawsuits over landholdings. The prosperity of market agriculture has made their land more valuable, since it is now a source of income as well as of subsistence. The increased expense of dowry and the demise of female infanticide have made financing good marriages for daughters more difficult. Commercial goods, once thought to be luxuries, have become necessities as the standard of living has increased. Increased population has necessitated the building of new houses, now constructed of concrete blocks rather than adobe. The new prosperity has new demands upon it, and disputes over money are inevitable.

CONCLUSIONS

Rajput women adhere to strict norms of conduct characteristic of elitist families. These norms are exacting, complex, and often contradictory. Women are expected to be chaste but passionate, proud but obedient, educated but traditional, cooperative but defensive of their rights, generous but covetous of their dowry goods. Rapid modernization has resulted in somewhat different norms and expectations for older and younger generations of adults. Most *bahus* are more educated than their *sasus*, more familiar with market goods, and more accustomed to travel.

The values of honor, duty to family, obedience to husbands, and the importance of dowry goods remain. In some important matters—for example, education of girls, increased husband–wife intimacy, separation of *chuulas* and food storage—as well as in some less important matters—for example, movie attendance and the wearing of commercial saris—the norms of the younger generation have prevailed. Other matters, however—religious observances, separation of *bahus* from older family men, *sasu* control of dowry in the early years of marriage—are still guided by tradition.

Although the changes that impacted them had caused some friction and a fair amount of grumbling, they had not engendered either social or psychological disintegration. *Sasu* reported that they did not see an overall change in the degree of harmony between *sasus* and *bahus*. Women retain their essential values while adapting them to changing realities, and manage this transition without serious disruption. Women still function as healthy individuals and families as intact groups.

One expects that the transition to modernism will continue to be made at a pace that does not fracture social bonds or violate basic values. The key customs of purdah are indeed disappearing, but not too rapidly to allow for the building of new customs, based on altered ideas, to take their place. Sita's daughters accept change as another face of Maya.

Three girls, returning home from their studies at the intercollege, walk across the bridge into Khalapur (1975).

15

Towards Equality

Realization of true parity between the sexes granted by the Constitution will be possible only when conceptions and attitudes of the people are brought at a par with it.
Towards Equality

In this final chapter I will place the information of my study in regional, national, international, and theoretical context. I will also suggest some topics for future research.

The International Decade of Women, sponsored by the United Nations, began in 1975. In connection with this effort to improve women's status, all U.N. members were asked to prepare reports on the status of women in their countries. The Indian government's report, prepared by some of India's most prominent women scholars, was published in December 1974 (*Towards Equality,* 1974). The sources of information used to prepare *Towards Equality* were: (a) basic documentary sources such as census records providing demographic data, (b) special studies on literature prepared at the request of the report's authors by scholars and specialists in the field, and (c) firsthand information from tours to different states and territories, empirical studies and discussions with specialists. In this chapter I will utilize relevant information from *Towards Equality* to place the information of my study in a state and national context. Whenever possible I use demographic information with comparable census figures for Uttar Pradesh (U.P.), the state in which Khalapur is located, as the comparison base.

Whyte's holographic study of women in preindustrial societies used information from the Human Relations Area Files to measure a variety of customs relevant to women's roles and status (Whyte, 1978). The majority of the 93 societies in Whyte's study are tribal, with simpler social structures than those of India. Nevertheless, the information of this study is often useful as an international base of comparison with the Khalapur data.

A number of the customs described in this book—purdah, large dowries, neglect of daughters' health, and occasional infanticide and sati—are still practiced despite government efforts to abolish them and widespread public opposition to them. Finally, I will venture some explanations for the persistence of traditional Indian customs that restrict women and impede their progress toward equality.

319

LAW

During trips to Delhi in the winter of 1974–75, I usually visited with the faculty of Lady Irwin College, my Fulbright sponsoring institution. Faculty women asked me what the current feminist issues were in the United States. When I told them that our efforts were concentrated on trying to pass a constitutional amendment guaranteeing equal rights for women, they were surprised and shocked because the Indian constitution does grant equal rights to women. "How is it possible that your American Constitution does not guarantee these rights?" they asked. Their question took me by surprise, but after brief reflection, I had the answer: "Because the U.S. Constitution was written in the eighteenth century."

This difference is important in understanding the problems faced by Third World women compared with American and European women in our progress toward equality. The United States and some other nations in the industrial countries have many educated women who know their legal rights, but many of these nations have laws that were written in previous centuries. Constitutions of postcolonial countries were written in the latter half of the twentieth century, after these nations became independent. They are based on the twentieth-century law of their colonial nation and include modern guarantees for civil rights. However, the uneducated women of these countries do not know their legal rights and are confined by custom and their lack of skills to their homes or to menial jobs in the workplace. Therefore, while the primary task of American feminists is legislative, the primary task of Indian feminists is educational.

The quotation from *Towards Equality* I have taken as the epigraph to this chapter— "Realization of true parity between the sexes granted by the Constitution will be possibly only when conceptions and attitudes of the people are brought at a par with it"—could apply to any country. The U.S. failure to pass the Equal Rights Amendment, the lack of sexual equality in the majority of states that have passed it, the opposition to equal pay for women, legalized abortion, and so forth, attest to the discrepancy between public opinion and legal rights.

Towards Equality found that 66% of U.P. women knew none of their constitutional rights and only 66% knew that Indira Gandhi was president. In 1975 we found that Khalapur women were most likely to know about the laws protecting rights they supported (i.e., dowry rights and widows' inheritance of family land). Fewer women knew that daughters could inherit land, and most opposed such claims. None knew that women could run for the village *panchayat,* and all opposed such action for themselves, although they generally supported the wife of the intercollege principal in her political post. In 1975 all women knew that Indira Gandhi was prime minister and were divided in their support of her leadership.

Ignorance and custom have prevented Indian women from obtaining the benefits of a number of laws passed during British rule and after independence. The British passed several laws protecting women, but because of their policy of noninterference in Indian customs, most of these laws were not enforced. Several laws were passed before the twentieth century. For example, female infanticide was made illegal late in 1795; sati was banned at different times in different states from 1829 to

1860; the Hindu Widow's Remarriage Act of 1856 legalized widow remarriage; and a law banning child marriage was also passed in 1856.

Muslim women were given the right of divorce in 1939. The Hindu Marriage Act of 1949 set the legal age of marriage at 18 for men and 15 for women. The Hindu Marriage Act of 1955 gave Hindu women the right of divorce and provided for the registration of marriages to prevent child marriage and ensure that marriages were legal.

Hindu Women's Property Acts were passed in 1929 and 1937. The Hindu Succession Act of 1956 gave equal inheritance rights to male and female heirs in the same kin category (e.g., brothers and sisters, sons and daughters). This act also abolished life estate rights for widows, giving them equal rights to inheritance along with mothers, sons, and daughters, but excluded dwellings from daughters' inheritance.

However, when passing the 1956 act, conservative legislators retained an older law of coparcenary, a group to which only male members of a patrilineage may belong. Property owned by a coparcenary group passes only to male heirs. Therefore, a father may deprive daughters of land by partitioning it among sons during his lifetime without reserving a portion for himself. Inheritance legislation in U.P., a state with one sixth of the Indian population, has more restrictions on women's inheritance than some other states. According to U.P. legislation: "The claims of a widow and unmarried and married daughters are preceded not only by the lineal male descendants in the male line of descent, but even by their widows who have not remarried" (*Towards Equality*, p. 137).

A Dowry Prohibition Act limiting dowry to 500 rupees was passed in 1961. The text of *Towards Equality* acknowledges the failure of this law, notes the rise in dowry-related murders of brides, and deplores "society's indifference to this social evil" (p. 115).

The majority of Indians polled for *Towards Equality* did not express the doubts voiced by Khalapur women about their political efficacy. Only 30% thought women should vote according to the wishes of family men, and only 30% thought that women should not become party members; 68% thought women should contest elections, and 71% thought women would make effective office bearers (p. 448). These results are encouraging for the future of women's political progress in India.

When Indian women are educated, and supported by their families, they can assume rights already guaranteed by their legal system. Until then, laws contrary to custom and belief will continue to be ignored. Equality, for any group, is ultimately won by the efforts of group members.

DESCENT AND RESIDENCE

Whyte found that men hold the important kin-group leadership positions in most societies. This is particularly true for patrilineal kin groups. As we have seen, Khalapur Rajput women do not belong to their husbands' lineages and are of little importance in their parental lineages.

Towards Equality recognizes the detrimental effect of patrilineal descent and patrilocal residence on the status of daughters, who must be raised to be given away to outsiders, and of wives, whose value depends on their dowry and their ability to bear sons. The report also notes that the inferior status of wives is likely to be most pronounced in rural areas, such as that of Khalapur, where brides move from one village to another rather than from one urban district to another.

The report comments on the contrast we observed between the roles of daughters and daughters-in-law in North India: "The contrasting norms of behaviour for the daughter and the daughter-in-law tend to make the life of a woman alternate between freedom and restrictions, between harsh and soft treatment and . . . does not allow her to become a person. She has roles but no personality" (*Towards Equality,* p. 65). Most of the women we knew accepted their dual roles with equanimity. Women always looked forward to visits home, where purdah restrictions would be in abeyance. Although wives' personhood was diminished in their husbands' homes, these women, despite normative expectations, were not without personality.

It should be noted that although the status of young brides is low, the executive *sasu* wields more power than mothers-in-law in societies with nuclear families. Brown & Kerns (1985) describes the position of older Rajput women that we observed as normal for women living in extended societies and contrasts their advantages with the situation of the American matron:

> In many societies, middle-aged women are freed from exhibiting the deferential and even demeaning behavior which they had previously been expected to display to the senior generation or the husband.
>
> One aspect of this major change is the greater geographical mobility that older women are often allowed. Child care has ceased or can be delegated, domestic chores are reduced, the hospitality of relatives living at a distance and religious pilgrimages may provide an opportunity to venture forth from the village. In some societies, all younger women are restricted to the household because they are believed to be sexually voracious and in need of constant supervision. Here older women are the supervisors because they are believed to be beyond sexual escapades that would bring dishonor to the entire kinship group. In many societies in which the young bride must move into the household of her husband and his family, she is at first mistrusted. It is only as the mother of grown sons that she is viewed as assimilated into her kin group by marriage. She is finally considered above disloyalty. . . . Thus, once a woman is the mother of adult offspring, she is no longer encumbered with elaborate rules concerning menstrual custom, modesty, and display of respect; nor is she confined. . . .
>
> A second major change brought on by middle age is a woman's right to exert authority over specified younger kin. This authority is of two kinds. The first is the right to extract labor from younger family members. The work of older women tends to be administrative: delegating subsistence activity tasks and making assignments to younger women . . . they oversee food distribution. Within the household the matron may have absolute control over who eats what and when. . . .
>
> The authority of older women also finds expression in shaping important decisions for certain members of the junior generation: what a grandchild is to be named . . . and who is eligible to marry whom. In some societies, older women

have specific responsibilities in the marital exchanges that solemnify a marriage. In the societies that maintain very separate worlds for men and women, older women are the go-betweens. . . .

Perhaps most significant are reports of many ethnographers concerning the tremendous influence that mothers exercise over grown sons. Often a man's relationship with his mother supersedes that with his wife. . . .

A third major change brought on by middle age is the eligibility that older women have for special statuses and the possibility these provide for recognition beyond the household. Societies vary in the number of special positions that their female members can occupy. . . . There are a variety of special offices: . . . holy woman, guardian of the sacred hearth, matchmaker. Such positions are typically not filled by younger women, sometimes because the exercise of spiritual power is considered harmful to a nursing child or to the baby the pregnant woman is carrying. Further, in many societies the belief that menstruation is disquieting to the spirit or dangerous makes women ineligible for dealing with sacred matters until later in life.

The circumstances of middle-aged women in industrial societies like our own differ from those suggested by the cross-cultural data. . . . There are reasons why middle age does not bring as many positive changes into the lives of women in our society as it does into the lives of women elsewhere. First, middle age does not usher in a life of fewer restrictions because these are negligible in the first place. . . . Second . . . American middle-aged women have far less power over their younger kin than their matron counterparts in other societies. Adult offspring often live at great distances from their mothers, since the location of employment determines the place of residence. The support given by adult children, so central to the definition of middle-aged women cross-culturally and so crucial to their relatively privileged position, often consists merely of occasional telephone conversations, letters, and brief holiday visits. Younger kin may seek advice, or may be manipulated covertly. The latter is seen as unbecoming meddlesomeness not as a maternal right. . . . Third, our society does provide the possibility for recognition beyond the household, either through volunteer activities in the community or through a career, but such opportunities are open to all women, regardless of age.

(Brown & Kerns, 1985, pp. 3–6)

With modernization, Khalapur is undergoing changes that make it more similar to industrial societies: Brown and Kerns' list of privileges of middle-aged women is being gradually extended to younger women; mothers' traditional control over sons is being threatened by greater intimacy between husbands and wives; and some sons do have jobs that take them away from their parental homes. It is this erosion of status and privilege that many older women resent; nevertheless, they retain advantages that matrons in industrial societies with nuclear family households have long since lost. *Sasu*s are still the recognized authorities in their *bughar*s. They direct the work of their *bahu*s, influence marriages of their children and the naming of grandchildren, and direct the religious rituals in their courtyards. They may leave their homes to visit other village houses or their parental homes, or to make pilgrimages to holy places. They may serve as holy women, matchmakers, and peacemakers (a role Brown and Kerns do not mention). It is likely that they will retain these privileges as long as the extended family survives.

MARRIAGE CUSTOMS

Whyte (1978) measured the degree to which men or women participate in marriage arrangements. Rajput women are low on Whyte's scale, which measures women's control over their sex lives. Among traditional Hindus, neither the bride nor the groom has much to say about the choice of spouse. However, we found that both male and female relatives are involved in choosing grooms. Married women make the first contact with prospective families, and men carry out the formal negotiations.

The section on marriage in *Towards Equality* begins with this statement: "Many problems of major importance for women are linked with marriage" (p. 62). The text notes that marriage is not an equal alliance, particularly in North India, where hypergamous marriages are widespread. Where marriage is hypergamous, bride-giving families are always inferior to bride-taking families. Brides are considered inferior to husbands by sex and by family status. This status distinction is emphasized by the unilateral flow of gifts from bride givers to bride takers.

The government survey showed that a majority of Indians interviewed opposed child marriage (73%) but believed that marriages should be arranged by parents (74%; p. 414). In Khalapur all Rajput marriages are still arranged. Child marriage was not practiced by Khalapur Rajputs within the memory of informants in 1955. Nevertheless, in 1975 we noted two marriages of underage daughters: Ranjeet's daughter, Maya, was 13 when she married, and Suraj's bride, Bala, was only 7. Ranjeet, a responsible father, was 70 years old and wanted to ensure a good marriage for his dark-skinned daughter before he died. Bala's greedy brothers told Suraj that the sister they were selling was 18 years old, and their lie was not discovered until the marriage had taken place and Bala was unveiled by Mamta, her gentle *sasu*.

In *Towards Equality* the task force women recommend that the registration of marriages be made compulsory as a deterrent to child marriage. It is difficult to see how this policy would be effective without also requiring registration of births. Khalapur mothers often lied to us about the ages of their unmarried daughters, always giving their ages as younger than their real age; obviously, parents could do the same when registering their daughters' marriages.

PURDAH

Whyte's study (1978) included measures of separation of men and women in work, ceremonies, and general activities. The Khalapur Rajputs would rank at the high point of sexual separation on all of Whyte's scales. *Towards Equality* does not report purdah observance in as much detail as our interviews. Where comparisons can be made, they show that Khalapur Rajput women observe more purdah than women in the majority of U.P. families. In the U.P. sample 46% observe purdah with their *soosar*s, 44% with their *jaith*s, and 20% with their *sasu*s. The pattern of more strict observance with men than women is the same as we observed.

Purdah customs are deferential rituals denoting the status of family members. All societies have deferential customs through which people recognize the status of persons of superior rank. These customs may be verbal (e.g., formal modes of address and titles); they may be gestural (e.g., bowing, walking behind, or sitting lower than a person of superior rank); they may involve allocation of resources (e.g., feeding superior people first; giving them better food, clothing, or preferred living space; avoiding superior persons by staying away from them or not talking to them). Examples of each of these types of deferential customs occur in Khalapur Rajput families. Seniors should always be addressed by their kinship terms rather than their names. The prohibition on speaking the names of senior men is so strong that a name not already taken by a man of either the husband's or the wife's family must be found for each newborn son. When men and women are together, women sit on the floor while men sit on the cots. When Hindu husbands and wives walk together, wives follow about 15 feet behind their husbands. Men are fed before women, and only men eat meat and eggs. Women avoid senior men and do not speak freely in the presence of senior women.

Most deferential customs recognize real power differences. Notable exceptions to the rule that deference is displayed as a recognition of power are cloistering and chaperoning. Cloistering, chaperoning, and limitations on the places where respectable women may go, or go alone, are based on an assumption of helplessness rather than power. Women are cloistered or chaperoned when it is assumed that they are unable to take care of or protect themselves. Men, on the other hand, are cloistered only when they have certain religious characteristics, such as monks or the Japanese mikado. High-status men are usually not barred from visiting places outside of their respectable communities (e.g., bawdy dance or drama performances, bars, or brothels). When custom decrees that high-status men not travel alone, the persons accompanying them are called escorts, body guards, or honor guards, but not chaperones.

High-status women, on the other hand, have restrictions on mobility in many societies. Often they cannot move as freely as either men or low-status women. Cloistering and chaperoning are extremes of the widespread custom of curtailing the mobility of high-status women. Papanek (1973) argues that purdah provides women with separate worlds and symbolic shelter. I think that prohibitions on free and private mobility of high-status women function to prevent potentially wealthy women from independently employing their wealth or utilizing their influence in ways that may not be in the best interests of family men.

Prohibitions on working prevent women from earning money and make them depend on their fathers, husbands, and sons for support. Under these conditions women have difficulty establishing legal claims to property because in so doing they incur the opposition of the men on whom they depend. Restrictions on women's travel, particularly alone, prevents women from checking land records or other legal documents and forces them to depend on men for information that may affect their legal rights or fortunes. Bahai's inability to testify in court prevented her from effectively disputing the land claims she had contested for most of her adult life. The belief that women who sit with men are "naked and shameless" prevented women from holding public office.

Khalapur women gave two reasons for accepting the restrictions of cloistering: They did not have to work in the fields, and cloistering was the mark of their high-caste status. These reasons are essentially the same as those most high-status women give for accepting restrictions on their freedom. Purdah is similar to the Western "cult of the lady." Ladies were not supposed to work outside their home, travel alone, go to places not considered to be respectable, converse with men except in the presence of a chaperone, swear, or behave in a vulgar manner. The "pedestal" on which the lady is supposedly placed is a totally symbolic shelter, as the *bughar* is partially a symbolic shelter. Both the *bughar* and the pedestal provide women with a place of deference but neither gives them room to move. These customs represent, in my opinion, a sort of pseudostatus based on attempts to curtail power rather than recognize it.

DOWRY

Dowry is rare in cross-cultural context, appearing in only 8% of Whyte's sample. (According to Schlegel & Eloul, 1987, some of these cases refer to indirect dowry.) Dowry is a consequence of cloistering or other customs that keep women from productive work. Wives who contribute to their husbands' incomes do not need dowries, since their labor over their life span is more valuable than dowry goods. But when wives cannot work, or when the value of their domestic work is not recognized, dowry provides a way of shifting part of the expense for their support expense to their parental families.

Towards Equality recognizes that dowry is "associated with women who are primarily housewives" (p. 75). The report finds that, despite legislation, dowry is common throughout India, does not decrease with education, and is increasing in incidence, particularly with upwardly mobile groups. Eighty percent of people interviewed said that dowry should be stopped, but 60% said that without a dowry it was not possible to get good husbands for daughters (p. 418). Khalapur Rajputs represent the upper class of their groups. More than 80% of the women we interviewed supported the practice of dowry, but all practiced it. Like other upper-class Indians, the necessity of getting good husbands locked them into the dowry system, even when they objected to it.

Poor women without dowries are reported to be more equal to their husbands than women with large dowries (p. 62). Evidently, the relative freedom from purdah that we noted for Mamta is a characteristic of poor families.

The report concludes:

> We would like to emphasize that the spirit of dowry and the transactions involved in it, particularly at the upper middle class and upper class levels, go against the goal of a socialist society. Such value patterns of marriage expenses tend to influence other socio-economic groups. It is an undeniable fact that, excepting a few rich, all have to spend beyond their means where dowry is concerned.
>
> (*Towards Equality*, p. 76)

The control of dowry goods, particularly jewelry, by modern wives observed in our Khalapur sample is widespread: 59% of the U.P. women interviewed for the government report said they had full or partial control of their dowry and jewelry (p. 433). Dowry legislation has apparently been successful in increasing women's rights to their property, although efforts to curb these expenses have failed.

Towards Equality recommends that the display of dowries be outlawed as a way of curbing comparisons among *bahus'* dowries and humiliation of poorer brides. It is difficult to see how such a law could be enforced, since it would involve invading *bughars* for inspections. Khalapur families had stopped the public display of *bahus'* dowries, displaying only the dowry goods of daughters. If this change becomes widespread, legislation concerning dowry display may not be necessary. The public display of daughters' dowries does not evoke invidious comparison and may serve to protect the dowry goods of orphaned girls. Khalapur women criticized a step-mother who had kept and worn a shawl after including it in her stepdaughter's dowry display.

It is the high-status, restricted daughter who is most likely to receive a large dowry. In part, dowry allows a young husband to support his wealthy wife in the manner to which her father has accustomed her. When, as in hypergamous marriage, women marry into families wealthier than their own, this expense is increased. It is my contention that Indian resistance to the abolition of dowry stems from hypergamous marriage, wherein women marry into families ranked higher than their parental group. Because wealthy families demand large dowries, it is reasonable to expect that daughters' dowries will usually be greater than those of daughters-in-law. During the interviews on family planning, we encountered the frequent answer: "It is best to have two sons and one daughter, then you can receive two dowries but give only one." Comparison between the amount of money and goods given to incoming daughters-in-law and outgoing daughters at initial fixing and *shadi* showed that, on average, daughters are given twice as much money as *bahus* bring. Daughters are also given somewhat more jewelry, clothing, bedding, and utensils than daughters-in-law bring in. The minimal acceptable amount of dowry goods for daughters is substantially higher than for incoming daughters-in-law. The comparison indicates that if a family had the dowry goods of two daughters-in-law they could indeed marry one daughter without drawing from their capital.

Project this dowry difference throughout the patrilineage and it becomes clear that hypergamous marriage of women moves their dowry wealth up the status hierarchy so that the wealthiest groups have the most to gain from the custom of giving large dowries. As land becomes scarcer and more expensive and daughters become more numerous and expensive, the dowries of *bahus* become increasingly important. As long as families must give substantially larger dowries to daughters than they receive from *bahus*, they must make every effort to maximize *bahus'* dowry wealth.

Women in the families I knew realized that daughters are more expensive now than they were in previous generations. The end of female infanticide and improved medical facilities had increased the number of daughters, and their education had become a condition for arranging good marriages. Therefore, daughters put new burdens on the family finances, which in turn added to the importance of incoming dowry wealth.

It would be valuable to trace the difference between daughter and daughter-in-law dowry through the hierarchies of *jatis*. This information would provide answers to several questions: Is this differential constant for a marriage hierarchy, or does it increase for families of increasing *jati* rank? Is this increased amount an increasingly greater percentage of family income, or are wealthier families better able to bear the financial burden of daughters' dowries? Is the incoming versus outgoing difference the same for high- and low-caste groups, or does it also increase by social status? If dowry differential varies, as seems probable, this information would identify those groups for whom it is greatest. These groups could then be enlisted in the campaign against dowry.

This conduction of dowry wealth up the socioeconomic status ladder is probably the basis for the persistent occasional female infanticide and sati among wealthy families who would be most able to support daughters and widowed daughters-in-law were it not for the dowry drain. Female infanticide prevented daughters from taking wealth way from the patrilineage, and sati freed families from the necessity of supporting young widows, particularly those without sons to contribute their labor and their wives' wealth to their families. Information on the daughter versus daughter-in-law dowry difference would serve to target those groups most likely to neglect their daughters' health or attempt to eliminate family widows.

Towards Equality does not report on indirect dowry. In commenting on the purpose of dowry authors note, "It is difficult to pinpoint what is being bought and sold: a secure future and leisure for their daughter? or a transfer of responsibility of the girl who was hitherto a liability of the parents?" (p. 75). It is interesting to note that although indirect dowry is called "buying a bride" by the poor and uneducated who resort to it, the cultural blinders of male superiority are so pervasive that even the foremost feminist scholars of India cannot recognize "buying a husband" as one possibility in this statement.

INHERITANCE

In evaluating women's rights to land inheritance, one must distinguish between Indian law that gives women relatively equal rights and custom that prevents them from establishing their claims. Indian women's actual control of property is low in comparison to Whyte's sample, but their legal control is average. None of the Khalapur women we interviewed reported that family men had used the coparcenary clause of the 1956 Succession Act to deprive daughters of their land claims. The utilization of this act requires legal division of land. Our inquiries showed that 84% of the land was legally undivided in the families we studied, even when men farmed their shares separately.

Married daughters living in their husbands' villages usually would have no reason to claim a portion of their parental house. However, widowed daughters, whose in-laws do not treat them well, might need a place to live in their parental villages. We heard of no instance of a daughter claiming a share of her family home, probably because daughters are welcome guests and, like Bahai, would usually be granted room to live if they returned to their parental village.

Under the succession rights laws, the women of Takadwar's family should have inherited their father's land. Their plight shows the difficulties faced, even by determined women, in winning legal rights. *Towards Equality* notes that where custom prevents women from appearing in public, the law provides that someone may stand in for women in court hearings and suggests that a social worker could fill this role (p. 109). Unfortunately, a spokesperson is difficult to find when women's opponents are wealthy, powerful men.

Sacks, in her comparison of sisters and wives, argues that women's status is more equal to men's status in the role of sisters, because sisters are owners and producers on the family land (Sacks, 1979). It is this sisterly role that is so strongly opposed in much of India. Daughters or sisters face strong family opposition if they press their land claims. They are still considered to be guests in their parental homes and do not work in the fields either as children or as adults. While it is true that among Rajputs sisters are more equal to their brothers than wives are to their husbands, this equality is based on the importance of blood line kinship versus affinal kinship.

Towards Equality expresses particular concern about land inheritance by women because land is the primary of inheritable property in India. While equal inheritance by sons and daughters is equitable, the concerns expressed by Khalapur women that land claims by daughters would take land from the patrilocal family are valid and important. These patrilineal inheritance rules account for the fact that Khalapur Rajputs and other landowners have been able to maintain control of their land through the vicissitudes of the past 400 years, including most recently the Zamindar Abolition Act.

Modern agriculture, essential to India's food supply, requires relatively large land plots. Despite the destruction of most of the wide irrigation dikes, many Khalapur landholdings are already too small to utilize modern farming equipment. Landholdings in poorer states are even smaller. Land inheritance by daughters and daughters' daughters would quickly divide landholdings among people living in diverse locations. Furthermore, it is the labor of sons that harvests the land and earns the money for investments such as tube wells and tractors. Sons may put in many years of labor between the time that their sisters marry and their parents die. Equal inheritance by daughters means that they benefit from this labor without having contributed to it. Daughters must hire people to work parental land, becoming absentee landowners, or sell their shares; unless they sell to their brothers, the patrilineage is deprived of ancestral property. The opposition to female land claims is understandable, and it seems unlikely that it will diminish.

Several of the women we interviewed said that the amount of daughters' dowries might be equal to or greater than sons' land shares. If true, it may be argued that daughters are receiving a fair share of their parental estates. It would be possible to document the shares received by sons and daughters by comparing the monetary worth of dowry goods, and goods and money given to daughters throughout their lifetimes, with the value of crops and land received by sons. Such comparisons might point the way for legislation that would equalize daughters' inheritance without dividing family landholdings.

DOMESTIC ECONOMY

Towards Equality recognizes that an important reason for the low status of Indian wives is that the value of their domestic labor is not recognized, a problem common to housewives in many nations. It also recognizes that "dowry encourages the belief that regards the value of women's work in the home as non-productive" (p. 75).

In fact, as we have seen, *bughar*s are workplaces as well as residences. In addition to cooking, women process the grain to be stored in the house. The government findings on sex division of labor is similar to ours. Cooking is exclusively woman's work (84%), as are sweeping and cleaning (96%). Men eat before women in 59% of rural families, a lower figure than in Khalapur. Only 5% of the people interviewed said that child care was exclusively done by women, an answer that probably reflects the prevalence of fieldwork done by boys with their fathers.

Like Khalapur wives, most high-caste wives do not work or have household allowances. Strangely, *Towards Equality* does not report on the funds wives bring from their parents. Apparently, Khalapur wives are more likely than the general population to make money from spinning and usury. Only 7% of U.P. women spin, and only 3% are engaged in money lending.

WIDOWS

Uttar Pradesh is one of India's more conservative states in the treatment of widows, and the high status of Khalapur Rajputs made them more conservative about widow remarriage than most U.P. citizens. The *Towards Equality* survey showed that 63% of the U.P. residents polled for the status of women report approved of widow remarriage (p. 421). To our knowledge, no Khalapur widows had remarried in 1975. The two young virgin widows we knew said that their fathers had wanted to find second husbands for them, but they refused.

Hindu widows face two strong impediments to remarriage, patrilineal descent and the belief in karma. Because of patrilineal descent, children belong exclusively to their father's lineage. A widow with children would have to marry a member of her deceased husband's lineage who lived in the same community or give up custody of her children. Even without children, a woman belongs, for better or for worse, to the family to which she has been given as a virgin bride. Returning a widow to her father is considered to be a breach of the affinal obligation to support her, one that might make it difficult for other family members to arrange good marriages. Karma, good and bad, is believed to be earned by actions in each life. Any serious misfortune is believed to come from the bad karma of previous lives. Therefore, Mrs. Hoshayar's belief that she was unlucky and would cause the death of her second husband if she married again is widely shared. Obviously, this belief would make it difficult to find a second husband for a widow. These two impediments combine to make widow remarriage doubly difficult. Faced with the possibility of a widow marrying a second man from the same lineage, some relatives would voice the concern that she would cause the death of another man of the family.

The discovery that all four of Khalapur's sati shrines honor virgin widows who were not necessarily immolated on their husbands' funeral pyres raises interesting questions for further investigation. If sati is an act of loving devotion to the husband, one would expect that most shrines would honor fairly elderly widows, since older women are more likely to be widowed and more likely to have established loving ties with their husbands. However, older women have paid their debt to the patrilineage by bearing sons and have reached an age when sexuality is no longer a matter of concern. It is older widows who are likely to have married daughters, grown sons, *bahu*s, and the responsibilities of executive *sasu*s. If a widow's daughters are already married and her sons old enough to work, and if the widow is directing the work of *bahu*s, then supporting her for the remainder of her life is a minor economic burden. Therefore, if sati is motivated by economics, one would expect that most sati shrines would have been erected for young, childless widows, whose support is an economic burden and who may disgrace the family.

Scholarly investigations of sati have been relatively rare. Historical accounts usually focus on the incidence and location of satis. Educated Indians have usually been opposed to sati and embarrassed by it. For villagers, on the other hand, local satis were among their village saints. Questions about sati shrines and their legends evoked enthusiastic and detailed reports. It would, therefore, be possible to canvass communities and obtain information about local sati shrines. The resulting information, judging from our stories, would be more mythical than factual. However, many myths have been based on fact, and one might put more credence on accounts of the age and status of satis than on the circumstances of their deaths. If indeed most sati shrines are found to be devoted to virgin or young widows, the publicizing of this information might be an effective propaganda weapon against the recent revival of the Sati movement.

FAMILY PLANNING

Towards Equality notes that in the past female infanticide was particularly prevalent among the higher Rajput *jati*s, because hypergamous marriages limited their choice of sons-in-laws (p. 65). In present times the mortality of female infants is still higher than that of male infants throughout rural India, and this difference is particularly great in rural sections of Uttar Pradesh (p. 17). The U.P. rates reported—154 boys versus 206 girls—are greater than the 5% excess of boys in our small Khalapur sample. The neglect of daughters' health, sometimes called "indirect infanticide," accounts for this male excess.

This report also recognized that the success of family planning efforts was not impressive. Uttar Pradesh is cited as one state in which family planning efforts had been particularly ineffective. Only 6.5% of U.P. families are protected by any birth control method (p. 29). (It is unlikely that this figure included celibacy, still practiced by older couples in Khalapur.) Apparently, the women we interviewed were fairly typical of U.P. women in their resistance to family planning.

In the context of increasing dowry demands, indirect female infanticide via poor medical care and bride murder may be seen as a substitute for the archaic custom of killing girls at birth. Neglect of daughters' health may eliminate sickly girls without breaking modern laws. The killing of poor *bahu*s increases the family resources available for the dowries of daughters who can no longer be killed.

SOCIALIZATION AND EDUCATION

Whyte (1978) found that women's authority was often highest in the domestic realm. It is not unusual for women to have equal or final say in matters pertaining to infants and children; however, he did not construct separate scales for sons and daughters. Khalapur mothers are likely to have final say where daughters are concerned, while fathers are likely to have more direct control over sons.

The traditional preference for sons is apparent in answers to survey questions in *Towards Equality*. Results showed that 44.5% of those interviewed said they are happier about the birth of a boy than the birth of a girl (pp. 57–58). In rural areas 30% said that boys get better access to food, clothing, education, and medical care, and 59% said that boys ate first (p. 409). Khalapur Rajput sons do get better education and medical care; most families we knew could afford food and clothing for all children.

School enrollment of girls had increased steadily since independence at all levels (p. 239). The statement that girls should receive no education was rejected by 79% of the people interviewed (p. 261), while an impressive 70% thought that girls should get the same type of education as boys (p. 275), and 64.5% thought that girls should be allowed to pursue higher education (p. 443). The support for higher education for girls expressed in the report's general sample was considerably stronger than it was among Khalapur Rajputs.

Concern for girls' virtue, so prevalent in Khalapur, was evident in the survey answers. Support for sex-segregated schools rose with school level and age of students: 50% thought there should be separate primary and middle schools, 60% separate high schools, and 70% separate colleges (p. 443). The absence of separate schools, cited as a problem by 67% of respondents, was the most frequently reported reason for not sending girls to school. Other important impediments to schooling for girls were the shortage of schools (60%), overcrowding of schools (63%), the school's distance from the house (63%), household and family responsibilities of girls (63%), cost of education (65%), early age of marriage (47%), and shortage of women teachers (47%; p. 445).

Khalapur is a relatively wealthy community where the lack of schools and overcrowded schools were not serious problems. The Khalapur intercollege is probably the best in the district and draws male students from surrounding villages. All schools were only a short distance from the houses they served. The only problem of access to school came when a liquor store was built near the bridge that intercollege students had to cross. The store was soon removed because harassment of girls by the store's drunken patrons led some families to take their daughters out of the intercollege.

Our Rajput families had enough money to finance their children's education, but despite the belief that girls are guests in parental homes, the headmistress of the girl's primary school complained during both of our field trips about parents' removal of girls to perform household chores. Both sons and daughters might be taken out of the intercollege when their marriages had been arranged.

According to the format of *Towards Equality,* questions about the purpose of education for girls were posed to respondents, who were asked to agree or disagree with several reasons presented by the interviewer. The majority of respondents agreed with all of the reasons, a "yea-saying" response pattern I found for Khalapur women. Reasons for educating girls, in order of frequency of agreement, were because education is good for a girl's development (88%); because education helps in case of emergency or misfortune (87%); because it brings prestige to the girl and her family (83%); because a girl will be able to earn a living (76%), so she can add to the family income (69%); and to improve marriage prospects (65%). In the families we studied, daughters were not expected to earn their living or add to their family income. For this group, prestige and improving marriage prospects were the most important reasons for educating both sons and daughters.

Reports of motivations for education are relatively rare in India. Sable conducted such a study in Bhubaneshwar and found, as did government interviewers and myself, that people had pragmatic attitudes toward education (Sable 1980). Educational aspirations depended on the kind of job that sons expected to hold, and families did not overeducate their children. Students showed little interest in education for its own sake; they thought that job qualifications were the primary reason for education and that teachers should only present material that appeared on examinations.

Sable notes that while much has been written about Indian education, the perspective of most writings is "from the top down"; that is, there is a tendency to espouse educational theory and goals without regard for the motives of those being educated. He argues that more studies "from the bottom up" would improve the efficiency of educational planning. I agree with his assessment. Few students, even in countries with long traditions of public education for the masses, are true scholars. The educational systems of postcolonial nations were developed by colonial governments primarily to train civil servants; thus some aspects of the educational systems are not particularly relevant to the needs of agriculturalists. It is to be expected that people new to literacy will be cautious and selective about their educational needs. Government attention to these needs should improve the educational level of the population.

RELIGION

Towards Equality notes that laws protecting women's rights are contrary to the Vedic laws of Manu that give religious sanction to the *varna* divisions, equate women with Sudras, and decree that women should always be subject to male authority. It cites the worship of the Mother Goddess as one indication that the status of women was higher in pre-Vedic times than it has been in later years (p. 40). The report deplores the inclusion of submissive heroines like Sita in school textbooks and argues that Indian girls should have more independent role models.

Some of the most intriguing puzzles concerning women's station lie in the realm of religion. The lack of predictable associations between the importance of female deities and women's roles and status is the most obvious enigma, and one that has been noted by a number of authors. Whyte included several measures of the sex of deities and religious leaders in his hologeistic measures and found they did not intercorrelate to form a factor, nor did they load on any other factor in his analysis (Whyte, 1978). Sanday found no systematic relationships between her measures of deities' sex and secular measures of women's power. In India reverence for independent, powerful goddesses seems to have no influence on the roles of women. Hindus would score relatively low on Whyte's scale of the value placed on women's lives.

Religion embodies societies' most central values. Religious songs and stories are usually taught to young children, who also observe religious rituals from early ages. Religion guides the moral lives of most people and permeates virtually all aspects of the lives of traditional people. It seems impossible that the characteristics of deities, including their sex, do not affect the beliefs of worshipers; it is more likely that scholars have not asked the correct questions, particularly since recent feminist scholars have noted the denigration of goddess worship in older writings.

The effect, if any, of goddesses as role models for women's self concept would seem to be an important field for investigation. On the basis of my experience, I second Bennett's (1983) contention that goddesses do give women a sense of power and self-esteem but, like Bennett, I have little concrete evidence for this conclusion.

The inability of uneducated people to answer abstract questions poses a problem for research on beliefs and self-concepts. However, these same people often have rich oral traditions of storytelling. I found that a small sample of stories told by Khalapur men and women showed an interesting and consistent difference. Women's stories told of faithful wives who overcame betrayal by their husbands, while men's stories told of faithful husbands betrayed by faithless wives. Analysis of larger samples of such stories might reveal significant aspects of beliefs about men's and women's character and sex differences in these beliefs.

Another topic for further investigation concerns belief in pollution, particularly from women's blood shed during menstruation and childbirth. (The blood that warriors shed in battle is not considered to be polluting.) Whyte (1978) was able to construct a Guttman scale for menstrual taboos, indicating that they are highly predictable across a wide sample of societies, but did not measure childbirth pollution. Khalapur Rajputs have only moderate menstrual taboos that forbid menstruating women from cooking or participating in ceremonies. However, although they believe that motherhood is sacred, they consider the blood of childbirth so polluting that the *dai* who changes bandages after a birth may be shunned by her own family. It would be interesting to know the reason for this contradiction.

RAMA'S SONS

Whyte found that sex segregation, patrilocal residence, and patrilineal descent were characteristics of warrior societies, and all of the culture traits predict low status of women. He also found that women's status is lower in societies with complex political hierarchies than in simpler societies (Whyte, 1978, p. 154). All of these conditions are present among Khalapur Rajputs.

Men's beliefs about goddesses and the influence of these beliefs on views of women would be of interest. An intriguing finding from Whyte's study (1978) may be applied to Khalapur men. He found that ritual fear of women, as measured by the belief that sexual intercourse is dangerous, and equal elaboration of the funerals of men and women appeared in societies where men were expected to be strong, aggressive, and sexually potent, a trait complex Whyte refers to using the Spanish term *machismo*. The warrior tradition clearly puts Rajput men into a high-machismo category. Khalapur Rajput men considered sex activity to be the cause of many illnesses. Funeral ceremonies were essentially the same for men and women, although the ghosts of men were usually considered to be more dangerous than women's ghosts.

Whyte's cluster suggests that macho men are compensating for underlying female identification, stemming from exposure to exclusive and prolonged authority of mothers during their early years. The assumption that men raised exclusively by women during their early years develop latent feminine personalities has been a theoretical basis for research by a number of scholars. (However, in her recent hologeistic study, Broude (1987) finds no evidence for this hypothesis.) Further investigation of societies where this cluster of culture traits exists is in order before this phenomenon can be explained.

Although the Khalapur men dominate most of the social realm of their society, Khalapur Rajputs do not fit Sanday's profile and the typical personality traits common among men in male-dominant societies (Sanday, 1973, p. 164). Whiting's characterization of them as manifesting "protest masculinity" is similarly inaccurate (Whiting, 1965). Sanday's definition of male-dominant traits embodies male aggression to women, and "protest masculinity" implies that men are protesting against underlying female identification.

Although Khalapur Rajput men value self-assertiveness, they do not value confrontation. They do not usually direct their aggression against women. Wife beating is known but rare, and rape of family women is very rare indeed. Nor do these men always oppose women's advances. The increased education of Khalapur daughters was clearly supported by men.

The error in both Sanday's and Whiting's analyses is the confusion of cultural tradition with personality traits. Rajput men are heirs to an ancient and honored tradition of rulers and warriors. Their dominance is based on ancient custom, not individual motivation. They are expected to behave in accordance with this tradition, irrespective of their individual inclinations, and to derive their self-esteem from adherence to it. A degree of prideful irascibility, as well as the exercise of severe discipline, is part of expected behavior for Rajput men. Their emotional dependence on their mothers is fostered by norms of loyalty to the blood kin and their patrilocal residence.

Because this warrior tradition is ancient and honored, it embodies norms of limits and restraints in the exercise of power and the display of aggression that are not characteristic of insecure individuals with immature personalities. Rama's sons are raised to the ideals of Rama, just as Sita's daughters are raised to the ideals of

Sita. They are men of honor, just as Rajput women are women of honor. In general, they behave with responsibility and restraint in dealing with subordinates, their servants, and their women. They behave with appropriate deference to their superiors, their elders, their daughters' in-laws. They, too, are ruled by *bhagwan* and will change with changing times.

CONCLUSIONS

It is difficult to alter customs that are sanctioned by religion or protect the vested interests of the wealthy. It is not surprising that attitudes of rural people are not on a par with the recent reforms of a distant central government. It is also not surprising that traditional customs, particularly those that benefit the powerful, have been resistant to change in a country that abolished a system of feudal landholdings as recently as 1952.

Our account ends in 1975, but the status of women's problems discussed in this book had not changed substantially by 1990. At the end of her book on sati, S. Narasimhan comments as follows on the contemporary Indian situation regarding female feticide, sati, dowry deaths, and widow status.

> [A]s long as the problems of dowry, widow denigration, the social obsession with male progeny, and the marginalization of women in the mainstream of life remain, bringing in laws, whether to curb dowry deaths, sati, female infanticide, or other aberrant customs can only be a partial measure. What needs to be tackled is the basic perceptions of society that give rise to these aberrations. The law prohibits the deed, but the background that was responsible for the occurrence (of sati, dowry deaths, infanticide, etc.) remains.
>
> (Narasimhan, 1990, p. 152).

As *Towards Equality* recognizes, "Realization of true parity between the sexes granted by the Constitution will be possible only when conceptions and attitudes of the people are brought at a par with it." Narasimhan's comments indicate that attitudes have been slow to change, even among government officials.

People change their customs at their own pace, and the pace of this change is particularly slow for traditional people. Nevertheless, the people of Khalapur are moving inevitably and successfully toward modernity. One may hope that greater equality of the sexes will come with this modernity, as it has in other regions.

APPENDIX A

Purdah Interviews with Mothers-In-Law

1. Do young daughters-in-law keep less purdah now than you did when you were a young daughter-in-law?
2. Do young daughters-in-law obey their mothers-in-law less now than they did when you were a young daughter-in-law?
3. Do you keep less purdah now than your mother-in-law did when she was your age?
4. Was there a difference in the amount of purdah kept by your mother and your mother-in-law?
5. Do women work in the fields now more than they used to?
   5a. When did this change occur?
6. Do women visit around the village now more than they used to?
   6a. When did this change occur?
7. Do young daughters-in-law have more control over their money now than they used to?
   7a. When did this change occur?
   7b. Do your daughters-in-law keep money they bring from home or do they give it to the mother-in-law?
8. Do young daughters-in-law visit their parents more now?
   8a. When did this change occur?
9. Do young daughters-in-law have more to say about how they will raise the children than they used to?
   9a. Who decides whether or not a child will go to the school?
10. Are young daughters-in-law more likely to demand separate *chuula*s now?
    10a. Are they more likely to want separate houses?
11. What do you think has caused these changes?
    11a. Is it that almost all men marry now?
    11b. Is it because people have more money now?

11c. Has the bus and *tonga* service made a difference in the frequency with which women travel out of the village?

11d. Do young men want their wives to keep less purdah than their fathers wanted?

11e. Has the education of women caused less purdah?

11f. Have radios and movies influenced any changes?

12. Do you think these changes are good?

12a. Do you think the young daughters-in-law are happier now than you were when you kept stricter purdah?

12b. Do you get along with your daughter-in-law as well as you got along with your mother-in-law?

12c. For most families do you think that the mothers-in-law and daughters-in-law get along as well now as they did when you were a young daughter-in-law?

13. Is there a difference in how well an educated and uneducated daughter-in-law will obey her mother-in-law?

13a. Is there a difference in how well she will obey her husband?

13b. Is there a difference in how well an educated and uneducated son will obey his father or mother?

APPENDIX B

Purdah Interviews with Daughters-in-Law

1. Do you keep less purdah than your mother did when you were a child?
2. What are the differences in the amount of purdah kept by you and your mother or aunts?
3. Do you keep less purdah from your mother-in-law than your mother did?
4. Do you keep less purdah from your father-in-law and older men in the house than your mother did?
5. Do you keep less purdah from your husband than your mother did?
6. Do you ever go to work in the fields? If yes,
    6a. What do you do?
    6b. How often do you go?
7. How often do you visit someone in the village?
8. When did you last go out of the house?
    8a. Where did you go?
9. Do you visit your parents more often than your mother did?
    9a. When did you last visit your parents?
10. Who decided that your children should go to school?
11. When do you expect to have a separate *chuula?*
    11a. How long have you had a *chuula?*
12. What do you think has caused you to keep less purdah?
    12a. Did your husband encourage it?
    12b. Do you keep less purdah because of education?
    12c. Did you ever see movies that made you want to keep less purdah? or Do you think movies may be one cause?
    12d. Do you think that the bus and *thonga* service have made it easier for you to travel?
    12e. Do you ever go alone on bus or *thonga?* If not,

12f. Who goes with you?

12g. Are there any other reasons?

13. Do you think that these changes are good?

13a. Do you think you are happier than your mother?

13b. Do you think that you get along with your mother-in-law as well as your mother got along with her mother-in-law?

13c. Do you want your daughters to keep as much purdah as you, or more or less?

14. Some mothers-in-law told us that they worry that their daughters-in-law will not cook for them. Do you expect your daughter-in-law to cook for you? If no,

14a. Who do you think will take care of you when you are old? If there is no one,

14a. What will you do?

14b. What would you do if she would not cook for you?

APPENDIX C

Dowry Items Classification

1. Money
2. Clothing
3. Bedding
4. Furniture
   a. sofa set
   b. table
   c. bed (*palang*)
   d. brass tray
   e. armoire (cupboard)
   f. chairs
5. Storage items
   a. trunks
   b. box
6. Household appliances
   a. sewing machine
   b. fan
   c. iron
   d. heater
   e. stove
7. Jewelry
   a. watch

   b. necklace
   c. belt
   d. anklet
   e. ring
   f. earrings, plugs
   g. bangles
   h. nose ring, plug
   i. button
8. Animals, bicycles
9. Utensils
10. Toys
11. Consumable items
    a. soap
    b. oil
    c. cosmetics
    d. fruit
12. Miscellaneous
    a. radio
    b. attaché case
    c. camera

APPENDIX D

Economic Control Interview

1. Who controls the money in this house?
   - a. self
   - b. husband
   - c. mother-in-law
   - d. father-in-law
   - e. parents-in-law
   - f. elder brother-in-law
   - g. grandfather-in-law
   - h. uncle-in-law
1a. Is land divided?
   - a. yes
   - b. no
1b. Are food supplies divided?
   - a. yes
   - b. no
2. Where do you get the money to buy your clothes or children's clothes when living in this village?
   - a. self
   - b. husband
   - c. mother-in-law
   - d. father-in-law
   - f. elder brother-in-law
   - g. grandfather-in-law
   - h. uncle-in-law
   - i. no need to purchase anything yet
   - e. parents-in-law

3. Do you buy most of your clothes here or do you bring them from your parents' house?
   a. here
   b. parents' house
3a. If you need more clothes, where do you get them?
   a. here
   b. parents' house
3b. Who pays for children's school, book fees, etc.?
   a. husband
   b. mother-in-law
   c. father-in-law
   d. parents-in-law
   e. brother-in-law
   f. parents
   g. uncle-in-law
   h. children not yet in school
4. Do you get money from your husband?
   a. yes
   b. no
   c. no need yet
5. Do you get money from your mother-in-law?
   a. yes
   b. no
   c. no need yet
6. When you bring money from your parents, what do you do with it?
   a. keep and spend it myself
   b. give it to mother-in-law
   c. keep it myself, but if mother-in-law asks for it, I give it to her
7. When you bring presents from your parents, who distributes them?
   a. self
   b. mother-in-law
   c. keep own, give rest to mother-in-law
   d. all kept in box—anyone can use them
8. When you brought your dowry, who decided how it was distributed?
   a. mother-in-law
   b. mother-in-law and grandmother-in-law
   c. mother-in-law and father-in-law
9. How much of your dowry do you still have?
   a. jewelry
   b. animals
   c. clothes
   d. furniture
   e. ornaments
   f. trunk
   g. utensils
   h. nothing
   i. everything

10. How much of the dowry has been given away?
    a. jewelry
    b. bicycles
    c. clothing
    d. money
    e. ornaments
    f. utensils
    g. nothing
    h. don't remember
    i. everything

10a. When was it given?
    a. marriage
    b. *chuchak*
    c. *gauna*
    d. birth of own son or daughter
    e. don't know

11. Do you think that you should have more control over the property you bring from your parents than you do?
    a. yes
    b. no
    c. sufficient control

11a. Would you like your daughters to have more control over their property than you have?
    a. yes
    b. no
    c. have control according to custom of that time
    d. parents-in-law should control until separated

12. What do you do with money from the Gandhi ashram?
    a. do not spin
    b. give to mother-in-law
    c. give to sister-in-law
    d. don't receive money, but do get cloth

13. Do you ever lend money on interest?
    a. yes
    b. no
    c. don't know
    d. in-laws lend money
    e. if yes, amount

14. People say that dowries are getting bigger. Do you think this is good or bad?
    a. good
    b. bad
    c. no comment
    d. both good and bad

15. The government is trying to stop dowries. Did you know this?
    a. have heard
    b. have not heard

15a. Do you think that this is good or bad, and why?
  a. good, poor can't afford big dowries
  b. good, treatment would be equal
  c. bad, big dowry means better family
  d. bad, a girl must have a dowry
  e. bad, a girl can't get articles of choice if she has no dowry
  d. bad, a girl should have a dowry, but it should be lowered

16. Do you know that now a girl can claim a share of the land along with her brothers?
  a. do know
  b. do not know

16a. Do you think this is good or bad?
  a. good
  b. bad

17. Is the share that a girl receives in gifts (*shadi, gauna, chuchak,* etc.) usually more or less than a brother's portion of the land?
  a. more
  b. less
  c. equal
  d. depends on individual family
  e. don't know

APPENDIX E

Legends of Local Sati Shrines

Khalapur has four Sati shrines and women still worship at all of them. The extension of the term *sati* to describe a shrine built for an unmarried girl is based on the reverence for virgins. Since the term can mean virginal, its use for such a shrine is understandable. The only shrine honoring a traditional sati (i.e., a living widow who joined her dead husband on his funeral pyre) was built for two Bania sisters who were members of an untouchable group. Two of the Rajput shrines were built to honor virgin widows, and a fourth shrine honors an unmarried girl. In 1975 we recorded women's accounts of the origins and nature of all village sati shrines. The descriptions of these shrines appear below:

SHRINE ONE

The largest and most prestigious sati shrine has 1.5 bighas of land around it and a shelter with cooking facilities for pilgrims from other villages. It was built for a Rajput girl whose husband died after her *shadi*.

> This girl told her parents she had an intuition that her husband had died, and asked her mother to take her to her husband's home. Since the final marriage (gauna) had not been held, her mother refused. She repeated her request to her father, who also refused. Then she went into her room and was never seen again. Legend says that, like Sita, she was swallowed up by the earth. Her intended husband had indeed died, and in his village his parents developed sore eyes. When asked why their eyes were sore they said that they had an intuition that their future *bahu* had become a Sati. The dead girl appeared to her *soosar* in a dream, and told him to come to Khalapur, carrying a hoe and make a shrine for her on the place where the hoe falls off of his shoulder. He came, as directed, and his hoe fell from his shoulder when he reached the fields of the dead girl's father. The shrine was built and the land

around it remains uncultivated. It is believed that everyone from Khalapur must worship at this shrine on the tenth day of the month of Kartik to prevent skin disease. Therefore this shrine is a place of worship for persons of all castes.

SHRINE TWO

A shrine behind the Cornell–Purena project house was built for a wife who was burnt on her husband's funeral pyre after he was cremated. Only the people of Jaroda puttii worship there.

The Sati of this shrine was engaged to a boy from Khalapur, who died before the *gauna*. When the girl received this news she grew very sad and lost weight. When her mother asked why she was growing pale, she replied that it was because her intended groom had died. The mother told her that there was no shortage of boys for her to marry. But the girl made her mother promise to do as she would direct. When her mother had promised, she asked her mother to bring a sacred coconut and get her married to her dead fiancé. She insisted that she did not want to marry anyone else and would die with her husband. She took the coconut in her hands and walked to her husband's village, tossing the coconut from one hand to another as if it were a ball. When she reached the cremation ground where her fiancé had been cremated, the coconut fell from her hands. She stopped on that spot and asked her parents to prepare a wooden funeral pyre. She lit the pyre with the lamp that was still there from her fiancé's cremation and entered into the fire.

SHRINE THREE

The oldest shrine is in the threshing field, just across from the village bridge. Its structure has been obliterated by overgrowth, so that it looks like a small hill. Only the people of Khalapur worship at this shrine, but its devotees include persons from all castes. The shrine was built in honor of a Rajput girl who lived at the time Khalapur was founded and died while still a child. She did not participate in family life but devoted herself entirely to worshiping God. At her death she walked into the earth, like Sita, as it opened to receive her. After her death she appeared to people and promised to bless the milk animals if she was worshiped. Legend has it that the shrine described in the following passage was constructed by a tribe of nomads.

Two hundred years ago people of a wandering tribe called Banjari camped near the spot where this shrine is now. They carried their luggage on the back of their donkeys. One of their donkeys broke his leg, and one of the bags it was carrying fell down from the donkey's back. When the owner picked it up, he found that the contents of the bag had turned into earth. He was very surprised and the whole tribe became afraid. They did not know whether they should go on without their luggage or return for it. The owner addressed the spot where the donkey broke its leg, saying, "Respected Sati Devi, please show us your divine power by converting the earth in this bag back into the original luggage. If you do this, I will always offer

you my prayers and my devotion. If you do not convert the earth, then I have lost valuable things at your shrine, where my donkey also got its broken leg."

While everyone stood and watched to see whether or not a miracle would occur, the Sati replied from the earth, "I have been bearing the weight of all of you while you were camped here, and now you are going without bothering [about] me. You must build me a house as large as the tomb of the Piir [Hindu saint]. Only then will your gold and valuables be returned to you and your donkey's leg healed."

So a large shrine was built by the Banjaris. Their gold and valuables were returned, and the donkey's leg got well. Since then people pray and make offerings at this shrine. The shrine is very old and has been broken for more than 50 years. No one has enough money to get it repaired.

The legend that this holy child entered the earth upon her death is clearly related to the tale of Sita's death.

SHRINE FOUR

The Bania shrine honors sisters who married two brothers. When the brothers died together and were cremated on a common pyre, both sisters threw themselves on their husbands' pyre. Only Banias worship at this shrine. Some Rajput women were scornful of the imitation of sati by this outcast group, contending that the only true satis were Rajput. Their scorn for low-caste pretentiousness did not, however, negate their respect for the Bania Sati sisters.

APPENDIX F

Family Planning Interview

1. Do you think that you have enough land to support the children of this house and their families when they are grown?
   a. If yes, probe for landholdings
   b. Why they are enough
   c. If no, probe for landholdings
   d. What the plans are for supplementing income (e.g., educating sons, buying more land, improving production)
2. Do you think there will be enough money to give good dowries to the daughters of this family?
   a. If no, what will they do?
3. The government thinks that people should have fewer children. Have you ever heard their radio broadcasts or seen any of their literature?
   a. Does the family planning worker ever come to see you? (I assume they know there is such a worker, but find out if they don't know this.)
4. What do you think of this government program to encourage women to have fewer children? Is it good to try to limit the number of children?
5. Why do you think the government is trying to make people have fewer children?
6. Have any of you ever considered using any method of family planning?
   a. Probe for what, including male methods
   b. Probe to find out if any method has actually been used
7. What methods do you like the least?
   a. Why?
8. Are there any methods you would use, if they were available?
   a. Probe for medicine
9. Do the men in the family object to family planning?

10. How many sons would you like to have?
11. How many sons would your husband like to have?
12. How many daughters would you like to have?
13. How many daughters would your husband like to have?

Glossaries

N.B.: The Aliteration system for use of the Roman alphabet is taken from Gumperz et al. (1962)

HINDUSTANI SECULAR TERMS

Anna	Small coin, one eighth of a rupee
Baan	Narcotic-based drink
Baap	Father
Bahai	Brother
Bahen	Sister
Bahu	Daughter-in-law; husband's wife
Banya	An untouchable caste
Bara	Big
Beta	Son
Beti	Daughter
Bhat	Contributions to wedding expenses of children of husbands' sisters.
Bhabhi	Brother's wife
Bharat	Groom's party
Bhudana	Railway town near Khalapur
Bigha	Unit of land measurement; 3,025 sq. yds; two thirds acre
Bindi	Cosmetic dot worn on forehead
Brahmin, Brahman	Highest-ranking *varna* of the priests and scholars; a person belonging to this *varna*
Bughar	Women's living quarters, including courtyard, rooms, and roof
Burka	Outer garment, worn by Moslem women
Chacha	Father's younger brother
Chachi	Wife of father's younger brother
Chaddar	White cotton headcloth worn over sari

351

Chamar	An untouchable caste whose traditional work is sweeping out latrines
Chapati	Unleavened bread
Charpoy	Cot constructed of bamboo frame and hemp webbing
Choopar	Men's living quarters, including platform and rooms
Chotili	Braid, usu. false braid of cotton string
Chuula	Cooking hearth
Chuchak	Gifts to husband's sisters when a wife's first son is born
Dai	Midwife from untouchable caste
Derani	Wife of husband's younger brother
Deva	God
Devi	Goddess
Dewar	Husband's younger brother
Dharma	Duty; to fulfill the caste obligations of one's karma or fate
Dhooti	Cotton cloth wrapped around waist and between legs; traditional male dress
Duge	Day
Gauna	Second stage of wedding, when brides go to live in their husbands' homes
Gher	Cattle compound
Ghi	Clarified butter
Gungat	Portion of sari worn over face as a veil
Halwar	Carrot candy
Harajan	Collective term for untouchable castes
Hindi, Hindustani	Official language of India
Hooka	Water pipe
Jaith	Husband's older brother
Jajmani	System of economic interdependence among members of different *jati*s
Jati	Basic social unit of caste system, usu. associated with a particular occupation
Jethani	Wife of husband's older brother
Jhinvar	Water-carrying *jati*
Karma	Fate
Kashatriya, Ksatriya	*Varna* of warriors and rulers: person belonging to this *varna*
Khala	Pond
Khandhan	Lineage
Latti	Bamboo staff sometimes used for fighting
Lota	Small brass pot
Maa	Mother
Naag	Snake

Namistee	Word of greeting meaning "we are one"
Nanad	Husband's sister
Panchayat	Town council
Patti	Smallest political division of a community; precinct
Pie	Smallest Indian coin
Pundeer	Largest kinship unit of Khalapur Rajputs, gotra
Purdah	Veil; customs of cloistering, respectful avoidance
Puri	*Chapatis* fried in *ghi*
Raja	Ruler, king
Rajput	North Indian division of the Kashatriya *varna,* orig. from Rajastan
Rani	Wife or daughter of raja; queen
Rupee	Basic Indian coin
Sadhu	Hindu holy man
Sanskrit	Ancient Indian language.
Sari	Cloth wrapped around waist and over shoulder or head; traditional female dress
Sasu	Mother-in-law; husband's mother
Shadi	Marriage ceremony
Soosar	Father-in-law
Sudra	Lowest-ranking *varna* of menial working groups
Taaya	Father's older brother
Taayi	Wife of father's older brother
Thonga	Two-wheeled horse-drawn cart
Tikka	Mark on forehead made with pigment; gold ornament hanging over forehead
Vaish, Vaisha	*Varna* of businessmen, merchants, and traders; person belonging to this *varna*
Varna	Color; the four major social groups (Brahmin, Kashatriya, Vaish, and Sudra) described in Vedic creation myth, original basis of caste system
Zamindar	Land-owning group; esp. used before land reform act of 1952 (Zamindar Abolition Act)

HINDUSTANI RELIGIOUS TERMS

Agni	God of fire
Ananta	Mythical serpent with 1,000 heads.
Arjuna	One of the Pandava brothers, hero of the Mahabharata
Aryans	Invaders from central Asia who conquered North India about 1500 B.C.

Avatara	Earthly manifestation of Vishnu
Ayodhya	Rama's capital city
Baalsundrii	Town and local name of Goddess Kali, whose temple is in the town
Baan	Narcotic-based drink, ceremony held before a groom leaves for his marriage
Bara Mata	Big Goddess
Bahai Duge	Brothers' day, a fast held by sisters in honor of their brothers
Bahari	Birth ceremony held for boys 1 to 6 days after birth.
Basant	Festival honoring Siva; day when marriage and engagement letters are sent.
Bhagavad Gita	Epic poem recording the advice given by Krishna to Arjuna on the eve of a battle.
Bhagwan	Name for nonpersonified deity; will of god; spirit of god.
Bhaktani	Holy woman
Bharata	Son of King Devaratha and his second wife, Kaikeyi, half brother of Rama and Laskhmana.
Bhumia	Shrine built when a village is founded
Brahma	God of creation
Buraa Babuu	Old man; shrine to a saint of water-carrying caste
Chotili	Birth ceremony held 5 days after birth for girls and 6 days after birth for boys.
Daksa	Father of Sati; one of Siva's consorts.
Darga	Name of Muslim saint whose tomb is in Khalapur; protector of the village
Deveratha	King; father of Rama
Dharma	God of fate
Divalii	Festival of lights; celebration of day Rama returned from exile to his capital of Ayudhia
Dravidians	Peoples who settled in Indus valley before 2000 B.C.
Durga	Consort of Siva; warrior goddess
Ekadsi	Fast day auspicious for widows
Flora Duge	Flower day; spring festival when girls go to fields to gather flowers and dance.
Ganesh	Elephant-headed God; son of Siva; scribe of the Mahabharata
Garuda	Steed of Vishnu; mythical beast; half man and half bird.
Ghas	Birthday of god Narayan
Ghoodhan	God of cattle; day honoring wealth derived from cattle
Gopis	Mythical milkmaids associated with Krishna

Gurshari	Prenuptial ceremony held on day groom leaves for bride's village.
Hanuman	Monkey god who helped Rama rescue Sita
Holi	Festival celebrating revels of Krishna and Gopis
Hooii	Goddess whose abstract image is painted on walls of women's bedrooms; fast held by mothers for health of sons.
Janaka	King; father of Sita
Janmashtmii	Celebration of Krishna's birthday
Jasutan	Birth ceremony held for boys 10 days after birth.
Kaikeyi	Second wife of Deveratha; Rama's stepmother, who sent Rama, Lakshmni, and Sita into exile.
Kali	Consort of Siva; dark, untamed goddess, possibly of pre-Vedic origin.
Kali Yuga	Iron Age
Kangana	Sacred-colored cord used during wedding ceremonies
Karwaa Chauth	Fast kept by wives for health of husbands.
Kausalya	Wife of King Deveratha; mother of Rama
Krishna, Krisna, Krsna	*Avatara* of Vishnu; god; in the Mahabharata Krishna is charioteer for Arjuna and author of the Bhagavad Gita
Kubera	Lord of demons
Kusa	Son of Rama and Sita
Lakshma or Lakshmana	Brother of Rama
Lakshmi	Consort of Vishnu; goddess of wealth
Launkaria	Brother of goddess Sanjii
Lava	Son of Rama and Sita
Mahabharata	Religious epic recounting war between royal brothers and their cousins
Manda Bandhan	Decoration composed of grass; used during wedding ceremonies
Maya	Brahma's consort; goddess of form and substance; goddess of illusion
Naag Panchmii	Festival honoring snakes
Nandi	Bull steed of Siva
Narayan	Ancestral god of Khalapur Rajputs
Pandavas	Royal brothers; heroes of the Mahabharata
Phaag	Day of drunken abandon held day after Holi
Piir	Tomb of Muslim saint named Darga; also used as title of saint.
Pitar	Ancestor shrine
Pithas	Sacred place; place where part of Sati's body was deposited.

Prakriti	Cosmic female principle
Prithvi, Parvati	Earliest representation of Earth Goddess; Siva's consort in the Rg Veda
Puranas	Sacred Hindu texts written during the Middle Ages
Purusha	Cosmic male principle
Puuran Maashii	Full moon, fast held during full moon
Radha	Lover of Krishna; goddess
Raghu	Race of Rama
Rama, Ram	*Avatara* of Vishnu; god; king; hero of the Ramayana; mythical ancestor of Rajputs
Ramayana	Epic religious story recounting life of Rama
Ravena	Demon of the Ramayana; king of Sri Lanka who captured Sita
Rg Veda, Rig Veda	Oldest of the Vedic texts
Sakut	Day devoted to worship of Kali and Durga
Sanjii	Local representation of Durga; water goddess
Sarasvati	Brahma's consort; goddess of wisdom
Sati	Siva's consort; embodiment of Shakti; name of widow who immolates herself on husband's funeral pyre
sati, suttee	Widow's act of immolation on husband's funeral pyre
Shakti	Female spiritual energy; basis of change; fertility
Shakumbrii	Town and local name of goddess Durga, whose temple is in the town.
Shatrughna	Son of King Devaratha and his second wife, Kaikeyi; half brother of Rama and Laskhmana.
Shiv Ratrii	Festival honoring Shiva
Sita	Earth Goddess; wife of Rama
Siva, Shiva	God of destruction and fertility
Tiijoo	Summer festival celebrated by unmarried girls and young wives; day on which brides receive presents from their husbands' families
Treta Yuga	Silver Age
Trimurti	Collective name for three major Gods (Brahman, Vishnu, and Siva); in sculpture, figure with three heads or faces.
Upanishads	Sacred Hindu texts, largely commentaries on the Vedas
Valmiki	Sage and scribe of the Ramayana
Vasumati	Earth Goddess of the Ramayana.
Vedas	Group of sacred Hindu texts
Visnu, Visnu	God of preservation; appeared on earth in 10 avatars, or lifetimes.
Yug, Yuga	One of four ages in life cycle of each universe

HINDI NAMES AND THEIR ENGLISH EQUIVALENTS

Abhaye	fearless
Ajab	strange
Amar Nath	immortal
Asali	real
Bahai	brother
Bala	young girl
Champa	flower
Darga	name of local Muslim saint
Daya	mercy
Dhooli	dust
Draupadi	wife of the Pandavas
Durga	goddess; consort of Siva
Ganga	goddess of river Ganges
Gopal	name for Krishna, lit. caretaker of the Gopis
Hoshiyar	wise one
Kanak	wheat
Kela	banana
Khajani	treasure
Kiran	sunbeam
Lakhpati	millionairess
Luxmi	goddess of wealth
Maina	singing bird
Mamta	affection
Maya	wealth
Mussadi	bandit
Nakali	not real
Om Prakash	God's glory
Phoolo	flower
Radha	Krishna's lover
Rama	god; avatar of Vishnu
Rambhool	God's forgetfulness
Ranjeet	winner of the war
Sarvasati	goddess of wisdom
Sher	tiger
Sita	Rama's wife
Succha	good; clean
Suraj	sun
Takadwar	strong
Tara	star

Bibliography

Beane, W. (1977). *Myth, cult and symbols in Sakta Hinduism*. Leiden, The Netherlands: Brill.

Bennett, L. (1983). *Dangerous wives and sacred sisters: Social and symbolic roles of high-caste women in Nepal*. New York: Columbia University Press.

Broude, G. J. (1987). The relationship of marital intimacy and aloofness to social environment: A hologeistic study. *Behavior Science Research, 24* (1–4), 50–69.

Brown, C. M. (1980). Kali, the mad mother. In C. Olson (Ed.), *The book of the goddess past and present* (pp. 110–123). New York: Crossroad.

Brown, J. K. (1963). A cross-cultural study of female initiation rites. *American Anthropologist, 65,* 837–853.

Brown, J. K., & Kerns, V. (Eds.) (1985). *In her prime: A new view of middle-aged women.* South Hadley, MA: Bergin and Garvey.

Brubaker, R. L. (1988). The untamed goddesses of village India. In C. Olson (Ed.), *The book of goddess past and present* (pp. 145–160). New York: Crossroad.

Campbell, L. B. (1971). *Sakti: Polarities of asceticism and fertility in the literature and mythology of the Devi.* Master's thesis, Columbia University.

Dexter, M. R. (1990). Indic goddesses. In Miriam Robbins Dexter (Ed.), *Whence the goddesses: A source book* (pp. 75–85). New York: Pergamon.

Dube, S. (1967). *Indian village.* New York: Harper & Row.

Fane, H. (1975). The female element in Indian culture. In Miriam Robbins Dexter (Ed.), *Asian folklore studies* (pp. 51–112). Nagoya, Japan: Nazar Institute for Culture and Religion.

Goody, J. (1973). Bridewealth and dowry in Africa and East Eurasia. In J. Goody & S. J. Tambiah (Eds.), *Bridewealth and dowry* (pp. 1–58). Cambridge: Cambridge University Press.

Gross, R. (1988). Hindu female deities as a resource for the contemporary rediscovery of the goddess. In C. Olson (Ed.), *The book of the goddess past and present* (pp. 217–230). New York: Crossroad.

Gumperz, J., Rumery, J., Singh, A. B., & Naim, C. M. (1962). *Conversational Hindi-Urdu.* Berkeley: Center for South Asian Studies.

Guttman, D. (1985). Beyond nature: Development perspectives on the vital older woman. In J. K. Brown & V. Kerns (Eds.), *In her prime: A new view of middle-aged women* (pp. 198–211). South Hadley, MA: Bergin and Garvey.

Hasan, S. N. (1974). *Towards equality.* Government of India: Report of the Committee on the Status of Women in India. New Delhi: Department of Social Welfare and Ministry of Education.

Jacobson, D. (1970). *Hindu and Moslem purdah in a central Indian village*. Ph.D. dissertation, University of Michigan, microfilm.

Jacobson, D. (1982). Purdah and the Hindu family in Central India. In D. Papanek & G. Minault (Eds.), *Separate worlds: Studies of purdah in South Asia*. Columbia, MO: South Asia Books.

Kinsley, D. (1986). *Hindu goddesses: Visions of the divine feminine in the Hindu religious tradition*. Berkeley: University of California Press.

Kinsley, D. (1989). *The goddesses' mirror*. Albany: State University of New York Press.

Kolenda, P. (1982). Pox and the terror of childlessness: Images and ideas of the smallpox goddess in a North Indian village. In J. Preston (Ed.), *Mother worship* (pp. 227–250). Chapel Hill: University of North Carolina Press.

Kolenda, P. (1984). Woman as tribute, woman as flower: Images of "woman" in weddings in North and South India. *American Ethnologist, 11*, 98–117.

Kurtz, S. N. (1992). *All the mothers are one*. New York: Columbia University Press.

Mahar, J. M. (1966). *Marriage networks in the northern gangetic plain*. Unpublished doctoral dissertation, Cornell University, Ithaca, NY.

Mandelbaum, D. G. (1988). *Women's seclusion and men's honor: Sex roles in North India, Bangladesh, and Pakistan*. Tucson: University of Arizona Press.

Marshall, J. (1931). *Mohenjo-Daro and the industrial civilization*. 3 vols. London: Arthur Probsthain.

Martin, E. (1972). *The gods of India*. Delhi: Varanasi.

Mazumdar, S. (1953). *Ramayana*. Vols. 1 & 2. Bombay: Hindustan Cellulose and Paper Co.

Mazumdar, V. (1978). Comment on suttee. *Signs: Journal of women in culture and society, 4* (2), 269–273.

Miller, B. D. (1981). *The endangered sex*. Ithaca: Cornell University Press.

Millser, B. D. (1984). Daughter neglect, women's work and marriage: Pakistan and Bangladesh compared. *Medical Anthropology, 8* (2), 109–126.

Minturn, L. (1984). Changes in the differential treatment of Rajput girls in Khalapur: 1955–1975. *Medical Anthropology, 8* (2), 127–132.

Minturn, L., Boyd, D., & Kapoor, S. (1978). Increased maternal power status: Changes in the socialization of Rajput mothers of Khalapur, India. *Journal of Cross-Cultural Psychology, 9* (8), 253–268.

Minturn, L., & Hitchcock, J. (1963). The Rajputs of Khalapur, India. In B. Whiting (Ed.), *Six cultures: Studies of child rearing*. New York: Wiley.

Minturn, L., & Hitchcock, J. T. (1966). *The Rajputs of Khalapur, India*. New York: Wiley.

Minturn, L., & Lambert, W. W. (1964). *Mothers of six cultures: Antecedents of child rearing*. New York: Wiley.

Minturn, L., & Stashack, J. (1982). Infanticide as a terminal abortion procedure. *Behavior Science Research, 17* (1, 2), 70–90.

Mukhopadhyay, C. C., & Higgins, P. J. (1988). Anthropological studies of women's status revisited: 1977–1987. *Annual Review of Anthropology, 17*, 461–495.

Narasimhan, S. (1990). *Sati: widow burning in India*. New York: Doubleday.

Olson, C. C. (1980). Sri Lakshmi and Radha: The obsequious wife and the lustful lover. In C. Olson (Ed.), *The book of the goddess past and present* (pp. 124–144). New York: Crossroad.

Papanek, H. (1973). Purdah: Separate worlds and symbolic shelter. In *Comparative studies in society and history: An international quarterly*, Vol. 15 (pp. 289–325). Cambridge: Cambridge University Press.

Papanek, H., & Minault, G. (1982). *Separate worlds: Studies of purdah in South Asia*. Columbia, MO: South Asia Books.

Piggot, S. (1950). *Prehistoric India*. Baltimore: Pelican Books.

Sable, A. (1980). Indian Education: A view from the bottom up. In S. Seymour (Ed.), *The transformation of a sacred town: Bhubaneswar, India* (pp. 157–182). Boulder: Westview Press.

Sacks, K. (1979). *Sisters and wives: The past and future of sexual equality*. Westport, CT: Greenwood.

Sanday, P. R. (1975). Towards a theory of the status of women. *American Anthropologist, 75*, 682–700.

Schlegel, A., & Eloul, R. (1987). A new coding of marriage transactions. *Behavior Science Research, 21* (1–4), 118–140.

Seymour, S. (Ed.) (1980). *The transformation of a sacred town: Bhubaneswar, India*. Boulder: Westview Press.

Seymour, S. (1980). Patterns of childrearing in a changing Indian town. In S. Seymour (Ed.), *The transformation of a sacred town: Bhubaneswar, India*. Boulder: Westview Press.

Sharma, U. (1978). *Women and their affines: The veil as a symbol of separation. Man, 13* (2), 218–233.

Sharma, U. (1980). *Women, work, and property in North West India*. London: Tavistock.

Sharma, U. (1986). *Women's work, class, and the urban household: A study of Shimla, North India*, London: Tavistock.

Stein, D. K. (1978). Women to burn: Suttee as a normative institution. *Signs: Journal of women in culture and society, 4,* (2), 253–268.

Tambiah, S. J. (1973). Dowry and bridewealth and the property rights of women in South Asia. In M. Fortes, J. R. Goody, E. R. Leach, S. J. Tambaiah (Eds.), *Cambridge Papers in Social Anthropology*, no. 7, Bridewealth and dowry. Cambridge: Cambridge University Press.

Whiting, B. (1963). *Six cultures: Studies of child rearing*. New York: Wiley.

Whiting, B. (1965). Sex identity conflict and physical violence: A comparative study. In L. Nadar (Ed.), *The ethnography of law* (pp. 123–140). Menasha, WI: American Anthropological Association.

Whiting, B., & Whiting, J. W. M. (1975). *Children of six cultures: A psycho-cultural analysis*. Cambridge, MA: Harvard University Press.

Whiting, J. W. M., Child, I. L., & Lambert, W. W. (1966). *Field guide for a study of socialization*. New York: Wiley.

Whiting, J. W. M., & Whiting, B. B. (1960). Contributions of anthropology to the methods of studying child rearing. In P. H. Mussen (Ed.), *Handbook of research methods in child development*. New York: Wiley.

Whyte, M. K. (1978). *The status of women in preindustrial societies*. Princeton, NJ: Princeton University Press.

Name Index

Abhaye, 112–13
Ajab, 32, 34, 278–79, 309
Amar Nath, 32, 33–39, 65–66, 91,
    112–13, 123–25, 128, 139, 230, 233,
    254, 277–78, 313
Asili, 68

Bahai, 227, 238–45, 309, 310, 325, 328
Bala, 32, 67–68, 227, 324
Bhaktani, 221, 236–38, 304, 310

Champa, 124
Chand, 303, 310

Darga, 32, 33–37
Daya, 31, 32, 37–39, 67–68
Dhooli, 32, 33–37, 65–67, 124–28, 131,
    136, 150, 180, 277–79, 307–10,
    315–17
Draupadi, 32, 33–37, 55–57, 66–67,
    123–28, 136, 139, 140, 150, 180,
    218, 233, 247, 258, 277–79, 305,
    307, 309, 311, 312, 314
Durga, 32, 37–39

Ganga, 32, 33–37, 113, 124–26,
    277–78, 306
Gopal, 32, 33, 254

Hoshiyar, 237, 309
Hoshiyar (wife), 241–44

Kanak, 32, 37
Kela, 31, 32, 37–39, 67–68, 107, 316

Khajani, 57–58, 252
Kiran, 32, 33–34, 55, 278–79, 309
Krishna, 212–16, 306, 309

Lakhpati, 32, 37, 56, 67, 123, 125, 140
Luxmi, 32, 33–36, 54–55, 65–67,
    123–28, 150, 278–79, 305, 307, 308,
    309, 311, 317

Maina, 228
Mamta, 32, 37–39, 67–68, 128, 224,
    227, 309, 310, 324, 326
Maya, 32, 36, 53, 56–58, 112, 123–24,
    126, 252, 306, 307, 310, 314, 317,
    324
Mussaddi, 32, 33–39, 309

Nakali, 64–65, 309

Om Prakash, 32, 33–39, 125–26, 312

Phoolo, 67–68

Radha, 166, 170, 173, 175, 199,
    212–16, 218–19, 223, 227, 228, 303,
    305, 306, 309, 312, 316
Rambhool, 112
Ranjeet, 32, 34–39, 53, 56, 112, 123,
    126, 306, 324

Sarvasati, 32, 33, 125, 278
Seema, 113

Subject Index

Agriculture, 11, 21, 22, 39, 93, 173, 288, 297, 313, 317, 329

Ancestor, 158, 163, 166, 173, 177, 184, 185, 191, 194, 195, 274, 275, 276, 312, 314

Arya Samaj, 17, 21, 178, 254, 312

Aunt
   as *chachi,* 23, 24, 48
   as *taayi,* 23, 24, 111, 311, 316

Baalsundri. See Towns
Baan. See Marriage ceremonies
Bahai, 24. *See* Brother: as *bahai*
Bahari. See Birth ceremonies
Bahen. See Sister
Bahu. See Daughter-in-law as *bahu*
Bara Mata. See Goddesses
Basant. See Calendric ceremonies
Bhabhi. See Sister-in-law: as *bhabhi*
Bhagwan. See Gods
Bhat. See Birth ceremonies
Bhudana. See Towns

Birth ceremonies, 273–76
   Bahari, 273–74
   Bhat, 146, 148–50
   Chotili, 274–75
   Chuchak, 115, 127, 146
   haircutting, 275–76
   Jasutan, 275–76, 275, 305

Brahma. See Gods

Brahmin, 17, 18, 49, 51, 56, 88, 114, 129, 158, 163, 166, 167, 174, 177, 179, 184, 186, 187, 191, 206, 229, 231, 250, 274, 275, 295, 309, 337

Bride, 41, 47, 49–59, 63–69, 103, 106, 111, 117, 118, 121–27, 150, 168, 170, 187, 190, 209, 210, 224, 227, 238, 240, 306–9, 311, 322, 324, 328, 330, 331

British, 20, 40, 78, 169, 183, 219, 221, 254, 310, 320

Brother, 22, 23, 24, 29, 30, 31, 33–35, 37, 39, 42, 44, 45, 46, 47, 48, 50, 51, 52, 53, 55, 56, 57, 58, 59, 60, 64, 66, 67, 68, 69, 74, 80, 82, 84, 87, 89, 90, 97, 98, 102, 103, 104, 109, 110, 111, 112, 113, 114, 115, 116, 117, 123, 126, 127, 128, 129, 130, 131, 139, 143, 147, 168, 170, 186, 191, 192, 193, 195, 199, 202, 203, 206, 207, 208, 212, 213, 214, 215, 224, 226, 228, 234, 235, 237, 238, 239, 241, 242, 243, 245, 263, 276, 287, 304, 305, 306, 307, 308, 311, 312, 316, 321, 324, 329
   as *Bahai,* 23, 186, 195, 227

Brother-in-law
   as *dewar,* 23, 142, 143, 148, 315
   as *jaith,* 23, 52, 224

Bughar. See Women's quarters

Calendric ceremonies, 187–95
   Basant, 189
   Diivalii, 187–88, 194, 195
   Flora Duge, 189
   Ghas, 180, 184, 186, 191, 194, 195
   Ghoodhan, 188, 195

365